Papers in Mediaeval Studies
6

Cover design by Leya Matalas

LOGOS ISLAMIKOS

Studia Islamica
in Honorem
Georgii Michaelis Wickens

edited by

ROGER M. SAVORY
and
DIONISIUS A. AGIUS

PONTIFICAL INSTITUTE OF MEDIAEVAL STUDIES

Canadian Cataloguing in Publication Data

Main entry under title:
Logos Islamikos

(Papers in mediaeval studies, ISSN 0228-8605 ; 6)
Bibliography: p.
Includes index.
ISBN 0-88844-806-6

1. Arabic philology - Addresses, essays, lectures.
2. Persian philology - Addresses, essays, lectures.
3. Civilization, Islamic - Addresses, essays, lectures.
4. Wickens, G. M., 1918- - Bibliography. I. Wickens, G. M., 1918- II. Savory, Roger. III. Agius, Dionisius A. (Dionisius Albertus), 1945-

PJ6024.W52L6 1984 492'.7 C84-099122-3

Pontifical Institute of Mediaeval Studies
59 Queen's Park Crescent East
Toronto, Ontario, Canada M5S 2C6

Contents

PART THREE: ISLAMIC WELTANSCHAUUNGEN

Contributors

Charles J. Adams is a member and former director of the Institute of Islamic Studies at McGill University in Montreal.

Dionisius A. Agius is Lecturer in Arabic at the Language Centre, Kuwait University.

Roger Allen is Association Professor of Arabic in the University of Pennsylvania in Philadelphia.

Eleazar Birnbaum is a professor in the Department of Middle East and Islamic Studies, University of Toronto.

Joshua Blau is a professor in the Institute of Asian and African Studies in the Hebrew University, Jerusalem.

C. Edmund Bosworth is Professor of Arabic Studies in the University of Manchester, and an editor of the new edition of the Encyclopaedia of Islam.

Jerome W. Clinton is an associate professor in the Near Eastern Studies Department, Princeton University.

Laurence P. Elwell-Sutton is Emeritus Professor of Persian in the University of Edinburgh.

George Hourani is a professor in the Department of Philosophy, in the State University of New York at Buffalo.

Georg Krotkoff is an associate professor in the Department of Near Eastern Studies in the Johns Hopkins University, Baltimore.

Bernard Lewis is a professor in the Near Eastern Studies Department at Princeton University and a member of the Institute for Advanced Study at Princeton. He is an editor of the new edition of the Encyclopaedia of Islam.

Michael E. Marmura is a professor in the Department of Middle East and Islamic Studies in the University of Toronto.

George Makdisi is a professor in the Faculty of Oriental Studies in the University of Pennsylvania in Philadelphia.

Jane D. McAuliffe is a doctoral student in the Centre for Religious Studies in the University of Toronto.

Charles Pellat is Professor honoraire in the Sorbonne, l'universite de Paris, and an editor of the new edition of the Encyclopaedia of Islam.

Erwin I. J. Rosenthal is Emeritus Reader in Oriental Studies at the University of Cambridge and Emeritus Fellow of Pembroke College, Cambridge.

Abdulaziz A. Sachedina is an assistant professor in the Department of Religious Studies at the University of Virginia in Charlottesville.

Roger M. Savory is a professor in the Department of Middle East and Islamic Studies in the University of Toronto.

George D. Sawa is Director of the Centre for Studies in Middle Eastern Music in Toronto.

R. Morton Smith is an emeritus professor in the Department of East Asian Studies in the University of Toronto.

Maria E. Subtelny is an assistant professor in the Department of Middle East and Islamic Studies in the University of Toronto.

Steven M. Wasserstrom is a doctoral student in the Centre for Religious Studies in the University of Toronto.

Preface

This Festschrift is presented to George Michael Wickens by his colleagues, to mark a lifetime of scholarly achievement in Middle East and Islamic Studies. Michael Wickens retired from the University of Toronto on 30 June 1984; in 1980, the University recognised his outstanding distinction in his field by conferring on him the highest accolade it can bestow, the title of University Professor.

This collection of essays is divided into three sections: Arabic Language and Literature (third/ninth–ninth/fifteenth centuries); Persian Language and Literature (fourth/tenth–ninth/fifteenth centuries); and Islamic Weltanschauung. This overall plan was decided upon in order to give the work a certain unity of theme, namely, medieval Islamic languages, literature and thought. The editors are acutely aware that, by making this decision, they have excluded important areas in which Professor Wickens has done very significant work, for example, modern Islamic literatures and comparative literature. In extenuation, the editors can only plead that the decision, at the time, seemed to be a necessary one.

The enthusiastic response to the editors' call for contributions to the Festschrift, from scholars in Canada, the United States, Great Britain and France, was eloquent testimony to Michael Wickens' international standing as a scholar. So, too, was the willingness of members of a distinguished editorial advisory board, consisting of scholars from Canada, the United States, France and Germany, to appraise the manuscripts which fell within their areas of competence, and the editors wish to take this opportunity of thanking them most sincerely for their help.

At the last moment, while this book was in press, the editors learned with profound regret that Laurence P. Elwell-Sutton, Emeritus Professor of Persian in the University of Edinburgh, and George Hourani of the Department of Philosophy in the State University of New York at Buffalo, both passed away in September 1984.

Roger M. Savory

Dionisius A. Agius

Acknowledgments

The editors wish to acknowledge with the deepest gratitude a number of generous grants-in-aid toward the cost of publishing this Festschrift.

In particular, the editors wish to express their thanks to Professor David W. Strangway, President of the University of Toronto, and to Dr. D. B. Cook, Assistant Provost; to Fr. John Kelly, CSB, Director of Alumni Affairs, St. Michael's College, and to Professor L. E. M. Lynch, former Principal of St. Michael's College; to Ms Carole Gillin, Director, Office of Research Administration, University of Toronto, and to Professor G. G. Ivey, Vice-President, Institutional Relations, University of Toronto; and to Professor K. R. Bartlett.

George Michael Wickens

G. M. Wickens
A Biographical Sketch

Roger M. Savory
The University of Toronto

By way of preamble, the author acknowledges his debt to the "oral history" communicated to him by Professor Wickens. In general, the traditions quoted in this biographical sketch are "sound," and the isnād of each consists of transmitters of unquestioned probity.

George Michael Wickens ("Michael" to his friends) was born in London on 7 August 1918. As he has wryly recorded, his home was "hard by the Caledonian Cattle Market and next-door to Pentonville Prison." His intellectual abilities were noted at his first elementary school, but it was the teachers at his second elementary school, on the outskirts of Highgate, who began to groom him for a scholarship to a high school, and in 1929 he entered Holloway County Secondary School. Once there, his goal became the winning of a scholarship to Cambridge. Fortunately for him, the School's strengths lay in the subjects for which he showed the greatest aptitude: languages, literature and history. He thus received a sound training in the Humanities, the branch of knowledge in which he was to make his subsequent mark as a scholar. His interests in philosophy and theology would come later.

After passing his matriculation examinations with distinction in 1934, Michael Wickens won the following year a London County Council Travelling Scholarship which enabled him to visit Germany. This visit not only broadened his intellectual horizons but enabled him to achieve an enviable mastery of spoken German. He was awarded a German Government prize for an essay in German on Thomas Mann's Death in Venice. "Fortunately or otherwise," he says, no copy of this early, handwritten work is extant.

In December 1935, Michael Wickens won an Open Major Scholarship to Trinity College, Cambridge, standing first in the list of

---

Logos Islamikos: Studia Islamica in honorem Georgii Michaelis Wickens, ed. Roger M. Savory and Dionisius A. Agius, Papers in Mediaeval Studies 6 (Toronto: Pontifical Institute of Mediaeval Studies, 1984), pp. 1-6.

scholarship winners, and he went up to Cambridge in the Michaelmas Term, 1936. Although his scholarship was in Modern Languages, before the end of his first year at Trinity he applied for permission to transfer to the programme in Oriental Languages. Given his linguistic ability, his choice might have fallen on Chinese, or Slavics, or even Old Norse. The principal criterion, he says, was that it should be something "unusual and difficult." In the event, he opted for the Oriental Languages Tripos; his decision to take Persian and Arabic appears to have been largely fortuitous, although The Arabian Nights had made a great impression on him when he was at elementary school. His College allowed him to study for the Oriental Languages Tripos on condition that he take Part I of the Modern Languages Tripos, that he complete the Oriental Course in two years, and that his Scholarship be forfeit if he fell below First Class.

Like many persons who won a place in that period at one of Britain's two senior universities by virtue of academic merit and not of social status, Michael Wickens looks back on his time at Cambridge as "probably the happiest in his whole life." "He revelled in his quasi-independent existence, in life in an ancient and aesthetically agreeable institution, in virtually unlimited access to books, and in long walks around the still healthy countryside. If he feared some black magic might take it all away, he was reasonably confident (despite some signs to the contrary) that he might well reach some inviolable security before the stroke of midnight." In 1939, Michael Wickens crowned his undergraduate career with a Double First and various prizes and scholarships, including the Yeats Prize, and was elected Senior Research Student at Trinity College. Nevertheless, a certain lack of confidence in his own outstanding abilities remained a permanent feature of his character.

The outbreak of World War II took the immediate control of affairs out of his hands. In February 1940, Michael Wickens was called up for military service as a private in the Royal Army Pay Corps (a defective right eye had debarred him from service with the infantry). Later that year, he took advantage of a thirty-six hours' leave to marry (9 November 1940) Ruth Lindop, whom he had been courting for several years. In the spring of 1941, he "committed the unpardonable offence" of asking the War Office for employment more consonant with his education and abilities. He was severely reprimanded for his temerity, but subsequently transferred to the Intelligence Corps. In the course of his training, he was gratified to face challenges once more, and "even to find among his colleagues quite a few sophisticated people and some engaging eccentrics"; among the latter were "former Soho waiters, Breton onion-sellers, and Armenian carpetdealers." In the autumn of 1941, he was posted overseas with the rank of Lance-Corporal (unpaid Acting Sergeant), and eventually came to rest as a member of Iran-Iraq Command, where he spent most of the next four years.

From early 1942 to late 1945, Michael Wickens belonged jointly to a combined Army-Air Force unit and to the British Legation (later Embassy) in Tehran. In 1943, after he had carried out special missions to India, Turkey and the Western Desert, and had played a part in the capture of German agents in Iran, he was commissioned and mentioned in despatches, and was eventually demobilized with the rank of substantive captain. Like others who had had similar experiences, he had to decide whether to take up "an almost ready-made career in the forces or in the diplomatic service," or to return to academic life.

In January 1946, he returned to Cambridge without any assurance of more than a temporary position. Shortly afterwards A. J. Arberry, then Professor of Arabic at the University of London, offered him a temporary teaching post at The School of Oriental and African Studies. He accepted this, and remained at the School for three years. In 1949, Professor Arberry was appointed to the Sir Thomas Adams's Chair of Arabic at Cambridge, and invited Michael Wickens to join him. In addition to his other duties at Cambridge, Wickens assumed the administrative position of executive secretary to the Faculty Board of Oriental Studies.

Michael Wickens' return to Cambridge was in many ways a homecoming, but there were some clouds on the horizon. In the first place, his appointment, like most at that time, was a University one, and, since it was not in a discipline that was likely to bring financial benefit to his old College, the latter's welcome was belated and half-hearted. The second cloud was a darker one. "It began to form imperceptibly, grew steadily and insidiously, and eventually resulted in his decision to leave Cambridge for good." Although Wickens' appointment at Cambridge was nominally in Arabic, he was also required to teach Persian and other subjects. In 1953 Professor

Arberry urged him to apply for the newly vacated Lectureship in Persian, in order to strengthen his claim to a new Chair of Persian due to fall vacant within a few years. Unfortunately, Wickens' appointment to the Lectureship in Persian was almost blocked by the supporters of a rival candidate, and this incident permanently soured the atmosphere of Cambridge for him. He began to consider alternatives.

In 1957, at the age of 39, Michael Wickens was invited to the University of Toronto by Sidney Smith, then President of the University, and by F.C.A. Jeanneret, Principal of University College. Wickens was appointed to the Department of Near Eastern Studies at University College, the Chairman of which was F. V. Winnett, the distinguished South Arabian scholar. This Department, for more than a hundred years, had offered courses on the ancient civilisations of the Near and Middle East, in programmes called "Oriental Studies" or "Near Eastern Studies." Wickens' mandate was to establish a Departmental interest in what was initially termed "Modern Near Eastern Studies," dealing with the Middle East since the rise of Islam. Wickens soon came to the conclusion that his plans for this new (to the University of Toronto) area of study could not be fulfilled within the college system as it then existed, and he pressed for the establishment of a separate University department. His suit was successful, and in 1961 a new University department with the name of the Department of Islamic Studies was established under his chairmanship; the total faculty complement of the Department was four.

Michael Wickens was Chairman of the Department of Islamic Studies from 1961 to 1968. Although the Department expanded rapidly during those relatively affluent years, it had not acquired the ultimate shape originally planned by Wickens before the ever more severe budgetary restrictions of the 1970's not only put an end to expansion but introduced the principle of attrition, as successive University Presidents spoke of "cutting close to the bone" and "making the University a leaner but harder" place. By the time the cuts began to take effect, however, the Department had become recognized as a leading centre of Middle East and Islamic Studies. During the formative years of the Department, in his tireless advocacy of the cause of Islamic Studies, Michael acquired the reputation of being _zūd-ranj_, "quick to take offence." He would give vent to his indignation in hard-hitting communications to University administrators, and receipt of a "Wickens' letter" was regarded by administrators as constituting membership in an exclusive club. Advancing years have brought a degree of mellowing, and Michael, in common with others, has had to husband his energies and restrict his "saeva indignatio" to a few, selected targets. Nevertheless, Michael remains a master of the mordant phrase, and those guilty of a lack of logic in their thinking, of a failure clearly to express their ideas, or of ungrammatical or inelegant writing, will have these defects pointed out to them in his own inimitable style. Michael derives great pleasure from drawing attention to the solecisms, mixed metaphors and other linguistic barbarities with which contemporary English, particularly that used in newspapers and by the media generally, abounds. The author has on a number of occasions urged him to publish an anthology of these as a contribution to contemporary humour.

In 1965, Michael Wickens was elected a Fellow of Academy II (Humanities and Social Sciences) of The Royal Society of Canada; he was only the second scholar in the field of Middle East and Islamic Studies to be so honoured in Canada. In 1980, the University of Toronto appointed him to the rank of University Professor, thus conferring on him its highest accolade. Michael Wickens, who reached the age of 65 on 7 August 1983, will retire from the University of Toronto on 30 June 1984, and this Festschrift, the work of his colleagues and students in Canada, the United States of America, Great Britain and France, is dedicated to him in recognition of his lifetime of outstanding service to Middle East and Islamic Studies.

Michael has been a prolific scholar (as the Bibliography of his published work included in this Festschrift attests), and we trust that he will long continue to publish the fruits of his research. Unlike many of the more narrowly competent scholars of the younger generation, Michael is at home in the broad fields of both classical and modern Arabic and Persian literatures, of Islamic Weltanschauung and Religious Studies, and of Comparative Literature. In the last-named, his early training in French and German, and his wide acquaintance with French and German literature, have enabled him to do work of a genuinely comparative nature. His work has always been characterized by original insights, derived from a profound knowledge of the sources; by an elegance of style that stems from the belief that language is a precise tool, to be wielded as a rapier and not as a bludgeon; and by lucid and logical exposition. Michael is an excellent teacher, and graduate students in particular have benefited from his willingness to give unstintingly of his time. His wisdom and experience have been repeatedly called upon by the University, and he has served on numerous important university committees. For a year or two, when the Department of East Asian Studies was undergoing an internal crisis, Michael Wickens managed the affairs of that Department as well as those of his own.

In his personal life, Michael had been blessed with a happy marriage, and he and Ruth have brought up eight children in circumstances of at times considerable economic hardship. Of recent years, Ruth's affliction with Alzheimer's disease has, naturally, caused Michael deep distress and additional labour, and has been a source of sorrow to his family and friends alike. The Roman Catholicism to which he and Ruth became converts in the late 1940's continues to be, despite their disillusionment with trends in the Church since the 1960's, of great importance in their lives, and Michael has remained a lay member of the Dominican Order. Michael has always been a person of decided opinions (some have found his manner abrasive), but can be relied upon to give his opinion honestly, without fear or favour. His friendship, once given, is steadfast. His many friends salute his achievements, and wish him God-speed in the years to come.

Part One
Arabic Language and Literature

The Contribution of Middle Arabic to the Vocabulary of Modern Standard Arabic

Joshua Blau
The Hebrew University of Jerusalem

It is imperative for any study dealing with Middle Arabic to clarify this term, since its use is by no means unequivocal. I use Middle Arabic to denote the mixed language of texts in which Classical Arabic, Neo-Arabic and pseudo-correct (including hyper-correct)[1] elements alternate. Classical Arabic is the chief representative of the Old Arabic lingual type, as opposed to Neo-Arabic, in modern times reflected by the contemporary Arabic dialects, whereas the Neo-Arabic component of medieval Middle Arabic texts constitutes its early layer.[2]

It is often overlooked that Modern Standard Arabic, although modelled on the orthography and morphology of Classical Arabic, is not devoid of Middle Arabic syntactic features.[3] Modern authors read medieval philosophic and scientific literature, in which the Neo-Arabic component is comparatively limited, as well as popular tales and romances, in which the Neo-Arabic layer is quite conspicuous, and thus absorb Neo-Arabic constructions contained in these Middle Arabic texts.[4] More Middle Arabic elements have penetrated Modern Standard Arabic vocabulary, and this is the topic of this paper.

Two caveats have, however, to be observed. First, Neo-Arabic vocabulary influences modern writers because they speak modern Arabic dialects. Therefore, it is often impossible to decide whether a certain word reflects the influence of a modern dialect or of a Middle Arabic text, or rather the joint impact of both.[5] Moreover, we do not possess historical Arabic dictionaries. Therefore, we have to rely on our rather partial knowledge of the Arabic vocabulary, and shall accordingly frequently err in attributing words to Middle Arabic

---

Logos Islamikos: Studia Islamica in honorem Georgii Michaelis Wickens, ed. Roger M. Savory and Dionisius A. Agius, Papers in Mediaeval Studies 6 (Toronto: Pontifical Institute of Mediaeval Studies, 1984), pp. 9-20.

although they occur in Classical texts as well. This, however, will not alter the general picture.

In the following I shall cite early occurrences of Modern Standard Arabic words in medieval Judeo-Arabic texts, i.e., in Middle Arabic sub-standard texts written by Jews. They are arranged in alphabetical order; translations are taken from Wehr (without mentioning Wehr *expressis verbis*). Words with meanings occuring in Lane (except when dubbed post-classical) or in Hava/Belot are not adduced, since they have to be regarded as belonging to the standard vocabulary of Arabic. Whenever the meaning dealt with is attested in Ayalon-Shinar's *Arabic-Hebrew Dictionary of Standard Modern Arabic*, I content myself with simply stating "AS." Square bracketed Roman numerals mark the century. In default of anything better, Middle Arabic quotations are vocalized in some kind of simplified classical Arabic.

(1) *uhba*; ^{c}*alà uhba*, "to be prepared, ready." AS, Blachère (who dubs also *akhadha uhbata-hū* modern, although Nöldeke cites it from *Ḥamāsa*; Nöldeke also cites *kūnū fī uhbatī* from *Kitāb al-Aghānī*): *Finkel* 1974, 122, -3 [XI] *li-yakūn* ^{c}*alà uhba fī 'n-nuzūl*, "to be prepared to go down."

(2) *battan*, "definitely." Dozy (Bocthor): Goitein 1983, 151, 13 [XVII] *bay*^{c}*an me*^{c}*akhshav thābitan akīdan lāziman* . . . .

(3) *bittun* (!); *batlan nāfidahan*, "a lasting, definite, binding and valid sale, from now once and for all, finally."

(4) *biṭāla*, "idleness, unemployment." AS, Blachère (mod.): Gibb 276, 2 [XII] ^{c}*arraftu-hū biṭālat-ī wa ta'akhkhur-ī*, "and I informed him that I was out of work and in straits."

(5) *bikriyy*, "first-born." Dozy (Bocthor): Maimonides [XII], *Responsa* 50, 9 *fa-kabur al-walad al-bikriyy*, "and the first-born son grew up."

(6) *tābāha*, "to be proud of." AS, Dozy (Bocthor), yet according to Blachère (who quotes *Lisān al-*^{c}*Arab*) it was used in all periods: *Perek* [XIV?] 67b, 7 *wa 'in kān yatabāhā wa yaftakhir*, "and if he glories and boasts."

(7) *bayyat*, "to contrive, hatch." AS, Blachère (mod.): *Tarbiz*, xxxiii, 193, b1 [XIII] *ittasal bi-nā ma bayyata-hū* ^{c}*alay-ka*, "we have been informed of what he had contrived against

you."

(8) jabar khāṭira-hū, "to console." AS, Doby (Bocthor), Blachère (mod.): Perek [XIV?] 91b, 10 wa yajbur khāṭir kull qalb munkasir min-nā, "and he will console every broken heart among us"; also Perek 1b, 11 jabar bi-khāṭiri-hī.

(9) ijrā'āt, "measures, steps." AS, Blachère: Goitein 1980, 101, 5 [XI] tamna^c nafsa-ka min ijrā-āt mā bi-sabab al-maqādisa, "you will restrain yourself from any measures for the Jerusalemites."

(10) injamad, "to freeze." AS, Dozy (Bocthor), Blachère (mod.): Saadya Gaon [X], translating Exodus 15:8 injamadat al-ghumūr, "the depths were frozen" (so ed. H. Dérenbourg; Tāj, jamad al-ghamr.

(11) jayb, "pocket." AS, Lane, Dozy (jayba from modern sources): Maimonides [XII], Mishna, ii, 55, -1 afmām tilka 'l-juyūb; Perek [XIV?] 106, 14 fārigh al-jayb, "with an empty pocket."

(12) ḥujja, "pretext." Dozy (Bocthor, Humbert), Blachère [Ibn Muqaffa^c, VIII]: Maimonides [XIII], Responsa 52, 8 ja^{c}al al-ḥujja.

(13) ḥaḍīḍ; nazal ilà 'l-ḥaḍīḍ, "to sink low." AS: Yefet, Daniel [XI] 12, 12 nazalū ilà 'l-ḥaṭīṭ(!).

(14) (naqd) ḥāḍir, "ready money, cash." Maimonides [XII], Responsa 45, 6; 83, 6; 84, -7.

(15) ḥāḍira, "city, district." AS: Ibn Ezra [1100] 48, 50 ḥawāḍir khurāsān; 50, 57.

(16) aḥaṭṭ, "lower." Maimonides [XII], Mishna i, 337, 13 tilka 'l-bilād aḥaṭṭ rutba min ereṣ yisra'el, "these countries have a lower rank than Palestine"; ii, 243, -4.

(17) ḥāffa, "border, edge, brink"; a later variant of ḥāfa. AS; Belot (vulgar), Hava (Syrian), Muḥīṭ al-Muḥīṭ: Perek [XIV?] 83b, 20 wa qa^{c}ad ^{c}alà ḥaffat 'l-līwān, "and he sat at the end of the sitting room"; one might note that with ḥaffat, the short (first) |a| attests to double |f| since in Middle Arabic |ā| tends to be shortened when standing in a syllable terminating in a double consonant (Blau 1981, 71).

(18) ḥafaz ^{c}alà, "to urge, prompt." AS: Maimonides [XII], Mishna ii, 120, 15 kull wāḥid min-hum ḥāfiz ^{c}alà ṣāḥibi-hī wa lā

yatruku-hu yata^c^adda hadda-hu; Friedlander.

(19) ḥaqqaq, "to study, examine." Perek [XIV?] 62, -7 wa yuḥaqqiq asrāra-hā; 62b, 12 darasū al-'umūr wa ḥaqqaqū as-sarā'ir ... wa ^c^arafū ghāyata-hā wa ḥaqqaqu ṣiḥḥata-hā; 69b, 3 ḥaqqaqnā wa daqqaqnā wa fattashnā.

(20) khass, "to decrease, diminish." Dozy (Bocthor, Muḥīṭ al-Muḥīṭ): Maimonides [XII], Responsa, 83/4 yaksud sūqu-hā takhass ^c^an dhālik as-si^c^r; Perek [XIV?] 37, 12 wa takhass quwwatu-hū; 65, 9 lā takhass sarmiyat-ō, "his assets will not diminish."

(21) bi-khuṣūṣ, "as to, concerning, as regards." AS, Dozy (Bocthor), Hava (Syrian): Perek [XIV?] 86, 10 wa tatakallam ma^c^a-hū bi-khuṣūṣ-ī; 89b, -5 wa 'aḥkā la-hom bi-lladhī jarà la-hū bi-khuṣūṣ al-waladayn.

(22) dashshan, "to consecrate, inaugurate." AS, Dozy (Muḥīṭ al-Muḥīṭ), Hava (Syrian), Graf: al-Fāsī [X] I, 564, 41 tadhsīn; Saadya Gaon [earlier X] uses dashn, as in Numbers 7:11 Psalms 30:1.

(23) dallal, "to pamper, coddle spoil." AS, Dozy (Bocthor, Humbert), but Belot, Hava cite it as Classical and not vulgar: Saadya Gaon [X], Deut. 28:56 al-mudallala ... min ad-dalāl (Dérenbourg: ad-dalala; read ad-dalāla?) wa 'r-rakhṣa; dalāl, "pampering, coddling" (also AS) also occurs in al-Fāsī [X] ii, 411, 64 dalāl wa tafannuq; Ibn Janah [XI] 536, 6 we he^c^anog ... ma^c^-nà al-jamī^c^ rafāhiya wa dalāl (var. lec. wa tadallul).

(24) indahash, "to be astonished." AS, Dozy (Bocthor, Humbert, Arabian Nights, Hava (Syrian); al-Fāsī [X] i, 200, 53; Yefet [X], Hab. i, 5; Pseudo-Maimonides, 7, 15.

(25) dhimma, barra'/abra' dhimmata-hū, "to exonorate, to release from a charge (Wehr s.v. abra'); to relieve one's conscience." AS, Dozy (Arabian Nights), Hava (Syrian): Goitein 1980, 318, 3 [1170] barra't dhimmat hiba al-madhkūr, "I exonorate the above-mentioned Hiba"; Maimonides [XII], Responsa 134, 10 wa 'abra' dhimmata-hū min-hu; Perek [XIV?] 47b, 18 wa [imma an tubrī dhimmat-ī min alḥaq wa 'anti ṭāliqa min-nī; fa-mā kān min-hā illā anna-hā abra'at dhimmata-hū fa-ṭallaqa-hā. Similarly Perek 64, 9 dhimmatu-hū barī'a, "he is not

indebted."

(26) rasāsiyy, "lead-coloured." Dozy (Bocthor): Tustaris [XI] 70, 11 wa 'th-thawb ar-rasāsiyy; 72, 25 thawbayn rasāsiyy.

(27) rayyah, "to give rest." Dozy (Bocthor), Hava (Syrian): Perek [XIV?] 64, 3 idhā ijtanabta qatᶜ al-dīn rayyahta nafsa-ka min al'ēva, "if you avoid passing a verdict, you save yourself from enmity"; 107b, 4 wa rayyihnā min shiᶜbud malkhuyot "and save us from servitude to the empires!"

(28) zaghal/zaghlan, "to adulterate, debase." AS, Dozy (from late sources), Hava (Syrian): Goitein 1983, 118, 24 [XII] harīr bi-kattān bi-ghayr zaghl.

(29) zahad, "to abstain, to renounce." With direct object; Dozy (Bocthor, Arabian Nights): Perek [XIV?] 22b, 7; 95b 10; 106, 18; 107, 7.

(30) sakat ᶜan, "to pass over in silence." AS, Dozy (Bocthor): Maimonides [XII], Responsa 34, 2 wa ma huwa amr an yuskat ᶜan-hū, "it is not something that can be passed over in silence."

(31) tasaltan, "to become ruler." AS, Dozy (from late sources), Hava (Syrian): Perek [XIV?] 105b, 14 lā yatasaltan ᶜalay-him illā sana wāhida; saltan, "to establish as ruler" (AS, Hava [Syrian]) occurs ibid., 12 yusaltinū-hu ᶜalay-him.

(32) (darb) sālik, "passable, clear, open (road)." AS, Dozy (Bocthor)" Perek [XIV?] 55b, -2.

(33) shakhat, "to shout." Spiro: Perek [XIV?] 3b, 4; 4b, 9; 4b, 19; 50b, 16.

(34) inshighāl, "apprehension, concern, anxiety." AS, Dozy (Bocthor): Perek [XIV?] 70, 20 wa hom bi-'awjāᶜ wa qalaq wa hamm wa nshighāl bāl.

(35) saffā, "to settle, straighten out." AS: Tarbiz xxxvii, 168, 33 [XI] nusaffī umūrī.

(36) dawwā, "to shed light." Dozy (late sources): Perek [XIV?] 103b, 13 kān wajh-ak judawwi mithl al-qamar.

(37) taᶜim, "tasty, delicious." Dozy (Bocthor), Spiro: Perek [XIV?] 52, 18 lahm al-jady ahsan wa 'atᶜam.

(38) tasa, "drinking vessel." AS, Dozy (Bocthor, Arabian Nights): Sefunot viii, 125, 24 [XII].

(39 tālamā, "how often!, often, frequently." Siddur Saadya [X] 69, 3

wa tāl mā nāla-nī min aḍ-ḍarr wa 'd-dīqa, "and how often did loss and anguish afflict me"; Perek [XIV?] 28, 17 fa-lā-tālamā maddayta yada-ka li-māl ghayri-ka.

(40) tālamā, "as long as, while." AS, Dozy (Bocthor): Maimonides [XII], Mishna ii, 81, -9; vi, 57, 3; Tanhum [XIII], s.v. qṣṣ.

(41) ^{c}aṭṭal, "to hinder, stop, impede." Dozy (Bocthor): al-Fāsī [X] i, 221, 81 fa-^{c}aṭṭalū at-tujjār min an yadkhulū ilay-hā bi-'t-tajā'ir.

(42) ^{c}azam, "to invite." AS, Hava (Syrian) Dozy (late sources): Perek [XIV?] 46, 11 kān marra wāḥida ma^{c}zūm; 83b, 19 anta^{c}azamta-nī; 83b, -5.

(43) lil-ghāya, "extremely, very (much)." AS, Spiro: Perek [XIV?] 29b, 23 fa-ghtamma bi-qalbi-hī jiddan fa-ḥazina lil-ghāya; 50b, 4 ^{c}alim lil-ghāya; 84b, -5 jayyid lil-ghāya.

(44) muftakhir, "excellent, superb, magnificent." Dozy (Bocthor, Arabian Nights), Spiro (who vocalizes muftakhar): Perek [XIV?] 63b, 20 ḥāja-muftakhira, "an expensive article."

(45) mufarraq, "retail." AS: Tarbiz xxxviii, 30, 13 [XI] wa kuntu bi^{c}tu la-ka mufarraq.

(46) bi-'t-tafṣīl, "in detail, elaborately, minutely." Maimonides [XII], v. Friedländer s.v.; he also uses (Mishna ii, 215, 16) ^{c}alà 't-tafṣīl.

(47) fawqa dhālika, "moreover, besides, furthermore, in addition to that." Perek [XIV?] 65, 9.

(48) istafād, "to derive advantage from." Also governs bi: Perek [XIV?] 63, 11 ma arād yastafīd bi-tāj at-tora, "he did not want to derive advantage from the study of the Law."

(49) muqbil, "succeeding, prosperous." AS (qbl IV; Wehr, however, only of crops and in phrases like aqbala ^{c}alay-hi 'd-dahru, Hava (Syrian), Dozy (Bocthor): Gibb 277, 40 [XII] mahmā anta fī 'l-maḥyāti anā manḥūs, law mutta, kuntu muqbil, "as long as you are alive, I will be a good-for-nothing; if you were dead, I would be successful."

(50) qasam, "to give someone a share, to allot." Dozy (Arabian Nights): Perek [XIV?] 100b, 21 ya'hkudh mā qusim la-hū.

(51 qaṭ^{c}iyy, "final, definitive." AS: Goitein 1983 [XVII] 151, 13-15 bay^{c}a qaṭ^{c}iyyan.

(52) qafal, "to shut, close." AS, Dozy (Bocthor): Sefunot viii, 116, 13 [1137] khizāna maqfūl ^{c} alay-hā.

(53) qahr, "sorrow, grief." Marked by Wehr as Egyptian; Dozy (Bocthor, Arabian Nights): Perek [XIV?, Egyptian as well], 72, 7 qahr wa 'amrāḍ wa humūm; 107b, 14 bilā qahr wa lā ghamm.

(54) kabsha (= kamsha), "handful." AS, Lane, Dozy (late sources), WKAS, Hava (Syrian): Perek [XIV?] 95b, 13 kabshat tibn.

(55) kābī, "dull, dim, pale." Dozy (Bocthor), Hava (Egyptian), Spiro; I have cited this item on purpose to demonstrate how misleading our dictionaries may be. However, this meaning is well attested in Classical Arabic, v. WKAS s.v. kabā: Saadya Gaon [X] on Leviticus 13:39 buqa^c kābiya bīḍ, and several times in this chapter.

(56) kasar khāṭira-hū, "to humble, humiliate." AS, Dozy (Bocthor), Hava (Syrian; s.v. maksūr), WKAS (post-classical): Perek [XIV?] 4b, 8 li-'ann al-^{c}aniyim (i.e., the poor ones) wa 'l-'arāmil wa 'l-aytām khāṭiru-hum maksūr; 46b, 14 kull man yaḥinn ^{c}alà 'l-maksūr al-khāṭir; 100b, 10.

(57) inkasaf, "to be ashamed." Cf. Dozy (from Bar ^{c}Ali, [IX]): Perek [XIV?] 9b, 7 lā shakk anna-hū yankasif; 13b, 17 inkasaf min al-ḥakham, "he felt embarrassed in front of the sage."

(58) ka^{c}b, "heel of a shoe." AS: Tanhum [XIII], s.v. sandal: min^{c}al kull mā la-hū ka^{c}b wa sandal mā laysa la-hū ka^{c}b, "everything that has a heel [is called in Hebrew] min^{c}al, and what does not have a heel [is called in Hebrew] sandal."

(59) laṭash, "to strike, hit." AS, Dozy (from late sources), Hava (Syrian), M.-T. Féghali, Memoires de la Société de linguistique de Paris, 27 (1920), 243: Perek [XIV?] 60, 11.

(60) la^{c}ib, "to play an instrument." AS, Hava (Syrian), Dozy (Muḥīṭ al-Muḥīṭ): Gibb [1131] 274, 30 wa 't-ṭabl wa 'z-zamr fī dār-ī wa 'l-la^{c}b, "and drum(s) and oboe(s) and music [were] in my house."

(61) māshik, "tongs." Dozy (Bocthor, Hélot), Hava (both s.v. māsik): Perek [XIV?] 80b, 8.

(62) istamlak, "to possess, to lay hold of, to dominate." AS, Hava (Syrian), Dozy (Bocthor): MS Bodl. Neubauer 793 [XII] 1b wa mukhtaṣṣun dūna-hū (scil. dūn al-ḥayawān) bi-'n-nuṭq wa

'l-^{c}aql al-ladhān bi-himā istamlaknā-hu wa stadhlalnā-hu.

(63) nashsh, "to drive away flies." AS, Spiro, Dozy (Arabian Nights): Perek [XIV?] 52b, 5 wa yanishsh bi-hī adh-dhibbān min ^{c}alà wajhi-h.

(64) nā^{c}im, "fine, powdery." Hava (Syrian), Dozy (Bocthor, Muḥīṭ al-Muḥīṭ): Tanhum [XIII], sv. mlḥ: inna-hū muhabbā ay nā^{c}im fī-'l-ghāya wa 'n-nihāya.

(65) nā'ib, "share, portion." Dozy (Bocthor): Maimonides [XII], Responsa 159, 5 inna-kum sukkān fī nā'ibi-hinna; 11 bay^{c} ḥissa min nāibi-hinna; Gil 287, 13 [XII] nā'ib al-qodesh "the share of the religious endowment"; 347, -3 ^{c}an nā'ibi-hī fī 'l-kiswa; Perek [XIV?] 52, 8 ta'khudhū nā'iba-kum min dhālika 'l-qurbān.

(66) nawāya, plural of niyya, "intention." AS, Hava (Syrian): Perek [XIV?] 92, 6 wa tafah-hum nawāyā-hom.

(67) harbān, "fugitive." Dozy (late sources), Hava (Syrian): Perek [XIV?] 83b, 21 wa ṭala^{c} yajrī harbān, "and he went out, running and fleeing."

(68) istahwan, "to esteem lightly." AS: Maimonides [XII], Mishna vi, 37, 7.

(69) wasaq, "to load, freight a ship." AS, Dozy (late), Hava: Tarbiz xxxvi 381, 12 [XI] yaqif ma-^{c}ī fī wasqi-hā ... wa 'in ittafaq la-hū wasqu-hā; Tustaris [XI] 81, 20 bi-wasqi-hā lil-qayruwān; Perek [XIV?] 83, 1.

R. Dozy in his Supplément aux dictionnaires arabes cited many Judeo-Arabic lexical items from Middle Arabic sources. Since it is not easy to determine the proper limits of Middle Arabic, I shall content myself with adducing Judeo-Arabic terms cited by Dozy from the Arabian Nights which could be considered as Middle Arabic:

bāshar, "to be in direct contact with" (also figuratively)

buq^{c}a, "spot, stain"

jawq, "company" (where the older sources cited by Dozy are Judeo-Arabic)

maḥẓiyya, "concubine"

istakhdam, "to employ, use"

kharaṭ, "to shape with a lathe"

tadammar, "to be ruined, to perish"

<u>qā'im bi-dhāti-hī</u>, "independent"

<u>bi-ra'si-hī</u>, "independent"

<u>marmūq</u>, "noted, of note, important"

<u>irtamà</u>, "to throw himself"

<u>zamr</u>, "a wind instrument resembling the oboe"

<u>zīja</u>, "marriage" (the reference to de Sacy's <u>Christomathy</u> is erroneous)

<u>mashrūb</u> "drink, beverage"

<u>ashraf ᶜalà</u>, "to supervise"

<u>shāṭir</u>, "clever, smart"

<u>istashᶜar</u>, "to feel, perceive, be filled with"

<u>ṣābūn</u>, "soap"

<u>ṣīniyy</u>, "porcelain"

<u>ṣīniyya</u>, "serving tray"

<u>ṭaraḥat</u>, "to miscarry"

<u>maṭraḥ</u>, "place"

<u>ṭawq</u>, "collar"

<u>ṭāqa</u>, "window"

<u>ᶜudda</u>, "implement, tool"

<u>ghibba</u>, "after"

<u>faraḥ</u>, "wedding"

<u>farraᶜ</u>, "to put forth branches"

<u>iftaqad</u>, "to examine, inspect"

<u>qaddar</u>, "to appraise, estimate, value"

<u>qidra</u>, "kettle, pot"

<u>qumāsh</u>, "fabric, cloth, material"

<u>qawwat</u>, "to feed, nourish, sustain"

<u>fī qayd al-ḥayāt</u>, "still alive, living"

<u>kulfa</u>, "expenses, expenditure"

<u>laqqan</u>, "to dictate, insinute, suggest"

<u>marragh</u>, "to roll in the dust"

<u>amᶜan an-naẓar</u>, "to examine closely"

<u>anᶜaẓ</u>, "to erect the membrum virile, to be sexually excited"

<u>istankar</u>, "to disapprove, reject"

<u>tanāwal</u>, "to take up, treat, deal with"

<u>tawāṣal</u>, "to form an uninterrupted sequence"

<u>waffar</u>, "to lay by, put by, save"

<u>tawaffar</u>, "to be saved (money)"

istawafà, "to complete, bring to a finish, go through with"

We have already called attention several times to the fact that, in default of historical Arabic dictionaries, words cited as Middle Arabic may well be Classical. We have indeed demonstrated this in the case of *kābī*, and to emphasize the importance of this fact we will conclude this paper with another word of this kind, the phrase *^{c}alà lisāni-hī*, "from his mouth, through him" (AS), which is marked by Hava as vulgar, although it is well attested in Classical Arabic, v. *WKAS*. It is not merely chance that in both cases it was with the help of the only existing partial historical dictionary, the *Wörterbuch der klassischen arabischen Sprache*, that the existence of these words in Classical Arabic could have been demonstrated.

Abbreviations

As	D. Ayalon and P. Shinar, *Arabic-Hebrew Dictionary of Standard Modern Arabic*, 2nd ed. (Jerusalem, 1952).
Belot	J. B. Belot, *Vocabulaire arabe-français*, 10th ed. (Beyrouth, 1910).
Blachère	R. Blachère, M. Chouémi and C. Denizeau, *Dictionnaire arabe-français-anglais* (Paris, 1967--).
Blau, 1981	J. Blau, *The Emergence and Linguistic Background of Judaeo-Arabic*, 2nd ed. (Jerusalem, 1981).
Dozy	R. Dozy, *Supplément aux dictionnaires arabes*, 2 vols. (Leiden, 1881).
al-Fāsī	David ben Abraham al-Fāsī, *Kitāb Jāmi^{c} al-Alfāz*, ed. S. L. Skoss (New Haven, 1936-1945).
Finkel	*J. Finkel Festschrift*, ed. S. B. Hoenig and L. D. Stitskin (New York, 1974).
Friedländer	I. Friedlaender, *Arabisch-Deutsches Lexikon zum Sprachgebrauch des Maimonides* (Frankfurt, 1902).
Gibb	*Arabic and Islamic Studies in Honor of H. A. R. Gibb*, ed. G. Makdisi (Leiden, 1965).
Gil	M. Gil, *Documents of the Jewish Pious Foundations from the Cairo Geniza* (Leiden, 1976).
Goitein, 1980	S. D. Goitein, *Palestinian Jewry in Early*

	Islamic and Crusader Times [in Hebrew] (Jerusalem, 1980).
Goitein, 1983	S. D. Goitein, *The Yemenites* [in Hebrew] (Jerusalem, 1983).
Graf	G. Graf, *Verzeichnis arabischer christlicher Termini*, 2nd ed. (Louvain, 1954).
Hava	J. G. Hava, *Arabic-English Dictionary* (Beirut, 1915).
Ibn Ezra	M. ibn Ezra, *Kitāb al-Muḥāḍara wa 'l-Mudhākara*, ed. A. S. Halkin (Jerusalem, 1975).
Ibn Janah	A. M. Ibn Janah, *The Book of Hebrew Roots (Kitāb al-Uṣūl)*, ed. A. Neubauer (Oxford, 1973-1975).
Lane	E. W. Lane, *An Arabic-English Lexicon*, Book 1 in 8 parts (London, 1863-1893).
Maimonides, *Mishna*	*Moses Maimonides' Mishnah Commentary*, ed. Y. Kafiḥ (Jerusalem, 1963-1969).
Maimonides, *Responsa*	Moses ben Maimon, *Responsa*, ed. J. Blau, 2 vols. (Jerusalem, 1957-1960).
Pseudo-Maimonides	*De Beatudine ... De Beatudine capita duo*, R. Mosi ben Maimon adscripta, ed. H. S. Davidowitz and D. H. Baneth (Jerusalem, 1939).
Muḥīṭ al-Muḥīṭ	B. Bustānī, *Muḥīṭ al-Muḥīṭ*, 2 vols. (Beirut, 1867-1870).
Nöldeke	T. Noldekes, *Belegwörterbuch zur klassischen arabischen Sprache*, ed. J. Kraemer (Berlin, 1952).
Perek	David Maimonides (attributed to), *Sefer Pirḳe Avot^{c}im perush belashon ^{c}aravi*, ed. B. H. Ḥanan (Alexandria, 1900-1901).
Saadya Gaon	Saadya Gaon, *Bible Commentary*. The Pentateuch commentary is, as a rule, cited according to the Yemenite tradition (in the *Tāj*); sometimes, however, Dérenbourg's edition is quoted.
Sefunot	*Sefunot*, periodical edited by the Ben Zwi Institute, Jerusalem.
Siddur Saadya	*Siddur R. Saadya Gaon ...*, ed. I. Davidson, S. Assaf, and B. I. Joel (Jerusalem, 1941).
Spiro	S. Spiro, *An Arabic-English Vocabulary of the Colloquial Arabic of Egypt* (Cairo/London, 1895).
Tanḥum	Tanḥum Hayerushalmi, *Al-Murshid al-Kāfī*, cited according to the dictionary entries. Letters |a|-|k| were edited by B. Toledano (Tel-Aviv, 1961); letters |l|-|sh| by H. Shay (doctoral dissertation, Jerusalem, 1975); and letter

	|t| by J. Dane (master's thesis, Jerusalem, 1969).
Tarbiz	*Tarbiz*, quarterly, Jerusalem.
Tustaris	M. Gil, *The Tustaris, Family and Sect* (Tel-Aviv, 1981).
Wehr	H. Wehr, *A Dictionary of Modern Written Arabic*, 4th edition, ed. J. M. Cowan (Wiesbaden, 1979).
WKAS	*Wörterbuch der klassischen arabischen Sprache*, ed. M. Ullmann (Wiesbaden, 1957).
Yefet, *Daniel*	Jephet ibn Ali, *A Commentary on the Book of Daniel*, ed. D. S. Margoliouth (Oxford, 1889).

Notes

[1] For this term cf. J. Blau, *On Pseudo-Corrections in Some Semitic Languages* (Jerusalem, 1970).

[2] J. Blau, *The Emergence and Linguistic Background of Judaeo-Arabic*, 2nd ed. (Jerusalem, 1981), p. 213.

[3] J. Blau, "Remarks on Some Syntactical Trends in Modern Standard Arabic," *Israel Oriental Studies*, 3 (1973), 173-182; idem, "Some Additional Observations on Syntactic Trends in Modern Standard Arabic," *Israel Oriental Studies*, 6 (1976), 158-161.

[4] I would prefer to call the language of philosophical and scientific writings Middle Arabic Standard, and that of popular literature, because of the prevalence of the Neo-Arabic layer, Middle Arabic Substandard. W. Fischer (ed., *Grundriss der arabischen Philologie* [Wiesbaden, 1982], p. 46) dubs the former post-classical, restricting Middle Arabic to texts reflecting regular deviations from Classical morphology. Yet I wonder whether many post-classical texts do not exhibit regular transitions of verbs III |ā| to III |y|. In my opinion, Middle Arabic Standard and post-classical Arabic are identical, the latter being looked upon from the vantage point of Classical Arabic.

[5] For the extent of subjective judgment, cf. S. Wild in Fischer, p. 53, n. 5.

Ṣafwān ibn Ṣafwān al-Anṣārī et Beshshār ibn Burd

Charles Pellat
L'Université de Paris (Sorbonne)

H.S. Nyberg, qui attribue légitimement une haute valeur documentaire au *Bayān* de Jāḥiẓ, fait état, dans l'article *Mu^{c}tazila* de la première édition de l'*Encyclopédie de l'Islam*, des poèmes de Ṣafwān b. Ṣafwān al-Anṣārī conservés par le grand écrivain, pour affirmer qu'à la suite de la scission qui se produisit entre Wāṣil b. ^{c}Aṭā' et ^{c}Amr b. ^{c}Ubayd, d'une part, et Bashshār b. Burd, d'autre part, après leurs entretiens avec ^{c}Abd al-Karīm b. Abī l-^{c}Awjā' et Ṣāliḥ b. ^{c}Abd al-Quddūs,[1] la lutte contre la *zandaqa* et la *thanawiyya* fut "un point cardinal du programme de la Mu^{c}tazila"; les poèmes en question, tout en apportant un écho de la polémique engagée contre Bashshār, seraient un "document fondamental de l'histoire de la dogmatique mu^{c}tazilite," car ils représentent, pour Nyberg, un spécimen d'une théologie de la terre opposée à la doctrine du feu professée par le célèbre poète de Baṣra. Par ailleurs l'orientaliste suédois tire des mêmes poèmes l'idée que Wāṣil et ses disciples ont pu prendre directement part à la propagande ^{c}abbāside.

J'ai déjà eu l'occasion de présenter une partie des vers de Ṣafwān al-Anṣārī conservés,[2] et si j'ai jugé bon d'y revenir, ce n'est point pour discuter en détail les opinions de Nyberg, mais pour essayer d'éclairer autant que faire se peut la personnalité d'un poète visiblement mu^{c}tazilite sur lequel Jāḥiẓ, et lui seul, fournit quelques renseignements, au demeurant bien sommaires.

Dès l'abord, se pose une question de chronologie. Des vers dont on trouvera plus loin un essai de traduction, il serait permis de déduire que Ṣafwān était le comtemporain de Bashshār (m. en 167 ou 168/784-785); il semblerait aussi avoir connu Wāṣil b. ^{c}Aṭā' (m. 131/748-749) dont il parle au présent et ^{c}Amr b. ^{c}Ubayd

Logos Islamikos: Studia Islamica in honorem Georgii Michaelis Wickens, ed. Roger M. Savory and Dionisius A. Agius, Papers in Mediaeval Studies 6 (Toronto: Pontifical Institute of Mediaeval Studies, 1984), pp. 21-34. © P.I.M.S. 1984.

(80-144/699-761). Or Jāḥiẓ, qui lui attribue des vers sur le palmier[3] sans intérêt immédiat, fait surtout de lui le transmetteur de fragments poétiques concernant particulièrement l'éléphant[4] et composés par un mawlà des Azdites, Hārūn b. Mūsà, dont il avoue ne connaître que le nom. D'une information fournie par Masᶜūdī,[5] il ressort que Ṣafwān ne put probablement rencontrer ce Hārūn qu'au Sind, où il se rendit, comme on le verra, entre 184/800 et 205/820, alors que Dāwūd b. Yazīd b. Ḥātim al-Muhallabī gouvernait la province. A se fonder sur ces dates, on est en droit d'avancer qui si Ṣafwān a pu à la rigueur rencontrer Bashshār, il est peu vraisemblable qu'il ait connu ᶜAmr b. ᶜUbayd et, à plus forte raison, Wāṣil b. ᶜAṭā'.

Sa présence au Sind après 184/800 est attestée par Jāḥiẓ, qui lui doit des observations directes sur les éléphants[6] et le compte parmi "les visiteurs"[7] du Muhallabide, sur qui nous possédons heureusement quelques données biographiques.[8] Désigné par son père Yazīd, gouverneur de l'Ifrīqiya depuis 155/772, comme son successeur pendant la maladie qui devait l'emporter en 170/786, il n'exerça ses fonctions que quelques mois et fut remplacé par son oncle, Rawḥ b. Ḥātim,[9] qu'al-Rashīd venait de nommer. Après son retour à Baghdād en 171/787, il reçut le commandement d'une armée envoyée au Khurāsān pour combattre les Kharijites, puis vécut dans l'entourage du calife, qui lui confia le gouvernement de l'Égypte en 174/790, le rappela l'année suivante, le garda, semble-t-il, au près de lui et le nomma enfin, en 184/800, gouverneur du Sind, où il demeura jusqu'à sa mort, survenue en 205/820. Au cours de son long séjour à Multān, il fut l'objet des louanges de plusieurs poètes parmi lesquels se distinguent Muslim b. al-Walīd[10] (m. 208/823), ᶜAbd Allāh b. Muḥammad b. Abī ᶜUyayna (m. après 204/819) et son frère ᶜUyayna (m. avant son aîné).[11]

Il se trouve qu'une pièce du cadet des deux frères[12] dans laquelle le poète compare Qabīṣa b. Rawḥ b. Ḥātim à son cousin Dāwūd b. Yazīd et marque sa préférence pour ce dernier, figure intégralement dans le Dīwān de Bashshār.[13] A. Ghedira, dans son commentaire, rejette à bon droit pareille attribution, en considérant comme peu vraisemblable que Bashshār ait pu adresser des louanges à Dāwūd qui, en 167/784, était encore obscur et vivait dans l'ombre de son père Yazīd, a qui le poète aveugle a d'ailleurs consacré au moins un panégyrique.[14] Plusieurs autres sont dédiés à Rawḥ b. Ḥātim[15] et, dans l'un d'eux,[16] est cité un fils de ce dernier qui s'appelait également Dāwūd. Il convient donc d'être circonspect dès l'instant que le nom du mamdūḥ est Dāwūd. Non seulement un Dāwūd b. Ḥātim figure dans l'introduction d'une pièce,[17] alors qu'il n'existe apparemment aucun personnage de ce nom, mais encore toute une urjūza[18] qui, d'après le recenseur du Dīwān, serait adressée à Dāwūd b. Yazīd, ne contient probablement aucun nom.[19] Il ressort de ce qui précède qui Bashshār, qui a connu plusieurs descendants d'al-Muhallab, n'a vraisemblablement pas fait le panégyrique de Dāwūd b. Yazīd lui-même.

En revanche, si la notation de Jāḥiẓ déjà citée (avec la correction qui s'impose,[20] car Dāwūd, n'étant pas poète, n'avait nul besoin de ruwāt), permet de considérer que Ṣafwān s'est rendu au Sind au plus tôt en 184/800, rien n'interdit de penser, d'abord qu'il eut l'occasion de fréquenter Bashshār pendant quelques années avant la mort de ce dernier vers 167/784, ensuite qu'il put rencontrer Dāwūd à Baghdad et même en Égypte, ainsi que pourrait le laisser supposer une allusion au Muqaṭṭam dans l'un de ses poèmes.[21]

Cela étant, et quelle que soit la date à laquelle remontent les premières relations des deux hommes, il conviendrait de savoir dans quel dessein Ṣafwān a pu entreprendre son voyage jusqu'an Sind. Il est probable que Dāwūd, homme de guerre et haut fonctionnaire de l'administration ᶜabbāside, ne s'intéressait aux doctrines politico-religieuses que dans la mesure où elles risquaient de troubler l'ordre public; sans doute était-il par atavisme et par devoir anti-khārijite, mais il ne voyait certainement dans les Khārijites que des rebelles dont il fallait réprimer les menées. Ibn Taghrībardī[22] rapporte que, durant son séjour en Égypte, il mit à la raison des troupes qui s'étaient mutinées et dispersa les rebelles en les expédiant vers l'Est, ce qui se comprend, et vers l'Ouest, c'est-à-dire a l'amīr umayyade Hishām Ier, qui avait alors à réduire la révolte fomentée par Maṭrūḥ à Barcelone en 173/789.[23] On ne sait comment interpreter cette collusion entre un gouverneur ᶜabbāside d'Égypte et un amīr umayyade d'Espagne; au demeurant, Dāwūd n'avait peut-être vu là qu'un moyen de se débarrasser d'une troupe turbulente, qui fut d'ailleurs capturée par les Francs en Méditerranée.

Il est par conséquent difficile d'établir un rapprochement entre l'activité de Dāwūd et la propagande muᶜtazilite à laquelle se serait livré Ṣafwān, et l'on ne saurait affirmer que ce dernier s'est rendu au Sind en qualité de *dā^{c}ī*, d'autant qu'à la fin du IIe/VIIIe siècle la *da^{c}wa* était certainement beaucoup moins intense que durant la période où le Mu^{c}tazilisme avait encore besoin d'être soutenu par une organisation perfectionnée.

Les poèmes de Ṣafwān nous apportent précisément un écho de cette activité initiale. Ils sont tous dirigés contre Bashshār et font allusion aux croyances des Kāmiliyya, tenants de la parousie (*raj^{c}a*) de l'Imām et du dogme de la supériorité du feu sur la terre que le poète baṣrien paraît avoir adopté avant 131/748-749, c'est-à-dire avant la mort de Wāṣil, puisque la brouille survenue entre les deux hommes date justement du revirement de Bashshār.[24] Une remarque de Jāḥiẓ[25] donne à entendre qu'après cette brouille, Bashshār, en butte aux attaques des premiers Mu^{c}tazilites, ne se montra plus jusqu'à la mort de ^{c}Amr b. ^{c}Ubayd (144/761). Quoi qu'il en soit, à en juger par les volumes publiés du *Dīwān* et la notice de l'*Aghānī* (où Ṣafwān n'est d'ailleurs pas cité), Bashshār ne semble effectivement pas avoir répondu aux poèmes de son détracteur, qui datent peut-être de cette période de silence.

Il est intéressant de voir comment ces derniers sont amenés dans le *Bayān*, qui est fondamentalement consacré à l'analyse des moyens d'expression. C'est le défaut d'élocution de Wāṣil, sa *luthgha*, qui sert d'introduction.[26] Un interlocuteur à qui Jāḥiẓ demande comment procédait Wāṣil pour dissimuler cette *luthgha* qui lui interdisait d'employer des mots contenant un *rā'* et comment il s'arrangeait pour exprimer les nombres ^{c}*ashra*, ^{c}*ishrīn*, *arba^{c}īn*, répond en citant ce vers de Ṣafwān,[27]

> Objet d'une suggestion et d'une inspiration en ce qu'il entreprend, riche d'idées, grand voyageur,

ce qui n'est guère explicite, mais laisse déjà entendre que l'auteur de ce vers était sinon un panégyriste, du moins un défenseur de Wāṣil, certainement après sa mort. Cette remarque conduit Jāḥiẓ à expliquer le surnom de Ghazzāl donné à Wāṣil, notamment par Bashshār qui, après l'avoir comblé de louanges avant sa conversion à la *raj^{c}a*, lui adressa ces vers:[28]

> Pourquoi accompagner un fileur de laine[29] au cou aussi long, par devant et par derrière, que celui d'une autruche du désert,
> Un cou de girafe? Pourquoi traiter d'impies des gens qui ont excommunié cet (?) homme?

C'est alors que Jāḥiẓ cite[30] un premier poème de Ṣafwān à la gloire de Wāṣil et de son action exercée par l'intermédiaire des du^cāt,[31] puis un vers isolé:[32]

> Il n'a ni palpé un dīnār, ni empoché un dirham; jamais n'a connu de vêtement taillé à sa mesure.

Ayant ensuite rappelé que Bashshār, après avoir proclamé la supériorité du feu sur la terre, prononcé son vers célèbre,[33]

> La terre est sombre, et le feu, éclatant de lumière; le feu est adoré depuis qu'il existe,

et attaqué Wāṣil, Jāḥiẓ reproduit tout naturellement un deuxième poème de Ṣafwān consacré à la réfutation de la doctrine de Bashshār[34] puis un troisième[35] encore destiné à prouver la supériorité de la terre sur le feu, mais dont il subsiste principalement un fragment à la louange de Wāṣil. Il est probable qu'à ces pièces s'ajoutaient des épigrammes plus acides, à en juger par ces deux vers également conservés par Jāḥiẓ:[36] s'adressant à la mère de Bashshār, Ṣafwān s'écrie,

> Tu as mis au monde une taupe,[37] une hyene mâle d'une laideur repoussante, puis un lièvre qui peine dans les montées,
>
> Trois [fils] qui sont affiliés à trois sectes différentes. On peut ainsi déceler la part de l'oncle maternal dans un enfant.[38]

Le premier poème, reproduit et traduit en appendice, concerne les du^cāt; il a servi à Nyberg d'argument en faveur de la collusion entre les propagandistes ^cabbāsides et mu^ctazilites. D. Sourdel[39] ne rejette pas la possibilité de l'envoi, par Wāṣil, de tels émissaires, mais il tend à rattacher leur activité aux mouvements d'inspiration shī^cite et à mettre l'accent sur l'attitude commune des Mu^ctazilites et des Zaydites au début de l'époque ^cabbāside. En fait, rien, dans les poèmes de Ṣafwān qui nous sont parvenus, ne prouve que les du^cāt mu^ctazilites aient travaillé au profit des ^cAbbāsides. Touchant les Shī^cites, les attaques du poète sont dirigées contre la croyance à la raj^ca professée par les Kāmiliyya extrémistes et adoptée par Bashshār, et aucun vers ne permet de tirer des conclusions précises.

La qaṣīda à la louange de la terre paraît avoir joui d'une certaine renommée, bien que la personnalité de Ṣafwān reste obscure[40] pour les auteurs qui ont copié Jāḥiẓ. Quoiqu'il soit dangereux de vouloir tirer du titre d'un ouvrage des indications sur son contenu, il n'est pas impossible que cette pièce ait figuré dans le Kitāb al-Ma^cādin de cet auteur, mais il est visible que les écrivains postérieurs se sont fondés sur le *Bayān*. D'abord Baghdādī[41] (m. 429/1037), puis, fort curieusement, Abū 'l-Ḥasan ʿAlī b. Yūsuf al-Ḥakīm (VIIIe/XIVe siècle), qui, dans *al-Dawḥa al-mushtabika fī ḍawābiṭ dār al-sikka*,[42] fait précéder les vers qu'il cite de la mention *qāl Ṣafwān*, comme dans le *Bayān*. Nyberg estime que la "philosophie de la terre" s'inspire des alchimistes, mais il est bien certain que les vers dans lesquels Bashshār proclame la supériorité du feu sur la terre, c'est-à-dire prend position en faveur du Mazdéisme, ne pouvait qu'appeler une riposte de la part de lettrés rompus a l'exercice de la *disputatio*, et il n'est nullement nécessaire de faire appel, pour expliquer cette attitude, à une quelconque philosophie.

Appendice A

Mètre *ṭawīl*, rime *-rī*; *Bayān*, 1: 25-26.

13.[43] L'unique de son temps a pris pour surnom[44] al-Ghazzāl. Qui donc [s'occupera] des orphelins et des tribus qui rivalisent de nombre?[45]

14. Qui [répondra] aux Ḥarūrites, aux Rāfiḍites, aux Murji'ites et aux tyrans?[46]

15. Qui ordonnera le bien, réprouvera le mal, fortifiera la religion contre tout impie?

1. Ô Ibn Ḥawshab,[47] quand a-t-on pu voir à un fileur de laine un *famulus*[48] de la qualité de ʿAmr [b. ʿUbayd] ou de ʿĪsà b. Ḥāḍir?[49]

2. ʿUthmān b. Khālid al-Ṭawīl[50] ou l'éminent Ḥafṣ[51] n'étaient-ils point parfaits pour répondre à qui les défiait?[52]

3. Il avait,[54] au delà du peuple de Chine, dans chaque contrée, jusqu'au Sūs al-Aqṣà,[54] par delà les Berbères,

4. Des hommes, des propagandistes dont l'esprit de décision n'aurait pu être entamé par les menaces d'un tyran, ni par les ruses d'un malin.

5. Quand, en hiver, il disait "partez," ils obéissaient docilement; si c'était l'été, le mois de la canicule[55] ne les effrayait point.

6. Ils quittaient leur patrie, payaient de leur personne,

subissaient des épreuves, affrontaient les dangers et enduraient les fatigues de la route.

7. Assurant le succès à leurs efforts, il a fair jaillir de leur briquet l'étincelle d'une éclatante victoire sur l'adversaire.

8. [Ils étaient], dans chaque ville, les piliers de la terre de Dieu, le centre des consultations juridiques et de la science de la controverse.

9. Saḥbān[56] n'aurait pu rivaliser avec eux, ni les membres des deux clans des Hilāl b. ʿĀmir,[57]

10. Ni le disert Nakhkhār,[58] ni le shaykh Daghfal,[59] lorsqu'ils tenaient un bâton dans leur dextre,[60]

11. Ni les orateurs éminents du clan de Mukaḥḥal,[61] lorsqu'ils partaient pour rétablir la paix entre les tribus,

12. Dans une réunion groupant des Bakr et des Tamīm,[62] satisfaits ou irrités, alors que les Bédouins s'étaient rendus en foule vers les aiguades [où l'on se rassemblait].

[13-15. Voir supra.]

--.[63] Nous avions une caravane puissante[64] formée de chamelles à haute bosse et de chevaux nombreux.

--. Les membres de cette troupe se sont dirigés vers le royaume de Syrie et, dans ce pays, se sont emparés, en rois, des chaires.

16.[65] Dans chaque lieu,[66] ils trouvaient les paroles décisives, comme le couteau du boucher s'applique juste sur la jointure des os.

17. [Ils étaient si graves qu'] ils semblaient porter des oiseaux sur la tête,[67] au-dessus de turbans connus dans les tribus.

18. Ils étaient eux-mêmes reconnaissables à leur visage, à leur démarche de pèlerins ou à leur façon de monter à chameau,

19. A leurs génuflexions qui duraient toute la nuit, à leurs propos pareils à leurs intimes pensées,

20. A leur manière, qui sautait aux yeux, de se couper les [sour]cils, de se raser la moustache, de rouler leurs turbans autour de leurs cheveux blancs,

21. A la mouche taillée qu'ils portaient sous la lèvre, à leurs sandales munies de deux lanières qu'ils mettaient dans leurs larges manches.[68]

22. Voilà des signes qui les décrivent totalement. L'ignorant, dans la tribu, n'a point le savoir de l'expert.

Appendice B

Une association d'idées tout à fait normale conduit Jāḥiẓ à citer le long poème qui contient, selon Nyberg, la philosophie de la terre caractéristique des premiers Muᶜtazilites. "Lorsque Bashshār," écrit-il dans le Bayān (1: 27), "se mit à excuser Iblīs d'avoir prétendu que le feu était supérieur à la terre et à dire de Wāṣil ce qu'il a dit de lui," Ṣafwān composa le poème suivant:

Mètre ṭawīl, rime -dī. Bayān, I, 27-30; Baghdadi, 39-42 (v. 1-3, 5-6, 8-13, 15, 17-18, 21-22, 27-29, 33); Dawḥa, 26-27 (v. 1-4, 9-16, 22).

1. Tu as prétendu que le feu était un élément plus noble, alors que c'est dans la terre qu'il vit, à l'état latent dans la pierre et le briquet,
2. Et que sont créées dans le sein, dans les racines de la terre, des merveilles que l'on ne saurait dénombrer ni avec des [chiffres] écrits ni en comptant sur les doigts.[69]
3. Au fond des gouffres de la mer se trouvent les richesses formées de perles cachées et d'ambre rose.
4. Le secret de la terre se dissimule ainsi dans toute la mer autant que dans la forêt luxuriante et la montagne aride.
5. Tout ce qui vole a besoin de la terre, comme tout ce qui nage dans les flots a besoin d'un rivage;
6. Il en est de même de tout ce qui rampe en se traînant sur le ventre et en déviant de la ligne droite,
7. En avançant sur une peau dont les écailles ondulent comme l'eau du ruisseau sur une pente raide.
8. Sur les sommets des montagnes, au delà du Muqaṭṭam, on trouve la topaze des rois du genre humain à l'heure du rassemblement;
9. Dans la ḥarra brûlante,[70] on rencontre des mines pourvues de galeries d'où jaillit la monnaie
10. Faite d'or pur et d'argent clair qui transporte de joie l'homme le plus enclin à la simplicité et au renoncement.
11. [La terre contient] tous les produits: cuivre, étain, vif-argent et sel ammoniac,
12. Ainsi que l'arsenic, la rubrique, la litharge, la marcassite

inépuisable,

13. Toutes sortes de poix, d'alun, de cristaux, de soufre qui brûle lentement;

14. On en voit dans les mines apparaître les filons, comme la belle coupe les franges de son manteau.

15. On trouve aussi dans les mines de l'antimoine brun, de la chaux, de l'argent, de la tutie de l'Inde.

16. Il y a des mines dans toutes les dépressions, à la surface des plateaux unis, dans les déserts sauvages.

17. Tous les rubis du monde, tous les joyaux, toutes les pierres précieuses viennent de la terre.

18. C'est sur la terre que sont situés le Maqām d'Abraham, al-Ṣafā, l'angle de la Kaᶜba contenant la pierre noire que les pèlerins baisent et qui vient du paradis éternel.

19. Dans le rocher d'al-Khiḍr qui est près de son poisson,[71] dans celui d'ou jaillit spontanément de l'eau pour Moïse,

20. Et dans la roche dure qui s'entrouvrit miraculeusement pour laisser passer la mère du chamelon qui bramait en marchant à grands pas,[72]

21. Il y a des titres de gloire pour l'argile qui est notre origine; nous sommes ses fils, sans doute ni démenti possible.

22. Voilà une ordonnance, un bienfait, une sagesse qui sont la preuve la plus claire de l'Unique.

23. Considéreras-tu ᶜAmr [b. ᶜUbayd] et le très savant Wāṣil comme les adeptes de Dayṣān,[73] qui sont des épaves rejetées par la marée?

24. Et tireras-tu gloire d'al-Maylā'[74] et du barbare ᶜĀṣim[75] en riant du cou du grand Abū 'l-Jaᶜd?[76]

25. Tu exposes publiquement ses opinions honteuses[77] pour diriger les sentiments des âmes vers la croyance à la métempsycose.

26. Dans des poèmes, avec prolixité, tu l'as appelé al-Ghazzāl, alors que ton maître, quand il est victime d'une injustice, présente sa supplique au moyen d'une gaffe.[78]

27. O fils de l'allié de l'argile,[79] enfant de l'ignominie et de la cécité, ô toi qui, parmi les hommes, es le plus éloigné des voies de la droiture,

28. Vas-tu satiriser Abū Bakr et renier ensuite ᶜAlī, puis attribuer tout cela à Burd?

29. Tu parais irrité contre la religion tout entière et tu ressembles à quelqu'un qui, voulant se venger, ne pourrait attendre le lendemain pour manifester sa haine.

30. Tu est revenu dans les métropoles après [la mort de] Wāṣil, après avoir erré en exil dans les Tihāmas et sur les plateaux d'Arabie.

31. Feras-tu de Laylà al-Nāᶜiṭiyya[80] une abeille[81] ainsi que chacun de ceux qui sont noyés dans la métempsycose et le retour sur terre?

32. Tu as à ta disposition Daᶜd, al-Ṣadūf et Fartanā, les deux nourrices d'al-Kisf, les deux compagnes de Hind.

33. Tu t'attaques à [des femmes belles comme] des lunes, alors que tu es laid et que, de toutes les crétaures de Dieu, tu es celle qui ressemble le plus à un singe.

Appendice C

Mètre ṭawīl, rime -dū. Bayān, 1: 32.

1. Dans le sein de la [terre] est le séjour de l'homme le plus dissimulé; à sa surface, il accomplit ses devoirs religieux.
2. La terre rejette avec force le sel, mais garde pour elle des lingots qui ne rouillent jamais, aussi anciens soient-ils.
3. Aucun calcul, aucun chiffre, même au prix de beaucoup de peine, ne saurait dénombrer ce que recèlent ses flancs.
4. Interroge ᶜAbd Allāh[82] sur le jour de la réunion, cette séance à laquelle n'assistait aucun faible d'esprit.
5. Shabīb et Ibn Ṣafwān avant lui ont prononcé des propos d'orateurs éminents qui ne dévient pas de la voie droite.
6. Ibn ᶜĪsà s'est ensuite levé, puis l'a suivi Wāṣil, qui a fait merveille en prononçant un discours sans pareil au monde.
7. Le rā' ne lui a pas porté tort, car il était capable de l'éviter tout en ayant une élocution coulante et aisee.
8. ᶜAbd Allāh donna la palme au discours de Wāṣil et lui accorda double récompense lors de la distribution des présents.
9. Son remerciement a convaincu tous les assistants, et son

renoncement aux biens de ce monde lui a fait minimiser cette double part.

Notes

[1] Cf. *Aghānī*, ed. Beyrouth, 3: 140; il y avait également un Azdite qui devint samanéen.

[2] *Milieu baṣrien*, 175-177.

[3] *Ḥayawān*, 7: 78.

[4] *Ibid.*, 7: 76, 77, 78, 114. Dans *Ḥayawān*, 7: 76, l'éditeur a corrigé *anshada* en *anshada-nī*, ce qui obligerait a considérer que Jāḥiẓ l'a connu personnellement; la chronologie ne s'y oppose pas, mais le pronom de la première personne n'est employé avant aucune des autres citations.

[5] Dans *Murūj*, 3: 14-17 (= n°s 855-858), il présente Hārūn comme "un poète et un vaillant guerrier qui jouissait d'une grande autorité auprès des siens et d'une réputation de puissance dans la contrée du Sind voisine de Multān"; il ajoute qu'il habitait une forteresse qui lui appartenait. Voir aussi Nuwayrī, *Nihāya*, 9: 304 (d'après Mas^{c}ūdī).

[6] *Ḥayawān*, 7: 114.

[7] *Ibid.*, 7: 76, où il faut remplacer *ruwāt* par *zuwwār*, ainsi qu'y autorise un ms., et Mazyad par Yazīd (voir *infra* 22).

[8] Voir Ibn al-Kalbī- Caskel, Tab. 204 et 2: 232; Tabarī, 3: 649, 1044, 1098, 1100 et 1105; *Bayān*, 2: 238 et 4: 75; Ibn al-Abbār, *Ḥulla*, éd. Ḥ. Mu'nis (Caire, 1963), 2: 360; Ibn ^{c}Idhārī, *Bayān*, 1: 82; Kindī, *Judges*, 133 sqq.; al-Riqīq (?), *Ta'rīkh Ifrīqiya wa 'l-Maghrib*, ed. M. Ka^{c}bī (Tunis, 1967), 169-170; *Aghānī*, 20: 53; Ibn Qutayba, *Shi^{c}r*, 528, 560; Ibn Taghribardī, *Nujūm*, 2: 75-76, 116; Ibn Ṭulūn, *Umarā' Miṣr*, éd. Munajjid (Beyrouth, s.d.), 17; M. Talbi, *Émirat aghlabide*, 93-94 et index.

[9] Pour éviter toute confusion, voici le tableau généalogique de la famille:

Abū Ṣufra
|
al-Muhallab
|
Qabīsa
|
Ḥātim

Yazīd	Rawḥ	
Dāwūd	Qabīṣa	Dāwūd

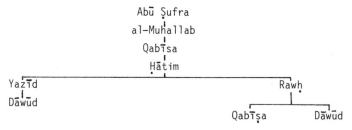

[10] *Sharh Dīwān Ṣarī^{c} al-Jawānī*, éd. S. Dahhān (Caire, s.d.), 151-171 (longue *qaṣīda* dont des fragments sont souvent cités; voir les

références p. 151).

[11] Voir A. Ghedira, dans Arabica 10.2 (1963), 163, 164, 167-168, 177; le même, dans BÉO [Damas], 19 (1966), 25/108, 13/120, 6/127, 4/129 et références citées.

[12] Voir A. Ghedira, dans BÉO [Damas], 19 (1966), 25/106.

[13] Éd. M. Ṭ. Ibn cĀshūr (Caire, 1375/1957), 3: 110-111.

[14] Ibid., 3: 178-192.

[15] Notamment 1: 232-239, 240-247, 332-340; 2: 242-256; 3: 50-56.

[16] 1: 339 lignes 4, 7-8, 240 ligne 1.

[17] 1: 278.

[18] 1: 134-140.

[19] A titre de pure hypothèse, on dira qu'il n'est pas impossible qu'à la ligne 7 de la p. 138 du t. 1, l'expression fa-ṣāfi dhā wuddin ait été lue fa-sāfi Dāwuda, ce qui expliquerait la confusion.

[20] Supra, n. 7.

[21] Voir infra, appendice B, vers 8.

[22] Nujūm, 2: 76.

[23] Ce Maṭrūḥ était le fils de Sulaymān b. Yaqẓān, allié, puis prisonnier de Charlemagne; il aviat pris part à la bataille de Roncevaux pour délivrer son père (E. Lévi-Provençal, Histoire de l'Espagne musulmane, 1: 126, 141).

[24] Voir Bayān, 1: 24; Aghānī, 3: 219.

[25] Bayān, 1: 25.

[26] Ibid., 1: 14 sqq.

[27] Ibid., 1: 22; mètre basīṭ, rime -āqī.

[28] Ibid., 1: 16, 23; Aghānī, 3: 139; mètre basīṭ, rime -lā.

[29] Jāḥiẓ (Bayān, 1: 33) montre que Wāṣil doit ce surnom à la fréquentation assidue du marché des fileurs de laine.

[30] Bayān, 1: 26.

[31] Voir appendice A.

[32] Bayān, 1: 27; mètre ṭawīl, rime -cuh.

[33] Ibid., 1: 16; mètre basīṭ, rime -dī.

[34] Voir appendice B.

[35] Voir appendice C.

[36] Bayān, 1: 31; mètre basīṭ, rime -dī.

[37] Allusion a la cécité de Bashshar.

[38] Ces affirmations demeurent énigmatiques.

[39] "La politique religieuse du calife cabbāside al-Ma'mūn," REI, 30.1 (1962), 30-31.

[40] C'est ainsi que Mascūdī (Murūj, 3: 17 = n° 858) ne le cite que sous sa nisba d'al-Anṣārī et que, dans la Dawḥa (voir infra), il est simplement appelé Ṣafwān.

[41] al-Farq bayn al-firaq, 4e éd. (Beyrouth, 1400/1980), pp. 39-42 (20 vers).

[42] Éd. Ḥ. Mu'nis (Madrid, 1379/1960), pp. 26-27 (13 vers).

[43] La qaṣīda est en désordre, et il a semblé légitime de placer en tête les vers 13-15 qui forment une sorte d'introduction; pour le reste, on suivra l'ordre adopté dans le Bayān, même s'il est évident que certains vers ont été déplacés.

[44] Il est peu probable qu'il se soit donné lui-même (talaqqaba) ce surnom; voir supra, p. 24.

[45] Dans cet hémistiche et les deux vers suivants, aucun verbe n'est employé, et la traduction est plutôt conjecturale, car on pourrait aussi bien dire: "Qui donc mieux que lui s'occupait ... répondait ... ordonnait ...?"

[46] Il s'agit vraisemblablement des Umayyades.

[47] Non identifié; on ne peut naturellement pas songer à Manṣūr

al-Yaman.

48 C'est sans doute ainsi qu'il faut rendre *ghulām* dans ce vers.

49 Familier de ^{c}Amr b. ^{c}Ubayd qui était probablement mu^{c}tazilite, à en juger par une anecdote du *Kitāb al-Ḥayawān*, 1: 337-338.

50 Non identifié.

51 L'éditeur du *Bayān* l'identifie à Ḥafs al-Fard (cf. *EI*^{2}, s.v.), qui fut en désaccord avec Abū 'l-Hudhayl à la fin du IIe/VIIIe siècle; cette identification est suggérée par l'expression *al-qarn Ḥafs*, mais se pose alors une question de chronologie, car Ḥafs n'était pas le contemporain de Wāṣil.

52 Il y a peut-être là une allusion aux discussions avec Abū 'l-Hudhayl.

53 Ici commence le passage relatif aux *du^{c}āt*; dans *la-hu*, le pronom parait bien se rapporter a Wāṣil.

54 L'éditeur du *Bayān* lui donne comme capitale Tanger (!) et confond le Sūs al-Adnà avec la Susiane (!).

55 *Nājir*, mois de juillet dans l'ancien calendrier arabe.

56 Saḥbān Wā'il, personnage plus ou moins légendaire dont l'éloquence était proverbiale.

57 Allusion probable aux Hilāl b. ^{c}Āmir b. Ṣa^{c}ṣa^{c}a, parmi lesquels se sont illustrés par leur éloquence Zur^{c}a b. Ḍamra et son fils al-Nu^{c}mān (voir *Bayān*, 1: 354), mais on ne sait comment interpréter "les deux clans."

58 al-Nakhkhār b. Aws al-^{c}Udhrī, généalogiste et beau parleur contemporain de Mu^{c}āwiya, dont il fut le compagnon. Jāḥiẓ dit de lui que lorsqu'il réglait des différends entre tribus, il répétait certains mots pour inspirer de la crainte; parfois, dit-il, il s'échauffait au point de renifler (*nakhara*), d'où son surnom; voir *Bayān*, 1: 105, 237, 333 et 2: 89.

59 Daghfal b. Ḥanẓala al-Sadūsī, généalogiste proverbiale du Ier/VIIe siècle, tué par les Azraqites; voir *Bayān*, index; Maydānī (*ansab min D.*); *Iṣāba*, n° 2395.

60 Le 2e hémistiche du v. 10 et le 1er du v. 16 ci-dessous constituent aussi un vers reproduit dans un group de 3 (*Bayān*, 1: 371 et 3: 117), ce qui prouve que la *qaṣīda* est incomplète et en désordre.

61 Surnom de ^{c}Amr b. al-Ahtam al-Minqarī, compagnon du Prophète; voir *EI*^{2}, s.v. ^{c}Amr.

62 Jāḥiẓ dit, pour expliquer ce vers, que le mot al-Juffānī désigne les Bakr et les Tamīm, comme al-Rawqānī désigne Bakr et Taghlib et al-Ghāranī désigne Azd et Tamīm.

63 Le texte des deux vers suivants se trouve dans *Bayān*, 1: 371 et 3: 116-117.

64 Ibid., 3: 116--*dhāt sudūd*; 1: 371--*dhāt sawra*.

65 Dans ibid., 1: 371 et 3: 117, le 2e hémistiche fait suite au 1er du v. 10 ci-dissus.

66 Ibid., 1: 26--*mawṭin*; 1: 371 et 3: 117--*khuṭba*: dans chaque discours.

67 Proverbe bien connu pour désigner la gravité du maintien.

68 Les sandales sont souvent portées dans les manches par mesure d'économie et par humilité; mais on peut également comprendre: et a leurs larges manches.

69 C'est-à-dire en usant de la dactylonomie.

70 Plus exactement: dans le sol rocailleux où il est difficile de faire marcher des chameaux ou des chevaux au point que l'on est obligé d'aller à pied.

71 al-Khidr est assimilé ici au serviteur de Moïse qui a oublié leur poisson près d'un rocher (voir Qur'ān, 18: 60 sqq.).
72 Allusion à la chamelle du prophète Ṣāliḥ (voir Qur'ān, 7: 71-73, 75-77; 11: 67; 17: 61; 26: 155-157; 54: 27 sqq.; 91:13).
73 Sur Bardesane, voir EI[2], s.v. Dayṣāniyya.
74 Nourrice d'Abū Manṣūr, chef des Manṣūriyya, surnommé al-Kisf.
75 Non identifié.
76 Serait la kunya de Wāṣil d'après l'éditeur du Bayān.
77 On ne voit pas à qui le poète fait allusion ici.
78 Commentaire de Jāḥiẓ: ton maître est un marin, et les marins, lorsqu'ils ont à se plaindre, lèvent leurs avirons.
79 Le père de Bashshār était potier.
80 Sur cette Shīᶜite notoire, voir Bakhalā', index.
81 L'éditeur du Bayān a lu niḥla = pour lui, madhhab.
82 Allusion à une réunion tenue chez ᶜAbd Allāh b. ᶜUmar b. ᶜAbd al-ᶜAzīz (gouverneur de l'Iraq en 126/744; voir Milieu, 280); y assistaient Bashshār, Khālid b. Ṣafwān, Shabīb b. Shayba, al-Faḍl b. ᶜĪsà al-Raqāshī et Wāṣil; c'est à cette occasion que ce dernier prononça son fameux discours ne contenant aucun rā' (Bayān, 1: 24) et plusieurs fois glorifié par Bashshār.

3

Musical Humour in the *Kitāb al-Aghānī*

George D. Sawa
Centre for Studies in
Middle Eastern Music, Toronto

Neither Abū 'l-Faraj al-Iṣbahānī nor his Kitāb al-Aghānī need any introduction to scholars in the field of Middle Eastern studies.[1] Too well-known is the medieval as well as modern consensus that the monumental Kitāb al-Aghānī is a unique source for the study of Arabic and early Islamic history, biographies, social life, literature and music. Yāqūt said that it was the best of its kind,[2] Ibn Khallikān reported that it was unanimously agreed that it was unequalled,[3] whereas Ibn Khaldūn called it the "register of the Arabs."[4] H. A. R. Gibb, on the other hand, saw in it an "immense panorama of Arabic and early Islamic life and manners probably unequalled in any literature down to modern times."[5]

Despite these ritualistic, pious assessments, however, the fact is that al-Iṣbahānī and his work have not received proper scholarly attention from Eastern and Western Arabists,[6] and that such "a most remarkable collection" is "still practically untranslated and only lightly tapped for its riches."[7]

Of these, the musical riches have probably suffered the most, for there has prevailed in Middle Eastern studies a misplaced belief that any matter musical should exclusively fall into the domain of the music specialist.[8] The truth of the matter is that musicologists and ethnomusicologists alike lack the proper historical, cultural and philological training to deal competently with the subject. Arabists on the other hand, with their background, can easily deal with an array of musical matters which are of a non-technical nature.

In fact, the old-fashioned idea that musical studies concern themselves with sound alone (technical matters) has been laid to rest by the modern school of American ethnomusicology. The late A. P.

Logos Islamikos: Studia Islamica in honorem Georgii Michaelis Wickens, ed. Roger M. Savory and Dionisius A. Agius, Papers in Mediaeval Studies 6 (Toronto: Pontifical Institute of Mediaeval Studies, 1984), pp. 35-50.

Merriam clearly articulated this viewpoint in the following statements:

> The technical side of ethnomusicology . . ., represents but one of the aims and responsibilities of the discipline. Equally important, and coming to be more and more understand, is the view that music involves not only sound but the human behaviour which is a prerequisite for producing sound.[9]

> . . . there is little validity for treating [music sound] as though it were divorced from social and cultural considerations for . . ., music is inevitably produced by humans for other humans within a social and cultural context.[10]

A thousand years before Merriam's statements, al-Iṣbahānī implicitly believed that the study of music involved more than "musical sound and theory," inasmuch as he wrote extensively about musical practices of an era (the Umayyad and part of the ᶜAbbāsid) whose musical repertoire had largely become extinct by his own time. A thousand years before Merriam, al-Iṣbahānī explicitly believed that there was far more to music than just sound for, in his collection, he selected songs around which revolved interesting anecdotes concerning the poet or singer/composer of the said songs, or around which revolved stories indicating the reason for which such songs were composed and performed. This made the mentioning of the songs more attractice and bettered by the narration of such anecdotes (KA, 1: 1). Thus the reader not only learns technical facts about a song (rhythm and melodic mode) but also the context--so dear today to ethnomusicologists--in which songs were composed and performed.

Thus on the non-technical level, an Arabist can successfully study anthropological matters such as the uses and functions of songs, verbal and physical behaviour of audience and musicians, social status and role of musicians, process of learning, oral transmission, process of musical and textual change, criteria for musical evaluation, and conceptualization.[11]

Besides being a forerunner of modern music anthropology, al-Iṣbahānī was a consummate educator. He intended his collection to be educational for young and old people alike (KA, 1: 2). As well, he intended it to be entertaining. This dual purpose guided his choice of anecdotes:

> . . . not all songs have a story [which we know], not all

> that which has a story has usefulness, and not all that which has some usefulness has beauty to delight and entertain the reader (KA, 1: 2).

Furthermore, to stimulate his readers, al-Iṣbahānī purposely arranged his anecdotes so as to constantly introduce variety and avoid tiring his reader by going:

> . . . from anecdote to anecdote, from old stories to new stories, from [stories about] kings to [stories] about common people, and from seriousness to comicality (KA, 1: 4).

It becomes clear, therefore, that humour in the Kitāb al-Aghānī had not only the function of entertainment per se, but also entertainment to relieve seriousness, and hence facilitate education by making it more palatable.

When dealing with humour in early Islam, Rosenthal concentrates on the personality of Ashᶜab, and divides the humour into three classes: the "political," the "religious," and the "Urban middle class."[12] In this paper, I shall not deal with general humour, but specifically with musically-related humour, its nature and its reasons, whether motivated by the musicians or by their audience. This type of enquiry is just one of the many examples where an Arabist can significantly contribute to the history of Middle Eastern music, without any prior knowledge of musicology.

From the Kitāb al-Aghānī we learn that the qualifications of a good musician were not confined to musical excellence, such as vocal and/or instrumental virtuosity, command of a large repertoire, musical creativity in the form of improvised ornaments, improvisation or composition. A good musician was to be careful in the choice of song texts, to cater to audience taste for particular poets or poetical styles, and to be able to improvise text and music on request.[13] A good musician was also to be endowed with the characteristics of a boon-companion, that is, one having refined and elegant manners, good behaviour, neatness of attire, regularity of physiognomy, wit and humour, as well as a well-rounded education which included competence in poetry, prosody, grammar, history, narration of anecdotes, Qur'ān, jurisprudence, astrology, medicine, the art of cooking, wine-making, horse-breeding, hunting, backgammon, and chess. With such qualifications musicians befriended, educated and entertained their patrons.[14]

Musicians thus used humour and musically-related humour as part of their boon-companionship baggage. In this paper I shall select and study six categories of musically-related humour.

A. Musical Humour Induced by Dramatic Effects

The majority of reported musical performances occurred in the rather undramatic indoor musical *majlis*, where the musicians mainly performed from a sitting position. They occasionally resorted to dancing while singing in order to add more excitement to their performances. Sometimes such extra effects were badly needed, as when a musician was indirectly to ask for forgiveness from a patron he had angered. The ^{c}Abbāsid court singer ^{c}Allūyah, who had arrived intoxicated and late to the *majlis* of al-Ma'mūn, was well aware that his lateness could anger his patron. He therefore burst into the *majlis* dancing to a song he had just composed. The wit, humour, and drama involved in this rather uncommon musical practice greatly amused the caliph, who granted the singer forgiveness.

B. Musical Humour Induced by Textual Change

Musical humour was sometimes a by-product of textual change. The latter was motivated by the necessity to adapt to the requirements of a given situation, where failure to adapt could in many cases bring corporal or financial punishment to the careless singer. Carelessness might consist in singing to a patron a song praising his rival, or praising a dynasty which rivalled his. It also consisted in singing songs which ridiculed certain traits (i.e., grey hair, old age) which happened to be those of a patron.

The following anecdote will illustrate how a clever female slave singer caught herself just in time so as to turn a panegyric to a satire, thereby possibly saving her life. At the same time her wit and the ensuing humour pleased and amused her patron, who in turn, gave her splendid rewards.

> We were informed by Muḥammad ibn al-^{c}Abbās al-Yazīdī who said: We were informed by Aḥmad ibn Zuhayr who said: We were informed by al-Zubayr ibn Bakkār who said: I was informed by my uncle on the authority of my grandfather ^{c}Abd-Allāh ibn Muṣ^{c}ab who said: Al-Rashīd happened upon a *qayna* (female slave singer) who sang:

People only hate the Umayyads/
Because they exercise magnanimity when angered

[And the Umayyads are lords among kings/
Only with them would the Arabs thrive].[15]

As soon as she started the song al-Rashīd's countenance changed. She immediately realized that she had made a mistake in her choice of song, and that should she go through with the song she might well be killed. She therefore sang, [but improvising the following textual change]:

People only hate the Umayyads/
Because they behave foolhardily when angered

And the Umayyads are the source of hypocrisy/
Only with them would the Arabs decay.

[Impressed], al-Rashīd said to Yaḥyà ibn Khālid: "Did you hear what she said O Abū ᶜAlī!" So he said: "O Commander of the Faithful she should be bought, a rich reward should be bestowed upon her, and its authorization should be speeded up to reassure her." Al-Rashīd said: "This is her reward." [To the girl:] "Get up and go, for you may stand with me as you please." Thereupon, the jāriya fainted . . . (KA, 5: 85-6).

The next anecdote will illustrate a less critical, more humorous situation of a textual change in which a realistic singer, realizing the impossibility of receiving an expensive reward he had alluded to in a song, improvised a minor textual change to settle for a lesser reward. The humour resulting from textual change insured a complete success.

I was informed by Jaᶜfar ibn Qudāma who said: I was informed by Mūsà ibn Hārūn al-Hāshimī who said: I was informed by my father who said: I was standing in front of al-Muᶜtaṣim while he was sitting in ḥayr al-waḥsh (a zoological garden attached to the caliphal palace). Horses were being paraded before him while he was drinking, and [two of the most famous ᶜAbbāsid singers] ᶜAllūya and Mukhāriq were singing before him. A reddish-brown horse was led out before him, the like of which I had never seen. ᶜAllūyah and Mukhāriq signalled to one another and ᶜAlluya sang to the Caliph:

If they drink and become intoxicated/
They give away every fine race horse.

Al-Muᶜtaṣim ignored him, then Mukhāriq sang to him:

He gives away white-skinned women like gazelles, swift horses/
Under their horse-clothes, and white camels [too].

> Al-Mu^c^taṣim laughed then said: "Shut up O you two sons of whores, by God neither of you will ever own it." [Hārūn al-Hāshimī] said: Then the turn came to ^c^Alluya who sang:
>
> If they drink and become intoxicated
> They give away every mule and every donkey.
>
> Al-Mu^c^taṣim laughed and said: "As to that, all right," and ordered for one of them a mule and a donkey for the other (KA, 11: 352-53).[16]

C. Musical Humour Induced by Poetical and Musical Improvisations

Textual changes in the above section consist of word-replacement to fit the requirement of a situation. One may accordingly term such textual changes "partial textual improvisations." In this section we will deal with total textual improvisations, recited to fit the demands of a circumstance, more specifically poetical satires of a humorous and even obscene nature, and attempt to show that when set to music, these satires had a more powerful humorous effect still.

This anecdote is too long to be translated in its entirety, therefore, parts of it will be paraphrased. The scene is the majlis of al-Mutawakkil, where two rival poets are present. The poet ^c^Alī ibn al-Jahm had claimed both privately and publicly that he was a better poet than Marwān al-Aṣghar. Al-Mutawakkil then decided to have a duel between them, giving the first chance to ^c^Alī, the claimant to better poetry, to satirize Marwān. ^c^Alī backed down with the excuse of being too drunk. The caliph then asked Marwān to go ahead. Marwān recited thus:

> Ibn al-Jahm in my absence criticizes me/
> Whereas when he meets me he says to me "Well done!"
> His prestige has waned while his belly has been swelled/
> As though it held twins.
> Alas for Ibn al-Jahm, he has no mercy upon his mother/
> For had he had any he would not be hostile to me.
> So when(ever) we meet, my poetry screws his/
> And my demon leaps on his.

The assembly laughed while Ibn al-Jahm sat defeated, unable to match Marwān's satire. Al-Mutawakkil then asked Marwān to continue and not to spare his insults. Marwān recited:

> By your life al-Jahm ibn Badr is no poet/
> And here is ^c^Alī after him claiming poetical skill.
> But my father used to be a neighbour of his mother/
> So when he claimed poetical craft it made me suspect something.

Al-Wutawakkil laughed and asked for more, so Marwān recited:

> O son of Badr, O ^{c}Aliyya/
> You said you were a *Qurayshite*.[17]
> You said that which was not true/
> So shut up, O *Nabatean*.[18]
> Shut up, O *daughter* of Jahm/
> Shut up, O woman with the diseased womb from your unsatiated sexual appetite.[19]
>
> [At this point] ^{c}Abbāda took these lines and sung them to the accompaniment of his drum, joined by those who could sing. Al-Mutawakkil laughed, and clapped his hands and feet [sic] . . . (*KA* 12: 81-3).

The musical improvisation to the last poem and the group-singing greatly enhanced the comic element, as one can easily deduce from the audience reaction: in the first two satires al-Mutawakkil was reported to have simply laughed, whereas in the third, the additional comic element provided by music made al-Mutawakkil not only laugh but also "clap his hands and feet" [sic].[20]

D. Musical Humour Induced by Funny Behaviour

To break away from the routine of a musical *majlis*, patrons sometimes encouraged their musicians to compete with each other. As well, musicians knowing their patrons' liking for such a musical format, themselves offered it as an added entertainment to their patrons.[21] These entertainments took sometimes a humorous turn, especially when they involved music plagiarism, in which an original composer had his new song stolen, and was then accused of musical theft. Often a musical spy was sent to steal a song, or more flagrantly, a song was stolen in front of its composer's nose right in the middle of a *majlis*. The operation was done with great skill by a rare breed of musicians such as Muḥammad al-Zaff, whose proverbial musical memory--almost as good as a modern tape recorder--allowed him to learn a song after one or two hearings.

The following anecdote shows a case of a group of musicians who entertained Hārūn al-Rashīd by stealing Ibn Jāmi^{c}'s newly composed song, then by accusing him of plagiarism:

> I was informed by Ibn Ja^{c}far Jaḥẓa who said: We were told by Ḥammād ibn Isḥāq on the authority of his father who said: One day Ibn Jāmi^{c} sang in the presence of al-Rashīd:
>
> Bold to forsake me, cowardly about union with me/

> Habitual liar, one given to following a promise by procrastination.
> Setting one foot forward towards union but withdrawing/
> The other, he mixes seriousness in this matter with jest.
> He is concerned for us, but whenever I say "He has come close [to us]/
> And shown generosity," he turns away and leans towards avarice.
> His abstention becomes greater as my passion grows/
> And my desire intensifies as he grudges giving.

> [Ibn Jāmi^c] went on to excel and beautify his rendering in whatever way he wished. At this point I [Isḥāq] made a sign about him to the singer, Muḥammad al-Zaff, who immediately understood my intention. Al-Rashīd liked Ibn Jāmi^c's singing, drank to it and asked for two or three encores.
>
> I then got up to pray, made a sign to al-Zaff who follows me, and I motioned the singers Mukhāriq, ^{c}Allūya and ^{c}Aqīd who also joined me. I asked al-Zaff to repeat the song: he not only did but performed it as if [Ibn Jāmi^c] were singing it. Al-Zaff kept on repeating it to the group until they sang it correctly.
>
> I then returned to the majlis, and when my turn came to sing, I started first of all by singing the aforementioned song. Ibn Jāmi^c stared at me blankly whereas al-Rashīd turned to me and said: "Did you use to transmit this song?" I replied: "Yes, my lord." Ibn Jāmi^c then said: "By God he has lied, he got it from none other than me just now!" I said: "This song I have been transmitting for a long time, and every singer attending this majlis once took it from me."
>
> I then turned towards al-Rashīd, and ^{c}Allūya sang it, then ^{c}Aqīd, and then Mukhāriq. Ibn Jāmi^c jumped up and sat in front of al-Rashīd, swore by his life and at the risk of divorcing his wife, that he had composed the melody only three nights ago, and that it had not been heard from him till that time. Al-Rashīd turned to me and said: "By my life, tell me the truth about this whole business." I did and this caused him to laugh and clap and say: "Everything has its fated end, and Ibn Jāmi^{c}s is al-Zaff" (KA, 14: 187-88).

Patrons enjoyed musical competitions which they sometimes encouraged for entertainment purposes. For the same reasons, patrons teased a certain type of musician who was predictably liable to behave hilariously if provoked. For instance, the unfortunate singer Abū Ṣadaqa, famed for his constant requests for rewards, was constantly provoked. His uncouth behaviour could have caused him to be banned from the court, for after all it was at odds with the qualities of a ẓarīf. It was however tolerated because patrons by teasing him gave rise to a great deal of laughter. The following anecdote, too long to be translated, will be partly paraphrased.

In the *majlis* of Hārūn al-Rashīd, Ja^{c}far ibn Yaḥyà was relating an incident which had happened to him on the previous night, in his musical *majlis* where Abū Ṣadaqa was present. After a good performance, Ja^{c}far praised him, and Abū Ṣadaqa seized the opportunity to ask Ja^{c}far to grant him furnishings for his new house. Ja^{c}far ignored him, but after the praise/request sequence was repeated twice with Abū Ṣadaqa becoming more persistent, Ja^{c}far was induced to swear on al-Rashīd's life to furnish the musician's house. Ja^{c}far did not however specify the type of furnishings. His cunning behaviour appealed to al-Rashīd who suggested to him to offer *bawārī* (mats made of bulrushes). Al-Rashīd then ordered the musician to be brought so that the *majlis* might enjoy the hilarious dénouement:

> Ja^{c}far said to Abū Ṣadaqa: "Choose: if you wish I will furnish it for you with mats of bulrush, and if you wish I will furnish it with mats of papyrus." Abū Ṣadaqa shouted and became agitated. Al-Rashīd then said to him: "What was it all about?" He told him and al-Rashīd said: "You made a mistake O Abū Ṣadaqa, for you did not name the type and did not specify the value, so if he furnishes it with bulrush or papyrus or even less than those two he will have fulfilled his oath. But he duped you for you were not aware of his stratagem, and you did not take the necessary precaution. As a result you have lost your just due." Abū Ṣadaqa fell silent and then said: "We will save him even the bulrush and papyrus too. May God give him glory."
>
> Then the singers sang until the turn came to him to sing, so he proceeded to sing songs of sailors, masons, and water carriers, and other songs of the same category [i.e. workers' songs as opposed to refined court music]. Al-Rashīd said to him: "Woe unto you, what sort of singing is this?" He replied: "The one whose house is furnished with bulrush and papyrus will sing much of this type of songs and will also sing much of it to those whose gifts are as such." Al-Rashīd laughed, was transported with joy and clapped. He then ordered for him one thousand *dīnārs* from his own money and said: "Furnish your house with this!" Abū Ṣadaqa replied: "By your life, my lord, I am not taking them unless you make a judgment against Ja^{c}far to give me what he promised, for otherwise I shall die of regret for losing what I had desired and what was promised to me." Al-Rashīd ordered Ja^{c}far to award him five hundred *dīnārs*. Ja^{c}far agreed and gave them to him (*KA*, 19: 297-98).

No doubt the audience enjoyed the humorous confrontation between the vizir and the singer, but far more humorous than the confrontation--judging by al-Rashīd's emotional and physical reaction--was Abū Ṣadaqa's unacceptable socially clashing choice of workers' songs to an aristocratic audience as well as his ensuing sharp remarks. His clever and musically humorous action, well summarized by the French proverb: "à malin malin et demi," ensured him a magnificent reward.

E. Musical Humour Induced by a Pun in a Song Text

In the following anecdote the musically-related humour is exclusively audience-motivated. Since the musician is not responsible for the humour, this story falls only in the domain of al-Iṣbahānī's technique of mingling seriousness with jest, i.e., entertainment to relieve seriousness and facilitate education:

> I was told by al-Hasan ibn ᶜAlī on the authority of Muhammad ibn al-Qāsim on the authority of Abū Hiffān who said: We were in a majlis with a qayna (female-slave singer) singing for us. The host was in love with her. She proceeded to make him jealous by showing to others signs of playfulness and flirtation. She infuriated him by her endeavours, making him almost die of anxiety and worry, and his day was thus spoiled.
>
> She persisted in her behaviour and at one point the pick [with which she was to play her ᶜūd] fell from her hand. As she bent over to the ground to pick it up she passed wind, which everybody present heard. She became embarrassed, and not knowing what to say she turned to her lover [the host] and said: "What is it you desire me to sing for you?"

At this point the host found a golden opportunity to get back at her, and so he asked for a love song which started as follows:

> O wind what are you doing to the remains of the encampement
> [of the tribe of my departed beloved].

However, the plural word diman which is conventionally translated in such poetry (KA, 23: 134) as "remains of the encampement," really means "heaps of manure," for this was all such nomad camps left behind them. Therefore the above hemistich also translates as:

> O wind what are you doing to the heaps of manure,

with the implied meaning of the wind passing through the buttocks of his beloved.

> The girl became embarrassed, and the guests and the host laughed uproariously. The girl wept, stood up and said: "By God you are a base crowd, God's curse upon whoever associates with you." And becoming furious, she left . . . (KA, 23: 138-39).

In this anecdote the musical element of humour is only by association, for the humour consisted of a pun in a song text which was after all not sung. Rather, humour was induced by a crude use of a human failing.

F. Musical Humour Induced by Hilarious Musical Statements

Statements about music and musicians are probably the richest musical aspect of *Kitāb al-Aghānī* and they certainly deserve by themselves a thorough investigation.[22] They deal with criteria for performance and compositional excellence, aspects of theory, compositional techniques, styles and forms. Hilarious musical remarks deal with two extremes: musical excellence and musical incompetence.

Perhaps the most colourful and brilliant praise of a musician's sense of rhythm came in the following anecdote:

> Isḥāq al-Mawṣilī said: I was informed by ^{c}Umar ibn Shabba who said: I was informed by Yaḥyà ibn Ibrāhīm ibn ^{c}Uthmān ibn Nahīk who said: One day my father invited al-Rashīd[23] who came with [the vizir] Ja^{c}far ibn Yahyà. Both stayed at his place where Ibn Jāmi^{c} arrived and sang for them. On the next day al-Rashīd left and Ja^{c}far stayed. [Then the rival singer] Ibrāhīm al-Mawṣilī came in and asked Ja^{c}far about [the musical *majlis* of their previous] day [in which he was left out]. Ja^{c}far informed him thus: "Ibn Jāmi^{c} kept on singing except that he would lose the *īqā^{c}* (the *īqā^{c}* is a concept encompassing musical meter rhythm, rhythmic mode, tempo, timbre and dynamics)[24]--and by so saying he meant to appease the mind of Ibrāhīm al-Mawṣilī. So Ibrāhīm said to him: "Are you trying to appease my mind with that by which it will not be appeased! No, by God, never has Ibn Jāmi^{c} passed wind for the last thirty years but within an *īqā^{c}*, so how can he get off the *īqā^{c}* [now]!" (*KA*, 6: 304).

Though it is quite unlikely that Ibn Jāmi^{c} consistently passed wind according to the *īqā^{c}*s used in ^{c}Abbāsid times, the *īqā^{c}* must have been second nature to him. Such a superb sense of rhythm Ibrāhīm eloquently clothed in humour, thereby making his statement the more stronger.

A concise statement of "musical ignoramuses unlimited" in the field of music analysis and theory came in a letter from Ibrāhīm ibn al-Mahdī to Isḥāq al-Mawṣilī, two relentless rivals:

> I was told by Jaḥẓa who said: I was told by Hibat-Allāh ibn

> Ibrāhīm ibn al-Mahdī who said: My father wrote to Isḥāq about a matter on which he disagreed with him concerning the *tajzi'a* (poetical divisions) and the *qisma* (related musical divisions): "To whom can I refer you for a decision when people around us are donkeys" (*KA*, 5: 372).

A funnier anecdote depicts a musician's incompetence in the field of composition:

> . . . [Abū Aḥmad ^{c}Ubayd-Allāh ibn ^{c}Abd-Allāh ibn Ṭāhir] said: I brought [Abū ^{c}Abd-Allāh] al-Hishāmī with me to Samarra . . . and brought him into al-Mu^{c}tazz, who was drinking while [the female singer] ^{c}Arīb was singing. Al-Mu^{c}tazz said to him: "O Ibn Hishām sing!" He said: "I have repented of singing since the time my master al-Mutawakkil was murdered." So ^{c}Arīb said: "By God you did well to repent when you did, for your singing had little intrinsic qualities, it lacked craft, perfection and *ṭarab* (quality in the music, and sometimes the text, which caused an acute emotion of joy or grief). She caused all the people in the *majlis* to laugh at him and as a result he got very embarrassed (*KA*, 21: 157-8).

In addition to the entertaining value of this anecdote we have useful educational insight in the concept of a good composition, that is the duality of "technicality" and "feeling". Whereas al-Isbahani uses humour to educate, ^{c}Arīb uses it sarcastically to make a stronger statement of her colleague's incompetence and consequently embarrasses him more effectively.

Incompetence in all areas of music is illustrated in the following anecdote:

> I was informed by Aḥmad ibn ^{c}Alī ibn Yaḥyà who said: I heard my grandfather ^{c}Alī ibn Yaḥyà who said: I was informed by Aḥmad ibn Ibrāhīm al-Kātib who said: I was informed by Khālid ibn Kulthūm who said: I was with Zabrā' in al-Madīna while he was its *wālī* (he is from Banū Hāshim, one of Banū Rabī^{c}a ibn al-Ḥārith ibn ^{c}Abd-al-Muṭṭalib). He ordered the musicians jailed and the singer ^{c}Aṭarrad with them. He set up a meeting to investigate their case, but there came prominent people of al-Madīna to intercede on ^{c}Aṭarrad's behalf, and told the *wālī* that ^{c}Aṭarrad was a man of standing, knightly virtues, charity, and religion. The *wālī* called him, set him free, and ordered him to submit any requests he might have. ^{c}Aṭarrad invoked God's blessings on him, and as he was leaving saw the singers brought in to be investigated. ^{c}Aṭarrad returned to the *wālī* and said: "May God make the *amīr* prosper, is it because of singing that you have jailed these people?" He said: "Yes." He said: "Don't treat them unjustly for by God they have never excelled in any part of it yet!" The *wālī* laughed and set them free (*KA*, 3: 307).

This anecdote shows how, in medieval Islam, musicians suffered from the vicissitude of life. It is true that they might amass great fortunes and command respect, but it is equally the case that they suffered the consequences of the "unlawfulness of music." In short, the samā^c (lawfulness or impermissibility of music) was not a theoretical matter debated by theologians, but a problem for musicians of serious practical consideration.[25] We also learn from this anecdote that a musician can effectively use musical humour to save his--supposedly incompetent--music colleagues from jail.

* * *

Before coming to the conclusion of this paper, it is only appropriate to translate a musical anecdote concerning Ash^cab, the prince of laughter. The clever joker-musician resorted to musical humour to escape the punishment of his patroness Sukayna bint al-Ḥusayn ibn ^cAlī:

> I was informed by my uncle who said: We were told by ^cAbd Allāh ibn Abī Sa^cd who said: I was told by Muḥammad ibn ^cAbd Allāh ibn Mālik on the authority of Isḥāq who said: I was told by Ibrāhīm ibn al-Mahdī on the authority of ^cUbayda ibn Ash^cab who said: Sukayna (bint al-Ḥusayn ibn ^cAlī) became angry at my father about a matter on which he had disagreed with her. She swore to have his beard shaved off, and brought a barber and told him: "Shave his beard." The barber said to him: "Puff out your cheeks so that I can get a grip of you." So Ash^cab said: "O son of an uncircumcised woman, she asked you to shave my beard not teach me to blow a wind instrument.[26] What about your wife, if you want to shave her vulva do you blow its side!" The barber got angry, swore not to shave his beard, and left. When the news reached Sukayna of what happened between them, she laughed and forgave Ash^cab (KA, 19: 175).

In his Kitāb al-Aghānī, al-Iṣbahānī used humour as a part of the entertaining elements with which he infused, relieved, and contrasted the educational elements of his work. His motto was to teach by way of fun and laughter. Thanks to al-Iṣbahānī's psycho-educational insight, today, ten centuries later, when we read his work, we are amused, we laugh, and we certainly learn a great deal with little effort.

Musical humour was one of the many qualities required of a really good court-musician. It was an added attraction which entertained and amused the patrons, and as a result often benefited the musicians with greater material rewards. Musical humour was also a tool used to calm an angered patron, to be granted forgiveness, to receive freedom from slavery or from jail, and even to save one's skin. Whereas musical statements were rendered more effective by the use of humour, the reverse equally obtained, namely, that humour was made more effective by the addition of the musical factor. Along these lines, other areas of investigation in Middle East studies can benefit from the study of the above-mentioned musical factor. As for the study of non-technical musical matters, Arabists can greatly contribute to ethnomusicology by bringing to light an area of Middle East studies unfortunately neglected for too long. This paper, it is hoped, will stimulate interest in this direction.

Notes

The research for this paper was supported through grants from the Canada Council, the Social Sciences and Humanities Research Council of Canada, and the Institute for Arab Studies.

1 For this paper I have used the Dār al-Kutub edition: Abū 'l-Faraj ʿAlī ibn al-Ḥusayn al-Iṣbahānī, *Kitāb al-Aghānī*, 4th ed., 16 vols (1927; rpt. Cairo: al-Mu'assasāt al-Miṣriyyat al-ʿĀmma li- 'l-Ta'līf wa 'l-Tarjama wa 'l-Ṭibāʿa wa 'l-Nashr, 1963); vol. 17, ed. ʿAlī Muḥammad al-Bajāwī and vol. 18, ed. ʿAbd al-Karīm Ibrāhīm al-ʿIzbāwī (Cairo: al-Hay'at al-Miṣriyyat al-ʿĀmma li- 'l-Ta'līf wa 'l-Nashr, 1970); vol. 19, ed. ʿAbd al-Karīm Ibrāhīm al-ʿIzbāwī (Cairo: al-Hay'at al-Miṣriyyat al-ʿĀmma li- 'l-Kitāb. Dār al-Ta'līf wa 'l-Nashr, 1972); vol. 20, ed. ʿAlī 'l-Najdī Nāṣif, vol. 21, ed. ʿAbd al-Karīm al-ʿIzbāwī and Maḥmud Muḥammad Ghunaym, vol. 22, ed. ʿAlī 'l-Sibāʿī, ʿAbd al-Karīm al-ʿIzbāwī and Maḥmud Ghunaym, vol. 23, ed. ʿAlī 'l-Sibāʿī, and vol. 24, ed. ʿAbd al-Karīm al-ʿIzbāwī and ʿAbd al-ʿAzīz Maṭar (Cairo: al-Hay'at al-Miṣriyyat al-ʿĀmma li- 'l-Kitāb, 1972-1974). For death dates and other biographical notices of persons mentioned in this paper, the reader should refer to Islamic biographical dictionaries.

2 Yāqūt al-Rūmī al-Ḥamawī, *Muʿjam al-Udabā'* or *Irshād al-Arīb ilà Maʿrifat al-Adīb*, ed. D. S. Margoliouth, Gibb Memorial Series, 6 (London: Luzac, 1907-1926), 5: 149.

3 Ibn Khallikān, *Wafayāt al-Aʿyān wa Anbā' Abnā' al-Zamān*, ed. Muḥammad Muḥyī 'l-Dīn ʿAbd al-Ḥamīd (Cairo: Maktabat al-Nahḍat al-Miṣriyya, 1948-1949), 2: 142.

4 Quoted in Reynold A. Nicholson, *A Literary History of the*

Arabs (1907; rpt. Cambridge: Cambridge University Press, 1969), p. 32. For more Eastern opinions on the worth of Kitāb al-Aghānī see Muḥammad ^{c}Abd al-Jawwād al-Asma^{c}ī, Abū 'l-Faraj al-Iṣbahānī wa Kitābuhu al-Aghānī. Dirāsat wa Taḥlīl li-Azhà 'l-^{c}Usūr al-Islāmiyyat (Cairo: Dār al-Ma^{c}ārif, 1951), pp. 163-190.

[5] H. A. R. Gibb, Arabic Literature, 2nd ed. (1963; rpt. London: Oxford University Press, 1974), p. 97.

[6] For bibliographic details as well as for documentation of the most recent scholarship in the Arab world, see George D. Sawa, "Music Performance Practice in the Early ^{c}Abbāsid Era, 132 AH/750 AD - 320 AH/932 AD," Ph.D. diss., University of Toronto, 1983, p. 35.

[7] G. M. Wickens, "Literature in Arabic," in The Persian Gulf States: A General Survey, ed. A. J. Cottrell (Baltimore: Johns Hopkins University Press, 1980), pp. 334-353.

[8] I should like to express my gratitude to Prof. L. M. Kenny, Prof. M. E. Marmura, and Prof. G. M. Wickens of the Department of Middle East and Islamic Studies (University of Toronto) who, in 1976, took exception to such a belief, and whose foresight allowed me to undertake a doctoral dissertation in Middle East studies on a musical topic (see note 6, above).

[9] Alan P. Merriam, The Anthropology of Music (1964; rpt. [Evanston:] Northwestern University Press, 1976), p. 14.

[10] Ibid., p. 29.

[11] Some of these points have been studied in Sawa, "Music Performance Practice."

[12] Franz Rosenthal, Humor in Early Islam (Philadelphia: University of Pennsylvania Press, 1956), p. 34.

[13] Sawa, "Music Performance Practice," pp. 212-218, 222-247.

[14] For the qualities of a boon-companion see Muhammad Manazir Ahsan, Social Life Under the ^{c}Abbasids: 170-287 AH/786-902 AD (London: Longmans, 1979), pp. 56-58; Anwar Chejne, "The Boon-Companions in Early ^{c}Abbasid Times," JAOS, 85 (1965), 327, 331-332; Mhammed Ferid Ghazi, "Un Groupe social: 'Les Raffinés' (Ẓurafā')," SI, 11 (1959), 39-71; Sawa, "Music Performance Practice," pp. 138-139, 216-218; Abū 'l-Tayyib al-Washshā', Kitāb al-Muwashshà (Beirut: Dār al-Ṣādir, 1965), pp. 21, 54-55, 60-65, 178-180, 191-193.

[15] Since only the incipit is given in this anecdote, I have supplied the second line in square brackets to clarify the meaning.

[16] For more details on textual change in performance see Sawa, "Music Performance Practice," pp. 244-247. For an interesting parallel in modern times in the Arab world see G. D. Sawa, "The Survival of Some Aspects of Medieval Arabic Performance Practice," Ethnomusicology, 25.1 (1981), 78.

[17] Marwān here "insults ^{c}Alī's manhood" by addressing him in the feminine, hence ^{c}Aliyya.

[18] The nasab of ^{c}Alī ibn al-Jahm is given in KA, 10: 203. Here Marwān satirizes ^{c}Alī by mocking the family's fake Quraysh descendance, calling them "Nabatean," which in ^{c}Abbāsid times denoted inhabitants of al-^{c}Irāq who were neither shepherds nor soldiers. It was also applied contemptuously to the Aramaic speaking peasants (Honigman, "Nabateans," in EI^{1}). In this line the satire therefore consists in attacking ^{c}Alī's "lower class origin" (Nabatean) and in accusing him of lying to be of the "highest class" (Qurayshite).

[19] Marwān uses the word woman to refer to ^{c}Alī's swollen belly mentioned in the first poem. To add crudity to the satire Marwān qualifies ^{c}Alī "the woman" as ḥalaqiyya. The word ḥalaqiyya applies to a she-ass with a disease in its womb as a result of copulating with a number of asses in turn. Ḥalaqiyya also carries the meaning of ḥulāq,

which was applied to a she-ass or to a woman with a unsatiable sexual appetite (KA, 12: 83, n. 1; al-Murtaḍà al-Zabīdī, Tāj al-ᶜArūs [Cairo, 1888; rpt. Beirut: Dār Maktabat al-Ḥayāt, n.d.], 6: 321).

[20] This anecdote is only one of many examples in which music beautifies and strengthens the meaning of a poem (Sawa, "Music Performance Practice," p. 158).

[21] For a detailed discussion of competitions in the musical majālis see Sawa, "Music Performance Practice," pp. 222-232.

[22] For verbal expressions on performance see Sawa, "Music Performance Practice," pp. 212-218.

[23] The Arabic text has al-Rashīd as the subject, but the context of the anecdote clearly indicates that al-Rashīd is the object.

[24] The wide concept of īqāᶜ was obtained by the newly discovered manuscript, Kitāb Iḥṣā' al-Iqāᶜāt of Abū Naṣr al-Fārābī. For details on the theory and practice of the īqāᶜ in ᶜAbbāsid times see Sawa, "Music Performance Practice," pp. 23-27, 48-82.

[25] G. D. Sawa, "The Status and Role of Musicians in the Kitāb al-Aghānī," paper delivered at the Columbia Symposium on the Muslim Musicians, New York, February 1981. For the social status of early ᶜAbbāsid court musicians see Eckhard Neubauer, "Musiker am Hof der frühen ᶜAbbasiden," Ph.D. diss. (Frankfurt am Main: J. W. Goethe-Universität, 1965), pp. 15-24.

[26] The word zamr means playing a mizmār, and the word mizmār in medieval times applied generically to mean wind instruments, that is, reedless (flute), single reed (clarinet family), and double-reed (oboe family). We therefore do not know which of the three is meant in the anecdote, and thus should not translate it as flute as Rosenthal did (Rosenthal, p. 94).

4

An Analysis of the "Tale of the Three Apples" from *The Thousand and One Nights*

Roger Allen
The University of Pennsylvania

The great scarcity of copies . . . is, I believe, the reason why recitations of them are no longer heard; even fragments of them are with difficulty procured; and when a complete copy of "The Thousand and One Nights" is found, the price demanded for it is too great for a reciter to have it in his power to pay.

To a Western audience which is generally aware of the influence of The 1001 Nights on Europe at the time of its translation into French and thereafter, the above quotation from Edward Lane's Manners and customs of the modern Egyptians may come as somewhat of a surprise.[1] Until quite recently interest in this world-famous collection of narrative has tended to focus on the origins of the work, the various recensions, and other essentially external features. Indeed, if we look at scholarship written in Arabic about the narrative tradition during the earlier period, we discover that the same situation applies with regard to other genres such as the maqāma and even the more philosophical tales of Abū 'l-ᶜAlā' al-Maᶜarrī and Ibn Ṭufayl. Studies of these works do, of course, exist, but if they venture any comments of a literary nature, they remain very much within the framework of a literary-historical approach. As a result there is a shortage of material on which to make any judgments concerning what one might call a tradition of narrative or of "fictionality" in Arabic literature before the modern period.

More recently a number of scholars have begun to analyse The 1001 Nights collection in particular as being something more than "dialect non-literature," availing themselves among other things of the advances in the study of epic, folktale and myth during the course of this century.[2] A variety of studies has appeared: of the larger ones, we would cite those of Gerhardt, al-Qalamāwī and Ghazoul, and in

Logos Islamikos: Studia Islamica in honorem Georgii Michaelis Wickens, ed. Roger M. Savory and Dionisius A. Agius, Papers in Mediaeval Studies 6 (Toronto: Pontifical Institute of Mediaeval Studies, 1984), pp. 51-60.

shorter form the contributions of Hamori and Molan.[3] In a recent work on a contemporary narrative genre, the novel, the present writer saw fit to question the views of those who would attribute the emergence of fictional genres in the modern Arab world entirely to Western influence.[4] It was suggested that, in view of our relatively scant knowledge about prose narrative in the earlier period, such a judgment was rash. Furthermore the interest expressed by a number of writers and critics in the earlier tradition since the 1967 conflict suggests that, while the influence of the West may indeed have been strong at certain points during the long process known as the nahḍa or renaissance, the indigenous tradition was never completely supplanted and has indeed emerged with great vigor in recent times. All of which points to the notion that an investigation of the nature of narrative in the earlier period might not only be of interest per se but also provide a framework within which to assess new experiments in fiction being tried today and indeed to re-examine the development of modern Arabic fiction as a whole. As an illustration of a narrative which seemed suitable for such analysis, I suggested "Ḥikāyat al-ṣabiyya 'l-maqtūla" ("The tale of the murdered young woman," usually known as "The tale of the three apples") from The 1001 Nights. In the context of this tribute to a great scholar who has devoted much of his attention to the process of analyzing and making accessible to others many of the riches of Middle Eastern literature, I would now like to make a contribution to this process by attempting an analysis of this short tale.

"The tale of the three apples" is a quintessential murder mystery.[5] It begins with the Caliph Hārūn al-Rashīd deciding to go down into the city in disguise with his wazīr, Jaᶜfar al-Barmakī, and his eunuch, Masrūr. This is, of course, a familiar theme to readers of the Hārūn tales in the 1001 Nights collection, providing as it does an obvious means whereby "local color" can be provided to tales set in ᶜAbbāsid Baghdad, or, as Hārūn himself puts it in the tale itself, in order to ensure that his people are being justly treated by those officials whom he has appointed to office. As we will see, the events of this story make Hārūn's pronouncement not a little ironic, but for the time being we may content ourselves with the observation that the Caliph's attitude to the entire exercise is well summed up by the description of his party as "going down" (nazala) into the city and later of "going up" to the palace. One is reminded of the terminology of Oxford and Cambridge Universities.

The first person whom the caliphal party meets is a shaykh who is bemoaning both the failure of mankind to appreciate the breadth of his learning and his own need to fish in the River Tigris in order to feed his family. Hārūn suggests to this shaykh-fisherman that he try fishing again, this time on his-Hārūn's-luck. But instead of a fish, the old man brings to shore a heavy box. Paying off the shaykh, the Caliph "goes up" to his palace carrying the heavy box and full of curiosity. The shaykh's role in the tale is at an end; this is not to be a story about the employment crises in academe.

When the box is opened, the Caliph discovers to his horror that it contains the dissected body of a beautiful woman. His horror is occasioned as much by the realization that, as ruler, he will be called to account for this crime in the next world as it is by the fact of the murder itself. He soon shifts the responsibility on to Ja^{c}far who is allowed three days to find the murderer. Unable to achieve this impossible task, Ja^{c}far (along with forty of his relatives) is taken out to be crucified; the populace of Baghdad is invited to watch the spectacle. At the crucial moment, a culprit comes forward, but this immediately poses yet another problem in that not one but two people insist that they committed the murder. One is a comely young man while the other is old. The young man then explains that the whole episode is a terrible mistake. He has obtained three apples for his sick wife at great expense of energy and money. When he sees a black slave carrying an apple and asks him where it came from, the young man is horrified to hear the slave tell him that he got it from his girlfriend while her husband was away. Suspecting his wife, the young man asks to see the three apples. She is unable to find the third one. In a rage he kills her, cuts her up and throws her body into the Tigris. Only later does he discover that his own son has taken the apple without his wife's knowledge and that the slave has snatched it from the boy.

Once again Ja^{c}far is given an impossible task, namely to find this slave. Despairing of carrying out the Caliph's orders, he is again saved in the nick of time when he discovers an apple in his little daughter's pocket when bidding her a last fond farewell. Asking her where the apple came from, he discovers that the culprit slave is none other than his own slave, Rīḥān. The mystery is thus finally solved, and Hārūn orders that the remarkable string of events be recorded. For, within the framework of the telling of stories each one more remarkable than the last, this one is certainly regarded as extraordinary.

The above synopsis of the events is, of course, merely the bare bones of the tale. Even so, it clearly illustrates one of the principal features of any murder mystery, namely the sequencing of events. Any murder story which introduced the fact of the murder on its final pages or which provided a solution soon after its beginning would fail in one area which is crucial to the success of this particular subgenre: the maintenance of ironic tension for the maximum amount of time possible. Indeed some writers of this type of fiction will challenge their readers relatively late in the narrative sequence. If we put a little flesh on the bare bones of "The tale of the three apples", we will see that this tension is maintained in a most skillful manner and that the process involves some novel twists. To be sure, the box with the murdered girl in it is found right at the beginning of the narrative (that is, once the background of the Hārūn and Jaᶜfar segment has been provided), but in this tale we do not have to wait to the end to find out who the murderer is. Not only are Jaᶜfar and Hārūn presented with a "choice" of two confessed murderers, but the actual culprit clearly identifies himself well before the conclusion of the tale. It is not so much a matter of "whodunnit?"--which is clear enough, but of who is responsible for the murder's occurrence. This leads in turn from a consideration of responsibility to that of justice. And it is here that the real irony arises through the palpable disparity between Hārūn's laudable aims expressed at the beginning of the tale and his demeanor throughout the course of events.

The reader's curiosity as to who killed the girl, who she is, how long she had been dead, and which of the two men--her husband or her father--committed the murder, is satisfied by the contents of the husband's own narrative. But throughout the tale other elements serve to maintain the tension. In the first place, the two deadlines which Hārūn gives to Jaᶜfar build up a tension of their own; the first is relieved by the appearance of the husband and father of the girl just as Jaᶜfar is about to be crucified; the second by the discovery that his own slave is in fact "responsible" for the entire tragedy through the theft of the apple and his own duplicity. And, if we read on beyond the end of the tale, we discover that this slave manages to escape punishment for his actions: Ja^c^far persuades the Caliph to forgive him in return for listening to the tale of Nūr al-Dīn and Shams al-Dīn. In the cause of the continuing stream of narrative, all loose ends have been conveniently tied up.

Beyond these features which seem to suggest a careful sequencing of events and their resolution so as to provide for the maximum of tension, there is another aspect of this tale which it shares with many others in The 1001 Nights, namely that of frames. Molan has treated some other tales from the collection in this way, and many of his points are applicable here too.[6] The outermost frame here is, of course, that of Shahrazād and Shahrayār. The situation in this frame is itself fraught with violence. In telling the vast collection of tales, Shahrazād is trying to prevent the King from killing her (as he has killed many virgin girls before her) as an act of revenge for his wife's infidelity with a black slave. In this context, the fact that a black slave in this story so close to the beginning of the collection is directly responsible for the tragic death of the girl is obviously of considerable significance.

It is Shahrazād, the potential victim of the violence of the King in the first frame of the tale, who narrates the contents of the second frame, namely the activities of Hārūn al-Rashīd and his retinue. Besides introducing a series of events, this frame provides the tale with authenticity of both place and character. The setting is Baghdad (as is the case with the tales of what Gerhardt terms "the Hārūn cycle"),[7] and this is emphasized by the use of the River Tigris as the initial focal point of the Caliph's attentions. We also have two authentic characters: Hārūn al-Rashīd and Ja^c^far. By "authentic" here I imply that two such people are familiar to students of the history of this period, but also that the means by which Ja^c^far al-Barmakī actually met his end at the hands of Hārūn--with his severed head impaled upon one of the bridges of Baghdad--seems fully reflected in this particular tale.[8] In this frame too the atmosphere is full of violence. Hārūn addresses his wazīr as "dog of a wazīr" and then proceeds to threaten him twice with a grotesquely public death. When Ja^c^far presents the Caliph with the dilemma of two men confessing to the murder, the latter's solution is to kill them both. He further expresses his amazement to the young man that he should have confessed without being tortured first.

Ja^cfar on the other hand emerges in a different light. He is portrayed for us by the narrator of the tale as a long-suffering servant of the Caliph--apparently a <u>sine qua non</u> for the office--although we must admire his one gesture of defiance when, knowing that he is to be crucified for failing to find the girl's killer, he asks his master how he is supposed to be able to "know the unseen." Ja^cfar is portrayed as a family man who "loves his little daughter more than all his other children," while to the young man who confesses to his wife's murder he is "prince of princes and haven of the poor."[9] Each time that he is charged with the impossible task of finding a particular person in Baghdad, the narrator gives us a glimpse of his thoughts through a short interior monologue, a process which arouses our sympathy, particularly when juxtaposed with the irascible and petulant comments of the Caliph.

As we noted above, this second frame begins with the discovery of the dead woman and is therefore relatively late in the time-frame of the complete story. But, apart from the three day deadlines which Ja^cfar is given, it is rather short on references to time. For that reason it stands in considerable contrast to the third and innermost frame in which the young man relates the sorry tale of how he came to kill his beloved wife. Almost every event is accompanied by a mention of when it occurred during the month or of how long it lasted. We are thus given not only the answer as to who killed the girl (although the reason for the grotesque violence with which it is done is never explained) but also a time-frame for the entire tale. No sooner has the young man recounted how he and his father-in-law mourned his wife for five days and are still sorrowing "until this very day" than the nineteenth night of the 1001 is over, and the narrator takes us back through the three frames in three sentences.

This framing technique whereby one story is embedded within another is a familiar one within <u>The 1001 Nights</u>, but in this case we may observe that it illustrates clearly the interconnections between the different situations in the story and points towards certain moral conclusions which might be drawn. There is firstly the parallel between the irascibility of Shahrayār and Hārūn al-Rashīd: that of the latter is amply demonstrated in the story itself, and of the former implicit in Shahrazād's very situation. Between the outermost frame and the innermost we may point to the theme of wifely infidelity, surely a touchy topic within the context of Shahrayār's feelings on the subject. The fact that the villain in the piece is a black slave only serves to amplify the similarities, while from the point of view of structure it also links the Hārūn frame with the innermost in that the black slave proves to be Rīḥān, a member of Ja^{c}far's own household. In contrast with the scheming, deceit and violence which punctuate this tale, the fact that two children are the agents of revealing the truth is surely not coincidental; even here violence intrudes in that the murdered girl's son is afraid that she may beat him once she discovers that the apple has been stolen. In a word, this tale might carry a subtitle "The wages of violence," and in that it comes so close to the beginning of the collection it may perhaps be viewed as a none too subtle commentary by Shahrazād herself on the very situation in which she finds herself.

Having now considered some of the structural details of the tale, let us look at the way in which some of the effects are achieved, particularly insofar as they concern language. We have already alluded to the narrator's use of interior monologue to give a more intimate picture of the character of Ja^{c}far. The reader's view is also manipulated in other ways, and no more so than through the means of describing the major participants in the tale. Those with a purely peripheral role are sparsely described: the learned fisherman at the beginning is said merely to have "a net and basket on his head and a stick in his hand," while the father of the murdered girl is simply "an old man." By contrast, the young man who is the girl's husband and killer is accorded the Hollywood treatment: "a young man, handsome and in spotless clothes; radiant of visage, with gorgeous eyes, gleaming forehead, rosy cheeks, a light down of beard, and a mole on his cheek looking like a grain of ambergris." This aspect is perhaps best seen in the treatment of the girl herself. At first her description is limited to the fact that she looks "like a silver ingot." At this point the narrator is more interested in the theme of the Caliph's anger and its effect on Ja^{c}far than on the personage or description of the victim herself. Later on however, when the husband relates how he came to kill her, she is described again. Once more the opportunity is used for a particular purpose; the young man characterizes his wife as an idealized life-partner, almost a stereotype: "This girl is my wife and my cousin too. This old man is her father and my uncle. She was a virgin when I married her and through God's will she gave me three sons. She used to love me and serve me, and I have never found any wrong in her." All of which makes the savagery with which he eventually kills her so seemingly inexplicable.

Our narrator then is at some pains to make his principals conform with his overall purpose. The same can be said of more detailed aspects of language. Each frame is enlivened with a generous amount of dialogue, but there are also subtle ways in which the frames are differentiated. Characteristically, the story told by Shahrazād is dotted with formulaic phrases often in *saj*^{c} (rhyming prose), a stylistic feature beloved of Arabic prose from earliest times. On the other hand, it is surely no coincidence that the young man's story (the innermost frame) contains the use of the colloquial word "*ḥaṭṭayt--hā*" ("I put her") which may well reflect the Egyptian period of the collections's compilation but may also be seen as an attempt to lend a popular touch to the inner narrative.

My aim in the preceding analysis has been to show that this tale is an interesting fusion of characteristics of traditional narrative and of features which modern critics might search for in a piece of contemporary fiction. It is, in a word, a finely crafted mystery story.

* * *

Returning to the theme with which I began, litterateurs in the Arab world showed an interest in *The 1001 Nights* from a relatively early period in the modern renaissance. For example, Mārūn al-Naqqāsh (1871-55) wrote a play entitled *Abū 'l-Ḥasan al-Mughaffal* and he was closely followed by Abū Khalīl al-Qabbānī in Syria with *Hārūn al-Rashīd ma^{c}a Ghānim ibn Ayyūb wa Qūt al-Qulūb*.[10] Within the realm of drama in recent times, Alfred Faraj and Sa^{c}dallāh Wannūs (to name just two figures) have made successful use of tales from *The 1001 Nights* to create dramas of considerable contemporary import and popularity.[11] Some contributors to contemporary fiction are also scholars within the field of traditional narratives: we sould mention Fārūq Khūrshīd, Shawqī ^{c}Abd al-Ḥakīm, and Jabrā Ibrāhīm Jabrā. The first chapter of

Al-Baḥth ᶜan Walīd Masᶜūd (In Search of Walīd Musᶜūd, 1978) by Jabrā contains the replay of a long message on cassette tape made by the character who is the focus of the work. In ᶜAbd al-Raḥmān Munīf's novel, Al-Nihāyāt (Endings, 1978) the action of narrative is suspended at one point while the men of a village tell each other a whole series of animal tales. Certainly Jabrā would wish to be seen through his many critical articles as drawing a firm link between the old and the new.[12]

The links between contemporary Arabic fiction and Western genres have been clearly drawn. At certain stages in the development of the fictional genres in the modern Arab world the influence of the West was certainly strong and even overwhelming. The connections between today's fiction and the narrative tradition of earlier Arabic literature, however overt or covert, conscious or unconscious they may be, are not as obvious and have been little investigated. This present study hopes to add to the relatively few works which may foster such a purpose.

Notes

[1] See Edward Lane, An Account of the Manner and Customs of the Modern Egyptians (London: Everyman, 1954), 420. This work is discussed in some detail in Leila Ahmed, Edward W. Lane (London: Longman, 1978), 127-170. Among more recent studies of the reception of The 1001 Nights, we would mention C. Knipp, "The Arabian Nights in England: Galland's Translation and its Successors," JAL 5 (1974), 44-54.

[2] Cf. Bridget Connelly, "The Structure of Four Banī Hilāl Tales," JAL 4 (1973), 18.

[3] Mia Gerhardt, The Art of Story-Telling (Leiden: E.J. Brill, 1963); Suhayr al-Qalamāwī, Alf Layla wa Layla (Cairo: Maṭbaᶜat al-Maᶜārif, 1943); Feryal Ghazoul, The Arabian Nights: A Structural Analysis (Cairo: Institute for the Study and Presentation of Arab Cultural Values, 1980); Andras Hamori, On the Art of Medieval Arabic Literature (Princeton: Princeton University Press, 1974), 145-180. See also Studia Islamica 43 (1976), 65-80; Peter Molan, JAOS 98.3 (Jul.-Sept., 1978), 237-247 and Edebiyat 3.2 (1978), 121-135.

[4] Roger Allen, The Arabic Novel, (Syracuse: Syracuse University Press, 1982), 16.

5 I have used the edition of Rushdī Ṣāliḥ (Cairo: Dār al-Shaᶜb, 1969), 86-90. In the older Būlāq edition (reprint 1960), the tale begins in Volume I, page 66.

6 See references in note 3 above.

7 Gerhardt, Section VI, pp. 417-470.

8 The event is described in P. Hitti, *History of the Arabs* (London: MacMillan, 1961), 295-296.

9 This reflects the historical picture of Jaᶜfar. There is a good illustration of the affection in which Jaᶜfar and the Barmakids were held in al-Qāḍī Abū ᶜAlī 'l-Tanūkhī's (940-94) work, *al-Faraj baᶜda 'l-Shidda* (Baghdad: Maktabat al-Muthannà, 1955), 7: 223-226.

10 For reference to the work of Naqqāsh, see Matti Moussa in *JAL* 3 (1972), 111-114. For the work of al-Qabbānī, see Muḥammad Yūsuf Najm, *Al-Masraḥ al-ᶜArabī* Vol. 7.

11 I have discussed the works of Faraj in *Edebiyat* 4.1 (1979), esp. 109-11, and of Wannūs in *JAL* 14 (forthcoming).

12 Jabrā's articles are scattered through his collections of critical articles: *Al-Hurriyya wa al-Tūfān* (Beirut: Dār Majallat Shiᶜr, 1960); *Al-Riḥla al-Thāmina* (Beirut: Al-Maktaba 'l-ᶜAṣriyya, 1967); *Yanābīᶜ al-Ru'yā* (Beirut: Al-Mu'assasa 'l-ᶜArabiyya, 1979).

Part Two
Persian Language and Literature

5

The Tragedy of Suhrāb

Jerome W. Clinton
Princeton University

A. Introduction

More than a decade ago, G. M. Wickens began an essay by lamenting the fact that the Shāhnāmah, like virtually all major works of Persian literature, ". . . had received very little analysis in purely literary terms, and even less in the context of really modern literary criticism."[1] Despite the fine example Wickens set in the essay from which I quote, and despite the generally encouraging upsurge in the number of literary studies devoted to Persian literature in the course of the last decade, his lament for the parlous state of Shāhnāmah studies is as true today as it was a decade ago. The national epic of Iran continues to be a major work of world literature that has received far less than its due of critical attention. Since I have long studied and taught what Wickens calls Iran's "royal work," but never written about it, it seems appropriate that as my contribution to this volume I should offer an essay that attempts, as he suggests, to address the Shāhnāmah in purely literary terms. As Wickens took as his subject the portion of Iranian national epic that he had first read when a student, I have taken as mine that famous story which has served as the introduction to Firdawsī and his work, for so many students of Persian literature, including myself.

No story in the Shāhnāmah has more engaged the interest and sympathies of audiences in the West than that of the tragic encounter between Suhrāb and his father, Rustam. It was translated repeatedly in the nineteenth century, and Arnold's brilliant paraphrase introduced it to a far broader audience than these translations could have reached by themselves.

The theme of filicide is a powerful and compelling one,

Logos Islamikos: Studia Islamica in honorem Georgii Michaelis Wickens, ed. Roger M. Savory and Dionisius A. Agius, Papers in Mediaeval Studies 6 (Toronto: Pontifical Institute of Mediaeval Studies, 1984), pp. 63-77.

particularly when both father and son are figures of great appeal. Although the theme is found in many literatures, it is usually somewhat rare within them.[2] The more usual, even archetypal pattern is of the son who kills his father, whether symbolically or in fact. However frightening and appalling that outcome is, it has the sanction of natural process. We accept the necessity of sons killing their fathers as part of their own process of growth and maturation. By reversing that fundamental pattern, The Story of Suhrāb violates our sense of the natural order of things and adds a nightmarish element to a confrontation that is already freighted with meaning.

As I have already suggested, the story, despite its appeal, has received little comment or study. The general view of it is that it is built upon tragic accident, but that the effects of accident are compounded by a certain meanness of spirit or failure of will on the part of Rustam. Bertel's, for example, says that Suhrāb dies only because of a misunderstanding, and that Rustam's fault is all the heavier for his having resorted to a ruse to defeat his son.[3]

In these comments, Bertel's, along with most other commentators on the story, seems to be echoing the line which begins the prologue to the tale, and seems to offer a guide to its interpretation, as well.

> It is a story that is filled with weeping.
> The gentle heart will be angry at Rustam.[4]

This line, or its placement, rather, poses something of a problem. While it appears at the beginning of the prologue in many, even most, of the manuscripts of the Shāhnāmah, produced since the fourteenth century, and so in the modern editions based on them, in the two oldest manuscripts it does not. In both of these it is placed at the very end of the tale, and serves as a final comment, not an introduction.[5] Textual evidence aside, the line as anomalous within the prologue. All the other lines address the moral dilemma raised by the death of a young man in the abstract, and have a general, homiletic quality. Only this line is so specific in its reference to one of the characters, and only this line sanctions our feelings of grief and anger at the outcome of the tale. In the older manuscripts, the first counsel of the prologue is to have faith that such apparent accidents are in fact the workings of divine justice.

> If a sharp wind springs up from some quarter,

And casts an unripe fruit to the ground,
Shall we call this tyranny or justice?
Shall we consider it as right or wrong?
If death is just, how is this unjust?
Why this wailing and complaining at what is just?
Your soul has no knowledge of this mystery.
You cannot proceed beyond this veil. (1 - 4)

It goes on from this to offer all the familiar consolations: nothing endures forever; death is not the worst thing that could happen to a young man; old age is no treat; heaven is a better place than this. Yet the dominant theme is the first one — all apparent accident is part of God's mysterious plan.

I would like to look at the story of Suhrāb anew here, and to try to see beyond this veil of mystery. That is, I would like to understand what justice is served by Suhrāb's death at the hands of Rustam, and how. But there are other themes here than the relation of fate and justice, and in the end, I too will return to the question of why the gentle heart should be angry with Rustam.

Since there is no good modern translation of the story of Suhrāb in English, I will include here an extended summary of the tale before proceeding with my interpretation of it.

B. The Story

The story of the birth and death of Suhrāb begins one morning when Rustam, the paramount hero of the epic, wakes up sad and decides to lift his spirits by going on a hunt. He sets out alone for the border of Iran's traditional enemy, Tūrān, and there falls upon a herd of onager. He roasts and eats his kill, then, sated, falls sound asleep, having first unsaddled his famous mount Rakhsh and turned him loose to graze. A party of Tūrānians passes by, spies Rakhsh, captures him, and leads him off to the nearby town of Simingān.

Rustam awakes to find himself unmounted and deep in enemy territory. He picks up his saddle and bridle and follows the tracks of Rakhsh and his captors, lamenting his misfortune as he does.

What will the heroes say? "They took his horse.
"Thus Rustam slept, and thus was he slain." (35)

However, no misfortune befalls him and the tracks quickly lead him to the city. Rustam's reputation has preceded him, and on his arrival there he is greeted with a mollifying deference by the Shāh of Simingān and his nobles. The Shāh promises that Rakhsh will be returned as soon as he is found, and invites Rustam to spend the night with them in drinking and celebration.

That night, when Rustam has retired, the Shāh's daughter, Tahmīnah, comes in secret to his room and declares her love for him. She is both noble and chaste, but like Desdemona she has been enraptured by her hero through hearing tales of his heroic exploits. She vows that she will have no other husband if Rustam refuses her, and begs him to give her a child. Rustam is enchanted by her, and when she adds that she knows where Rakhsh is hidden, he finds her request irresistable. The next morning, he gives her his armlet and says that if their child is a daughter, she is to braid it in her hair, and if a son, to bind it on his arm. He then mounts Rakhsh and returns to Iran.

Nine months later Tahmīnah bears a son whom she calls Suhrāb. Suhrāb manifests all the physical traits of a hero. He is large from infancy and grows at an extraordinary rate. At ten, he seems a grown man already, and at twelve, no warrior in Tūrān can stand up to him in battle. Suhrāb now demands that his mother tell him who his father is. She answers that he is the son of Rustam, but that he must guard that secret from the ruler of Tūrān, and overlord of Simingān, Afrāsiyāb, since he is his father's mortal enemy. Suhrāb rejects her advice and makes a bold and fateful declaration. He vows to lead a Tūrānian army into Iran to overthrow the Shāh, Kay Kā'ūs, and set his father in his place. That done, he will return to Tūrān to unseat Afrāsiyāb so that together he and his father may rule the world.

"When Rustam is the father and I the son
"Who else in all the world should wear a crown?
"When sun and moon fill up the world with light,
"Why should the stars boast their crowns are bright?"
(40 - 41)

And, suiting action to words, he quickly gathers about him the army he needs.

Afrāsiyāb has learned who Suhrāb is by this time, and when he hears of his plans to invade Iran, he sends him troops and arms. He also sends him the generals, Humān and Barman, ostensibly to serve him, but with the more important task of keeping Suhrāb and Rustam from recognizing each other.

Suhrāb and his army advance on Iran. At the border fortress of Safīd Dizh he encounters two heroes--Hajīr, whom he easily defeats and takes captive, and Gurdāfrīd, the only warrior maiden in the Shāhnāmah. Suhrāb's encounter with Gurdāfrīd is a baffling one for him. He easily defeats her in single combat, thinking her a man. Then she reveals herself to be a woman by loosing her long hair from under her helmet. Suhrāb is both smitten with her, and embarrassed to have been fighting a woman. Gurdāfrīd shrewdly plays on both these emotions to trick him into letting her regain the fortress, where she slams the gate in his face and taunts him from the battlements.

Gurdāfrīd and the garrison slip away from the fortress during the night, but before they go, she sends a letter to Kay Kā'ūs warning him of the impending invasion and describing its leader as more than a match for any of Iran's heroes. Alarmed by this, Kay Kā'ūs sends a messenger to Zābulistān at once to summon Rustam. Years of easy victories against extraordinary odds have lulled Rustam into an overweening confidence in his strength, however. All he needs to put any army to flight, he says, is to show his banner on the field of battle. He briefly considers the possibility that this new hero might be his son, but rejects it. Tahmīnah, fearing to lose her son to his warlike father, has written him to say that their son is still a boy, and unskilled in the arts of war. He does not set out for the court immediately, as Kay Kā'ūs had ordered, but delays instead for three days, which he spends in drinking and carousal.

When he reaches the court at last, Kay Kā'ūs, incensed by this delay, orders his champion Ṭūs to execute him. Rustam explodes at this insult.

> "Each thing you do is worse than the last.
> "Sovereignty befits you not at all.
> "You place Suhrāb alive upon the stake.
> "You abase that fierce and warlike enemy."
> (384-385)

And with this, he storms out of the court.

The other Iranian heroes, appalled at the catastrophe they see impending, immediately set about reconciling the two. The senior warrior there, Gūdarz, tells the Shāh he is a fool to drive away his champion just at the moment when Iran is threatened by a Tūrānian warrior without equal. Kā'ūs agrees, and sends him with a deputation to persuade Rustam to return. This they do by telling Rustam that while the Shāh behaved insultingly, others will attribute Rustam's departure not to that but to fear. The argument is persuasive, and

Rustam and Kā'ūs are reconciled. The Iranian army then sets out to meet that of Suhrāb.

With the two hosts now in direct confrontation, and with Suhrāb bent on discovering his father, it hardly seems possible that the two should fail to recognize each other. Yet fate is busy to prevent it. An aged warrior, Zhindarazm, who knows Rustam and whom Tahmīnah has sent with Suhrāb to point out his father to him, is killed by a disguised Rustam when he encounters him while spying on Suhrāb's camp. Suhrāb presses the captive Hajīr to point out Rustam's pavilion to him, but Hajīr, loyal to Rustam and fearful for his life, says Rustam's standard is nowhere to be seen in the camp, and that the pavilion which Suhrāb rightly surmises must be Rustam's does in fact belong to a prince newly arrived from China.

Finally, when the two do at last meet in single combat, Rustam refuses to identify himself. Instead, using a deceit he has employed before to put awesome opponents off their guard, he says that he is not Rustam but a warrior much inferior to him. Suhrāb also fails to reveal his parentage, though he is all but certain that the man before him is his father. The motive for his reticence is not clear. Firdawsī intrudes his voice to say that neither was stirred by love at this moment, but then adds:

> Each wild creature knows its own child,
>   From the fish in the sea to the wild ass in the plain.
> But man, out of the agony of ambition,
>   Thinks his own child an enemy. (707–708)

Suhrāb also seems to feel that it is his father who has failed at this point, for he rebukes his father later, when it is too late, for not having known his own son.

Suhrāb and Rustam fight three battles on three successive days. In the first, they fight each other to exhaustion with no clear advantage gained. In the second, Suhrāb defeats Rustam and has his knife drawn to behead him when the wily veteran dissuades him by saying that among the Iranians two falls are necessary for a decisive victory. In the third, Rustam throws Suhrāb to the ground and quickly thrusts his sword through his chest, wounding him mortally.

Now, when all hope for him is past, Suhrāb reveals who he is and shows the horrified Rustam the very jewels bound on to his arm that Rustam had sent to Tahmīnah as a gift for his child. The scene of recognition is unbearably poignant. Rustam in desperation sends to

Kay Kā'ūs to beg the imperial panacea for his son, but the Shāh refuses to save the life of one who has made war against him. Rustam sets off to plead with him in person, but he has gone only a little way when word of Suhrāb's death is brought to him.

The armies now part. Rustam carries his son's body back to Zābulistān to introduce him posthumously to his illustrious ancestors, Zāl and Sām, and to give him the burial his birth merits. In later versions of the tale a section is added showing Tahmīnah's grief at learning of her son's death.

C. The Making of a Tragedy

As Wickens points out in his essay, the stories of the Shāhnāmah have the quality of drama. The action is fast-paced. Scenes are brief and follow each other briskly and usually with very abrupt transitions. In the presentation of the events of the narrative, the emphasis is also very much on dialogue and action. Descriptions of the physical setting of the scene, or the appearance of the characters are brief and conventional. Only when Suhrāb describes the appearance of the pavilions of the Iranian nobles ranged before him in an effort to discover that of his father, do Firdawsī's descriptions become vivid and detailed. But here the art of description has been used to very practical ends. For only those formal and heraldic features of each pavilion that are emblematic of their owners are mentioned.

The character of Suhrāb provides another link with drama, and specifically with tragedy. Like the greatest tragic heroes, Suhrāb is a good and noble man who precipitates his own destruction by a fatal error in judgement. Moreover, his crime is a crime against the state, an assault upon the throne. His death is necessary to assure the security of that throne and state. Once he declares his ambition to overthrow the Shāh of Iran and set his father in his place, we know that he must inevitably be defeated and killed. In the Shāhnāmah, the one crime that cannot be allowed to go unpunished is armed opposition to the Shah.

Where Suhrāb differs from the great tragedies of Greece and England, is that it has two protagonists, not one. Only Suhrāb dies, but in defeating his son, Rustam suffers a loss that is a kind of death for him. Suhrāb is ideally suited by strength and disposition to succeed his father as the paramount hero of Iran. When Rustam slays him he slays his own successor. More than that, Suhrāb is the only son he will ever have. When Rustam dies himself, the great line of Sistanian heroes who have served the nation of Iran in the role of chief hero for generations will come to an end.[6]

There is also the same fateful quality about his role in this tragedy as there is about that of Suhrāb. We know from that same moment that Suhrāb makes the choice that will lead to his destruction, that it is Rustam who will be the agent of that destruction. Rustam is the paramount hero of Iran, and from virtually his first appearance in the Shāhnāmah, he and he alone has had the responsibility for defending Iran from such attacks as Suhrāb has prepared, and from such attackers as Suhrāb. If the identity of the champion who must confront Suhrāb is ever in doubt, the report of Gūdarz to the Shāh that Iran has no hero to match Suhrāb, puts the matter beyond doubt. Only Rustam has a hope of victory.

The inevitability of the confrontation between the two is never stated explicitly in the story, but it is implicit in the repeated intrusions of fate to thwart that recognition of son by father which would avert it. In reconnoitering the Tūrānian army, Rustam slays the one warrior there who is both willing and able to reveal his identity to Suhrāb. Hajīr puts his own life in jeopardy rather than threaten Rustam's by revealing to Suhrāb that he is in fact in the Iranian camp. Rustam is so intimidated by the stature and ferocity of this young challenger, and so fearful that he will try to deceive him, that he hides his own identity when they at last do meet, hoping to gain some advantage for himself by appearing to be less than he is. And finally, Humān, who knows Rustam by sight, confirms his lie in order to promote the tragedy, and his master's ends.

One cannot read far in the Shāhnāmah before discovering that within it fate is a powerful force in men's lives, and usually a malignant one. It is a dark presence, waiting in the wings to dash human hopes and aspirations. The commonest epithet for it, "the hunchbacked heavens," gives a sense of how it is viewed as the shadowy side of the future. In the story of Suhrāb, it has become more than a lurking, offstage presence, that intrudes at random. Here it is an actual participant in the drama, shaping events to its particular purposes. The tragedy is inevitable because fate, in the guise of justice, requires it.[7]

But how is justice served by this double tragedy? The simple answer is the one already given - a serious threat to the throne of Iran has been defeated by Iran's greatest warrior. Another chapter in the continuing struggle between Iran and Tūrān has ended once more with God giving victory to the nation he favors above all others. But this answer simply draws attention to the formal dynamics of the Shāhnāmah, and takes no account of the personalities who act out this drama. There is surely more to what the story has to say about justice than this. The questions that are left unanswered by this formal answer are essentially two: why does Suhrāb, who has such an illustrious parentage, wish to overthrow both Kay Kā'ūs and Afrāsiyāb; and why must Rustam, the national hero, pay such a heavy price for his victory? The roles of hero and villain are strangely confused here.

The question of why Suhrāb wishes to overthrow Kay Kā'ūs and Afrāsiyāb must begin, I think, with a second look at the nature of his crime. For at first glance, his rebellion does not seem all that wicked. A modern reader, in particular, may well be tempted to see Suhrāb's hostility to these two rulers as a sign of innate virtue and good sense. They are, after all, such unattractive monarchs. Kay Kā'ūs is weak, impulsive and foolish — failings which even his loyal supporters recognize. As Gūdarz says to the Shāh himself after he has so enraged Rustam, "Whoever has a warrior like Rustam,/ If he drives him away, he is a fool" (410). And later, when he is attempting to cool Rustam's wrath, he freely acknowledges the Shāh's failings, "You know that Kā'ūs is a fool./ His angry words are without sense" (422). Even without these explicit statements, the audience of the Shāhnāmah will by this point in the story have seen how Kay Kā'ūs' ineptitude as a ruler has brought his country to the brink of disaster repeatedly, only to have it saved at the last moment by the heroic Rustam. To summarize these episodes very briefly, Kā'ūs has led his army into unnecessary and ruinous battles with both the dīvs of Māzandarān and the kingdom of Hamāvarān. He has also attempted to have himself carried into heaven by trained eagles, only to crash ignominiously in Tūrānian territory. In later editions of the text there are specific allusions to these labors of Rustam both in the scene of confrontation, and in that where Gūdarz attempts to bring Rustam back to the court. The effect is to draw the contrast between the two all the more sharply.

Afrāsiyāb, as the principal enemy of Iran, is, virtually by definition, the epitome of a bad ruler - cruel, vicious, cowardly and untrustworthy. Rustam, particularly as he must have been described to Suhrāb by his mother, Tahmīnah, is the hero of godlike virtues. There is an appealing logic to Suhrāb's ambition to put his father on the throne. Since it is the weakness and folly of Kay Kā'ūs that most threatens Iran's safety, and Rustam's courage and strength that preserve it, is not Rustam indeed a more reasonable choice for Shāh?

Suhrāb's wish to substitute personal merit for divine designation in the selection of the Shāh of Iran does, as we know, place him in sharp conflict with the fundamental political conception of the Shāhnāmah, that Iran will endure for so long as it is ruled by a line of divinely appointed rulers. Yet here that conception is being tested in the most extreme fashion. The monarchs against whom Suhrāb wishes to contend present the very poles of badness in monarchical types. The one who is of principal importance to us is completely incompetent, but the other is actively evil. While Suhrāb and, in particular, Rustam, are figures of contrasting goodness. The effect of presenting the conflict in this way is to make clear that the key element in the ideology of the Shāhnāmah is that the choice of monarchs is God's, and that his reasons are as unfathomable as his choice is unchallengeable. As the prologue puts it, the proper attitude of man in the face of such unexplainable events as Suhrāb's death,

> Fill your heart with faith and be silent,
> You are a slave and silence befits you best.
> The secret of this act of God's is not yours,
> Unless your soul is partners with the devil.
> Strive here in the world as you pass.
> And in the end, take goodness as your cargo.
> (11 - 13)

Suhrāb's rebellion is not an act that can be weighed simply in human, political terms for at bottom it is an act of impiety. And, indeed, the quality of impiety is strong in his declaration that after having unthroned Kā'ūs, he will thrust his spear "above the sun" in challenging Afrāsiyāb, and that he and his father are in the orbit of the sun and moon. In the Iranian cosmology the Shāh was the brother of sun and moon, dominant in his sphere as they were in theirs.[8] Suhrāb wishes by his own efforts to make himself and Rustam into semi-divine beings subordinate only to God.

The contrast between him and his father in this respect is sharp and revealing. After their first battle, which ends in an exhausted stalemate, Rustam acknowledges to himself that the outcome of the next battle is in the hands of God (Yazdān), and Kay Kā'ūs says that he will himself pray to him that night. Then, after the second battle, from which Rustam escapes alive only by guile, he repairs to a stream and prays to God for strength and victory in the next.[9]

Suhrāb, on the contrary, neither prays to God nor refers to him at any point in the story. His loyalty and devotion are fixed exclusively on his father. At the moment of death, Suhrāb appears to gain an insight into the measure of his responsibility for his fate, and the forces against which he has been contending. When he has been mortally wounded, he absolves his still unknown opponent of responsibility for slaying him.

> He said to him, "This came to me from me.
> "Fate placed my key in your hand.
> "You are guiltless of this, for this hunchback
> "Thus raised me up and swiftly cast me down."
> (892-893)

The question of why Suhrāb challenges monarchy is thus refined into one of why the son of such a pious father wishes to commit an act of such striking impiety. Let us leave that question at this point, and turn for a moment to that of why Rustam must kill his son, since the answer to that has much to do with the question of Rustam's own piety and his relation to the ruler.

Rustam's first reference to God occurs in a very different context than those I have just mentioned. It comes much earlier in the story, at that point when the Shāh is enraged by Rustam's failure to obey his command to the letter. "Who is Rustam," he says, "that he ignores my order and turns from his bond to me," and he orders Ṭūs to take him out and execute him. Rustam replies with equal heat, that he is one who has no need of the Shāh.

> He went out in anger and mounted Rakhsh.
> "I am," he said, "the lion-killer and crown-giver."
> "When I am angry, who then is Kā'ūs Shāh?
> "Why does he turn on me? And who is Ṭūs?
> "The earth's my servant and Rakhsh my throne.
> "The mace my signet and the helm my crown.
> "With my blade I light up the dark night.
> "I scatter heads upon the field of battle.
> "Spear point and blade are my companions.
> "This heart and these two arms my Shāh.

"Why does he reproach me? I'm not his slave.
"I am the slave only of the Creator."
(388-393)[10]

The message of both these statements by Rustam is that he wishes to separate his obedience to God from his obedience to the Shāh so that he may abandon the latter. He has no need of the Shāh as a mediator between himself and God. He is his own Shah. He is the crown-giver who brought Kay Kā'ūs to the throne, and more, he is a ruler like the sun, whose sword lights up the dark night.

While Rustam's contempt for the Shāh only explodes at court, and under the extreme provocation of Kay Kā'ūs' order of execution, it has, as these quotations suggest, been building for a long time ("My head's grown weary, my heart full"). The first evidence of its existence in the story is Rustam's failure to heed the Shāh's command that he hasten at once to the court to deal with this new crisis. He cannot believe that the threat is a serious one. How could the Turks produce a warrior who was in any sense a challenge to him? Nor does he feel he owes the Shāh total and unquestioning obedience. The reason for Rustam's lapse in fealty, in short, is to be found as much in his high opinion of his own abilities as in his low opinion of the Shāh's. Alas that both opinions are well founded.

I have already mentioned Kā'ūs' unhappy disposition for involving himself and his army in disastrous and unnecessary battles, and the heroic daring with which Rustam has rescued them. More than that, the tale just before that of Suhrāb shows Rustam single-handedly defeating the army of Tūrān and very nearly taking Afrāsiyāb captive.

Rustam's lapse in fealty is temporary. Gūdarz does succeed in reconciling him to the Shāh, and on his return to the court, Rustam makes the humblest acknowledgement of his authority. But such a lapse cannot be allowed to pass unpunished. And if the price Rustam must pay seems excessively high, there is the example of Suhrāb before us to make clear why it is necessary. For Suhrāb is Rustam released of the constraints of piety and loyalty to the state.

Kay Kā'ūs sees the threat all too well. When Rustam sends Gudarz to him for the panacea that will cure Suhrāb, the Shāh refuses it because he believes that a live Suhrāb will strengthen Rustam against him. He even fears that Rustam might even slay him one day, and explains his fear by alluding to Rustam's words. "You heard him say, 'Who is Kā'ūs?'" (972).

Let us turn one last time to the question of why Suhrāb finds himself in the role of villain. Even with the evidence of his impiety before us, he seems strangely cast in that role. The dominant impression he gives is one of innocence and guilelessness, and even of futility. Since we know from the very first line of the story that he is doomed to an early and painful death, it is difficult to perceive him as posing any real threat to Iran or its monarch. Moreover, that defeat is anticipated repeatedly throughout the story by the many episodes in which each new evidence of Suhrāb's awesome strength and skill in combat is diminished by some example of this guilelessness.

He gathers a mighty army around him, but when Afrāsiyāb sends one of his own generals to assure Suhrāb's failure, he blithely accepts him as one of his advisers.

He defeats Gurdāfrīd, a worthy opponent despite her sex, but then lets her escape to warn Kay Kā'ūs because he is too smitten by her to see through the cunning in her appeals to his pride and reputation.

He defeats Rustam, now knowing who he is, but then throws this victory away by his naive acceptance of his opponent's desperate and transparent deceit. He has the tragic quality of a prince cut off in his prime, not of a villain.

Why is Suhrāb unable to benefit from the great strength and martial skill that are his genetic inheritance? And, when he is in so many ways a worthy son to his father, why is he so fatally unable to worship God or be obedient to monarchy?

The reason has little to do with Suhrāb, and everything to do with Rustam. For the root cause of all of Suhrāb's limitations and his ultimate failure is that he lacks a father. Though physically a giant, Suhrāb is still a boy in years and experience. He can hardly be expected to cope with the intrigues of an Afrāsiyāb or the wiles of seasoned warriors like Gurdāfrīd or Hajīr, let alone Rustam. He wants the advice and counsel that his father is suited before all others to give him. More fundamentally, he has been raised in such a way that he has no natural allegiance to either Shāh. He is an Iranian, but raised in Tūrān and with his only connection to Iran through his idealized accounts of his father as the hero who is the real mainstay of the state, not the Shāh. He is essentially stateless, and being so, essentially without religion as well, since in terms of the Shāhnāmah, religion is a state institution. He has not rejected religion and state, he has been raised without them.

Suhrāb seems strangely cast as a villain to us because we recognise this and know that he is largely blameless of the crimes he commits. And by the same token, we sense that the final reason that Rustam must bear the burden of destroying his own son is that he is a partner in his crimes. It is not just Rustam's reliance on a ruse that makes the gentle heart angry with him, it is the recognition that he has betrayed his son twice before they ever meet in battle. First, he abandoned him at birth and was not there to teach him to be his son in spirit as well as in strength and courage. And second, he did not know him when they met.

Notes

[1]"The Imperial Epic of Iran: A Literary Approach," Acta Iranica, première série, p. 261.

[2]S. A. Hatto finds only four exemplars in European languages--one each in Germanic, Russian, Irish and Persian; "On the Excellence of the 'Hildebrandslied': A Comparative Study in Dynamics," in Essays on Medieval German and Other Poetry (Cambridge University Press, 1980), pp. 820-838. M. A. Potter had earlier found a good many more, but he both looked well beyond European literature and took this theme as a subgroup of the larger category of blood feuds between relatives; Sohrab and Rustem: The Epic Theme of a Combat between Father and Son, A Study of its Genesis and Use in Literature and Popular Tradition (London, 1902); reissued as no. 14 in the Grimm Library Series by AMS Press (New York, 1972).

[3]Ye. E. Bertel's, Istoriia Persidsko-Tadzhikskoi Literatury (Moscow, 1960), p. 204. I would like to except from this general stricture the thoughtful study by Muṣṭafà Raḥīmī ("Dil az rustam āyad bih khashm," Alifbā, 3 (1352), 1-18), which sees the desire for power and precedence as the shaping forces of the story.

[4]All quoted lines are taken from volume two of the edition prepared under the general editorship of Ye. E. Bertel's Firdawsī, Shâh-Nâme, Kriticheskii Tekst (Moscow, 1962), and the numbers in parenthesis refer to the line numbers of that text. All translations from the text are my own.

[5]The two oldest manuscripts of the Shāhnāmah thus far to come to light are those of the British Museum, dated 675/1275-6, which is the basis for the only modern scholarly edition of the whole of the Shāhnāmah, the Soviet edition edited by Bertel's and others mentioned in the previous note, and the recently discovered Florence manuscript, dated 614/1217, which includes only the first half of the text (A. M. Piemontese, "Nuova luce su Firdausi: uno Šāhnāma datato 614 H./1217 a Firenze," Istituto Orientale di Napoli, Annali 40 (1980), 1-38 and

189-242).

[6]Rustam cannnot, of course, know that this will be the case, but he appears to sense that it is when he says with regard to the tomb he is having built for his son:

". . . Though I make his bier of gold,
"And surround it with black musk,
"When I have gone, it will not remain.
"Yet what else can I do?" (1051-1052)

[7]H. Ringgren notes in passing that the actions of fate often seem reasonable, but does not consider how such reasonableness may determine the events of a story; "Fatalism in Persian Epics," in Uppsala Universitets Arsskrift (1952), pp. 17 and 61. Hatto has drawn attention to the centrality of fate or accident in the story, but since he has no general familiarity with the Shāhnāmah, he misreads its function, seeing it as a lapse in narrative technique that destroys the sense of logic and probability he prizes so highly; ibid., pp. 99-100.

[8]John R. Hinnels, Persian Mythology (Hamlyn, London, New York: 1973), p. 100.

[9]Olga Davidson has shown the symbolic significance of Rustam's association with water in her thesis, "The Crown Bestower" (Princeton, 1982), pp. 140-155 (to be published shortly by Acta Iranica. In later manuscripts this passage is expanded to include a curious account of how Rustam had at first been so heavy and powerful that when he walked upon the ground he sank into the earth up to his knees. He asked God to reduce his power to more manageable proportions then, and in his prayer now he requests that his former strength be returned to him.

[10]Virtually this same passage is repeated in the next scene where Rustam has abandoned the Shah and Iran to their fate in his rage, and Gūdarz has pursued him to plead that he overlook the Shāh's insulting behavior. Rustam is eventually reconciled, but at first he responds that he has no need of monarchy or the monarch.

Tahamtan (Rustam) thus answered him,
"I have no need at all of Kay Kā'ūs.
"The saddle is my throne, this helm my crown.
"Chainmail's my cloak, and my heart is set on death.
"What have I to fear from Kā'ūs' anger?
"He is no more than a fistful of earth to me.
"My head's grown weary, my heart full.
"I fear no one save the Pure God." (426-429)

6

An Early Persian Ṣūfī
Shaykh Abū Saᶜīd of Mayhanah

C. Edmund Bosworth
The University of Manchester

By the fourth/tenth century, Ṣūfism was reaching the stage in which informal circles had grown up around individual mystics or saints, who became the spiritual directors, murshids, of the novices, murīds, shāgirds, who came to seek guidance from one who had already traversed the stages of the Ṣūfī path.[1] Many of these groups or circles had no fixed centre, and the murīds merely followed the wandering saint around; such holy men depended on alms, thank-offerings for working cures or miracles, and labour performed en route. But some of these wanderers settled in fixed spots, which became like monasteries or retreats for the adepts. In the Arab lands, the terms usually found for these are ribāṭ (originally a frontier post, literally "tethering place,"[2] where warriors for the faith congregated for holy war, jihād, against the infidels), and zāwiya "hermitage, retreat," literally "corner, angle." In the Persian world originally, but spreading westwards as far as Syria and Egypt and eastwards into India, the term khānaqāh was employed.[3] These expressions are all used in the general sense of "Ṣūfī monastery," though it must not be thought that these were necessarily like the monasteries of contemporary western Europe, the ones following St. Benedict's rule and the reformed way of Cluny, and, a little afterwards, those of St. Bernard's Cistercian rule. The Ṣūfīs in these monasteries were not necessarily contemplatives at all, but might include fierce and bellicose fighters for the faith, and there was no particular stress on celibacy. An oft-quoted, anti-ascetic tradition attributed to the Prophet stated that there was no "monkery" (rahbānīya) in Islam, with a variant, "no celibacy" (ṣarūra) in Islam, and most of the best-known Ṣūfī mystics are known to have been married.[4] As early as the end of the second/eighth

Logos Islamikos: Studia Islamica in honorem Georgii Michaelis Wickens, ed. Roger M. Savory and Dionisius A. Agius, Papers in Mediaeval Studies 6 (Toronto: Pontifical Institute of Mediaeval Studies, 1984), pp. 79-96.

century, there was a ribāṭ on the island of Ābādān at the head of the Persian Gulf, and the very name here, originally ᶜAbbādān, means "devotees, worshippers of God."[5] The late fourth/tenth century geographer al-Maqdisī describes an encounter with a Ṣūfī shaykh and his circle in the mountains of Jawlān (i.e., the Golan Heights region) of southern Syria: "I met Abū Isḥāq al-Ballūṭī (literally, "the acorn-eater") with forty men, all wearing wool (ṣūf), who had a place for worship where they congregated. I discovered that this man was a learned jurist from the school of Sufyān al-Thawrī and that their food consisted of acorns, a fruit the size of dates, bitter, which is split, sweetened and ground up and then mixed with a wild barley which grows in that locality."[6] In Persia, the spread of khānaqāhs for pious devotees at this time seems to be particularly associated with the Karrāmīya, the followers of the spiritual leader from Khurāsān Muḥammad b. Karrām al-Sijistānī (d. 225/869), although these sectaries were to prove themselves amongst the most strenuous opponents of Shaykh Abū Saᶜīd in Khurāsān; it is very probable that the two groups, those of the Shaykh's followers and the partisans of the Karrāmīya, were competitors for the adherence, hence the financial support, of the urban and rural masses there.[7]

Shaykh Abū Saᶜīd Faḍl Allāh was born in 357/967, the son of a pious druggist and grocer called Abū 'l-Khayr of Mayhanah, a little town of northern Khurāsān on the edge of the Qara Qum desert and now just within the Turkmenistān SSR.[8] He began his education in the traditional way for a Muslim scholar and member of the ᶜulamā' class by sitting at the feet of prominent teachers of theology, tradition and Islamic law in Khurāsān. Obviously of a restless, enquiring spirit, he spent several years as a wandering scholar before an all-transcending mystical experience came over him through his contacts with a Ṣūfī shaykh, one Luqmān of Sarakhs, who is described as one of the ᶜuqalā' al-majānīn "intelligent madmen," apparently something like the wise simpletons and fools for Christ of early Christianity, and who had a convent (khānaqāh) of Ṣūfīs at the nearby town of Sarakhs. Persuaded that the door of spiritual grace would be opened to him if he persisted in ascetic exercises, he retired for seven years to the private oratory of his house in Mayhanah and there sat repeating the name of Allāh. Repetition of the name of God, or one of His ninety-nine names, or some other pious phrase, had become a traditional component of the Ṣūfī practice of dhikr, following the Qur'ānic injunction "To God belong the most beautiful names -- pray to Him, using these names," often supplemented by breathing exercises and, later, by whirlings or bodily gyrations, as means to induce ecstasy, the forgetting of self and the approach to God. Abū Saᶜīd relates that whenever during these seven years he nodded off or became negligent, the terrifying spectral figure of a soldier with a flaming spear would loom up before him, enjoining him, "O Abū Saᶜīd, say Allāh." Abū Saᶜīd continues that "The fear of this ghostly apparition used to keep me burning and trembling for whole days and nights, so that I did not again fall asleep or become inattentive; and at last, every atom of me began to cry aloud 'Allāh, Allāh, Allāh'!"[9]

This account of mystical conversion is of a familiar pattern: the failure of and rejection of book-learning and intellectual means as a way of finding God, and instead, the seizing of the soul by a spiritual force, compelling concentration of the whole being on the struggle for contact with God, or even for certain mystics of advanced powers, absorption into God. Once thus converted, Abū Saᶜīd sought spiritual guidance from the then head of the Sarakhs Ṣūfīs, Shaykh Abū 'l-Faḍl Ḥasan, and by this means attached himself to a spiritual silsilah or geneological chain which went back through celebrated Ṣūfīs like al-Junayd of Baghdād, Maᶜrūf of Karkh and al-Ḥasan of Baṣra to the Imām ᶜAlī and the Prophet Muḥammad himself.[10] In this way, Ṣūfīs could claim that they fitted with perfect legitimacy into the framework of mainstream Islam, and were indeed the rightful heirs and transmitters of the esoteric, secret teaching of the Prophet; this teaching was veiled from the simple minds of the ignorant masses and also from the official religious classes, the ᶜulamā' and lawyers, with their sterile formalism, and was communicated only to those who had cultivated the gift of gnosis, maᶜrifah. Such a chain of affiliation was indeed a valuable means of anchoring Ṣūfism to the main body of Islam, for such a diffuse and intellectually far-ranging trend of thought as Ṣūfism could easily move towards a contempt for official creeds and practices and into antinomianism and heresy. Hence it was the constant concern of some of the foremost Ṣūfī scholars that connections with official Islam should be maintained and the basic orthodoxy of Sufism affirmed. In Abū Saᶜīd's own time, his fellow-shaykh of Khurāsān, Abū 'l-Qāsim al-Qushayrī of Nīshāpūr, composed his apologetic work, the Risālah Qushayrīyah, with the express aim of demonstrating how the traditions and practices of Ṣūfism still required observance of the Sharīcah or religious law;[11] and only a few decades later, another Khurāsānian, al-Ghazālī, after his conversion to a mystical view of the faith, described in his apologia, the Munqidh min al-ḍalāl, how some forms of Ṣūfism and orthodoxy were perfectly compatible and even, for those of great insight, complementary.

Mention of al-Ghazālī's Munqidh, which though brief, is a classic account of a man's search for God in the Islamic context, reminds one of the necessity of saying something about the sources for Shaykh Abū Sacīd's life and religious experiences. There is extant a short treatise in Persian on the Shaykh's life and sayings, the Ḥālāt va sukhanān-i Shaykh Abū Sacīd, put together about a century after the Shaykh's death. This was ulitised for a much more extensive and detailed biography, the Asrār al-tawḥīd fī maqāmāt Shaykh Abi Sacīd "The secrets of divine unity concerning the spiritual stages of Shaykh Abū Sacīd," composed by the Shaykh's great-great-grandson Muḥammad b. al-Munawwar of Mayhanah as a work of family piety. This must have been written in the second half of the sixth/twelfth century, probably in the years after 574/1178-9, when Khurāsān was being racked by warfare and disorders consequent upon the decay of the eastern empire of the Great Seljuks and when many of the Shaykh's descendants had been massacred at Mayhanah and there was no memorial left of him but his tomb (see below, n.48).[12]

Biography on the scale of this work -- the original printed edition by Zhukovski runs to 450 pages and the Tehran one of Dhabīḥ Allāh Ṣafà almost to 400 pages, and Meier's study based essentially on it also, extends to 590 pages -- is rare in Islamic literature. There abound biographical dictionaries, some on a gigantic scale, dealing with theologians, mystics, traditionists, poets, physicians, etc., in groups or in generations, but individual biographies are much rarer. Muslim authors tended to start from the view that a man's character and nature were divinely decreed and fixed almost from the womb. Thus no room was left for the interplay of character development and for the influence of the external events which might mould it, the very essences of successful biography as we understand it in the West. Abū Sacīd's biography is no exception from the normal model of the Islamic biographical approach. It is essentially a hagiography, with everything which happens after the Shaykh's own mystical conversion depicted in black and white. On one side there is the saint and his followers, and on the other, the ensemble of his enemies -- representatives of the religious and civil official classes, rival shaykhs, Zoroastrians, Christians and Jews. When there are disputations and clashes between the two sides, the Shaykh and his partisans invariably come off best; often the opposition collapses under the spell of the Shaykh's barakah or charisma; the one who came to scoff remains to pray and henceforth becomes a fervent admirer of the Shaykh. Within the framework of early Persian prose literature, the Asrār al-tawḥīd is virtually the first work with the life of an individual mystic as its subject-matter. It contains graphic descriptions of Abū Saᶜīd's miracles and of the ways of life of him and his devotees, with much valuable historical detail on the social and religious life of early fifth/eleventh century Khurāsān. Although five generations separated Muḥammad b. al-Munawwar from the Shaykh, the Islamic practice of oral transmission (riwāyah) of a person's sayings or aphorisms could well have ensured that the substance, if not the exact wording, of his sayings was preserved by his descendants. Whether the sayings describe authentic happenings cannot often be checked against other sources, but Meier in particular has constructed a highly detailed and generally convincing picture of the Shaykh's personality and his circle, even if an analysis of some of the Shaykh's doings and of the reactions of persons in his environment seems to fall more within the sphere of the psychologist, or even the pathologist, of religion.

The Khurāsān in which Shaykh Abū Saᶜīd spent his mature years was under the control of the Ghaznavids, the dynasty of Turkish military slave origin which from a base at Ghaznah in Afghanistan, had built up a mighty empire extending from western Persia to northern India. Abū Saᶜīd's father had been a great admirer of Sultan Maḥmūd of Ghaznah, an Islamic hero famed as a hammer of the pagan Hindus and of heterodox Muslims, and he had had inscribed the names of the Sultan and his followers on the walls of his house.[13] However, when Shaykh Abū Saᶜīd arrived at Nīshāpūr, the centre of government for Khurāsān, he speedily clashed with the official religious classes, the ᶜulamā' of both the Ḥanafī and Shāfiᶜī law schools, with the ᶜAlids or

Shīcites, and with the heads of the Karrāmīya sect there, who enjoyed particular favour from the Ghaznavid leaders. The root of the trouble seems to have been resentment at the Shaykh's material excesses and extravagant life style, a reprehensible outlook on life for many Muslims since the Qur'ān specifically denounces israf, excess and extravagance, as a waste of God's bounty and even as being something near to kufr or unbelief -- "The extravagant (al-musrifīn) are amongst the people of hell fire."[14] The religious leaders of Nīshāpūr drew up an indictment and sent it to the Sultan's court at Ghaznah:

> A certain man has come here from Mayhanah and pretends to be a Ṣūfī. He holds sessions during which he declaims and in the course of this recites from the pulpit poetry but does not quote from the Qur'ān commentaries or the traditions. He is continually holding sumptuous feasts, and music is played by his orders and he holds dancing sessions. He gets the young men to dance, and he eats sweetmeats made of almonds and walnuts, roasted fowls and all kinds of fruits and feeds them with these comestibles. He claims to be an ascetic, but this is not the displaying of either asceticism or Ṣūfism. The populace have instantly flocked to him and have gone astray. The greater part of the masses have fallen into dissension. Unless measures are taken to correct this, the discord will speedily become [universally] apparent.

Here we have expressed a common fear in mediaeval Islam -- as in mediaeval Christendom -- that religious innovation and heterodoxy are the concomitants of social unrest and political disorder. In this case, the decree comes back from Ghaznah that the culamā' are to review the accusations and then pronounce judgement and inflict punishment as the sharīcah provides. The Shaykh's enemies duly decree that the Shaykh and his adherents should all be hanged en masse in the market place of Nīshāpūr. The rest of the story is in broad outline predictable. Before this ultimate penalty can be exacted, the Shaykh's enemies are won over by a demonstration of his astonishing powers of telepathy or second sight (see further on these, below), and no further hindrance is ever placed in his way at Nīshāpūr.[15]

Towards the end of Abū Sacīd's life, Khurāsān was taken over by Turkish steppe nomads coming in from Central Asia under the leadership of the Seljuk family,[16] and various anecdotes connect the Shaykh to the conquerors. Their two leaders Ṭoghrïl and Chaghrï Beğ are said to have visited the Shaykh at Mayhanah in the course of their campaigns to take over the province (hence in the late 420's/1030's). They found him seated on his throne, they kissed his hand and stood before him, and in return he bowed his head. Then he told the two Seljuks that "We (i.e., the divine influence in the world, as embodied in the Shaykh) have given Khurāsān to Chaghrī Beg and Iraq (i.e., ʿIrāq ʿAjamī, western Persia) to Ṭoghrīl Beg" -- this being cited as an instance of his prophetic powers.[17] There is also mentioned in the Asrar al-tawḥīd an anecdote from the great Seljuk vizier Niẓām al-Mulk of Ṭūs, who was a great patron of the Ashʿarī theologians and Shāfiʿī lawyers, and who gave an impetus in the eastern Islamic lands to the building of madrasahs or colleges of higher learning, the Niẓāmīyahs, and who was also well known as a patron of Sufis. Nevertheless, the story continues that Niẓām al-Mulk came to visit Abū Saʿīd in his convent at Nīshāpūr and presented him with a fine girdle which he had made himself. In return, the Shaykh prophesied that one day Niẓām al-Mulk would have at his instant command 4,000 retainers wearing golden girdles like the one which he had just received. All that later came to pass, and the vizier was consequently wont to say, "Everything which I have achieved has come from the barakah of Shaykh Bū Saʿīd."[18]

These tales illustrate the fact that, as in the vitae of so many other Ṣūfī saints, the exercise of telepathic or prophetic powers played a great role in building up their image as a holy man possessed of supernatural powers. The term used here and commonly elsewhere is firāsah, a concept which formed the basis for a substantial corpus of literature in mediaeval Islam about divination, and, in particular, about divination by inductive reasoning based on sharp observation of physical features and attributes, e.g., through physiognomy or the study of facial features, through birthmarks, through the practice of palmistry, etc.[19] This technique of making what must often have been inspired guesses about psychological states, moral qualities and defects, etc., through observation of external physical features, derived its validity from certain Qur'ānic references to this technique, called there the scrutiny of a person's sīmā "marks,"[20] and this and firāsah became quasimystical terms since they were regarded as special gifts from God, this power of intuitive vision, one indicative of profound spiritual qualities.

Many of the miracles recorded about Shaykh Abū Saʿīd depend on this gift of firāsah, and he obviously acquired much of his reputation as a wonder worker through a studied exercise of this power, apparently on account of his ability to make large numbers of people -- and especially, the more credulous masses, since it is usually the more educated people, ᶜulamā' and civil officials, who are depicted as his enemies -- believe that he possessed these miraculous gifts.[21] Popular Islam could hardly conceive of a holy man who did not possess thaumaturgic powers, whether the publicly-performed evidentiary miracles of prophets, muᶜjizāt, or the marvels and charismatic acts of saints, karāmāt, which come from the abundance of God's special favour.[22] Many of the accounts of these invite scepticism, as do the similar miracles of early Christian saints, and undoubtedly, tricksters abounded. There exists a certain amount of literature in mediaeval Islam aimed at exposing tracks and swindles and at protecting the public from exploitation; one of the best-known works of this type, the Kashf al-asrār wa-hatk al-astār ("Revealing of secrets and drawing aside of veils") by the seventh/thirteenth-century Syrian author al-Jawbarī, is notably concerned with showing up the tricks of fraudulent Ṣūfīs, a class which the author describes as the most consummate rogues of all.[23] E.W. Lane, who lived amongst the Muslims of Cairo in the late 1820's and early 1830's and wrote penetratingly of the pre-modern, pre-industrial society of Egypt in almost its last phase, remarked concerning the Egyptian dervishes, "Various artifices are employed by persons of this class to obtain the reputation of superior sanctity, and of being endowed with the power of performing miracles. Many of them are regarded as welees (i.e., saints)." But he also relates how he witnessed the inexplicable clairvoyant powers of a Maghribī magician in Cairo, exercised through a boy and with the aid of a magic mirror of ink; one of his boys successfully described Lord Nelson to Lane, down to the amputated right arm. [24]

Shaykh Abū Saᶜīd and his followers comprised essentially the murīds or novices making up his household, but also on the fringes of this was a group of sympathizers, muḥibbs or "lovers," like the lay-brethren or tertiaries of the Christian religious orders in the West, who carried on their normal trades and vocations whilst binding themselves to a certain rule of spiritual life. The Shaykh caused to be written down for the guidance of his novices ten rules, something like a monastic rule in mediaeval Christendom, and these enjoined several of the eighteen ascetic practices which Abū Saᶜīd had bound himself to perform during his own novitiate (see below), together with such duties as keeping open house for the poor and destitute and spending leisure time in the study of theology or devotional literature or in good works for others.[25] The maintenance of this extensive household would have been a constant headache for the Shaykh had it not been for his supreme confidence in God's providence for his community. His biographer frequently recounts how the Shaykh's group were often on the verge of penury and starvation but would be saved by an opportune gift from a sympathizer. However, sometimes subsidies and presents would be peremptorily demanded and methods used which approached spiritual blackmail. When a military commander, who had once paid off the Shaykh's debts, refused to be mulcted a second time, he was torn to pieces that very night by the savage guard-dogs in his own camp which had unaccountably failed to recognise him. Episodes of this type, even if founded on a lucky coincidence, must have had a powerful effect on superstitious minds in building up an image of the Shaykh's remarkable gifts.[26]

Much of the contemporary opposition to the Shaykh clearly arose from the fact that in certain ways he approached close to that class of dervishes known as Malāmatīyah "those who [deliberately] incur blame," i.e., that type of antinomians who did not consider themselves as bound by the law. There is a distinct tendency in certain of the higher religions for an inner group of initiates into the faith to regard themselves as marked off from the grosser masses by possession of superior gnosis vouchsafed to them by God or attained through ascetic and other practices. Such a group often comes to consider itself as not bound by the laws and precepts of formal religion, which it views as aids to spirituality only for those incapable of rising higher by their own spiritual efforts. Raised to a higher degree, such attitudes may lead to a contempt for organized religion and a deliberate flouting of the religious law in order to demonstrate the adept's freedom from such unnecessary shackles, as was done by the Qalandarī dervishes in later mediaeval Islam.[27] Hence extravagant and even blasphemous behaviour ensues, with the aim as much as anything else of shocking; but on the level of belief, such antinomianism may reach a position approaching interconfessionalism in which the pure essence of religion finally attained is regarded as an element common to all faiths. Naturally, the defenders of orthodoxy have in the past reacted strongly against such claims of freedom from the law and have often imputed excesses and license to the esoteric groups. We can discern such a reaction in mediaeval Western Christendom against the Albigenses in thirteenth century France and against the Templars in the early years of the following century; whilst in Islam, the extremist Shīᶜī Ismāᶜīlī movement, notorious in Syria and Persia as the Assassins, elicited a reaction of fear from the orthodox, Sunnī and Shīᶜī alike, at times approaching the psychotic, and the excesses of the Qalandarīyah excited vigorous condemnation in such a standard Ṣūfī manual as Shihāb al-Dīn al-Suhrawardī's ᶜ<u>Awārif al-maᶜārif</u>.[28]

However, Shaykh Abū Saᶜīd, in the tradition of the less blatant Malāmatīyah rather than that of the deliberately provocative Qalandarīyah, always observed rigorously a considerable proportion of the requirements of the <u>sharīᶜah</u>. In his youth, as a Ṣūfī novice, he had neglected nothing here. As he relates,

> At the beginning of my novitiate, I bound myself to do eighteen things, so that by means of them I might free myself from the burden of 18,000 worlds. I fasted continually; I abstained from unlawful food; I practiced <u>dhikr</u> uninterruptedly; I kept vigils at night; I never reclined on the ground; I only slept in a sitting posture; I sat facing the direction of the Kaᶜba; I never leaned against anything; I never looked at a beardless youth with a lascivious glance, nor at women whom it would have been unlawful for me to see unveiled; . . .;[29] I did not beg; I was content and resigned to God's will; I always sat in the mosque and did not go into the market because the Messenger of God has said that the market is the worst of places and the mosque the best. In all my acts I was a follower of the Messenger of God. Every twenty-four hours I completed a recitation of the Qur'ān. In my seeing I was blind, in my hearing deaf, in my speaking dumb. For a whole year I conversed with no-one.[30]

He continued these observances later in life, thereby protecting himself against charges that he was not fulfilling the law, with the exception of the Pilgrimage to Mecca; this he refused to perform. Many Ṣūfīs came to terms with rites which they regarded as basically pagan in origin by viewing them allegorically and as having a mystical significance: the Pilgrimage was valuable only if it were an act of mortification, <u>mujāhadah</u>, with the aim of achieving contemplation of

God, mushāhadah, says the Ṣūfī biographer and exponent of mysticism of a decade after Abū Sa^c^īd's time, (Hujwiri).[31] Shaykh Abū Sa^c^īd would not even go as far as this concession to orthodox practice. When asked why he had never gone on the Pilgrimage, he replied,

> "As for what you say about the spiritual masters (pīrān) having accomplished the Pilgrimage to the Ḥijāz, whereas you have never performed it, well, it is nothing much that you should tread beneath your feet a thousand parasangs of ground to visit a house of stone. The genuine man [of God] is the one who sits where he is [and] the Khānah-i Ma^c^mūr (i.e., the heavenly archetype of the Ka^c^ba) comes several times in a day and a night to visit him and perform the circumambulation above his head. Look and see!" All those who were present looked and indeed saw it.[32]

The true pilgrimage for the mystic is thus an internal one, once he has reached the highest levels of the Ṣūfī path; for those of his followers who had not yet attained these heights, the Shaykh used to enjoin instead a visit to the tomb of his own former master, Abū 'l-Fadl, in the nearby town of Sarakhs as fulfilling the desideratum of pilgrimage. This is really illustrative of a tendency which subsequently grew in popular Islam to regard the veneration of a local saint or walī, and the seeking of his intercession at his tomb, as more efficacious spiritually and more satisfying personally than cultivation of the remoter, less real Prophet Muḥammad in Mecca and Medina.

However, although the Shaykh could be regarded as orthodox in regard to the prescriptions of the sharī^c^ah, except for his low opinion of the value of physical performance of the Pilgrimage to Mecca, his general life style grated excessively on many of the more staid and orthodox believers. Islam, and especially mystical Islam, extolled the virtues of tawakkul or tuklān, day-to-day dependence on God for all one's needs, in the confidence that the Lord will provide; the truly trusting Muslim thus becomes the ibn al-waqt "son of the moment," living only in the immediate present and taking no thought for the morrow.[33] But there is obviously a difference between simple faith like this and a feckless extravagance, the Qur'ānic sin of isrāf, an accusation launched against Shaykh Abū Sa^c^īd, apparently with justice. For when he was in funds, the Shaykh lived not like a simple ascetic but like a prince of the church in luxury and profligacy. This pomp was, as noted above, specifically denounced by the religious leaders of Nīshāpūr in their remonstrance to the Ghaznavid court. The Shaykh always rode forth on a fine horse, with his faithful assistant and major-domo Ḥasan-i Mu'addib holding his stirrup, whereas the modest ass was the traditional mount for holy men in the Near East. Another Ṣūfī Shaykh, ᶜAbd Allāh Bākū, visiting Abū Saᶜīd found him lolling back on four cushions and propped up "just like a sultan."[34] His biographer mentions several times the splendid open-air feasts which he gave on occasion to all his sympathizers. These affairs were invariably arranged on a munificent scale, with rich dishes of meat and almond confectionery and with fragrant aloes wood and candles burnt, and the food spread out on freshly laundered cloths. Thus there is described one occasion when the Shaykh gave an open invitation to the people of Nīshāpūr and over 2,000 people, both high and low, came to the village of Būshangān, situated outside Nīshāpūr and noted as a picnic spot.[35] A thousand candles were burnt, even though it was daytime. This reckless expenditure excited the criticism of one of the Shaykh's opponents, but he was won over by the unanswerable argument that laying out money for God is never profligacy; he became one of the Shaykh's novices and placed all his money at Abū Saᶜīd's disposal, the usual requirement of someone becoming a _murīd_.[36]

Shaykh Abū Saᶜīd's joy for living, indeed, showed itself in many aspects of his life, and Meier has spoken of "Abū Saᶜīds _dolce stil nuovo_," pointing out that the norm in the literature of Ṣūfism and the Ṣūfī _vitae_ is sadness and resignation as the inevitable background to this present life; only in the hereafter will joy characterize the lives of the saved. Abū Saᶜīd, on the contrary, more than once insisted to his disciples that joyfulness and a soaring of the spirit, _shādhī_, _istirāḥah_, were not merely desirable put positive duties for the believer who is genuinely filled with a feeling of thankfulness to God for his good fortune in life.[37] Not surprisingly, this search for salvation through joy led the Shaykh to place a strong emphasis on the recitation of poetry, the playing of music and dancing as integral parts of his sessions of _dhikr_; these he regarded not only as outward expressions of joyfulness but also as means of heightening mystical awareness and even as a mode of divine worship, anticipating the later emphasis on such arts by the Mawlawīyah or "dancing dervishes." He was thus in the line of those Muslim thinkers and mystics who saw in music and dancing an earthly reflection of the harmony and the procession of the heavenly spheres and of the aesthetic entertainments which the blessed will enjoy in paradise.[38]

Mortification of the flesh might require sexual abstinence, and the eighth/fourteenth century Moroccan traveller Ibn Baṭṭūtah mentions meeting dervishes of the Ḥaydarīyah order in Khurāsān and India who loaded their hands, necks and ears with iron chains and who placed iron rings round their penises in order to prevent copulation and to signify victory over the lusts of the flesh.[39] But, as noted at the outset, celibacy and continence were by no means mandatory for the Ṣūfī, and those of antinomian tendencies who delighted in flouting the law not infrequently made a parade of sexual excess, the debauching of women sympathizers and of attractive boys. The accusations of vice, natural and unnatural, which are a standard feature in the attacks of the orthodox on esoteric groups (see above) must often have been exaggerated, but in the case of Ṣūfism clearly had an element of truth. It is well known that the great corpus of Ṣūfī mystical poetry in all the great Islamic languages, in which the beloved is addressed in an erotico-religious vein, can be understood on the two levels of divine love or earthly love, and that in the latter case the absence of gender differentiation for pronouns and verbs in Persian and Turkish, and the often deliberately ambiguous differentiation in Arabic poetic style, means that such poetry can appear to be addressed either to women or to boys. Homosexuality had its place amongst the Ṣūfīs of Khurāsān -- the pro-Arab opponents of the Shuᶜūbīyah such as al-Jāḥiẓ had often accused the Khurāsānians of bringing the vice into the Arab lands at the time of the ᶜAbbāsid revolution[40]-- and in one of the tales in Abū Saᶜīd's biography we read that the leader of the moderate group of Ṣūfīs in Nīshāpūr, Abū 'l-Qāsim al-Qushayrī, deprived one of the dervishes of his cloak, upbraided and ill-treated him, and drove him out of the town because of his unnatural passion for the Imām al-Qushayrī's brother-in-law Ismāᶜīlak Daqqāq. Shaykh Abū Saᶜīd, however, was more indulgent to human frailty here; he deliberately ignored the four years' long passion of one of his dervishes for his own son Bū Ṭāhir until the dervish in question was shamed into abandoning this and going off on the Pilgrimage to Mecca.[41]

There is interesting information in the Asrār al-tawḥīd about the adherents of other faiths in Nīshāpūr. The holy man who by his preaching, his example or his miracles converts non-Muslim People of the Book to Islam in a stereotype of Muslim hagiography, so that it is not surprising to find Shaykh Abū Saᶜīd depicted thus. In the early fifth/eleventh century, Persia was by no means as monolithically Muslim as it later became. The ancient faith of Zoroastrianism persisted in the more mountainous and inaccessible parts of the land, such as Fārs, Azerbaijan, the Caspian region and Khurāsān, though by now it was entering its last phase of survival as a living faith. The towns of Khurāsān and Central Asia, such as Nīshāpūr, Herat, Merv and Bukhārā, had within them anciently-established communities of Jews which sent contributions to the Exilarch of Head of the Dispersion in Iraq, and it was for instance scholars from these places who provided the polymath al-Bīrūnī with information about Jewish chronology and history.[42] Sasanid Persia had been the refuge for Nestorian Christians escaping from persecution by the Byzantines, and from its base in eastern Iran the church had carried on important mission work amongst the peoples of Central Asia and Siberia as far as Mongolia and northern China. The remnants of a Nestorian hierarchy in Eastern Persia and Inner Asia persisted into the Il-Khānid and Tīmūrid periods, and it was only the extensive conversions to Islam of the Turks of Central Asia and South Russia which extinguished Christianity there.[43]

The conversion of the Shaykh's Zoroastrian physician took place through the holy man's barakah, as did that of a rich Jew.[44] But of special interest are the accounts in his biography of his visits to the churches of the Christians in Nīshāpūr. He was there one Sunday and noted that the Christians had constructed a raised arcade in front of the church in which were images of Jesus and the Virgin Mary, before which they were prostrating themselves. The Shaykh recited the Qur'anic denunciation of the Trinity, placed in the mouth of God addressing Jesus, "Did you say to the people, 'Take me and my mother as gods, apart from [the One] God'?"[45] At this, the images immediately fell to the ground with their faces turned towards the Kaᶜbah. At this miracle, forty of the congregation of Christians embraced Islam, casting off the characteristic girdle, zunnār, of the dhimmis and donning the patched cloak, khirqah-'i muraqqaᶜah, of the dervishes.[46]

On another occasion, Abū Sa^c^īd and his band of adherents entered a church in Nīshāpūr and entertained the congregation by reciting the Qur'ān melodiously before departing. Someone remarked that, if the Shaykh had shown the slightest sign of encouragement, all the Christians there would have become Muslim; Abū Sa^c^īd, however, replied that on this particular occasion the time was not opportune for that.[47]

Abū Sa^c^īd returned from Nīshāpūr to a rural life in Mayhanah, and continued to live in his accustomed way until the end, with his community placing particular stress on social and charitable work amongst the people of the town. When in 440/1049 he felt near to death, being then 83, he was oppressed by the thought of the weight of debt remaining on the khānaqāh, amounting to 3,000 dinars. Hence he sent one of his disciples, Bū Sa^c^d Dūst-i Dādā, to the court at Ghazna to seek help from the sultan there (there seems to be an anachronism here; northern Khurāsān had been lost to Ghaznavid control nine years before,[48] and the obvious goal for such a mission would have been one of the courts of the Seljuk leaders, whose greatness the Shaykh had prophesied [see above] either Chaghrī Beğ's at Merv or Toghrïl's at Rayy). Naturally, the sultan willingly paid the debt, adding a further 1,000 dinars for a funeral banquet, ^c^urs, to be held at the Shaykh's tomb (or possibly, according to another reading, ^c^arsh, for a canopy to be erected over the tomb) and yet another similar sum for the envoy's travelling expenses.[49]

Although the Asrār al-tawḥīd goes on to relate that Bū Sa^c^d Dūst-i Dādā eventually travelled after the Shaykh's death to Baghdad and founded there a Ṣūfī convent which continued to benefit from the Shaykh's charisma and to be a centre of Ṣūfī spirituality in the capital of the caliphate,[50] no definite dervish order or ṭarīqah grew out of the Shaykh's work. Outside the region of Mayhanah, and outside Baghdad, further khānaqāhs founded by his disciples are mentioned as amounting only to two in northern Khurāsān and one in Shīrwān, i.e., in eastern Caucasia.[51] Abū Sa^c^īd's eldest son Bū Ṭāhir continued his father's homilectic and charitable activities in Khurāsān, but did not apparently have the organizing ability or spiritual intensity to found an order, as did Mawlānā Jalāl al-Dīn Rūmī's son, Sulṭān Walad, after his father's death. The political and military catastrophes which befell Khurāsān in the two centuries after Abū Sa^c^īd's death, such as the ravages of the Ghuzz, the warfare of the Ghūrids and Khwārazm-Shāhs, and above all the incursions of the Mongols, cannot have been favourable to the growth of a cult of sainthood and of a Ṣūfī order based on the Shaykh's teachings. Even so, Abū Saᶜīd's fame and example did to a perceptible extent continue throughout the mediaeval Persian world, and thanks to his recorded sayings and his biography, his is a more substantial -- if at times not always credible -- figure to us today than many other Ṣūfī personalities.

[1] The process is well described by J.S. Trimingham, The Sufi Orders in Islam (Oxford, 1971), ch. i: "The Formation of Schools of Mysticism," pp. 1-30.

[2] Echoing Qur'ān, 8:62, "Prepare against them [sc. God's enemies] whatever forces and places for tethering horses (ribāṭ al-khayl) you are able."

[3] See J. Chabbi, "Khānkāh," in EI², 4: 1025-1026.

[4] For this tradition, see A.J. Wensinck, A Handbook of Early Muhammadan Tradition (Leiden, 1927), p. 143, and the discussion in L. Massignon, Essai sur les origines du lexique technique de la mystique musulmane, 2nd ed. (Paris, 1954), pp. 145-153 and 233.

[5] See ibid., pp. 157 and 234-235.

[6] Aḥsan al-taqāsīm, ed. M.J. de Geoje, in Bibliotheca Geographorum Arabicorum (Leiden, 1906), p. 188; French trans. by A. Miquel, Aḥsan at-taqāsīm fī maᶜrifat al-aqālīm (La meilleure répartition pour la connaissance des provinces) (Damascus, 1963), p. 238 #235.

[7] On the sect in general, see C.E. Bosworth, "Karrāmiyya," in EI², 4: 667-669, and, for the sect in Khurāsān at the time of Shaykh Abū Saᶜīd, idem, The Ghaznavids, Their Empire in Afghanistan and Eastern Iran 994-1040 (Edinburgh, 1963), pp. 165-166, 185-189 and 192.

[8] See C.E. Bosworth, art. s.v., in EI² (forthcoming); F. Meier, Abū Saᶜīd-i Abū 'l-Ḫayr (357-440/967-1049), Wirklichkeit und Legende (Tehran/Liège, 1976), pp. 39-40; for editions of the works about Abū Saᶜīd and studies on him, see below, n. 12.

[9] Muḥammad ibn al-Manawwar, Asrār al-tawḥīd fī maqāmāt Shaykh Abī Saᶜīd, ed. Dhabīḥ Allāh Safā (Tehran 1332 s./1954), pp. 15 ff.; French trans. by Moḥammad Achena, Les étapes mystiques du shaykh Abu Sa'id, mystères de la connaissance de l'Unique (Paris, 1974), pp. 31 ff.; R.A. Nicholson, Studies in Islamic Mysticism (Cambridge, 1921), pp. 3-15; Meier, pp. 39 ff.

[10] Asrār al-tawḥīd, p. 27, trans. pp. 48-49; Nicholson, pp. 10-11.

[11] Shaykh Abū Saᶜīd's relationship to al-Qushayrī is discussed by Nicholson, pp. 33-36, and Meier, pp. 56-57.

[12] The Ḥālāt were first published in critical edition by V.A. Zhukovski as Zhizn'i ryechi startsa Abu-Sa'ida Meykheneyskago (St. Petersburg, 1899), who also produced in the same place and year the

editio princeps of the Asrār al-tawḥīd, Tainī edineniya s Bogom v podvigakh startsa Abu-Sa'ida, cf. C.A. Storey, Persian Literature, a Bio-Bibliographical Survey (London, 1927), 1: 928-930. More recently, Ahmad Bahmanyār produced a text (Tehran 1313/1934-1935) based on Zhukovski's edition and with a Persian translation of the Russian editor's introduction; and then Dhabīḥ Allāh Ṣafā issued one (Tehran 1332/1954), taking into account an Istanbul manuscript, Selim Ağa 238/488, copied in 700/1300-1301 and thus older than the two manuscripts used for the previous texts. Further manuscripts are now known, and Meier notes that "complete, improved editions of the two principal works are necessary" (pp. 19-21). A French translation, not quite complete, of the Asrār al-tawḥīd has been made by Mohammad Achena: Mohammad Ebn E. Monawwar (sic), Les étapes mystiques du shaykh Abu Sa'id (see n. 9 above).

Of studies of the Shaykh, the pioneer one was that of Nicholson (n. 9 above), to which should be added H. Ritter's article in EI, s.v.; J. Rypka et al., History of Iranian Literature (Dordrecht, 1968), pp. 220 and 451 and the references given in p. 458 n. 98; and above all, Meier's very detailed book which amongst many other things sets Shaykh Abū Saᶜīd in the context of the historical development of eastern Islamic Ṣūfism and examines his own particular form of spirituality. The language and prose style of the Asrār al-tawḥīd were reviewed by Malik al-Shuᶜarā' Bahār in his Sabk-shināsī, 2nd ed. (Tehran 1337 s./1958-1959), 1: 197-205; cf. also G. Lazard, La langue des plus anciens monuments de la prose persane (Paris, 1963), p. 120.

13 Asrār al-tawḥīd, pp. 16-17, tr. 32-33. For the general political background of Khurāsān under the Ghaznavids, see Bosworth, The Ghaznavids, pp. 145-202.

14 Qur'ān, 40:46.

15 Asrār al-tawḥīd, pp. 77-78, tr. 85-90; Nicholson, pp. 28-33.

16 See Bosworth, The Ghaznavids, pp. 206-268, and idem in The Cambridge History of Islam, 5: The Saljuq and Mongol Periods (Cambridge, 1968), pp. 15-23.

17 Asrār al-tawḥīd, pp. 170-172, tr. pp. 164-166; Meier, pp. 326-329.

18 Asrār al-tawḥīd, pp. 98-99, tr. pp. 107-108; cf. also pp. 372-373, tr. pp. 359-360, where the Shaykh's son, Khwājah Bū Ṭāhir, meets Naẓam al-Mulk at Iṣfahān; Meier, pp. 331-333.

19 See T. Fahd, "Firāsa," EI^2, 2: 916-917.

20 In particular, Qur'ān, 47:32, "If We Willed, We should let you see them [sc. the Hypocrites of Medina] and you would know them by their marks (sīmāhum)."

21 Cf. Nicholson, pp. 65 ff.

22 See D.B. Macdonald, The Religious Attitude and Life in Islam (Chicago, 1909), pp. 49-52.

23 See on this work and on the author's exposé of mountebanks and swindlers, C.E. Bosworth, The Mediaeval Islamic Underworld, the Banū Sāsān in Arabic, 1: The Banū Sāsān in Arabic Life and Lore (Leiden, 1976), pp. 106-118. The Kashf al-asrār has now been translated into French by Rene Khawam.

24 An Account of the Manners and Customs of the Modern Egyptians (London, 1836 and later editions), chs. x, "Superstitions," and xii, "Magic, Astrology and Alchemy."

25 Asrār al-tawḥīd, pp. 330-332, tr. pp. 324-325; Nicholson, p.46; Meier, pp. 310-311.

[26] Asrār al-tawḥīd, pp. 197-198, tr. pp. 186-187; Nicholson, pp. 38-42.

[27] Trimingham, appendix B: "Ṣūfīs, Malāmatīṣ, and Qalandarīs," pp. 264-269; and Tahsin Yazıcı, "Ḳalandariyya," EI², 4: 473-474.

[28] Trimingham, p. 267.

[29] Corrupt phrase in text.

[30] Asrār al-tawḥīd, p. 37, tr. p. 50; Nicholson, pp. 15-17; Meier, pp. 69-70.

[31] Kashf al-maḥjúb, the Oldest Persian Treatise on Ṣúfism, trans. R.A. Nicholson (Leiden/London, 1911), pp. 326-329.

[32] Asrār al-tawḥīd, p. 278, tr. pp. 268-269; Nicholson, Studies in Islamic Mysticism, pp. 61-62.

[33] The concept of tawakkul was particularly studied by I. Goldziher, "Materialen zur Entwicklungsgeschichte des Ṣûfismus," Wiener Zeitschrift für die Kunde des Morgenlandes, 13 (1899), 41-50; reprt. in idem, Gesammelte Schriften (Hildesheim, 1967-1973), 4: 179-188.

[34] Asrār al-tawḥīd, p. 94, tr. p. 103; Nicholson, p. 36.

[35] For Būshangān or Bushtaqān as a tamāshāgāh, see Bosworth, The Ghaznavids, p. 153.

[36] Asrār al-tawḥīd, pp. 105-107, tr. pp. 114-116: cf. pp. 89-90, tr. pp. 98-99, etc.; Nicholson, pp. 40-41, cf. pp. 37, 71.

[37] Meier, pp. 134 ff.

[38] Ibid., pp. 210-260.

[39] Riḥlah, ed. C. Defrémery and B.R. Sanguinetti (Paris, 1853-1859), 3: 79-80; trans. H.A.R. Gibb, The Travels of Ibn Baṭṭūṭa (Cambridge, 1958-1971), 3: 583; cf. Trimingham, p. 39 and Massignon, pp. 147 and 233, on this infibulation with a chain, silsila, and on perforation of the penis with a ring, tathqīb al-iḥlīl, citing also Christian ascetic parallels.

[40] Cf. A. Mez, The Renaissance of Islam (Patna, 1937), p. 358.

[41] Asrār al-tawḥīd, pp. 90-92, tr. 99-101; Nicholson, pp. 35-36.

[42] See W. Fischel, "The Jews of Central Asia (Khorasan) in Mediaeval Hebrew and Islamic Literature," in Historia Judaica (New York, 1945), 7: 29-50.

[43] See J. Richard, "Le Christianisme dans l'Asie Centrale," Journal of Asian History, 16 (1982), pp. 105-113.

[44] Asrār al-tawḥid, pp. 123 and 141, tr. pp. 131 and 146-147.

[45] Qur'an, 5:116.

[46] Asrār al-tawḥīd, pp. 102-103, tr. pp. 109-112.

[47] Ibid, p. 226, tr. p. 215.

[48] Bosworth, in The Cambridge History of Iran, 5: 20-23.

[49] Asrār al-tawḥīd, pp. 361-362 and 368, tr. pp. 351-352 and 361-362; cf. Nicholson, pp. 44-45. The tomb, buqᶜah, continued to be a goal of pilgrimage until the town of Mayhanah was destroyed by the Ghuzz in the chaos following the Seljuq Sulṭān Sanjar's death (see Asrār al-tawḥīd, p. 360, tr. p. 349) although a tomb and a shrine, turbatī wa mashhadī, of Abū Saᶜīd were, it seems, alone spared by the Turkmens (see ibid., p. 7, tr. p. 23). The question of historicity involved in the story of Dūst-i Dādā and his activities, and in particular of his mission to Baghdad (see below), are discussed in detail by Meier, pp. 369-383.

[50] Asrār al-tawḥīd, pp. 362-367, tr. pp. 352-358.

[51] Meier, pp. 426-427.

7

Colour and Number in the *Haft Paykar*

Georg Krotkoff
The Johns Hopkins University

> That which is new and also old is speech,
> and on this speech some speech is to be used.
> Niẓāmī

Many students of Persian letters have lavished their praise on the poetic works of Niẓāmī Ganjavī[1] in general, and on his romance Haft Paykar [henceforth HP] in particular. The latter has been called "one of the most sophisticated works of world literature,"[2] and there is little need to expand on this point any further, since even a single reading of the HP convinces the sensitive reader that he is dealing not only with a superb example of artfully formed language, but also with a highly complex and multilayered system of meanings and cosmic relationships.

In spite of the popularity of Niẓāmī's Khamsah or quintet,[3] tantalizingly little is known about the person himself. We do not know how he made a living, or what made him tick. Since biographical works give only scanty, and often contradictory information, scholars have tried to glean personal data from his literary works. In them he mentions a much beloved, but early lost wife, as well as a son Muhammad, whom he addresses as seven years old in Khusraw and Shīrīn, and as fourteen years old in Laylà and Majnūn. On the latter occasion he also gives his own age as seven times seven. Scholars have seized upon such items for the sake of dating his works and establishing a chronology of his life.[4] It must be pointed out, however, that all these references to age happen to be multiples of seven, which is a number loaded with symbolic meaning. Ages seven, fourteen and twenty-one have traditionally been considered important stages in the life of man, and they have retained their significance in educational and legal contexts until this very day. In view of this, one would do

---

Logos Islamikos: Studia Islamica in honorem Georgii Michaelis Wickens, ed. Roger M. Savory and Dionisius A. Agius, Papers in Mediaeval Studies 6 (Toronto: Pontifical Institute of Mediaeval Studies, 1984), pp. 97-118.

well to mistrust the value of these data for chronological purposes.

At the end of the Sharafnāmah some manuscripts have a curious postscript, which, in view of its style and placement, is an obvious forgery.[5] In it, Niẓāmī is made to address his seventeen-year-old son, who has "now acquired the seventeen properties (khiṣal)." Although useless for purposes of dating, this postscript is valuable in so far as it shows that the writer of these lines was aware of an esoteric meaning in Niẓāmī's romances and must have considered them valid for purposes of initiation of some sort.[6] The only biographical information about Niẓāmī himself which would point in the direction of a possible membership in a secret, or at least hierarchical, association is Dawlatshāh's assertion that he had been an adept (murīd) of Akhī Faraj (or Farrukh) Zanjānī.[7]

Of all the works of Niẓāmī, the HP has the most obvious numerical structure, with the cosmic number seven in its title and visibly displayed in its centrepiece, the seven stories told by seven princesses in seven coloured pavilions on seven consecutive days of the week. Previous studies of the HP have duly noted the open cosmological references, and some have made general statements about possible deeper, especially mystical, levels of meaning. Nobody, however, has shown such deeper meanings in detail. Thus, to C.E. Wilson the HP "depicts, so far as the esoteric sense is concerned, the progress of the Ṣūfī through the seven Stages,"[8] but he does not show how the content of the seven stories relates to these stages. According to him "a sub-current of the mystic doctrine runs through"[9] all of Niẓāmī's poems.

In his review of Wilson's translation and commentary, H. Ritter denied any justification for the interpretation of the HP as a Ṣūfī path, saying that a slight mystic colouring was quite normal for a Persian poet of that time. He thought, on the contrary, that the poem merely demonstrates an astrological method of counteracting the evil eye, and he compared it to Marsilio Ficino's Vita coelitus comparanda, with the sole difference that the HP showed also the futility of such a method, and that the latter could, and should, be overcome by true religion. Only in one respect did Ritter concede an underlying "mystical, or rather gnostic," intent, namely in the description of the ascent to heaven (miʿrāj) of the prophet Muhammad. In the miʿrāj he saw an echo of the "heavenly journey" of the soul, as it is known from the Hermetic book Poimandres.[10]

Ye. E. Bertels, author of the fullest account of Niẓāmī's life and works, who had not only written two monographs and several articles on him, but also had supervised the critical edition of several of his poems and their translation into Russian,[11] did not discuss any mystical or esoteric levels of meaning, but concentrated solely on the sociopolitical views of Niẓāmī, as they can be gleaned from the overt text of the poems. He also praised the mastery of composition, the harmony and the mutual echoing of various parts of the HP,[12] but at the same time he stressed the absence of typical Ṣūfī terminology and "pathological self-observation."[13]

Among Iranian contributions to the study of Niẓāmī's work, Dastgardī's annotated edition stands out. It is very useful for the understanding of detail, of linguistic difficulties and allusions, but it is of no help in uncovering hidden levels of meaning. An ambitious Analysis of the Haft Paykar of Niẓāmī by Muḥammad Muᶜīn is disappointing, because it only attempts to trace separate elements of the HP, especially numbered items, to their origins in ancient Near Eastern religions, mythologies, and cosmologies, without contributing to an understanding of the work itself. The origin of a motif, as interesting as it may be, does not necessarily explain its function within a new literary work, just as the knowledge of the quarry from which the stones for a particular building were cut, does not tell about the purpose and function of the building itself.

More recently, scholars have begun to see structural elements hidden under the surface fabric of the stories, comparable to the warp and weft of rugs. The pictorial content of the rug, just like the narrative part of the poems, is in its pile, but the pile is held together by the invisible warp and weft. In the Nachwort to his partial translation of the HP, R. Gelpke speaks of this work as "an artistic image of the all-embracing cosmic order,"[14] and he recognizes a structural feature shared by the first and the last stories, which thus seem to be framing the five stories between them. The shared feature is simply that these two stories are not told directly by the princess, but in a third-hand manner, on the authority of a set of other persons.[15] Gelpke also published an analysis of the astrological aspects of the HP. Finally, P.J. Chelkowski in his commentary on a condensed translation of the HP discussed briefly some cosmological implications of the colours and numbers involved.[16]

The goal of the present essay will be to uncover more of the warp and weft of the HP, and to reconstruct the blueprint which, if this writer's intuition is right, must have been in Niẓāmī's mind when he set out to compose the poem.[17] First it will be good to give the reader a quick survey of the main features of the narrative.

The legendary image of the Sasanid king Bahrām Gūr (420-38 A.D.) as it is presented in the Shāhnāmah is that of an insatiable 'ladies' man' and passionate hunter. In making Bahram the hero of the HP, Niẓāmī clearly used the Shāhnāmah as a source, but he changed and rearranged biographical elements at will, or substituted completely alien ones for them. The most important feature of the HP, the building of the seven coloured pavilions and the visits with the seven princesses is not part of the preexisting legend, but Niẓāmī's own invention. It also provides a tangible link with Hermetic literature.[18]

After a series of invocations, dedications, and an apology for writing the romance,[19] the actual story begins with the birth of Bahrām, whose cruel and unpopular father Yazdigird soon sends him, upon the advice of his court astrologers, to Arabia to be educated there by his vassal, king Nu^{c}mān. Bahrām grows up and acquires all the necessary knowledge and the skills of a royal prince. Nu^{c}mān builds him a luxurious castle in the desert,[20] in which Bahrām lives in expectation of his father's demise, whiling away his time by hunting. Among the exploits of this period are the killing of an onager and a lion with a single arrow, and the pursuit of another onager to the mouth of a cave in which a dragon guards a treasure. Bahrām kills the dragon and takes the treasure.[21]

One day the prince discovers a locked door in the castle. Curious to know what is behind it, he obtains the key from the chamberlain and enters a room which is decorated with the portraits of seven beautiful princesses from seven different parts of the world. In their midst he discovers a picture of himself. All this had been secretly painted by the architect, and as we shall see, represents the prediction, or a vision of the future. Bahrām is delighted and often spends his time in this room. Eventually his father dies, but the nobles are afraid of Yazdigird's offspring and quickly elevate another man to the throne. Bahrām gathers an Arab army and moves into Iran.

The nobles meet him and negotiate an agreement according to which they will welcome him as king if he can take the crown from between two lions. On the appointed day, Bahrām kills the two lions, takes the crown and becomes ruler of Iran.

Another famous adventure, a popular theme for Persian miniaturists and rug weavers, is inserted at this point. Bahrām's favourite slave girl and companion on the hunt, Fiṭnah, challenges him to show his markmanship by turning a female gazelle into a male, a male into a female, and to pierce a gazelle's hoof and ear with one arrow. Undisturbed by this seemingly impossible task, Bahrām puts two arrows into his bow and shoots them into a gazelle's head providing her with horns like a male. Then he takes an arrow with two points, and with one shot razes the horns from the head of a buck. Finally, he takes a crossbow and shoots a pellet of clay at the ear of another gazelle. In pain, the gazelle puts her hoof to her ear, at which moment Bahrām pierces both with an arrow.[22] The backdrop for this adventure is provided by the king's wise and humane rule and the general prosperity, albeit interrupted by famine, of the country. Bahram expands his domain, gains the respect of his peers, and remembering the mural with the seven portraits, he obtains and marries seven princesses from the seven climes of the earth.[23]

During a banquet which celebrates Bahrām's success in every sphere of life, a wise and skillful architect, pupil of the builder of Khawarnaq,[24] advises Bahrām to live according to the stars and suggests the construction of seven pavilions, or domes, each of which would harmonize in colour with the regent of a given day of the week, and be inhabited by the princess from the astrologically related clime. Bahrām should then spend each day and night in the corresponding dome and thus escape the evil eye, which he has to fear because of his absolute success.[25] Bahrām consents, the seven domes are built, and now begins the central and apparently most important part of the poem, namely the stories as told by the princesses to the king during his visits on seven consecutive days, beginning with a Saturday, whose colour is black, and ending with a Friday, whose colour is white.[26] To call the stories love stories would be an oversimplification, but the pursuit of love plays a very prominent role in them.[27] They are also replete with folkloric motifs known elsewhere, especially from the 1001 Nights. Before going into the stories themselves, it will be expedient to look first at the end of Bahrām's career, which provides the frame for the whole.

After the night of Friday we are not told how long Bahrām continued to circulate among the seven pavilions, but subsequent events clearly imply that he must have done so for at least seven years, and that he had become oblivious of what was going on in the world outside his palace. One day a messenger arrives with the news that the emperor of China is preparing to invade Iran.[28] Bahrām sends for his army and his gold reserve, but there are no soldiers, and the treasury is empty. Now he discovers that his minister had badly abused his power, and has even had treacherous contacts with the Chinese. The whole country is on the verge of ruin, and the people are suffering injustice. The king takes matters into his own hands, punishes the minister, and in short time restores order and prosperity in the land.[29] The keynote of the relevant passages is <u>justice</u>. Seeing that Iran is recovering, the Chinese emperor abandons his aggressive plans and sends his apologies.

Following this, Bahrām does not return to his former way of life, but transforms the pavilions into places of fire worship.[30] He continues to rule justly for some time, retaining only his former passion for hunting. The story, however, is nearing a sudden and unexpected end. One day during a hunt, our hero notices an unusually beautiful onager and pursues her on his horse leaving his retinue far behind. The animal flees and enters a cave between some rocks, Bahrām follows and disappears forever.[31]

The overall message of the romance seems to be indeed, as H. Ritter thought, the futility of astrological practice and the need, in a successful life, for wisdom, justice, action, good deeds, and the acceptance of a higher order. But why did Niẓāmī contrive to substitute this inexplicable disappearance for the normal death mentioned in the <u>Shāhnāmah</u>? The posing of this question seems to be of crucial importance. It is also important to note that the description of the final chase[32] is not couched in terms that would indicate impending disaster, but on the contrary, it is made clear that Bahram is following a leader ("angel, four-winged messenger"), and that when both enter the cave, the life of the hero reaches its highest fulfillment.[33] There is no commiseration of his fate.

The question just raised, echoes of passages from Hermetic

literature,[34] and the continuous firework of astrological and cosmological references, including frequent statements of colour and number, will justify a close reading of the seven stories with particular attention to details of this sort. In doing so, we will make only the following assumptions: a) The seven tales are not "just so stories" thrown in for mere entertainment, but are an integral part of the total structure of the romance: b) Niẓāmī's terse style does not leave much space for banalities and truisms; every little detail is, therefore, potentially significant. As we proceed, we will enter all items which catch our attention in a table with seven columns.

On Saturday, the black princess from India tells Bahrām about a king who had heard of a town in which the inhabitants all dress in black, but refuse to tell the reason for this. Driven by curiosity, he travels to that town, and after many vain efforts he finds a man who is willing to show, but not to tell, him the reason.[35] The man leads him to a tower and bids him to climb into a basket. The basket is suddenly lifted by magic to a high platform where the king remains bewildered and full of fear for a while, and whence he is later carried, having attached himself to the leg of a huge bird who had come to roost, to a distant land.[36] There the king ultimately finds himself in a beautiful garden in the company of maidens. The fairest of them shows him a favourable disposition, but when he desires to possess her she puts him off for later, allowing him meanwhile to become intimate with one of her handmaidens. Their meeting is repeated thirty[37] times with the same result. On the thirtieth time he loses his patience and tries to force her. She makes a show of giving in and asks him to close his eyes so she can undo her garments. He complies and instantly finds himself back in the basket at the foot of the tower.[38] His friend is waiting and laconically states that a hundred years of explanations would not have sufficed to get across what this experience has. Henceforth the king and all close to him are wearing black.[39]

As noted by Gelpke, this tale is set in a little frame of its own and thus somehow relates to the Friday story. The general mood is determined by notions of yearning, fear, desire, regret, repentance,[40] and the pervasive black colour.

On Sunday, the tale of the princess of Rūm deals with a king who had been warned in his horoscope that there was danger for him in marriage. He, therefore, lives as a bachelor and avoids permanent attachment to women.[41] Instead, he buys slave girls, but the latter, being spoiled by an old woman, soon become negligent in their duties, which leads to their frequent exchange. Once a dealer shows him a girl of rare beauty but warns him that she strictly refuses to give her favours to a man. The king is, nevertheless, so overwhelmed by her charm that he acquires her in spite of the handicap. They live together in harmony, except for the one thing which he desires but cannot obtain from her. Intrigued by her firmness, he decides to discover the reason for it. In order to encourage her to tell the truth, he first tells a story of Solomon and Bilqīs who have a paralysed child. They are instructed by an angel that they can cure him by telling each other the absolute truth. They do so, and the child is cured. Thereupon the girl admits that the women of her clan die during childbirth, and that she is simply afraid to die. Again the old woman enters the scene and advises the king to make the girl jealous. He succeeds, she admits her love for him, and they are happily united in terms which the English translator chose to render in Latin. The leitmotiv of the story is clearly truthfulness, but auxiliary themes are fear and jealousy. Even in Western culture, the yellow colour is symbolic of jealousy, and according to a German proverb, the truth is brought to light by the sun.

On Monday, the princess of the green pavilion[42] tells a story whose psychological insights are worthy of the Freudian age. A young godfearing and goodhearted man, while walking in the streets of his town, happens to catch a glimpse of a beautiful woman's face when the wind lifts her veil for a moment. His first impulse is to follow her, but he restrains himself and goes home. No matter how hard he tries to forget, he cannot find peace from his thoughts and decides to seek consolation in a pilgrimage to Jerusalem. He performs the ritual and on his way back finds himself in the company of another man who very soon turns out to be evil and a gabbler, who pretends to know and understand everything. There is no doubt that the other man is a projection of the negative forces within the hero, and that the visit to the holy place has had an effect similar to the one psychoanalysis is trying to achieve. The evil which was in the man and disturbed him is now set free and travels beside him in a personified form. It can now be fought and overcome.

Whenever the two travellers see a natural phenomenon, Malīkhā, the evil one, asks Bishr[43] for its meaning and cause. Bishr retorts that it is so by the will of God, and does not try to explain what he does not know. Malīkhā then laughs, boasts with his knowledge, and embarks on his, the scientific explanation. They traverse a desert and reach a tree under which there is water surrounded by a rim of clay. It looks as if a large vessel were buried in the ground. Immediately the bad fellow begins to formulate a theory about its origin, but first he asks Bishr. The latter says that a good man must have put the vessel there as a good deed to provide wayfarers with water. The former laughs and says that nobody would do so for no profit at all, and that it must be a means for attracting animals installed by a hunter.

They quench their thirst and rest. Having rested, the gabbler declares that he is going to bathe in the water and then destroy the vessel. Vainly Bishr tries to prevent him, and then walks away in sadness in order not to have to witness the crime. What had looked like a buried vessel, however, was in reality a deep well protected by a rim of clay. Not having recognized its true essence, Malīkhā is drowned. This, in Niẓāmī's own words, is the punishment of the evildoer, the gabbler, the scientist who collects information which is useless because he lacks the wisdom to use it for the good.[44] Malīkhā may also represent death because water, the symbol of life as well as of wisdom, destroys him, while Bishr, who takes from it only what he needs and does not defile it, is saved. All this harmonizes with the extremely complex symbolism of the moon with its changing phases, of water, and of the green colour, a symbolism which includes life and death.[45]

Bishr returns to the well, finds his companion drowned, retrieves his body with considerable difficulty, and buries it. Then he collects the other's valuables in order to return them to his lawful heirs. Using the dead man's turban for identification, he is able to find his house in the city. When he knocks at the door, it is opened by a woman in whom he recognizes the lady who stood at the beginning of all his troubles. Impressed by Bishr's honesty and his kind features, but also glad to be rid of her wicked husband, she proposes to him on the spot. As they agree to get married, Bishr changes her clothes from yellow to green. As the outstanding virtues of this story, self-restraint and trust in God can be identified.

On Tuesday, the Slavic princess, adorned in red, tells Bahrām the story which has become the prototype of Turandot in Western literature.[46] The beautiful and learned daughter of a king has an impregnable fortress built for herself, the path to which is protected by powerful talismans.[47] At the city gate beneath the fortress she affixes her portrait and four conditions under which she would be willing to accept a suitor: He must be of noble descent, disarm the talismans, find the entrance to the fortress, and, finally, he must solve four riddles posed by her. Unsuccessful suitors will be beheaded. Many were those who fell in love with the picture,[48] tried their luck, failed, and lost their lives. Blood flowed in streams, and the severed heads piled up.

Eventually the <u>right</u> prince arrives. Instead of foolhardily trying on his own, he repairs to the hermitage of a wise man who instructs him and prepares him for the task. Through various tricks, and acting as the avenger of all previously lost lives, he solves the first three problems and is hailed by the populace as the redeemer from a bloody nightmare. The riddles which he has to solve before the king and his court turn out to be silent actions.[49] The princess, from behind a curtain, sends the prince two pearls, he adds three equal ones and returns the five to her. She weighs them, and pounds them to powder, and mixes the powder with sugar. He adds milk to the mixture, she drinks the milk, and finds the weight of the residue equal to the weight of the pearls. She sends him a ring from her finger. He puts it on his finger and returns a large pearl. She matches the pearl with one from her necklace, and he adds a blue bead. Thus ends the trial.

Being questioned by the king who is just as baffled as the reader, the princess gives an explanation which seems at once superficial and unsatisfactory. The wedding is immediately prepared, and the marriage is consummated in terms for which Wilson again preferred the use of Latin.

It is here that a few pieces of the game begin to fall into place. Since Mia Gerhardt's discovery of rigorous structure in the Sindbad story and the fact that its climax is in the centre,[50] it is not surprising to find that the central story in the <u>HP</u> is loaded with meaning and may contain the key for the understanding of the entire structure. If such a key is provided, it is only logical that it will have to be looked for in the riddles. Disregarding the given explanation, we can extract from them some quantifiable information and keep it in evidence as follows: 2 + 3 = 5 (pearls), 1 ring, 1 + 1 = 2 (pearls), 1 blue bead, sugar, milk.

It is well to remember at this point that Bahrām is the Persian name of Mars and that, therefore, the king is in his very own sphere on Tuesday (= mardi, martedi etc.). Following an intuition we check the numerical values of b, h, r, ', m: 2 + 5 + 200 + 1 + 40. The total of digits is 248 = 14 = 5. The magic square assigned to Mars is 5 x 5.[51] Five is also the numerical symbol for love, and the result of the first exchange between princess and prince (2 + 3) certainly derives significance from this fact.[52]

The heroic prince in red has no name, and it is certainly legitimate to identify him with Bahrām who, in some mystical or gnostic fashion is going through the stages of initiation or perfection represented by the seven stories. If we look at the days and planetary spheres traversed so far, we realize that according to medieval cosmological doctrines these first four spheres correspond to the four elements Earth, Fire, Water, and Air. In an initiatory context this should imply that the adept has now passed the ordeals by the four elements, and that the quadruplicity of conditions imposed by the princess, as well as of the final "questions,"[53] is a reference to them. We also note that this is the first of three consecutive stories in which the hero's success or salvation depends upon the intervention of a benevolent old man. The admixture of sugar and its dissolution in milk may simply mean that the true meaning is covered by the surface stories (sugar) and can be uncovered by the application of esoteric knowledge (milk).[54] As for the blue bead, a ubiquitous good luck charm and protection against the evil eye, its main function seems to be merely to indicate a connection to the next day whose colour is blue.

In order to complete the chart, we must now take a rapid look at the remaining stories. On Wednesday, the blue princess speaks of an Egyptian young man named Māhān, who is called away from a party under the pretence of business by a jinn impersonating an acquaintance of his. He is then abandoned in the wilderness, and after many tribulations and encounters with ghouls and monsters is finally brought back to civilization by Khiḍr. There is an almost dramatic retardation in the story when Māhān on his way through the wilderness decides to spend the night in a pit. There he sees a ray of light falling through a crack in the wall.[55] He widens the opening and climbs into a beautiful garden where he is discovered by an angry owner. The latter takes pity on him and eventually promises to adopt him. He bids Māhān to spend the night on a sandal tree and not to come down under any circumstances. Māhān, however, yields to the temptations of a beautiful girl in a manner reminiscent of the Saturday story, except that the girl turns into a monster before Māhān finds himself transferred back into the wilderness. When Khiḍr comes to the rescue he bids Māhān to close his eyes,[56] and when Māhān thereupon is rejoined with his friends, they are wearing the blue colour of mourning.[57] These last elements also recall some features of the Saturday story. The sandal tree in the garden, however, forms a link with, and anticipates the next day.

On Thursday, the Chinese princess tells of two travellers named Good and Bad, whose characters correspond to their names. In the desert, when Good runs out of food and water, Bad robs him of his possessions and of his eyesight. The daughter of a chief of Kurdish nomads finds the helpless man and brings him to her family's camp. Her father has the knowledge of a tree with two kinds of leaves, one restores sight, the other cures epilepsy. Good's eyes are healed in five days, and he becomes the son-in-law of the Kurd. When, on their wanderings, they come into the territory of a king whose daughter has epilepsy, Good, who has stored some of the leaves from "the sandal-scented tree," is able to cure her. She also becomes his wife,[58] and he embarks on a profitable career at the kings court, curing the vizier's blind daughter in the process and receiving her as a wife as well. There is no sign of jealousy on the part of his wives, and it is quite clear that they symbolize three qualities acquired by Bahrām. One day, Bad is recognized in town, brought before the king, and executed by the Kurd.[59] Of further significance must be that two gems taken by Bad from Good are now returned, but Good passes them on to the Kurd in gratitude for his rescue.

On Friday, the white princess tells a story which had been heard by her mother.[60] It is about the owner of a garden who surprised a group of women feasting in it. Two women in charge of security take

Saturday	Sunday	Monday	Tuesday	Wednesday	Thursday	Friday	[Sophia]?	[Logos]?
MACROCOSM:								
Saturn	Sun	Moon	Mars	Mercury	Jupiter	Venus		
Black	Yellow	Green	Red	Blue	Sandal	White		
3 x 3	6 x 6	9 x 9	8 x 8	4 x 4	7 x 7			
Earth	Fire	Water	Air					
MICROCOSM:								
Black	Yellow	Phlegm	Blood					
Bile	Bile							
Melancholic	Choleric	Phlegmatic	Sanguinic					

4 Elements (Matter)

7 Planetary Spheres

3 (Spirits)

STRUCTURAL DIVISIONS:

frame   colour link   colour link   frame

Old Man

PEARLS:

1   2   5   3   7   1

[2 + 3 + 5 + 7 = 17]

Feminine Trine   Masculine Trine

Grand Trine = Total Cosmos

him for a thief, but upon identification they hide him in a nook and become instrumental in procuring him the beauty of his choice. There follow four attempts at consummating the love affair, but collapsing beams, falling gourds, and other technical mishaps frustrate the would-be lovers.[61] Finally, a formal commitment through legal marriage leads to the desired result, for which Wilson, as before, has recourse to Latin.

* * *

The basic grid of the chart is provided by the seven days of the week, their planets and colours. The corresponding four elements and humours happen to fit under the first four planets, so that the cosmic seven becomes easily divided into four and three which stand for matter and spirit. A review of the themes of the first four stories furthermore confirms that the characters of the heroes are in harmony with the humour they represent. The melancholic black king who is aware of something beyond his reach and who mourns a missed opportunity. Then the choleric king who speaks up, determined to learn the truth, and who speaks the truth. Further, the phlegmatic, self-restrained Bishr in whose story water played such an important part. Finally, the streams of blood which flow because of the princess who has her unsuccessful suitors beheaded until she is conquered by the active, sanguinic prince.

This division of the seven into four and three is accentuated by the fact that both series begin with colours of mourning, both initial tales end with the mere survival of the hero, without success in marital or sexual terms. We also noted other parallels between the two stories.

What makes matters so complicated, is that there seem to be several simultaneous numerological levels indicated by different means. We have already noted that the first and last stories are set off from the rest by their introductions. Besides, there is a colour link between stories 2 and 3 (yellow garments changed to green), 4 and 5 (blue bead), 5 and 6 (sandal tree), through which device a series of two and one of three are created, both framed by the single stories at the ends. This brings to mind the riddles of the cruel princess in which pearls appear in precisely these quantities: 2, 3, 1, 1. Thus, within the seven, the numbers 2, 3, and 5 are made "visible." They, including 7, happen to be the first four prime numbers whose sum is 17.[62]

One other numerological level is virtually certain. It is made "visible" mainly through the fact that stories 4, 5, and 6 are connected by the feature of intervention by an old man (hermit, Khiḍr, Kurdish chief).[63] This leaves the first three stories opposed to them as a triad whose feminine character seems to be born out by the intervention of the old woman in the Sunday story. Searching for other clues, we notice that within each of these groups of three the degrees of success are evenly distributed. Stories 1 and 5 end with a failure to obtain the desired woman. Stories 3 and 6 end with marriage, while stories 2 and 4 end with a description of the physical union of the lovers. The odd story number 7 is of the third type with the added feature that two women are instrumental in the union with the beloved. The meaning of this appears to be that in the seventh stage the adept is invested with the powers represented by the two preceding trines.[64]

In the context of trines, however, one does not expect a structural sequence 3 + 3 + 1, but rather 3 + 3 + 3. In astrology, for instance, a Grand Trine is precisely this, three trines, the symbol of perfection, "the most perfect of all aspects."[65] Niẓāmī himself makes explicit reference to nine spheres in the chapter on the miᶜrāj.[66] To complete the third trine we obviously have to go beyond the seven tales into the concluding portion of the frame. There are, however, no clear, externally marked divisions or events which could be taken to represent the two missing spheres. It becomes necessary to scrutinize Bahrām's behaviour in order to discover further steps towards perfection. The first is, no doubt, his recognition of the true situation in the world outside, the gaining of insight.[67] The second must be then the translation of this insight into action and the assumption of active and just government. Wisdom and justice are the ultimate goods.[68]

If we accept this as a working hypothesis and represent the three resulting trines as triangles, we can easily imagine how, upon completion of the last triangle, all three of them combine into a pyramid, thus creating a new dimension. Similarly, Bahrām is suddenly elevated from the plain of life to a point beyond description.

No claim is made at this juncture that all problems presented by the HP have been solved, nor is the reader expected to conclude that Niẓāmī was simultaneously a Zoroastrian, Druze, Ismāᶜīlī, or a member of the Ahl-i Ḥaqq, and so forth. What is certain, however, is that he was familiar with a vast reservoir of traditions at least partially shared by these various groups, and that he was able to play the many registers of this unique cosmological organ with virtuosity. It is probable that he was a member of the Akhī movement whose ideals he undoubtedly expressed most eloquently,[69] and it is possible that the main message of this grandiose symphony of Celestial Music is that all cosmological systems are ultimately compatible, and that each is only part of God's design for this world. It is not impossible that Niẓāmī was an alchemist.

Notes

[1] Ilyās ibn Yūsuf, named Ganjavī after the place of his birth and life-long residence, Ganjah in Azerbaijan (later Yelizavetpol', now Kirovabad). Niẓāmī was the poet's takhalluṣ. After much controversy, the dates of his life have been determined as 535/1141-605/1209. See Jan Rypka, Iranische Literaturgeschichte (Leipzig: VEB Harrassowitz, 1959) and History of Iranian Literature (Dordrecht: Reidel, 1968).

[2] G.E. von Grunebaum, Medieval Islam, 2nd ed. (Chicago: University of Chicago Press, 1953), p. 291.

[3] The five components of the Khamsah are: Makhzan al-Asrār, Khusraw va Shīrīn, Laylā va Majnūn, Haft Paykar, and Iskandarnāmah. The Iskandarnāmah consists in fact of two books with separate titles and dedications: Sharafnāmah and Iqbālnāmah. It looks as if they were made to count as one in order to yield a quintet, because of the special significance of the number five (see notes 51 and 52). Niẓāmī may have originally planned seven poems.

[4] For the most detailed discussion see Wilhelm Bacher (Nizami's Leben und Werke, Beiträge zur Geschichte der persischen Literatur und der Alexandersage [Leipzig, 1871]), Ye. E. Bertels (Nizami, tvorcheskiy put' poeta [Muskva, 1956] and Nizami i Fuzuli, Izbrannyye trudy [Moskva, 1962]), and Gholām Dārāb (Makhzanol Asrār, the Treasury of Mysteries of Niẓāmī of Ganjeh, trans. Ghulām Husayn Dārāb [London: A. Probsthain, 1945], introduction).

[5] It was still taken seriously by Bacher (p. 6), but since then Dastgardi (Niẓāmī Ganjavī, [Works], ed. Vaḥīd Dastgardī, 7 vols. [Tahrān, 1934-1939; 2nd ed. Tahrān, 1954-1956], 5: 528) and the editors of the Baku edition (Niẓāmī Ganjavī, Sharafnāmah, ed. A.A. Ali-Zade [Baku, 1947], p. 503) have recognized it as a later addition.

[6] The significance of the number 17 has been shown by Irène

Mélikoff ("Nombres symboliques dans la littérature épico-religieuse des Turçs d'Anatolie," Journal Asiatique, 250 [1962], 435-445).

[7] Dawlatshāh bin ^{c}Alā'u 'l-dawla . . . of Samarqand, The Tadhkiratu sh-shu^{c}arā', ed. E. G. Browne (London/Leiden, 1901), p. 129. A discussion of the merit, probability, and further implications of this assertion is given by Ye. E. Bertels (Nizami . . . poeta, pp. 73 f.; Nizami i Fuzuli, pp. 90 and 110 f.), who prefers the reading "Farrukh." See also Niẓāmī, Makhzanol Asrār, trans. Darab, p. 5. On the brotherhood of the Akhīs, see note 69 and EI^2, s.v. Akhī.

[8] Niẓāmī Ganjavī, The Haft Paikar (The Seven Beauties), trans. C.E. Wilson, 2 vols. (London: Probsthain, 1924), 1: xv.

[9] Ibid., p. xviii.

[10] Helmut Ritter, review of The Haft Paikar, trans. C.E. Wilson, in Der Islam, 15 (1926), 113. See also his Über die Bildersprache Niẓāmīs, Studien zur Geschichte und Kultur des islamischen Orients, 5 (Berlin/Leipzig, 1927), pp. 27 and 50. It is interesting to note that Ritter's reference to Ficino and to Hermetic literature coincides with his association with the circle of A. Warburg, founder of the famous institute.

[11] The history of his involvement with Niẓāmī is surveyed in the preface to his Nizami i Fuzuli.

[12] Ibid., pp. 340 f.

[13] Ibid., p. 448.

[14] Niẓāmī Ganjavī, Die sieben Geschichten der sieben Prinzessinen, trans. Rudolf Gelpke (Zurich: Manesse, 1959), p. 290.

[15] Ibid., p. 291.

[16] Peter J. Chelkowski, Mirror of the Invisible World, Tales from the Khamseh of Nizami (New York: Metropolitan Museum of Art, 1975), p. 113. No reference is given. The title of this book is derived from a passage in Laylà va Majnūn (ed. Dastgardī, 3: 40 line 12; ed. A.A. Alesker-Zade and F. Babayev [Moskva, 1965], p. 72 line 3) in which Niẓāmī boasts to be called āyīnah-'i ghayb. On the subject of mirrors reflecting the world, see Iraj Dehghan, "Jāmī's Salāmān and Absāl," Journal of Near Eastern Studies, 30 (1971), 121.

[17] I am encouraged in this undertaking by the insights gained, not too long ago, by Charles S. Singleton, ("The Poet's Number at the Centre," Modern Language Notes, 80/1 [Jan 1965], 1-10) into the numerical structure of the Divine Comedy. This structure had remained invisible to readers for over six centuries.

[18] The famous manual of magic, Picatrix, has the following quotation from an unknown Hermetic book: "Hermes built a tower, 30 cubits high, with a dome which every day took on a [different] colour, until seven days passed and it would return to [its] first colour. The [entire] city would be enveloped in that colour." (Maslamah al-Majrīṭīl[?], Das Ziel des Weisen, Arabic text ed. H. Ritter, Studien der Bibliothek Warburg 12 [Leipzig/Berlin: Teubner, 1933], p. 310; "Picatrix," das Ziel des Weisen, trans. into German by H. Ritter and M. Plessner, Studies of the Warburg Institute 27 [London, 1962], p. 323.) The fundamental similarity between the contents of this passage and the motif of the seven domes in the HP is too striking to be brushed aside. The latter is clearly an expansion of the former. It is this passage which, in 1965, provided the initial impetus for the research which led to this article. One may only wonder why H. Ritter, who had edited both the Picatrix and the HP, did not notice the connection. It may be that preoccupation with philological detail had blocked the vision of the whole.

[19] One of these introductory chapters is the description of the

mi^c^rāj mentioned above. On the subject of the heavenly journey, see W. Bousset, "Die Himmelsreise der Seele," Archiv für Religionswissenschaft, 4 (1901), 136-169 and 229-273; reprt: (Darmstadt, 1960).

[20] The historical Lakhmid king, Nu^c^man of Hirah, is placed by both Firdawsī and Niẓāmī in the Yemen. The palace of Khawarnaq was an actual structure whose ruins are located in Mesopotamia (EI, s.v.).

[21] In the Shāhnāmah, the killing of the dragon and the finding of the treasure are not connected. There seems to be an intended parallelism between this adventure and Bahrām's last hunt, with an onager acting as psychopomp (cf. note 33). The motif of following an animal to some destination occurs in Jānshāh's story which is embedded in the "Queen of Serpents" (1001 Nights, night 500 [1830 Calcutta edition count]).

[22] Fitnah ("temptation" is Niẓāmī's fitting replacement for Firdawsī''s Āzādah ("noble"). In the Shāhnāmah, the girl is killed on the spot for taking Bahrām's skill lightly; in the HP she offends him by attributing his skill to "mere practice". He orders her killed, but she persuades the officer charged with her execution to spare and hide her. By starting to carry a little calf up sixty steps and by continuing to do so as the calf grows into a bull, Fitnah develops enormous strength. When Bahrām is again hunting in the neighbourhood, she has the opportunity to prove her point, and they are reconciled. Aside from inventing a humane ending for the story, Niẓāmī is using the motif of the great athlete of antiquity, Milo of Crotona, who developed his muscles in precisely the same way. It would be interesting to know how this motif reached Azerbaijan in the twelfth century A.D.

[23] The names of the princesses are given only once in the context of the description of the fresco of Khawarniq (Niẓāmī Ganjavī, Haft Paykar, ed. H. Ritter and J. Rypka, Monografie archiv orientālnīho 3 (Praha/Istambul, 1934), p. 60; trans. Wilson, 1: 56). It was tempting to examine them numerologically, but the totals of digits do not appear significant in themselves, or as a sequence: 9,2,9,6,4,2,8. The total of the totals, however, is 40 (= 4). This could be an allusion to the fact that they all represent the material world. The name of the Iranian princess is written drsty. The meter requires the reading Dursitī (name of the daughter of Nūshīrwān [F. Steingass, A Comprehensive Persian-English Dictionary (London, 1892)], but if vocalized durustī it would mean "rightness," which is probably an intended pun. Cf. Schuyler V.R. Cammann, "The Interplay of Art, Literature, and Religion in Safarid Symbolism," Journal of the Royal Asiatic Society, (1978), pp. 126-131. The numerical values of these letters are 4 + 200 + 60 + 400 + 10 = 674; the intermediate total of digits is 6 + 7 + 4 = 17. This might again be significant. Without intending to push the numerological interpretation too far, it is useful to remember that Niẓāmī was not above such games, as is evident from his analysis of his own name in Laylī va Majnūn (ed. Dastgardī, 3: 44, ed. Alesker-Zade and Babayev, p. 77; see also Bacher, p. 8, and Bertels, Nizami i Fuzuli, p. 92).

[24] The older architect, Simnār by name, had paid with his life for his boastful claim that he could build a more beautiful castle than Khawarnaq. Nu^c^mān had him pushed from the top of a tower. For Simnār as a reflection of a Babylonian name see J. Halévy, "Khawarnak et Sinimmar," Revue Sémitique, 15 (1907), 101-107.

[25] HP, ed. Ritter and Rypka, p. 116; trans. Wilson, 1: 110. This is reminiscent of the following passage quoted from a

pseudo-Aristotelian work in Picatrix (Arabic text, p. 310; German trans., p. 323): "O Alexander, if you are able to make no movement without complete coordination with the heavenly movement, which cannot be achieved except through astrological election, you will reach whatever you desire and hope for."

26 The obvious harmony between each day of the week, its planet, colour, and astrologically related clime has been discussed too often to need repetition here. All these items appear in the chart below, and the reader may wish to take an advance look for orientation. For the relationship between planetary spheres and earthly climes, see Seyyed Hossein Nasr, An Introduction to Islamic Cosmological Doctrines (Cambridge: Harvard University Press, 1964), p. 146, and Steingass, s.v. kishvar.

27 According to C.G. Jung (Man and his Symbols [New York: Doubleday, 1964], p. 29) the deer hunt is "one of the countless symbolic or allegorical images of the sexual act." Thus Niẓāmī's combination of hunting and love as the two most prominent themes of his romance appears to be quite "archetypal." It is interesting that the hunt can be a religious theme as well, as the literature of Ahl-i Ḥaqq shows. See Mohammad Mokri, Le Chasseur de Dieu et le mythe du Roi-Aigle, Beiträge zur Iranistik (Wiesbaden: Harrassowitz, 1967). In a related context the arrow is mentioned as a symbolic instrument of esoteric knowledge (bāṭin; see Mokri, La grande assemblée des Fidèles de Verité au tribunal sur le mont Zagros en Iran [Paris: Klincksieck, 1977], pp. 95 and 172). In "The Concept of the Hunt in Persian Literature" (Boston Museum Bulletin, 69 [1971], 32) W.L. Hanaway Jr. states, " . . . the union of lover and beloved . . . is aptly expressed through the metaphor of hunting and capture." Niẓāmī is mentioned there only in passing.

28 Like many others, the theme of a Chinese attack occurs twice in the HP. The first instance is between the Fitnah story and the banquet scene. The motif of an enemy being tempted to attack by the prospective victim's neglect of good government has a parallel in Jānshāh's story (1001 Nights, night 516; cf. note 21).

29 In this context seven witnesses of the minister's wrongdoings are heard.

30 Here, in keeping with the historical setting, Zoroastrianism represents "true religion."

31 According to the Shāhnāmah, Bahrām dies of old age and is given a funeral. It is Kay Khusraw who disappears without a trace. Bertels, in discussing this (Nizami i Fuzuli, p. 341, where wrongly Kāvūs for Khusraw), is puzzled by Niẓāmī's choice "not to explain the mysterious disappearance" and suspects a different source. But there can be no doubt that Niẓāmī made the substitution intentionally, and for a reason. Historicity was not his concern here.

32 HP, ed. Ritter and Rypka, p. 291; trans. Wilson, 1: 276.

33 In the earlier episode which anticipates the final chase (cf. note 21), the cave yields material treasures which had to be gained by physical force (killing the dragon). Now the treasure is ultimate spiritual perfection, and therefore not subject to verbalization. Compare Seyyed Hossein Nasr's discussion of Avicenna's esoteric philosophy (Three Muslim Sages [Cambridge: Harvard University Press, 1964], p. 44): "The traveller learns from the Guide . . . what the structure of the cosmic crypt is . . . Then he accepts the challenge and makes the sojourn through the cosmic mountains and valleys until he finally comes out of the world of formal manifestation and meets at the end with death, which symbolizes birth into a new spiritual life

. . . He who has left the cosmos does not become imprisoned in it again." The lore of the Ahl-i Ḥaqq also contains an account of the disappearance of one of their theophanies, Shāh-Khōshīn, by riding on horseback into the river Māsināv (Mohammad Mokri, "Un kalām gourani sur les compagnons du Roi des Rois," Journal Asiatique, 257 [1969], 317-359 passim and esp. note 2).

34 See notes 18 and 25.

35 The motif of travelling to a distant land in search of knowledge, and of slowly working one's way into the confidence of a person able to show the way to it, is reminiscent of Barūyah's mission to India (!) in search of Kalīlah wa Dimna. Fittingly, this story is told by the Indian princess.

36 This method of transportation is identical with the one used by Sindbad to escape from an island during his second journey (1001 Nights, night 544), but it cannot be related to the flying contraption with four eagles used by Alexander (and Kay Kāvūs) as von Grunebaum thought (Medieval Islam, p. 302). The latter, aside from the essential difference in numbers, represents technical ingenuity and a hybris, while the former represents serendipity in its true sense (cf. S.V.R. Cammann, "Christopher the Armenian and the Three Princes of Serendip," Comparative Literature Studies, 4 [1967], 229).

37 Note that Hermes built a tower thirty cubits high (cf. note 18). Qāḍī Nu^c^mān makes a connection between the fast of thirty days and the occultation of the Imām (Y. Marquet, "Le Qaḍi Nu^c^man à propos des heptades d'imāms," Arabica, 25 [1978], 226).

38 Transfer through the closing of the eyes occurs in the story of Bulūqiyā also embedded in the "Queen of Serpents" (1001 Nights, nights 531 and 532).

39 The black colour and the general sombreness of this tale recall the character of Druze villages. Is it then a pure coincidence that the Druze rites of initiation as described by W.B. Seabrook begin with various temptations including the lure of a beautiful girl? (W.B. Seabrook, "The Golden Calf of the Druzes," Asia, 26 [Concord, NH, March 1926], 250; quoted by Klaus E. Müller, Kulturhistorische Studien zur Genese pseudo-islamischer Sektengebilde in Vorderasian, Studien zur Kulterkunde 22 [Wiesbaden: Steiner, 1967], p. 83).

40 Compare with this Abu Sa^c^īd's reply to the question, "When shall a man be freed from his wants?": " . . . First of all, [God] brings forth in him the desire to attain his goal. Then He opens to him the gate of repentance, etc." (Reynold A. Nicholson, Studies in Islamic Mysticism [Cambridge: Cambridge University Press, 1921], p. 51).

41 This motif is akin to an early version of Sālāman and Absāl translated by Ḥunayn, in which the king is unwilling to cohabit with women (Henry Corbin, Avicenna and the Visionary Recital, Bollingen Series 66 [New York, 1960], p. 211). "[Majun's] Layla states clearly, that in the religion of love close intimacy is perilous" (Rudolf Gelpke, in Niẓāmī Ganjavī, The Story of Layla and Majnun, trans. R. Gelpke [London: Cassirer, 1966], postscript).

42 The original text does not identify the homeland of the princess, nor does Wilson's translation. Other translators or summarizers decided as follows: Bertels - Khwarezmian; Gelpke - Moorish; Chelkowski - Tatar. This, of course, affects their identification of the princess on Wednesday, whose homeland is not mentioned either. The earlier list of princesses (see note 23) has no colour clues.

43 Scholars are divided as to the vocalization of this name.

Wilson and Chelkowski write "Bashr," Bertels and Gelpke "Bishr." "Bishr" is preferred here, because it is an existing name, and its meaning, "joy, happy face," is more fitting than that of the verbal noun bashr.

44 On al-Ghazali's contempt for the mere amassing of information see von Grunebaum, p. 236.

45 Although this story is not at all similar to the Hermetic Salāmān and Absāl, they share the feature that water separates the two characters by killing one and sparing the other. H. Corbin's subsequent discussion (Avicenna . . ., p. 215) of initiatory psychology is highly instructive in connection with the HP as well.

46 On the diffusion of the Turandot story, and on the history of some of its motifs, see Fritz Meier, "Turandot in Persien," Zeitschrift der Deutschen Morgenländischen Gesellschaft, 95 (1941), 1-27; idem, "Nachtrag zu Turandot in Persien," ibid., 415-421; Ettore Rossi, "La leggenda di Turandot," in Studi orientalistici . . . Levi della Vida (Roma: Istituto per l'Oriente, 1956), vol. 2; and Albert Wesselski, "Quellen und Nachwirkungen der Haft Paikar," Der Islam, 22 (1935), 106-119.

47 These so-called talismans must be pictured as sword-wielding automata. Also Hermes protected the city in which he built his tower (cf. note 18) with talismans.

48 Falling in love with a picture is a frequent motif in the 1001 Nights (Mia I. Gerhardt, The Art of Story-Telling, a Literary Study of the Thousand and One Nights [Leiden: Brill, 1963], pp. 122 f.). Here, it is also a repetition of Bahrām's earlier enamoration with the seven portraits.

49 Instances of sign language occur in the 1001 Nights, as, e.g., in "Azīz and Azīzah" (nights 113-130), where the intention to kill the inept lover is also an ingredient of the story. It is particularly interesting that sign language plays a part in the initiation ritual of the Nuṣayrīs (Müller, pp. 58 f.).

50 Gerhardt, pp. 255 f. Cf. Singleton, "The Poet's Number."

51 On the coordination of magic squares with planets, see W. Ahrens, "Studien über die 'magischen Quadrate' der Araber," Der Islam, 7 (1917), 198. According to a Druze author, "the sacred number of five serves as the basic principle for the organization of ᶜilm (Franz Rosenthal, Knowledge Triumphant [Leiden: Brill, 1970], p. 151). In the "Queen of Serpents" (1001 Nights, night 483), the essence of Dānyāl's knowledge survives his shipwreck on five sheets. It is fitting to remember at this point the late Vladimar Vikentiev who had devoted much thought to the "Queen of Serpents" in his "Rayonnement des anciennes légendes à travers le monde; Série de conférences," Revue des Conferences Françaises en Orient (Le Caire, 1945), 207-222, 396-411, 591-603; unfortunately his research is buried in a rather inaccessible periodical.

52 Matila Ghyka, The Geometry of Art and Life (New York: Dover, 1977), p. 113; Rudolf Hasse, "Harmonikale Symbolik und neue Pythagorasforschung," Symbolon, Jahrbuch fur Symbolforschung, 5 (Basel/Stuttgart, 1966), 81; cf. J.E. Cirlot, A Dictionary of Symbols (New York: Philosophical Library, 1962), p. 222: "The hieros gamos is signified by the number five, since it represents the union of the principle of heaven (three) with that of the Magna Mater (two)." H. Ritter's purely sexual interpretation as reported by Meier ("Nachtrag zu Turandot," p. 417) is certainly too simplistic and crude.

53 The number four is expressly stated by the princess (HP, ed. Ritter and Rypka, p. 190 verse 213; trans. Wilson, 1: 183 verse 8),

and it is the number of times that the princess sends the prince something which counts.

[54] According to Qāḍī Nuᶜmān milk symbolizes esoteric knowledge (Rosenthal, p. 150; cf. ibid., p. 80).

[55] This motif occurs at the beginning of the "Queen of Serpents" (1001 Nights, night 484) and in the fourth journey of Sindbad (ibid., night 554).

[56] Extensive wanderings, rescue by Khiḍr, and transfer through the closing of the eyes are all part of the story of Bulūqiyā (see note 38).

[57] For blue as a colour of mourning, cf. von Grunebaum, p. 352. It is also interesting to note that some of the early Islamic sects are associated with colours. The Azāriqah, although named after a certain Ibn Azraq, are, at least etymologically, associated with blue, the Muḥammirah (followers of Pāpak) with red, and the Mubayyiḍah (followers of Abū Muslim) with white (Bertold Spuler, Iran in früh-islamischer Zeit, Akademie der Wissenschaften und der Literature, Veröffentlichungen der orientalischen Kommission 2 [Wiesbaden, 1952], pp. 168 f., 198, 200 f.). Shahrastānī records the name of a sect called Māhānīyah (Māhān!), a subdivision of the Mazdakites (Muḥammad al-Shahrastānī, Book of Religious and Philosophical Sects, ed. William Cureton, 2 parts [London, 1842-1846], p. 194; idem, Religionspartheien und Philosophen-Schulen, trans. Theodor Haarbrücker, 2 vols. [Halle, 1850-1851], p. 298). On the associatioh of colours with religions, see also the story of the "Petrified Prince" (1001 Nights, night 8): Jews--yellow, Christians--blue, Magians--red, Muslims--white.

[58] The king had previously announced that whoever tried to cure his daughter but failed, would be beheaded. Good thus takes a calculated risk similar to that of the prince on Tuesday. This looks like an additional tie for the second group of three stories which are connected by the intervention of an old man.

[59] Bad's excuse that his name predestined him to be bad reflects the old controversy over the freedom of man's will. The reader is left with a feeling that Bad's execution in spite of Good's mercy is meant as a mockery of predestinatarianism.

[60] See the context before note 15.

[61] The four mishaps must be a reference to the vagaries and unreliability of the material world.

[62] Cf. note 6.

[63] Cf. notes 56 and 58.

[64] It is characteristic that the successful adept is met by two persons. Thus "two prudent counsels" greet the adept who has managed to enter the Hermetic citadel (Emile Grillot De Givry, Picture Museum of Sorcery, Magic and Alchemy [New York: University Books, 1963], p. 349), and the hero of the Song of the Pearl is met by two chancellors upon his return from Egypt (Robert Haardt, Gnosis, Character and Testimony [Leiden: Brill, 1971], p. 165). In the seventh journey of Sindbad (according to the Calcutta 1830 edition), in an otherwise confused and enigmatic context, two youths with golden staffs prove beneficial to Sindbad (night 565).

[65] Larousse Encyclopedia of Astrology, English edition (New York: McGraw-Hill, 1980), pp. 123 f. and 290 f.

[66] HP, ed. Ritter and Rypka, p.8 verse 8; trans. Wilson, 1: 6 ult. Also in Niẓāmī Ganjavī, Khusraw va Shīrīn, ed. L.A. Khetagurov (Baku, 1960), p. 5 verse 27; ed. Dastgardī, 2: 4 verse 11. The enneadic structure of reality in Neoplatonism (Stephen Gersh, From

Iamblichus to Eriugena, Studien zur Problemgeschichte der antiken und mittelalterlichen Philosophie 8 [Leiden: Brill, 1978], pp. 129 ff.) is reflected in, among others, the Rasā'il Ikhwān al-Ṣafā', epistles 3 and 16. Turkish guilds allied with the futuwwah had nine degrees (EI[2], s.v. Akhī).

67 Bahrām's eyes are opened by the tale of a shepherd whom he meets during a hunt. This is somewhat reminiscent of the story of King Nūshīrwān in the second discourse of Niẓāmī's Makhzan al-Asrār (ed. A.A. Ali-Zade [Baku, 1960], pp. 95 ff.; trans. Darab, pp. 157 ff.).

68 The notion of justice had already been advanced in the context of the fight with the dragon, which anticipates the final hunt (HP, ed. Ritter and Rypka, p. 57 verse 32; trans. Wilson, 1: 53 verse 8); cf. note 21. Justice was the principal attribute requested from the shaykh of a guild in Egypt (Gabriel Baer, Egyptian Guilds in Modern Times, The Israel Oriental Society, Oriental Notes and Studies 8 [Jerusalem, 1964], p. 56. The need to combine knowledge with action was stressed repeatedly by Muslim authors (Rosenthal, pp. 39, 92 and 268). Cf. Corbin, p. 109: "It is under [the] influence [of the Active Intelligence] that the gnostic progresses on the way, and finally, by uniting with it, the mystical Sage is put in the same situation as the Prophet."

69 The Akhī movement is not well documented for the period of Niẓāmī's lifetime, which led some critics to discount the possibility of his membership in it. The organization was, however, well established all over Anatolia a little over a century later. There they are described as "a brotherhood with a multiplicity of interests and functions, [which] wielded extensive political power, limiting the absolutist tendencies of Anatolian Turkish emirs . . ." (G.C. Arnakis, "Futuwwa Traditions in the Ottoman Empire, Akhis, Bektashi Dervishes, Craftsmen," Journal of Near Eastern Studies, 12 [1953], 247b). The silence of the sources should not be sufficient reason to deny that Niẓāmī could have been one of the ideologists of the brotherhood during its formative period.

8

A Royal Tīmūrid Nativity Book

Laurence P. Elwell-Sutton †
The University of Edingburgh

Although most collections of Islamic manuscripts contain numerous specimens of astronomical and astrological works, few have been studied in depth, partly perhaps because of their difficulty, but even more, I suspect, because astrology in this rational age is regarded as a discredited science, not worthy of the attention of serious scholars. This attitude is an unfortunate one, not because there is a case for the resurrection (if it ever died) of predictive or judicial astrology, but because so much of medieval Islamic literature, philosophy, history and science is permeated with astrological lore. Indeed the clear dividing line that we recognize today, between astronomy as the science of observing and measuring the heavenly bodies and their movements, and astrology as the art of determining the influences exerted on human affairs by the reading of the stars, did not exist in the medieval Islamic world. ᶜIlm al-hay'a covered equally the measurement of astronomical and of astrological phenomena, while ahkām al-nujūm was concerned with the interpretation of these phenomena; but both were regarded as part of the same science.

A variety of astrological document that is surprisingly rare in the library collections (surprising, because most people of any standing must have had one prepared, if not at birth, then on some other important occasion) is the individual horoscope or "nativity book" (kitāb-i vilādah). Presumably their disappearance may be accounted for by the fact that they were of interest only to the individual to whom they applied. Yet, judging by the specimens that are readily available, they can repay study, since they may constitute almost a complete treatise on astrological principles, complete with worked examples.

Logos Islamikos: Studia Islamica in honorem Georgii Michaelis Wickens, ed. Roger M. Savory and Dionisius A. Agius, Papers in Mediaeval Studies 6 (Toronto: Pontifical Institute of Mediaeval Studies, 1984), pp. 119-136.

The subject of the present paper is one such work - a nativity book compiled in Persian for one of the grandsons of Tīmūr-i Lang. It is now in the library of the Wellcome Institute for the History of Medicine in London, and I have in particular to express my thanks to Dr. Nigel Allan, Curator of Oriental Books and Manuscripts, and to Miss Fāṭimah Kishāvarz, to whom falls the credit of having discovered this manuscript and recognized its interest. Since Miss Kishāvarz is preparing a detailed description for the introduction to a catalogue of the Institute's Persian books and manuscripts, I do not propose to do that here, and will concentrate on the astronomical and astrological aspects of the work.

Iskandar Sulṭān, third son of Tīmūr's second son ᶜUmar Shaykh, was Governor of Fārs from 812/1409 to 817/1414, and also of Iṣfahān for the last two years of his reign. In the latter year he was deposed and blinded on the orders of his uncle Shāh Rukh, third ruler of the Tīmūrid line. Iskandar during his short reign achieved a reputation as a patron of the arts and sciences, and anthologies compiled for him (examples are in the British Library, the Yates Thompson collection, and the Gulbenkian Museum in Lisbon)[1] show the great breadth of his interests, covering poetry, Ṣūfism, philosophy, law, history, medicine, and mathematics, as well as astronomy and astrology.

The document under consideration establishes for the first time Iskandar's precise date of birth--3rd Rabīᶜ I, 786, equivalent to 25 April 1384. The horoscope was not however prepared at the time of his birth, but on 22nd Dhū 'l-ḥijja, 813/18 April 1411, when he was approaching his twenty-seventh (solar) birthday. The emphasis on the solar reckoning is not as misplaced as it might seem, since astrological predictions are normally based on the solar calendar, and in fact the present horoscope offers prognostications for Iskandar's twenty-eighth solar year onwards. There is nothing in the history books (e.g., Ẓafarnāmah, Ḥabīb al-Siyar)[2] to suggest why this date was important; it was some time after the murder of Iskandar's elder brother Pīr Muḥammad and his own accession to the rule of Fārs, but at least a year before his occupation of Iṣfahān in 815/1412. To those concerned with the history of Islamic science, however, the date is of particular interest, for this must be one of the last astronomical works to have been compiled before the exhaustive reobservations carried by Iskandar's cousin Ulugh Beg in 841/1437.

The nativity book was compiled by Maḥmūd ibn Yaḥyā ibn al-Ḥasan ibn Muḥammad ᶜImād al-Munajjim al-Kāshī, of whom nothing else seems to be known, and consists of 86 folios written in a small neat naskh hand. Dots are frequently omitted, and in general there is no distinction of the Persian letters pah, chīn, zhah and gāf. Figures are usually written in red, and in a number of cases the copyist (al-Kāshī himself?) has failed to insert them in the appropriate places. The folios have been numbered in reverse order in a European hand, so that the manuscript begins with folio 86 and ends with folio 1.

The work opens with a standard invocation of God, to which are added numerous quotations from the Qur'ān referring to the heavenly bodies, perhaps with the purpose of reconciling the practice of astrology with the tenets of orthodox Islam — though the passages are hardly specific enough to warrant such a conclusion: "Say: Consider ye whatever is in the Heavens" (10: 101); "He created the Sun and the Moon and the stars subjected to laws by His behest" (7: 54); "It is He who hath appointed the Sun for brightness and the Moon for a light, and hath ordained her stations that ye may learn the number of years and the reckoning of time" (5: 5); "Blessed be He who hath placed in the Heaven the signs of the Zodiac! Who hath placed in it the Lamp of the Sun and the light-giving Moon!" (25: 61).[3] Similar quotations from the Qur'ān occur at intervals throughout the book, as do citations from other authorities — the Samarah and Arbaᶜ Maqālāt of Ptolemy, the Kitāb-i Asās of Hirmis (Hermes Trismegistus), Dorotheus the Syrian, Abū Maᶜshar Balkhī, Kūshyār, The Jāmiᶜ-i Shāhī of Aḥmad al-Sajzī, the Mutawassiṭāt of Naṣīr al-Dīn Ṭūsī, and the Kitāb al-Mawālīd (no author given).

There follow laudatory descriptions of Iskandar (seven lines), of his father ᶜUmar Shaykh (three lines), and of his grandfather Tīmūr (five lines). The date of Iskandar's birth is then given in the Hijrī form (Monday, 3rd Rabīᶜ I, 786), Jalālī/Malikshāhī (15th Urdībihisht, 306), Yazdijirdī (17th Murdād, 753), and Rūmī/Iskandarī (255th Nīsān, 1695). These offer no unusual features, but there then follows a somewhat complex passage giving the same date according to the Chinese-Uygur reckoning,[4] which runs as follows:

104 1/10 fink elapsed of the 8th kih of the 12th

> chāgh, which is called in Khatā'ī khāy [and in Turkish] ṭunghūz, of the eighth day of the sexagesimal cycle, which in Qatā'ī [sic] is called sin vī, and in Turkish qūy . . . .

This is somewhat obscure, as in the Chinese-Uygur reckoning the day is divided into 10,000 fink (Chinese fen),[5] grouped into twelve chāgh (Chinese shi) of eight kih (Chinese ke) each; each kih therefore equals 104 1/6 fink. The last chāgh of the day is known as khāy (Chinese hai) or ṭunghūz (pig), and the passage would seem to imply that the birth took place 1/16 of a fink (i.e., about 6/10 of a second) before the end of the day in question. This day is described as sin vī (Chinese xin wei), which combines the eight elements in the duodecimal and decimal cycles, and so designates the eighth day of the sixty-day week. The term corresponds to the Turkish qūy (sheep), used for the eighth element in a series (double-hours, days, months, or years). This sixty-day week evidently began on 18 April, though how this could be calculated is not clear.

The passage continues:

> . . . According to the fourth cycle, which is favoured by the people of Qatā, on the fourth day called pin, described as khī, 3 days and 4,215 fink (in figures 3,1,10,15) past the beginning (madkhal) of dūrdinj āy . . . .

The fourth cycle, described by Ulugh Beğ as ikhtiyār-i rūz, or in Ideler and Ginzel's German Wahlzyklus, is a twelve-day cycle four of whose days are considered to be khī (Chinese hei), "black, unlucky"; these include the fourth day pin (Chinese ping). The figure of the number of fink is given (as also in the passage that follows) in both the decimal and sexagesimal systems; thus 3,1,10,15=3 days, 1x60x60 + 10x60 + 15 = 3 days, 4215 fink. Dūrdinj āy is the fourth month of the Turkish-Uygur year. Following Ginzel's method of calculation, we find that the fourteenth day of the fourth month fell on 30 April, which would make the fourth day 20 April, a discrepancy of five days. But the correlation of these months with the Christian and other eras is not very straightforward.

> . . . and 10 days and 8677 fink (in figures 10,2,24,37) past the beginning of the section (qism) of kūwū, which is the sixth section fo the first year of the khā vin cycle, which year is called kā zha in Khaṭā'ī and kiskū or sījqān in Turkish . . . .

Khā vin (Chinese hsia wan) the third of the three 60-year parts of the Uygur 180-year cycle, which began on 29 January 1384. Following Ulugh Beğ and Ideler, kūwū (Chinese gu yu) is the sixth half-month of the Uygur year and the last section of spring, and begins 76.0924 days after the beginning of the year; to this we add 10.8677, which gives us 86.9601--say, 87. Adding the 29 days of January we arrive at the 116th day of the Christian year, that is, 25 April. Kā and zhah (Chinese jia zi) are the first days respectively of the decimal and duodecimal cycles, and are combined to indicate the first day of the sixty-day week. Kiskū and sījqān are alternative names for the Turkish year of the Rat.

> . . . There had elapsed since the creation of the world 8863 complete vin, and of the incomplete vin 9860 years, the above-mentioned year being the incomplete year.

Vin (Chinese wan) is a period of 10,000 years. The reckoning is therefore 88,639,860 complete years elapsed of the world era, the event of Iskandar's birth taking place during the following year (or to put it another way, the creation of the world took place in 88,638,477 BC). Oddly enough Ulugh Beğ, calculating for a date (847/1444) sixty years later, gives exactly the same figure for the world date. In the absence of geological or archaeological confirmation, we can only speculate on the reasons for this discrepancy!

A brief section gives the place of birth as Ūzgand, in the fifth clime, 102° 55' east of the meridian of the Fortunate Isles (Jazāyir-i Khālidāt), and 44° north of the equator. The coordinates of the modern town of Uzgen are given (in the Times Atlas of the World) as 73° 14' E and 40° 48' N, which gives a difference between the meridians of Greenwich and the Fortunate Isles of 29° 41'. This is somewhat less than the usual reckoning, which ranges between 33° and 34° 30'. This, coupled with the substantial difference in latitude (more than can be accounted for by inaccurate observation) suggests that the old Ūzgand may have been some distance from the modern Uzgen.[6]

The time of birth, according to the rāṣid va mutaraṣṣid-i āftāb-i īn dawlat, was four equal hours of the night, and a series of calculations lead to the conclusion that the estimated Ascendant was 9s 0° 56', and the Tenth House 6s 27° 0'. However al-Kāshī, like many other astrologers, attaches more importance to the moment of conception, and this involves the use of namūdārāt, essentially methods of estimating this event. By the Ptolemaic method, the Dominant (mustawlī) must be found, which in this case turns out to be Venus, and a complex chain of calculations leads to the result that the estimated degree of the Ascendant is 9s 0° 26' 49". However, according to Hirmis, "the position of the Moon at the time of birth is the Ascendant of the Conception, and at the conception the Ascendant of the Birth." Calculating on this basis, al-Kāshī finds that the moment of conception was 286 days before the birth, or 5th Ābān 752 Yazdijirdī (equivalent to 25 July 1383). Further calculations give the relevant degree of the Ascendant as 9s 0° 8' 22". Finally, the namūdār of Abū Maᶜshar Balkhī, which according to our astrologer is the most accurate (bih-ṣavāb awlītar), is arrived at simply by splitting the difference between the other two, giving the figure 9s 0° 17' 35", while the Tenth House is 6s 27° 6' 24" (this latter figure is derived from tables). These figures are the basis of subsequent calculations.

Al-Kāshī now turns to the important task of demarcating the cusps of the other Houses (tasviyat al-buyūt), but unfortunately at this point there is some confusion in the manuscript. Folio 85 (it will be remembered that the folios are numbered in reverse order) is out of place, and should follow folio 83, while at least one folio is missing between folios 84 and 83. Thus the correct sequence is 86, 84, X, 83, 85, 82, 81 . . . We have therefore only part of the first of two methods approved by the astrologer, the so-called ṭarīq-i mashhūr, and that of the marākiz-i muḥaqqaqah. Although the first part is incomplete, it is accompanied by a diagram, and it is clear that the Alcabitian (al-Qabīsī) method is used, based on the temporal hours.[7] Details of the second method used are unfortunately lost; folio 83 starts with the last two lines of the calculation of the longitudes of Mercury and the Ascending and Descending Nodes at the time of birth (or conception). As the next section deals with the calculation of the latitudes of the planets, we may assume that the missing folio(s), as well as completing the equalization of the Houses, contained a calculation of the longitudes of the other planets.

Two brief notes follow on the sectors (niṭāqāt) and the direct motion (istiqāmah) and retrogression (rujūᶜ) of the planets, and then an even briefer note on the seven imaginary malevolent planets (*dhavāt-i adhnāb*), whose names are given as *ghaṭīṭ*, *gharīm*, *sar-i mūsh*, *kalāb*, *liḥyānī*, *dhū zu'āba*, and *kayd*. Unfortunately no further details are given, even though the heading to the note promises their positions (*mavāzi^{c}*).[8]

There follows a passage on the motions of Mercury at the time of the nativity, illustrated by a diagram.[9] This uses the Ptolemaic theories of deferents and epicycles to explain the apparently erratic movements of Mercury and (on a lesser scale) the other planets.

The astrologer's next task is to establish the distance (*bu^{c}d*) of the planets from the equator (*mu^{c}addil al-nahār*); this is also known as the *mayl-i awwal* (first declination). Following this comes the calculation of the *muṭāli^{c} al-mamarr*,[10] defined as "an arc of the equator between the vernal equinox and the point of intersection of the equator with the declination circle passing through the centre of the planet." The degree of transit (*darajah-'i mamarr*) is the point of intersection of the ecliptic with the above-mentioned declination circle. After calculation of the degrees of rising and setting (*maṭāli^{c} al-ṭulū^{c} wa 'l-ghurūb*) of the planets, al-Kāshī then turns to the *ufuq-i ḥādith* (the accidental horizon), "a great circle passing through the intersection of the meridian and the horizon and the centre of the planet." There is an illustration of this in geometrical form, followed by mathematical calculations of the *ufuq-i ḥādith* for the seven planets and the Pars Fortunae (see infra), and of the *mutāli^{c}-i muṣaḥḥaḥ*, which is defined as an arc of the equinoctial between the vernal equinox and the *ufuq-i ḥādith*. From these the *maṭāriḥ-i muṣaḥḥaḥ* (the projections of the rays) can be computed, that is, the aspects of sextile, quartile and trine to the right and left of the planet.

The astrologer now turns to the *sihām* or Lots, a set of mobile points in the heavens that, although they have no physical existence, are considered like the planets to exert influence on human affairs; their positions are generally arrived at by adding the distance between two given planets to the degree of the Ascendant. For instance, to find the position of the Lot of Fortune (*sahm al-sa^{c}āda*, Pars Fortunae), the difference in longitude between the Sun and the Moon at the time of the nativity must be added to the degree of the Ascendant, thus:

Sun	$1^{s}\ 12^{\circ}\ 39'$
− Moon	$2^{s}\ 21^{\circ}\ 29'$
	$9^{s}\ 21^{\circ}\ 10'$
+ Ascendant	$9^{s}\ 0^{\circ}\ 18'$
	$7^{s}\ 21^{\circ}\ 28'$

Similarly, for the Lot of Daemon (sahm al-ghayb) the figure is the difference between the Moon and the Sun (reckoning always against the direction of the Signs of the Zodiac). Other well-known Lots listed by al-Kāshī are the Lot of Victory (sahm al-ẓafar), the Lot of Courage (sahm al-shujāᶜah), the Lot of Life (sahm al-ḥayāt), and so on. It will be evident that each is relevant to a different aspect of the native's affairs. Maḥmūd al-Kāshī however does not explain how he calculates the positions that he lists at this point for 26 Lots, simply stating that he has used the method of Abū Maᶜshar. Elsewhere in the manuscript he lists 22 (all included in the above list), while in the table referred to later he has no fewer than 47. This compares with, for example, Abū Maᶜshar's list of 97, al-Qabīsī's 130, and Bīrūnī's 158.

This section completes the examination of the planets and other moving points in the heavens, and al-Kāshī now turns to the fixed stars, an important element in Islamic astrology, though generally ignored by western astrologers. Like Ptolemy, he regards them as being set in the eighth sphere, but he also states that, according to "the most learned of the moderns" (afzal al-muta'akhkhirīn), they travel with respect to the Zodiac one degree in seventy years. It is not quite clear when this figure was established, since earlier Islamic astronomers (for instance the compilers of the Zīj al-mumtaḥan [ca. 200/815], followed by al-Battānī [ca. 264/876] and, ᶜAbd al-Raḥmān al-Ṣūfī [354/965]) reckoned precession at one degree in 66 years. It has commonly been implied that the more accurate estimate of one degree in 70 years was established by Ulugh Beğ in the middle of the ninth/fifteenth century. However the seventh/thirteenth century Naṣīr al-dīn Ṭūsī also has a claim, for, though in his translation of Ṣūfī's catalogue of stars he repeated (presumably with approval) his figure of 66 years, a table in his own Zīj-i Il-khānī (ca. 658/1260)--or at any rate in the fifteenth century manuscript of this work in the Cambridge University Library (Browne O.2)--would imply that he had already arrived at the figure of 70. The point can only be settled by reference to an earlier manuscript of the work, but even if this table proves to be a fifteenth century interpolation, the al-Kāshī manuscript is evidence that this figure was not established by Ulugh Beğ, who was only sixteen when his cousin's nativity book was compiled.

Al-Kāshī follows Ptolemy (as subsequently did Ulugh Beğ) in giving the number of the fixed stars as 1022, classified into six magnitudes, and stresses their influence on the *tasyīrāt* (apheses, the directions of the progressed horoscope) and the *^{c}aṭāyā* (allowances, the years of life allotted to the native by the *hīlāj*), so that they can "raise a *bāzārī* to kingship or to high rank." He provides a selected list of the 84 most influential stars, and calculates their longitude, latitude, and degrees of rising and transit. This list is repeated later in the manuscript in tabular form, together with the *mizājāt* (temperaments), the latter expressed in the shape of the two planets whose qualities the star in question is held to share. The longitudes and latitudes all follow Ptolemy's list of 139 A.D., with the addition to the longitudes of 18° 56' for precession. Presumably al-Kāshī did not use the Ptolemaic tables directly, especially as, reckoning at 70 years to the degree, 1245 years would give only 17° 47'. Nor presumably did he use Ṣūfī's catalogue of 354/965, which was 12° 42' ahead of Ptolemy's figures, but to which he would only have added, at 70 years to the degree, 5° 59', making a total of 18° 41'. The figures point to a table compiled in about 658/1260 on the basis of Ṣūfī's catalogue, that is, 12° 42' + 4° 28' (295 years at 66 to the degree) + 1° 46' (124 years at 70 to the degree), making up the total of 18° 56'.[11]

Following the discussion of the fixed stars, al-Kāshī turns to an explanation of the concepts of the *hīlāj* and the *kadkhudāh*, whose function is to influence the native's length of life. "All things," al-Kāshī points out, "must have a cause," the ultimate First Cause (*sabab al-asbāb*) being God. The *hīlāj* is the indicator causing the movement of the *tasyīr* (aphesis, progress) of the native's horoscope throughout his life. According to tradition, the *hīlāj* is to be sought in five places: (a) the Lord of the Day of Night (*rabb al-nawba*), that is, the Sun by day and the Moon by night; (b) the Moon by day or the Sun by night; (c) the Degree of the Ascendant; (d) the Lot of Fortune; (e) the conjunction or opposition immediately before the nativity. The *kadkhudāh* is the planet dominant over the place of the hīlāj, that is, the Lord of the House, or the Lord of the Exaltation, and so on. The function of the hīlāj and the kadkhudāh in the astrologer's task is to determine the length of the native's life. As al-Kāshī puts it, the hīlāj corresponds to the body, and the kadkhudah to the soul. In the present case there are three hilajat — the Sun, the Pars Fortunae, and the juzw (conjunction), and one kadkhudāh — Venus. Venus being, at 11^s 27° 18', between the Succedent (zāyil) (11^s 15° 43' 47") and the Cusp of the Fourth House (0^s 27° 6' 24") gives an ^{c}aṭīya between its greater (82.0) and lesser (8) ^{c}aṭāyā. Venus' ^{c}aṭīya is strengthened by Jupiter and Mercury, both of whom are in sextile to Venus, and weakened by the Moon, which is in quartile. Venus' ^{c}aṭīya works out at 28° 41' 27", to which must be added the combined ^{c}aṭāyā of Jupiter and Mercury at 15° 19' 36", less the negative (nāqiṣa) ^{c}aṭīya of the Moon, 13° 10' 41", leaving a net total of 30° 50' 22", equivalent to 30 years, 10 months, 6 days, and 10 hours. Sceptics may care to ponder the fact that this must have been very close to Iskandar's actual age when he fell victim to his uncle's hostility!

The final calculation gives the positions of the planets on the falak-i mumaththal at the moment of conception, and the same calculations were evidently intended for the sihām, of which 22 are listed here; but the spaces for their positions have been left blank. There follows a table giving the zodiacal position, Lord (ṣāḥib), Lord of Exaltation (ṣāḥib al-sharaf). Lords of the Limits (arbāb al-ḥudūd), the Triplicities (muthallathāt), the Decans (wujūh) and the Dominant (mustawlī) in respect of each of the Twelve Houses, the seven Planets, the two Nodes, the juzw, the Asendant of the Conception (ṭāli^{c} al-masqaṭ), and 47 sihām. Much of this information has already been recorded during the processes of calculation, and is presumably repeated here for ease of reference. This is followed by the star catalogue already discussed, and with this is concluded the mathematical section of the nativity book.

However, inserted rather incongruously into the middle of this last table (but evidently part of the original manuscript, since it is on the obverse and reverse of two folios of the catalogue) is an elaborate two-page painting of the horoscope, presumably added by an artist other than al-Kāshī himself. It is not my intention here to discuss the artistic merits of this miniature,[12] but simply to indicate the contents. In the four corners are four angels (as in the "Kühnel" miniature) supporting a circle representing the twelve astrological Houses, each House being identified in a band of script surrounding the circle. Each of the twelve sectors contains a small circle with the conventionl representation of the corresponding Sign of the Zodiac, and between these and the centre of the design are listed the Limits, Lords of the House, Lords of the Triplicities, Lord of the Exaltation, the *Darījān*, and the Dominant. In four of the Houses are representations of the Planets: Venus in the Third House, Jupiter in the Fifth, Mercury, the Moon and Saturn and a fourth unidentified figure in the Sixth, and Mars in the Eleventh.[13] This chart is in fact the only representation of the horoscope in the nativity book, there being no diagram in the conventional square form. However we may tabulate its significant features as follows:

First House:	Cusp	9^{s} 0° 18'
Second House:	Cusp	10^{s} 6° 12'
	Descending Node	11^{s} 2° 58'
Third House:	Cusp	11^{s} 15° 44'
	Venus	11^{s} 27° 18'
Fourth House:	Cusp	0^{s} 27° 6'
	Sun	1^{s} 12° 39'
	juzw	1^{s} 9° 11'
Fifth House:	Cusp	1^{s} 19° 20'
	Mercury	2^{s} 0° 17'
	Jupiter	2^{s} 2° 28'
Sixth House:	Cusp	2^{s} 10° 14'
	Moon	2^{s} 21° 19'
	Saturn	2^{s} 15° 29'
Seventh House:	Cusp	3^{s} 0° 18'
Eighth House:	Cusp	4^{s} 6° 12'
	Ascending Node	5^{s} 2° 28'
Ninth House:	Cusp	5^{s} 15° 44'
Tenth House:	Cusp	6^{s} 27° 6'
	Mars	7^{s} 1° 25'
Eleventh House:	Cusp	7^{s} 19° 20'
	Pars Fortunae	7^{s} 21° 38'
Twelfth House:	Cusp	8^{s} 10° 14'
Hīlāj:	Sun, Pars Fortunae, *juzw*	
Kadkhudāh:	Venus	

The astrologer now turns to what was presumably the justification for the whole work, and yet turns out to be somewhat disappointing, that is to say, the interpretation of the astronomical findings (*aḥkām al-nujūm*). These he divides into two categories, the basic influences (*aḥkām-i aṣlī*) surrounding the conception and birth of the native, and the influences affecting him in later life, which are determined by the *tasyīrāt*, *intihā'āt* (profections), *tawāli^{c}-i* taḥwīlāt (ascendants of the anniversaries), fardārāt (planets ruling certain periods), and rabb al-nawba (Lord of the Day or Night). According to Ptolemy, says al-Kāshī, the astrologer can help the native to ward off any evil influences that may show up in his horoscope or its aphesis. "The wise soul manages the actions of the heavens, just as the farmer manages the power of nature by ploughing and watering."

The prognostications are classified under the twelve astrological Houses, each one of which affects a different aspect of the native's being. Thus the Ascendant relates to his life, body and soul, the Second House to his property, livelihood, helpers and friends, the Third House to brothers and relatives and to travel, and so on. Since the hīlāj and the kadkhudāh are strong in the Ascendant, the native will be long-lived, prosperous and successful. Mars, both as Lord of the Exaltation and being in Sextile in the Eleventh House, guarantees victory in war and conquest. ᶜAyn al-Rāmī (ν Sagittarii) in the Ascendant (at 9^s 4° 6') is a sign of danger, but with Mars in sextile this will soon pass. In general the prognostications maintain this favourable tone, and even where they do not (as in the last sentence above), the astrologer shows great ingenuity in offsetting any unfavourable suggestions with balancing favourable ones, so as to present his findings in the most attractive light. Other examples (chosen at random) are:

Third House:

> . . . since Mars is retrograde and Mercury also at the point of retrogression, this indicates that the brothers and relatives of His Excellency will envy his rank and status, and trickery, plotting and opposition will arise among them . . . but Jupiter in the Succedent indicates that this group will always be frustrated and despondent, and no misfortune will accrue . . .

Sixth House:

> . . . since the Lot of Illness is in Cancer, and the Moon and Saturn are in this (the Sixth) House, this indicates that His Excellency will enjoy balanced health and soundness of person, and ill-health will seldom occur. If sometimes a little deviation of the constitution takes place from excess of blood and phlegm, weakness of the stomach, and deficiency in digestion, since Mercury is with Jupiter, this indicates that with a little treatment the trouble will soon be removed . . .

Seventh House:

> . . . since the Lot of Enmity is in Gemini with Jupiter and

> Mercury, this indicates that there will be many enemies and opponents, but outwardly they will express concord, and they will always be ruined, distressed and despondent . . .

The next stage is the tabulating of the tasyīrāt and the accompanying features. The tasyīr is the movement of a particular point on the Ecliptic associated with the native across the heavens as in position at the moment of nativity. The movement of such points is thought of as being forced or "directed" by the hīlāj. Each degree of movement is reckoned as being equivalent to one year of life. The present horoscope is very detailed in this respect. Many horoscopes limit themselves to the movement of the four Angles (the Ascendant, Fourth, Seventh and Tenth Houses), but al-Kāshī's work gives tasyīr tables for each of the twelve Houses, the seven Planets, and the Pars Fortunae. Each of these, as we have already seen, is regarded as affecting a different aspect of the native's being. Each table lists, for 88 solar years of the native's life, the tasyīr reading for each year, the intihā' and the qāsim, that is, the point at which the tasyīr moves from the influence of one planet to another (from beneficent to maleficent, and so on), in some tables only the corresponding Malikī year, and the indications (al-dalāyil al-aṣlīya for each year. Under this last head are listed the significant astrological points encountered by the tasyīr — for instance, aspects (trine, quartile, sextile) with the planets, Lots, the degrees of certain fixed stars (jirm, taqwīm, darajah-'i mamarr, and various other points. The tables for Houses I and VII are stated as calculated for the horizon of the place of birth, for Houses IV and X the Equator, and the remainder, including the planets and the Pars Fortunae, for its accidental horizon (ufiq-i ḥādith). The table (ḥādith) for the Pars Fortunae carries an additional column showing the fardārāt and their degress (maṭāli^{c}-i ṭāli^{c} al-taḥwīl); for instance, Year One is ruled by the Moon at 295° 8' 47", and so on with various readings for the next eight years, when Saturn takes its place, to be followed in due course by all the other planets. These tables occupy 39 folios, and so constitute a major part of the manuscript. One folio is missing between folios 35 and 34, part of the tasyīr table for Jupiter. These tables are followed by monthly tables for each of the first twelve years of the native's life, the same tables being valid for the subsequent twelve-year periods up to his 84th year. All these tables will repay further study, especially as many of the *dalāyil* are expressed in abbreviated form, some elements of which are difficult to interpret.[14]

There now follow as before the *aḥkām* of these *tasyīr* tables, first of all a general one, and then for the individual years from the 28th to the 40th of his life. The years from 28 to 34 will be prosperous because the *tasyīr* of the Sun moves from the *ḥadd* of Mercury (of mixed influence) to that of Jupiter (beneficent), while the *tasyīrāt* of the Ascendant, the Lord of the House (Saturn), the Pars Fortunae, and Venus are all in favourable *ḥudūd*. Since the *tasyīr* of the Twelfth House will be in the *ḥadd* of Mars, the native will be victorious over his enemies. At the end of the 34th and beginning of the 35th years the *tasyīr* of the Tenth House comes under the influence of maleficent fixed stars (Qalb al-^{c}Aqrab (Antares) and Ra's al-Jabbār (λ Orionis), having the temperaments of Mars and Jupiter, and Mars and Mercury respectively), while the *intihā'* of the Ascendant comes under the influence of Mars and the opposition of the Sun; all this indicates a period of hostility, anxiety and fear. Sadly for Iskandar, this state of affairs had already risen by his 30th year, so that he was unable to benefit from his astrologer's warnings.

At this point a flowery Arabic colophon provides the name of the astrologer and the date (but not the place — presumably Shīrāz) of composition, and so signals the end of the book; but in fact there now follow tables for the Yazdijirdī years 781-791 (equivalent to 4 December 1411, to 27 November 1422, and thus to years 28 to 38 of Iskandar's life) giving the daily positions of the seven planets and the Moon's Ascending Node. Once again, a folio appears to be missing between folios 69 and 68, as only part of the first year's table is present. Finally, apart from some extraneous additions of a literary nature in a much later hand, the nativity book concludes with twelve *zāychas* (horoscope diagrams) for the ascendants of the above years (*ṭāli^{c}-i sāl*), with the addition of the Yazdijirdī year 792, showing the position of the planets in the Zodiacal Signs (together with some of the fixed stars, which of course do not change significantly within so short a period). Each *zāycha* is accompanied by a brief prognostication, which follows much the same pattern as before, though occasionally somewhat more specific:

Year 781: ". . . there will be rebellion in the neighbourhood of

Kirmān . . ."
783: ". . . there will be rebellion, disturbance and war in the area of Balkh and Kirmān . . ."
784: ". . . there will be an earthquake in ᶜIrāq . . ."
785: ". . . the armies of Fārs and ᶜIrāq will be on the move . . ."
787: ". . . there will be war and rebellion in the region of ᶜIrāq and Fārs . . . the lower classes will dominate some of the provinces of Khurāsān . . ."
790: ". . . there will be war in Gīlān and Māzandarān, and one of the governors of that region will be disgraced . . ."

The cynic might comment that such predictions (except perhaps for the earthquake) were pretty safe in that time and place.

The foregoing has provided a very general survey of the contents of this Nativity Book. Much more could be done in the way of checking and collating the calculations, while on the other hand it could be argued that it is of purely ephemeral interest, relating as it does to a particular individual at one point in time. I would not accept this criticism. Astronomy/astrology was one of the major medieval Islamic sciences; it was also evidently a much more complex affair than a reading of modern "newspaper" horoscopes would suggest, involving as it does abstruse arithmetical, geometrical and trigonometrical operations. Indeed it is arguable that it was to the compilation of "nativity books" that most of the very sophisticated mathematics and astronomy of the Muslim middle ages was directed.[15] Heinrich Friedrich von Diez, commenting in 1811 on his own translation of the Qābūsnāmah, made much the same point: "How many good inventions and contrivances would have been lost to the world if there had been no pursuit by chemists of the Philosopher's Stone, by mechanical scientists of perpetual motion, by geometricians of the square of the circle, by politicians of the balance of power, and by moralists of altruism."[16]

But even if no other justification were available, Islamic astronomy is a field of fascinating and inexhaustible interest that fully rewards the time and effort put into its study.

Notes

[1] British Library, MS Add. 27, 261; A Descriptive Catalogue of the Second Series of Fifty Manuscripts (Nos. 50-100) in the Collection of Henry Yates Thompson (Cambridge, 1902), pp. 358-363, No. 100. See also Basil Gray, Persian Painting (London, 1961), pp. 69-73. I am

grateful to Dr. Robert Hillenbrand for drawing my attention to these references, and to other sources on astrology in Islamic art referred to in this paper.

2 I have not yet had the opportunity of examining the anonymous biography of Iskandar Sulṭān, a copy of which is in the British Library, MS Or. 1566.

3 Rodwell's translation.

4 There is a description of the Chinese-Uygur calendar in the introduction to Ulugh Beg's Zīj-i Sulṭānī, of which a very full explanation summary was published by Ludwig Ideler, "Über die Zeitrechnung von Chata und Igur," Abh. der K. Akad. der Wiss. zu Berlin (1832), pp. 271-299. The Persian text is found in Maqālah I, Bāb 6 (Prolégomènes des tables astronomiques d'Oloug-Beg publiés avec notes et variantes et précédés d'une introduction par L.P.E.A. Sédillot [Paris, 1847], pp. 30-56). A French translation followed in 1853, the section on the Chinese-Uygur calendar being found on pages 32-61. A somewhat condensed version, with much other material, is to be found in F. K. Ginzel, Handbuch der mathematischen und technischen Chronologie (Leipzig, 1906), 1: 450-540.

5 I am indebted to Dr. J. D. Chinnery for identifying and transliterating the Chinese words that follow.

6 The problem of the position of the imaginary Fortunate Isles, the meridian of which was taken by the Islamic geographers, following the Greeks, as the starting point for reckoning the longitude of points on the terrestrial globe, seems to have been ignored by most scholars. D. M. Dunlop's article, "al-Djazā'ir al-khālida" (EI^2, p. 522), does not mention the point, but tends to identify them with the Canary Islands, which are some 20° too far east. G. R. Kaye, The Astronomical Observatories of Jai Singh (Calcutta, 1918), p. 25 suggests that the meridian was approximately 35° west of Greenwich, or the same of the Azores.

7 For a full description of this method see my The Horoscope of Asadullāh Mīrzā (Leiden, 1977).

8 These intriguing phenomena are discussed briefly by Willy Hartner in "La problème de la planète Kaïd," in Les Conférences du Palais de la Découverte, ser. D, no. 36 (Université de Paris, 1955); reprinted in idem, Oriens-Occidens (Hildesheim, 1968), pp. 268-286.

9 Similar diagrams are to be found in Willy Hartner, "The Mercury Horoscope of Marcantonio Michiel of Venice," in Vistas in Astronomy, ed. A. Beer, vol. 1 (London and New York, 1955), pp. 84-138; reprinted in Oriens-Occidens, pp. 440-495.

10 E. S. Kennedy, "The Sasanian Astronomical Handbook Zīj-i Shāh and the Astrological Doctrine of 'Transit' (Mamarr)," Journal of the American Oriental Society, 78 (1958), 246-262.

11 The date 658/1260 would suggest Naṣīr al-dīn Ṭūsī's Zīj-i Īlkhānī. I have only been able so far to consult the 15th-century manuscript of this work in the Cambridge University Library (Browne Coll., O.2), and there the longitudes are 4° 03' in advance of Ṣūfī's and 2° 11' behind al-Kāshī's, which would give a date for the Zīj of either 629/1232 (267 years at 66 years to the degree), which is certainly too early, or 646/1248 (at 70 years to the degree), still rather too early. The most probable explanation is that Ṭūsī was basing his figures not on Ṣūfī but on some intermediate catalogue; further study of the work might elucidate the problem.

The whole question of the figures estimated by Islamic astronomers for precession is somewhat confused. Ptolemy in 139 A.D. gave a figure of 100 years per degree, and the first Islamic scientists to correct this were the authors of al-Zīj al-mumtaḥan, compiled on Ma'mūn's orders in approximately 200/815, who worked on a figure of 66 years to the degree, and so added 10° 15' to Ptolemy's figures. Al-Battānī some years later used a figure of 11° 10', which would suggest that he was observing in 263/876 (according to C. Brockelmann, Geschichte der arabischen Literatur, Supplement Band 1 [Leiden, 1937], p. 397, he began his observations in 264/877). Al-Ṣūfī, who compiled his star catalogue in 354/965, makes it clear that he believed Ptolemy's figures were not his, but those of Menelaus (98 A.D.), to which Ṣūfī assumes Ptolemy added 25', representing 41 years at 100 years to the degree. Ṣūfī therefore calculated precession since Menelaus at 13° 09' (867 years divided by 66), from which figure he subtracted Ptolemy's assumed inaccurate addition of 25' to give him a figure of 12° 42' to be added to Ptolemy's longitudes. Ṣūfī's catalogue seems to have formed the basis of all subsequent catalogues prior to Ulugh Beǧ (for instance, ^{c}Umar Khayyām in 472/1079, and probably Ṭūsī in about 658/1260). Ulugh Beǧ in 841/1437 re-observed most of the 1022 stars in Ptolemy's catalogue, but he took Ptolemy's figures in at least 27 cases (E. B. Knobel, Ulugh Beg's Catalogue of Stars, Carnegie Institution of Washington Publication No. 250 [Washington, 1917], thinks considerably more), and added 19° 41' for precession. Since this would give a figure of 68 years to the degree instead of the 70 that Ulugh Beǧ adopted, Knobel speculates that Ulugh Beǧ's assistants may mistakenly have calculated in lunar instead of solar years - a most probably error! It is more likely that, like al-Kāshī, he used a later catalogue of, say, 658/1260, even though this had been calculated at 66 years to the degree, and only used the 70 ratio in reckoning the subsequent 177 years, making 17° 10' + 2° 31'.

[12] A miniature of about the same date, "formerly in Istanbul, Library of the Sultan," in what appears to be a similar style though representing the World Mirror, is reproduced on Pl. 41 of E. Kühnel, Miniaturmalerei im islamische Orient (Berlin, 1933); plate reprinted in Willy Hartner, "The Pseudoplanetary Nodes of the Moon's Orbit in Hindu and Islamic Iconographies," in Ars Islamica, vol. 5 (Ann Arbor, Mich., 1936), p. 130, fig 19 (reprinted in Oriens-Occidens, p. 375).

[13] Strictly speaking, Mercury is in the Fifth House and Mars in the Tenth. These apparent discrepancies may be due to the House cusps being reckoned as the centres of the Houses rather than the beginnings, or they may--together with other details--lend support to the possibility that the miniature was produced as a separate operation.

The conventional representation of the planets and the signs are described in D. S. Rice, The Wade Cup in the Cleveland Museum of Art (Paris, 1955); Willy Hartner, "The Pseudoplanetary Nodes" and idem, "Zur astrologischen Symbolik des 'Wade Cup'," in Aus der Welt der islamischen Kunst, ed. R. Ettinghausen (Berlin, 1959), pp. 234-243 (both reprinted in Oriens-Occidens, pp. 349-414); Eva Baer, "Representations of Planet-Children in Turkish Manuscripts," Bulletin of the School of Oriental and African Studies, 31.3 (1968), 526-533.

The darījān is an extension of the Planetary Domiciles system, in which the ṣāḥib al-bayt rules only the first third of each sign, the other two thirds being under other planets separated from the ṣāḥib and each other by three interverning planets. The third of a sign into which the House Cusp falls is ruled by the darījān.

[14] For instance, the letter rā' may stand for, in addition to the sounds |r| and |z|, the figure 7, the figure 200, the Moon, Scorpio,

Saturday, and the Sinister Aspect.

[15] E. S. Kennedy in a private letter.

[16] Quoted by Reuben Levy in Kai Kā'ūs ibn Iskandar, A Mirror for Princes (London, 1951), p. 176.

Scenes from the Literary Life of Tīmūrid Herāt

Maria E. Subtelny
The University of Toronto

The number of published editions of primary sources for the study of the Tīmūrid dynasty which figured so prominently in the cultural life of Khurāsān (east Iran and west Afghanistan) and Transoxiana (Central Asia) in the fifteenth century has been growing steadily since V.V. Bartol'd noted in his groundbreaking essay, "Mir Ali-Shir i politicheskaia zhizn'" (1928), that the difficulty for a researcher in this period lay not in the lack, but rather in the great abundance of materials that were scattered throughout various libraries and in need of critical editions.[1]

By 1936, when Walther Hinz wrote his overview of the historical sources for the Tīmūrid period, matters had not progressed appreciably.[2] Twenty years later, however, Hans Robert Roemer could report that a whole series of critical editions, as well as translations and scholarly studies had been published since Bartol'd's time[3] and, in the introduction to his edition and translation of the chronicle, Shams al-ḥusn, he enumerated an impressive list of publications in the field by, among others, Felix Tauer, Muhammad Shafīᶜ, Walther Hinz, V.V. Bartol'd as well as himself.[4] The following year, the Tajik scholar, Abdulgani Mirzoev, reviewed the significant contributions of Soviet scholars, such as E.È. Bertel's, V.V. Bartol'd, A.M. Belenitskii, A. Iu. Iakubovskii, I.P. Petrushevskii, A.N. Boldyrev, A.A. Semenov, to the study of the Tīmūrid period,[5] and he made the interesting observation that the political, social, cultural and literary life of the second half of the fifteenth and beginning of the sixteenth centuries in particular "has, thanks to Soviet scholars, been studied more thoroughly than probably any single period in the history of Central Asia and Khorasan."[6] B.V. Lunin's

Logos Islamikos: Studia Islamica in honorem Georgii Michaelis Wickens, ed. Roger M. Savory and Dionisius A. Agius, Papers in Mediaeval Studies 6 (Toronto: Pontifical Institute of Mediaeval Studies, 1984), pp. 137-155.

bibliographical guide to Soviet studies on the Tīmūrid period (1969) certainly appears to corroborate this statement.[7]

Bartol'd's charge that no monograph based on the sources existed for any major political or cultural figure[8] has also been answered in the form of separate studies on ᶜAlī Shīr Navā'ī, Jāmī, Hilālī, Binā'ī and Ulugh Beg, to name just a few.[9] However, although scholarship has come a long way from Lucien Bouvat's "Essai sur la civilisation timouride" (1926) and his L'empire mongol (2ème phase) (1927), both of which were severely criticized for their lack of scholarly method,[10] a definitive monograph on the Tīmūrids in English similar to C.E. Bosworth's work on the Ghaznavids or Roger Savory's recent work on the Safavids, remains to be written.[11]

The published sources for the Tīmūrid period encompass a wide range of genres. They are for the most part in Persian and include what are customarily referred to as "official" or commissioned histories such as Mīrkhvānd's Rawẕat al-ṣafa and Khvāndamīr's Ḥabīb al-siyar, which deal primarily with political events; local histories such as Muᶜīn al-Dīn al-Isfizārī's Rawẕāt al-jannāt fī awṣāf-i madīnat al-Harāt; biographical literature, including biographies of saints (such as Jāmī's Nafaḥāt al-uns), poets (such as Navā'ī's Majālis al-nafā'is), and even vizirs (Khvāndamīr's Dastūr al-wuzara); and collections of chancellery documents (such as ᶜAbd Allāh Marvārīd's Sharaf-nāmah).

The richness of available material is underscored by the fact that to this period also belong two works of an autobiographical nature: the Bābur-nāmah of Ẓahīr al-Dīn Muḥammad Bābur in Chaghatay Turkish,[12] and the Bādayiᶜ al-vaqāyiᶜ of Zayn al-Dīn Vaṣifī in Persian. The former is by now well known to Western scholarship on account of Annette Beveridge's excellent English translation, while the latter, although available in a critical edition since 1961, has not been utilized nearly as extensively.[13]

Neither of these works can, strictly speaking, be regarded as autobiography which does not appear in Persian writing, nor for that matter in medieval Islamic literature as a whole, until the twentieth century.[14] The reasons for this may perhaps be sought in the Islamic conception of personality which did not allow for the possibility of true self-sufficiency--and therefore of true self-expression--for the individual since it was the community (ummah) and not its several members that necessarily remained the prime focus.[15] Autobiographical elements, however, can be found to a greater or lesser extent, in various genres of medieval Persian writing, including the universally popular travel account, narratives of the lives of famous Ṣūfīs, and the political "memoir", usually written by rulers as a kind of apologia. This last type is especially well represented in Persian and is viewed by some scholars as the continuation of a pre-Islamic tradition.[16] To it belong such works as the memoirs of the Mughal emperor, Jahāngīr, and the Ṣafavid shāh, Ṭahmāsp, and, of course, the above-mentioned memoirs of Bābur, the founder of the Mughal empire in India.

The Badayi^c al-vaqāyi^c, which is in all probability the best example of medieval Persian memoir literature because of its strongly autobiographical character, was not, however, written by a political figure. Completed at the Uzbek court in Tashkent in 1538/9, it is an account of the adventures and experiences of its author, Vāṣifī, a professional poet and littérateur, at the courts of the Tīmūrid and Uzbek rulers of Khurāsān and Transoxiana. More entertainment than apologia, it also possesses a certain didactic strain in some of its anecdotal sections which are reminiscent of the "mirrors for princes" genre. The many descriptions it contains of various aspects of cultural life at the Tīmūrid and Uzbek courts make it an excellent source for the cultural history of Khurāsān and Transoxiana of the late fifteenth and early sixteenth centuries.[17]

The uniqueness of the Badayi^c al-vaqāyi^c as a source resides in the background and point of view of its author. Born in 1485 into the educated, petty-functionary class of Herāt (his father was probably an official secretary or munshī), Vāṣifī was a typical product of the Khurāsānian cultural milieu of the late fifteenth century.[18] Not always successful in obtaining a position as a court poet, he experienced a checkered career during the course of which he was, among other things, a tutor, preacher and chancellery scribe. He is mentioned by Ḥasan Nisārī Bukhārī in the Muzakkir-i aḥbāb (completed in 1566) primarily as a poet and munshī,[19] however, and his literary bent is amply reflected in his work, as most of the episodes he describes deal with literary, particularly poetic, activity.

Since it was a non-official and non-commissioned work, the Badāyi^c al-vaqāyi^c provides rare glimpses of the literary life of the medieval Central Asian court not usually found in the official historiographical writing or even in the critical literary anthologies (tazkirāt) of the time. The many descriptions of episodes relating in particular to the Tīmūrid court make it an especially valuable source for the cultural history of the late Tīmūrid period as represented by the rule of Sulṭān Ḥusayn Bāyqarā in Herāt (1469–1506).[20] Although these are usually in the form of anecdotes, the "historicity" of which may at times be questionable, nevertheless, it cannot be denied that they convey the flavor of the period and what they lack in fact they certainly make up for in feeling.

In the following excerpt, Vāṣifī describes an experience from his youth when, at the age of 16,[21] he was invited to an audience with ᶜAlī Shīr Navā'ī (1441–1501), the outstanding Tīmūrid poet and patron, and chief overseer of the literary life of the court of Ḥusayn Bāyqarā at Herāt. He relates how he mastered the muᶜammā,[22] the favorite poetical genre of the time (a fact corroborated by the Muzakkir-i aḥbab[23], how he was "discovered" by his uncle, Ṣāḥibdārā Astarābādī, who happened to be one of Navā'ī's personal attendants and intimate companions, and then invited through him to be tested by Navā'ī at a formal audience. Very touching is his expression of anxiety on the eve of his meeting with the great man.

A Young Talent is Introduced at Court[24]

One day, at the age of 16, when I had finished memorizing the Word of Omniscient God (i.e., the Qur'ān), and, having girded myself up for striving to acquire the sciences, was expending great effort therein, I was walking around the Malik Bazaar in Herāt with a group of poets and men of parts when that seditious troublemaker, Ḥāfiẓ Ḥusayn, nicknamed Ḥāfiẓ Ghamzah, joined us. In his hand he had a book and I asked him what text it was. He answered, "It's the treatise on muᶜammā by Mawlānā Sayfī Bukhārā'ī."[25]

Since at that time the ultimate goal and highest aspiration of all accomplished persons was to come to the attention of Amīr ᶜAlī Shīr and since there was no better means of gaining admission to him than through (one's expertise in) muᶜammā, I asked Ḥāfiẓ Ghamzah whether he would be so kind as to lend me the treatise so that I might copy it. But Ḥāfiẓ only laughed and said:

What do the mousehole and rosewater have in common?
And what the deaf ear and the lute?[26]

On account of this insult, the world became for me oppressive and dark like a mousehole. The rosewater of my tears trickled out of the rosewater bottle of my eyes onto the page of my face and the musician of pride so tightened the keys of the lute of scorn that the veins of my saddened heart moaned woefully just like the strings of a lute. Weeping, I made my way home. I sat down in a corner and shut the door on all acquaintances.

At the time of the evening prayer, I went to the mosque. After the prayer, I saw a man reclining in a corner of the mosque. He had pulled a coarse cloak over his face and was moaning sadly. I went up to him and removed the cloak from his face. It was as if the sun had appeared from behind the veil of the clouds for he was an exceedingly beautiful youth, but all the color had gone from his face and the dust and grime of travel had become caked on his cheeks. He was like the sun in the west that turns pale when it is about to set or like the full moon in eclipse . . .

I sat down beside him and asked him who he was. He answered, "I am from Tabrīz and they call me ^{c}Abd al-Raḥmān Chelebī. I wanted to go to Khurāsān, but my father wouldn't allow it. Without his permission, I set out for these parts with a sum of money. When we reached the dry river bed of the Sāq-i Salmān, which is one league from Khurāsān, the people in the caravan became very happy and said, 'Praise be to God, for we have been freed from fear and from the dangers of the road and we have been set at ease from the fear of brigands and highway robbers!' They ceased to be vigilant and cautious and felt safe and free from care. It just so happened that that same night a band of robbers, who had been lying in wait still from Tabrīz, took advantage of this opportunity to attack us. The merchants, who had been grouped together like the Pleiades, became scattered in all directions like the constellation of the Bear.

"Suddenly, during the fighting, an arrow lodged itself in my arm so that (when) the broker of calamity and affliction brought the goods of my life to the weigh scales of pain and affliction, (he found them to be) merchandise of little value. Most of the people in the caravan perished while I stumbled all the way here in a state that could not have been worse."

I burst into tears. I went home and brought back a litter and carried him home on it. In the neighborhood lived a surgeon . . . I fetched him and showed him his wound and in a short while he healed it.

One day, that young man demonstrated his sense of obligation and gratitude to me. He said, "In Tabrīz, I acquired mastery of two sciences: *mu^{c}ammā* and astrology, and I made the claim, 'I know what you do not,' among people of learning. It has occurred to me that, in order to repay your kindness to me, I might, in accordance with the Qur'ānic saying, 'Is the reward of goodness aught save goodness?'[27] inscribe those two sciences on the page of your mind and thus leave you with a keepsake from me."

When I heard the word "*mu^{c}ammā*," I thought that an epistle had been revealed from heaven on high in my name. I said, "O friend, it is imperative that I learn the science of *mu^{c}ammā*. If you strive to teach me that science so that I might become accomplished in it, that would be for me the ultimate kindness and favor."

He asked for pen and ink and, to invoke a blessing, wrote down, by way of example, a famous *mu^{c}ammā* by the Commander of the Believers and Prince of Muslims, the Victorious Lion of God, ^{c}Alī ibn Abī Ṭālib[28] (May God have mercy upon him!). He explained in writing all the rules and technicalities of the science of *mu^{c}amma* and he made a memorandum book of them for me.

In the meantime, people came from Iraq and took this noble youth back with them with great pomp and ceremony, thereby handing the heart and soul of this distressed one over to the warden of affliction and grief. But, thanks to his efforts, I had attained such a high degree of proficiency in the science of mu^{c}ammā that most of the mu^{c}ammās I heard I could solve without knowing the solution beforehand.[29] News of this spread among the professional mu^{c}ammā writers of the city of Herāt and it reached the point where many people made bets with each other and won when they bet on me. So, when a mu^{c}ammā writer from Anatolia came to Khurāsān and circulated difficult mu^{c}ammās of his composition throughout the city, one of my friends made a bet with him for 100 tangahs[30] that such-and-such a person (meaning myself) could solve a mu^{c}ammā of his without knowing the solution to it beforehand.

They came to my house with a group of people and it just so happened that five days earlier I had come down with the measles and was lying in bed. When they assembled at my bedside, they said, "Truly, we were not aware of this state of affairs." One from the group explained the situation to me and I said, "Read me the mu^{c}ammā!" They said, "This is not the time or place. The strain of thinking will only aggravate your illness!" I insisted and made them swear to read me the mu^{c}ammā. When they read it, I said after a little reflection, "The name, 'Saifī,' can be extracted from this mu^{c}ammā. But I do not know, is this (the solution) or not?"

The mu^{c}ammā writer was greatly astonished and he handed over the sum of money he had wagered and he gave me a cloak of cloth made in Yazd worth 50 royal tangahs.

* * *

Mawlānā Ṣāḥibdārā was one of the illustrious friends and dear companions of the great amīr, Amīr ^{c}Alī Shīr (May God refresh his soul and increase his triumph in Paradise!)[31]. . . Since the aforementioned Mawlānā (i.e., Ṣāḥibdārā) was set apart from the other attendants of that amīr by the preferential treatment that he enjoyed and since he was always the recipient of the latter's liberal favors . . ., he wrote an elegy on him that is (at the same time) a chronogram and that is distinguished from the poems of his peers and contemporaries by the great number of figures of speech and rhetorical flourishes it contains . . .[32]

I, the humble author was closely related to Mawlānā Ṣāḥibdārā on the maternal side. One day, I went to his house with my father. There were many accomplished and learned people present and Mawlānā Ṣāḥibdārā said to my father: "For a long time now we have heard that your son is an outstanding student, a sweet voiced reciter of the Qur'ān and a fine poet. We have learned that he solves every difficult mu^{c}ammā that is read to him without knowing the solution to it beforehand." He read a mu^{c}ammā to me and, after a little deliberation, I said, "The solution is 'Pāyandah'." Those present at the majlis[33] were greatly amazed. Mawlānā Ṣāḥib said, "I composed that mu^{c}ammā last night and had not yet read it to anyone; otherwise, I would have suspected that he had heard it before. This then represents the highest degree of intelligence and sharpness of wit."

A few moments after we had returned home, Mawlānā Ṣāḥib's footman arrived and said, "My master is asking for you." When I arrived in his presence, Mawlānā said, "I have been in attendance on Amīr ^{c}Alī Shīr. Now it is the Mīr's custom to call for me every day and to ask me, 'What interesting and unusual things have you seen or heard in the city today?' I said, 'I saw a person aged 16 or 17 who solves every difficult mu^{c}ammā that is read to him without knowing the solution to it beforehand. He also has a reputation as a student, a reciter of the Qur'ān and a poet.' The Mīr was quite amazed by this and asked, 'Have you put him to the test?' I said, 'Yes. I read him a difficult *muᶜammā* and he solved it as soon as I read it.' His Excellency the Mīr reproached me, saying, 'Why did you not bring him here?' I regretted having said anything, for meeting with the Mīr causes such consternation that, for example, if a person is called upon in the *majlis*, it is possible that he might not even be able to answer. What if someone reads you a *muᶜammā* and you are not able to solve it? That would put me to shame. At any rate, prepare yourself and come here early in the morning, because his Excellency the Mīr is intent on meeting you."

When I came home that evening, a strange feeling came over me. I tossed from side to side like someone who had been bitten by a snake and I just could not calm down. My father learned of my anxiety and asked:

> O soul of your father, what's wrong with you?
> Why are you so anxious?

I said, "Father, how can you ask? Tomorrow I am going to Amīr ᶜAlī Shīr's *majlis* and I don't know how things will go for me." My father wept and said, "My dear, can you be so afraid of conversing with a human being? Alas for our souls! On the Judgement Day, the book of our deeds will be handed to us in the presence of the Almighty Creator and, in the words of the Lord of Lords, 'Read thy book. Thy soul sufficeth as reckoner against thee this day,'[34] we will be commanded to make clear the enigma of our secrets. Alas, in that place of severity there will be no alleviation and at the time when fear wells up, God's ire will not be mitigated."

To make a long story short, I presented myself in the morning at Mawlānā Ṣāḥib's house. There were three other students at Mawlānā Ṣāḥib's besides myself. Mawlānā Ṣāḥib said, "You have come just in time. I have also talked to the Mīr about these three persons." One of them was a *muᶜammā* writer who was considered the equal of Mawlānā Ḥusain Nīshāpūrī.[35] The other was known as a writer of *qaṣīdahs*, while the third wrote good *masnavīs*.

When we arrived at the formal audience, all the intimates and boon companions of His Excellency the Mīr were assembled. His Excellency the Mīr glanced at us and then pointed to me, saying, "Is this the fellow who solves *muᶜammās* without knowing the solution beforehand?" Mawlānā Ṣāḥib answered, "Yes my lord, he is the one." Mawlānā Muḥammad Badakhshī[36] said, "O lord and sovereign, your ability to solve *muᶜammās* cannot compare with his." The Mīr said, "I can see that from his eyes, for in them are evident the signs of a thinker." Then he read me a *muᶜammā* . . . It just so happened that I knew it already. I wondered whether I should pretend that I didn't know it and leave the audience that way, or tell the truth. Finally, the decision to tell the truth prevailed and I said, "My lord, I already know this *muᶜammā*." His Excellency the Mīr lowered his head in thought for a moment and then said, "Friends, do you know the meaning of his words? He is showing his expertise by saying, 'Not this one, give me another one to solve!'"

His Excellency the Mīr did not read another *muᶜammā* at that audience. He was very gracious and said to Mawlānā Ṣāḥib, "We accept his claim."

* * *

No other source for the Tīmūrid period provides more vividly detailed descriptions of the medieval institution of the majlis than does the Badāyi^{c} al-vaqāyi^{c}. The term majlis designated any king of convivial social meeting--from the formal court audience (in which case it was called majlis-i ^{c}ālī) to an informal gathering--at which the customary forms of entertainment could include musical performance and singing, wine-drinking, engagement in witticism and the relation of anecdotes, and the recitation and discussion of poetry. When this last activity constituted the chief focus, the term majlis carried the connotation of a literary assembly, a kind of literary "soirée," and it represented the main forum for literary, particularly poetical, expression in the late Tīmūrid period.

Formal majlises that were held at court by Tīmūrid dignitaries could be quite sumptuous. The following description of the preparations for one held in Herāt by Majd al-Dīn Muḥammad, one of Ḥusayn Bāyqarā's vizirs,[37] who claimed to have spent close to 100,000 tangahs on it,[38] gives an idea of the actual physical and social setting for these literary entertainments. The list of those present reads like a who's who of the literary and entertainment world of the reign of Husayn Bāyqarā. The episode is related by Vāṣifī from his uncle, Ṣāḥibdārā.[39]

A Tīmūrid Vizīr Prepares for a Majlis[40]

Mawlānā Ṣāḥibdārā related that one day the great amīr, ^{c}Alī Shīr met with Khvājah Majd al-Dīn Muḥammad, who was also known as Mīr Kalān, in the Jahān-ārā Garden and said: "I have heard a lot about your majlises which are like paradise itself . . . and it has occurred to me that I would like to be present at such an entertainment." The Khvājah put his hand to his breast and said: "You would be doing me a great honour (by attending)," and he asked for a week's time to prepare for the majlis.

The place designated for the entertainment was the village of Parzah, which was half a league from Herāt and in which the Khvājah had set out a garden. It was such a (beautiful) garden that the Garden of Iram[41] would have bitten the finger of amazement at (the sight of) its pleasantness, and the architect of fancy would have been stunned by its charm and unusual touches. In it there was a pavilion with a dome like a glass decanter that would put Khavarnaq and Sadīr[42] to shame. It was built like a lofty palace on whose high towers the skies had placed their limits. The age had not seen anything like it except in the lustre of a mirror and the heavens could find its model only in abstract . . .

On the banks of every stream there were tall cypresses like the vision of the figure of the beloved on the (banks of the) stream of (tears from) the eyes of lovers. On every rosebush there were nightingales complaining like distressed (lovers) of separation from their rose-bodied beloveds. At the feet of the sunfaced tulips, grass sprouted like the enchanting down on the (cheeks of) beautiful boys, and in the shade of the chaste willows there was fragrant basil. On the meadow there were violets like the dishevelled locks of beauties with every hair out of place and, on the banks of the streams there were narcissi (looking) like the eyes of intoxicated beauties. Before the portico of that edifice, which was as high as the planet Saturn and which was the envy of the heavenly dome, nimble footmen erected silk canopies like the heavens themselves, woven with gold thread that dispelled the darkness, in accordance with the saying, "Thou makest the night pass into day."[43] *Maḥfūrī*, *muṣalṣal*, *kāfūrī* and *firang* rugs were spread on the ground and embroidered, multi-colored coverlets were laid out at every place.

Among the singers who were invited were: Ḥāfiẓ Baṣīr, Ḥāfiẓ Mīr, Ḥāfiẓ Ḥasan ʿAlī, Ḥāfiẓ Ḥājjī, Ḥāfiẓ Sulṭān Maḥmūd ʿAyshī, Shāh Muḥammad Khvānandah, Siyāhchah Khvānandah, Ḥāfiẓ Awbahī, Ḥāfiẓ Turbatī and Ḥāfiẓ Chirāghdān. Of the musicians there were present: Ustād Ḥasan Nā'ī, Ustād Qul Muḥammad ʿŪdī, Ustād Ḥasan Balabānī, Ustād ʿAlī Khānqāhī, Ustād Muḥammadī, Ustād Ḥājjī Kuhistī Nā'ī, Ustād Sayyid Aḥmad Ghijakī and Ustād ʿAlī Kuchak Ṭanbūrī. Of the poets and boon companions who were the pride of the *majlis* there were present Mawlānā Bināʾī, Khvājah Āṣafī, Amīr Shaykhum Suhaylī, Mawlānā Sayfī Bukhārī, Mawlānā Kāmī, Mawlānā Ḥasan Shāh, Mawlānā Darvīsh Rawghangar Mashhadī, Mawlānā Muqbilī, Mawlānā Ḥasan Shāh, Mawlānā Darvīsh Rawghangar Mashhadī, Mawlānā Muqbilī, Mawlānā Shawqī, Mawlānā Zavqī, Mawlānā Khalaf, Mawlānā Nargisī, Mawlānā Hilālī and Mawlānā Riyāẓī Turbatī. Of the wits there were: Mīr Sar-barahnah, Mawlānā Burhān Gung, Mīrkhvānd the historian, Mawlānā Muʿīn Shīrāzī, Mawlānā Ḥusayn Vāʿiz, Sayyid Ghiyās al-Dīn Sharfah, Mawlānā Muḥammad Badakhshī, Mawlānā Khalīl Ṣaḥḥaf and Mawlānā Muḥammad Khvāfī Khaṭṭāṭ. And of the "jeunesse dorée" of Khurāsān there were: Mīrak Zaʿfarān, Shāh Muḥammad Mīrak, Khvājah Jān Mīrak, Sulṭān Sirāj, Mīrzāy Naṭʿ-dūz, Ḥusayn Zar-dūz, Sarv-i Lab-i Jūy, Shimshād-i Sāyah-parvar, Mullā Khvājah Khvānandah, Yūsuf-i Mazāri-i Chilgazī, Yūsuf-i Sānī, Māh-i Samanānī, Sāqī and Bāqī-i ʿIrāqī.

Before the portico of that edifice there was a marble pool, the envy of Salsabīl and Kavs̱ar,[44] which was filled with sweet sherbet. It became known that 800 sugar-loaves had been used to make it. Experienced confectioners had also prepared countless sherbets, confections (*maʿjūn*), *birish*,[45] pickled foods (*āchār*), candied fruit and rice puddings (*palūdah*, *firnī*). Sulṭān Ḥusayn Mīrzā (i.e., Sulṭān Ḥusayn Bāyqarā) had a very famous cook by the name of Abū 'l-Malīḥ who prepared for this *majlis* 40 dishes, the names of which no one even knew.

* * *

In view of the absence of theoretical works from the fifteenth century that deal specifically with the problem of Persian literary criticism, the record of critical comments made at literary *majlises*, such as those described in the *Badāyiʿ al-vaqāyiʿ*, when analyzed together with the views expressed by the authors of the contemporary *taẕkirāt*, could provide the basis for the reconstruction of such a theory, a study of which is still lacking.[46] More immediately, however, the descriptions of critico-literary discussions held during these majlises help us to identify the aesthetic criteria by which poetry was judged and provide an idea of some of the concrete technical problems encountered by a fifteenth-century Persian poet. In general, they attest to a high degree of sophistication on the part of literary critics of the time in terms of familiarity with the works not only of contemporaries, but also of past masters.

The following excerpts are from the description of a majlis held in Herāt by ᶜAbd Allāh Marvārīd (d. 1516), a notable of Ḥusayn Bāyqarā's court, who, besides being a poet and composer of chancellery prose, was also an accomplished musician.[47] Vāṣifī mentions that he set to music a Turkish ghazal by Navā'ī, entitled Sarmast va yaqam chāk ("Drunk and dishevelled"), and that the song was so popular that "there wasn't a house or palace in Herāt where it couldn't be heard."[48] Bābur refers to him as being a good critic of poetry.[49]

Vāṣifī, whose own literary pretensions appear to be somewhat inflated, relates how he pointed out defects at the majlis in the poetry of some famous Tīmūrid poets. Most noteworthy in his criticisms is his insistence on adherence to "established" (muqarrar) poetical practice in the use of certain expressions and images. His remarks are entirely in keeping with a fundamental principle of medieval Persian literary theory that set the reordering of relationships between stock images above the creation of entirely new ones.

The Critic Has the Last Word[50]

One day, at a majlis held by Khvājah ᶜAbd Allāh Ṣadr Marvārīd, there were present such poets and accomplished persons of Khurāsān as Mawlānā Muḥammad Aṣīlī, Mawlānā Hilālī, Mawlānā Ahlī, Faẕlī, Zulālī, Harātī, Rūḥī, Ḥālī, Mawlānā Amānī, Qābilī, Muqbilī, Anvarī Dīvānah and others. It happened that the Dīvān of His Excellency Mawlānā Nūr al-Dīn ᶜAbd al-Raḥmān Jāmī[51] (May God have mercy on his sublime tomb!) was available at the majlis. Khvājagī (Marvārīd) said: "Let it be opened at random," and the following ghazal was the first one that they came upon:

> O sāqī, bring on the wine, for a cloud has appeared
> in the east, all white.[52]

Mawlānā Jānī said: "Many great and accomplished persons have composed ghazals with a radīf in the word "white" (safīd).[53] But I dare say that no one has composed one as elegant as Khvajah Āṣafī's,"[54] and he recited the following opening verse:

> When, with the fire of wine, you lit up your face,
> all white,

The grey-headed old candle set fire to its hair,
all white.[55]

Mawlānā Muḥammad Aṣīlī leaned over to me and said, "Do you recall that you once said that there was a defect in this verse?" (Just then) Khvājah Āṣafī came in and asked, "What's all the talk about?" Mawlānā Muḥammad Aṣīlī said: "He (i.e., Vāṣifī) thinks that there is a defect in this verse." Everyone turned to me, wondering what the defect could possibly be since no one had noticed it before.

Khvājah Āṣafī got set to argue with me about this, but I said: "It occurs to me that there is some doubt that a candle would set fire to its hair out of envy. Where have you ever seen the practice or the custom of setting fire to one's hair out of envy? This would be the equivalent of an old woman setting fire to her hair out of envy whenever (she saw) the cheeks of a beauty become inflamed with the fire of wine!"

As soon as I said this, those present at the majlis started to laugh and Khvāhah Āṣafī was overcome with great shame. A group of those present started to dispute this, but Khvājah (Āṣafī) said: "I do not approve of this quarrel of yours. He is right," and he accepted my judgement.

* * *

There ws at that majlis a person from Transoxiana who was a great admirer of the poet, Riyāẓī, whom he regarded as being superior to all the poets of Khurāsān.[56] Khvājagī (Marvārīd) turned to me and, with a wink, indicated that I should take him on. So I said to the fellow: "Be so kind as to recite some of Mawlānā Riyāẓī's verses that are held in such esteem by his admirers." He recited this opening verse:

Deprived of your beauty, I pull thorns of despair out
from the garden,
Instead of rosebuds, I pluck spear-points from the
rosebush.

I said: "The expression 'deprived of your beauty' (bi-jamalat) alludes to the time of separation and it is established practice to say that, at that time, the thorn of despair springs forth from the garden of the heart and not that the thorn of despair is pulled out from the garden of the heart. Moreover, it is not common (poetical) usage to pluck rosebuds from the rosebush, as some poets have noted:

I am always saying that I will renounce that
statuesque beauty,
But, I repeat, how can I pluck a rosebud from
the rosebush?

(Consequently,) that man became upset, but he wasn't able to say a single reasonable thing in his defense.

* * *

One of the most colorful figures of the late Tīmūrid period was Binā'ī (variously, Banā'ī and Bannā'ī [d. 1512/13]), who is mentioned by Bābur in his list of professional poets at the court of Ḥusayn Bāyqarā as well as in his list of musicians and composers.[57] His poetry was extremely popular in both Khurāsān and Transoxiana[58] and, during the course of his professional career, he served such rivals as the Aq Qoyunlu, the Tīmūrids and the Uzbeks. One of the main points of interest about Bināʾī as a personality was his long-standing conflict with ʿAlī Shīr Navāʾī whose service he entered while in Herāt. Bābur calls the two men "opponents."[59] Personal differences aside, however, Navāʾī had a high opinion of Bināʾī's poetical talent, if not of his character.[60]

Numerous anecdotes are preserved in the sources about the conflict between the two poets. Some scholars have regarded it basically as a difference in politico-cultural orientation, for Bināʾī, a native of Herāt in Khurāsān--traditionally the heartland of Persian culture--was opposed to the pro-Turkic sympathies of Navāʾī who represented the political interests of the ruling Tīmūrid dynasty[61] and who sought to elevate Chaghatay (Eastern Turkish), which he regarded as a language superior to Persian, to the status of literary language.[62] Vāṣifī relates the following anecdote, in which Bināʾī's stand is clearly formulated, on the authority of Muḥammad Badakhshī, one of Navāʾī's closest friends and long-time servitors.[63]

<u>Linguistic Tensions at the Tīmūrid Court</u>[64]

One day after Mullā Bināʾī had returned from Iraq,[65] at a <u>majlis</u> held by Mīr (ʿAlī Shīr Navāʾī) at which there were many accomplished and notable persons present, ʿAlī Shīr said to him: "What interesting things do they say about Sulṭān Yaʿqūb Beğ?" Mawlānā Bināʾī replied: "Nothing about Yaʿqūb Beğ is more pleasing and excellent than the fact that he does not recite Turkish poetry." Navāʾī retorted: "O Bināʾī, your hardness and coldness have no bounds. You deserve to have your mouth stuffed with dirt!" To this Bināʾī replied: "That would be easy, since all I would have to do is recite some Turkish verses!"

* * *

ʿAlī Shīr Navāʾī has traditionally been portrayed in the official sources,[66] as well as in the scholarly literature, in an idealized fashion as a modest and kindly old man, a kind of father figure who helped along aspiring young talents.[67] The fact is that his literary and philanthropic achievements notwithstanding, the chief character trait noted most often by his contemporaries was his extreme sensitivity which verged on what might best be described as "touchiness." Bābur, for example, wrote that, "The over-sensitivity (<u>nāzuklūk</u>) of his temperament was well-known,"[68] and Muḥammad Ḥaydar that, "He had no other faults except for his sensitivity (nāzukī) and the fact that he was quick to take offence (zūd ranjīdan)."[69]

Navā'ī's high personal standards were reflected in his dealings with those around him and he was known as a stern task master. Vāṣifī records a young student with whose education Navā'ī had been entrusted, as complaining that, "To live in conformity with the temperament of the Mīr (i.e., ᶜAlī Shīr) and to live up to his standards is a difficult, or rather an impossible task."[70] His stand on literary matters was equally uncompromising and the literary critic, Dawlatshāh, refers to the exclusivity of his majlises to which those whom he did not deem worthy were not admitted.[71] The following episode, related by Vāṣifī from Ṣāḥibdārā, demonstrates how unsparing he could be in his treatment of those who just didn't measure up:

Navā'ī Disposes of a Dull Wit[72]

His Eminence, Mawlānā Faṣīḥ al-Dīn Ibrāhīm, who had been His Excellency Mīr (ᶜAlī Shīr)'s teacher and master,[73] had honored Amīr Ṣadr al-Dīn Yūnus with the cloak of son-in-lawship.[74] This, however, did not meet with the Mīr's approval because, as the Mīr was well-acquainted with the science of physiognomy, he could read in the book of Mīr Dāmad's[75] (i.e., Ṣadr al-Dīn Yūnus) outward form and on the pages of his behaviour the signs of stupidity. (Nevertheless,) Faṣīḥ al-Dīn took great pains to have his son-in-law accepted and approved of by the Mīr . . . He took it upon himself to bring him to the Mīr's majlises; but, whenever he appeared, the Mīr would sing this verse:

I want to get so far away that, if the revolving sphere
  should, whirlwind-like,
Sift through the garbage-can of fate, it would not even
  be able to find the dust!

One day, Mīr Dāmad was seated at the Mīr's majlis at the very front of the audience chamber and was showing off his literary attainments. Suddenly, a strong wind, reminiscent of the loud talk of the afore-mentioned Mīr (Dāmad), started blowing and slamming the panels of the door together. His Excellency the Mīr became vexed and said to Ṣadr al-Dīn Yūnus, "Would you be so kind as to bolt the door?" (Ṣadr al-Dīn Yūnus) got up immediately and put his hand to the lock, but the Mīr said, "I meant bolt it from the other side." (Ṣadr al-Dīn) did not grasp the subtlety of this witticism. He bolted the door and sat down, (thus) shutting the door of enjoyment in the faces of those present at the majlis.

Just then, an extremely mangy and ugly cat appeared in the assembly and tried to climb into the Mīr's lap. The Mīr struck it and said, "My God this cat is repulsive!"[76] The participants of the majlis who had quick minds all laughed. But, just by looking at Ṣadr al-Dīn Yūnus' face, the Mīr knew that he was only laughing in imitation of the others and that he had not grasped the point of the joke. So he asked him, "What would you be laughing at?"

He blushed and lowered his head,
Confused, he couldn't utter a word.

His Excellency the Mīr said:

The laugh which is ill-timed,
Weeping is better than such a laugh.

To laugh every moment in a flash,
Shortens the life to a spark.

He went on: "Most people know only three types of laughter. One type is like the laughter of Mīr Ṣadr al-Dīn Yūnus which is in imitation of others. Another type is the laughter that comes only after reflection. And the third type is the laughter that says to itself of the first type, 'How asinine it is!'"

When Ṣadr al-Dīn Yūnus heard this, he cringed, but his pride dictated that he raise the flag of his disgrace. He said, "The reason for my laughter is obvious. You said, Īn gurbah ᶜajab shakl-i karīhī dārad ('My God, this cat is repulsive') and you used the kāf of comparison."[77] A great cry went up from those at the majlis and they all said, "He is living proof of the saying, 'His apology is worse than his sin.'" The Mīr said . . .[78] and the wits and literati laughed so hard that Mīr Ṣadr al-Dīn Yūnus had to run from the majlis in tears.

* * *

The colorfulness of these vignettes from the Badāyiᶜ al-vaqāyiᶜ might obscure the fact that they often inadvertently contain important factual information not found in other sources. For instance, in his description of how poets presented verses containing chronograms (tārīkh)[79] to ᶜAlī Shīr Navā'ī to commemorate the completion of the restoration of the cathedral mosque (masjid-i jāmiᶜ) of Herāt, that had been conducted under the latter's supervision, Vāṣifī records the texts of two chronograms composed by Ikhtiyār al-Dīn Ḥasan.[80] Not only does he indicate the exact locations in the masjid-i jāmiᶜ where they were inscribed,[81] but one of them even yields the precise date on which the restoration was completed: the 10th of Rabīᶜ al-avval, 904 (=Wednesday 26 October 1498).[82]

The single most outstanding feature that emerges from all the episodes, however, is the degree to which the life of Tīmūrid Herāt in the late fifteenth century was permeated with literary concerns, in particular, with poetry. The biographical sources in fact attest to a very large number of poets who were active in the city at that time and the literary critic, Dawlatshāh, even complained that, "Wherever you listen, you hear the murmur of a poet, and wherever you look, you see a Laṭīfī or a Ẓarīfī or a Nāẓirī."[83] Undeniably, Vāṣifī's descriptions add to our appreciation and enjoyment of what was certainly the most "literate" of all periods in medieval Islamic Central Asian history.

Notes

I would like to express my thanks to the National Endowment for the Humanities, Washington, DC, for its generous support during the period in which translations for this paper were completed.

[1] V.V. Bartol'd, Sochineniia, 10 vols. (Moscow, 1963-1977), vol. 2,2: 199.

[2] Walther Hinz, "Quellenstudien zur Geschichte der Timuriden," Zeitschrift der Deutschen Morgenländischen Gesellschaft, 90 NF 15 (1936), 357-398.

[3] Hans Robert Roemer, "Neuere Veröffentlichungen zur Geschichte Timurs und seiner Nachfolger," Central Asiatic Journal, 2 (1956), 220.

[4] [Tāj al-Salmānī], Šams al-Ḥusn: eine Chronik vom Tode Timurs bis zum Jahre 1409 von Tāǧ as-Salmānī, ed. and trans. Hans Robert Roemer (Wiesbaden: Franz Steiner Verlag, 1956), pp. 1-4.

[5] A.M. Mirzoev, Kamal ad-Din Binai (Moscow, 1976), pp. 6-11.

[6] Mirzoev, Binai, p. 10. See also Richard Frye's short study, "Soviet Historiography on the Islamic Orient" in Historians of the Middle East, ed. Bernard Lewis and P.M. Holt (London: Oxford University Press, 1962), p. 367 where he suggests some of the reasons for this.

[7] B.V. Lunin, "Istoriia, kul'tura i iskusstvo vremeni timuridov v sovetskoi literature: Bibliograficheskii ukazatel'," Obshchestvennye nauki v Uzbekistane, 8-9 (1969), 101-145.

[8] Bartol'd, Sochineniia, 2.2: 199.

[9] See for example: E.É. Bertel's, Izbrannye trudy, vol. 4: Navoi i Dzhami (Moscow, 1965); Agâh Sırrı Levend, Ali Şir Nevaî, 4 vols. (Ankara: Türk Tarih Kurumu Basımevi, 1965-1968); ^{c}Alī Aṣghar Ḥikmat, Jāmī (Teheran, 1320/1942); A.M. Mirzoev, Kamal ad-Din Binai (Moscow, 1976); Kamol Aini, Badriddin Khiloli (Stalinabad, 1957); V.V. Bartol'd, "Ulugbek i ego vremia" in Sochineniia, 2.2: 25-196.

[10] Bartol'd, Sochineniia, 2.2: 201-202.

[11] Clifford E. Bosworth, The Ghaznavids: Their Empire in Afghanistan and Eastern Iran 994-1040 (Edinburgh: Edinburgh University Press, 1963); Roger Savory, Iran under the Safavids (Cambridge: Cambridge University Press, 1980); for a review of the latter, see International Journal of Middle East Studies, 15 (1983), 300-302.

[12] Bābur, The Bābar-nāma, facs. ed. Annette S. Beveridge (Leiden: E.J. Brill, 1905) and Bābur-nāma: Memoirs of Bābur, trans. Annette S. Beveridge (London, 1922; rep. ed., New Delhi: Oriental Books Reprint Corp., 1970).

[13] Zayn al-Dīn Vāṣifī, Badāyi^{c} al-vaqāyi^{c}, ed. A.N. Boldyrev, 2 vols. (Moscow, 1961).

[14] Ann K.S. Lambton, "Persian Biographical Literature" in Historians of the Middle East, ed. Lewis and Holt, p. 149; see also Bert G. Fragner, Persische Memoirenliteratur als Quelle zur Neueren Geschichte Irans (Wiesbaden: Franz Steiner, 1979), p. 8.

[15] See R.A. Nicholson, The Idea of Personality in Sufism

(Lahore: Muhammad Ashraf, 1964), pp. 100-101; also Franz Rosenthal, "Die arabische Autobiographie" in Studia Arabica 1, ed. Fr. Rosenthal, G. von Grünebaum and W.J. Fischel (=Analecta Orientalia, 14 [1937]), p. 11.

16 Fragner, Persische Memoirenliteratur, p. 11; Rosenthal, "Die arabische Autobiographie," pp. 8, 10.

17 The Badāyi^c al-vaqāyi^c was dedicated to Abū al-Muẓaffar Ḥasan Sulṭān, the six year old son of Kīldī Muḥammad (d. 1532/3), the cousin of Muḥammad Shībānī Khān, the founder of the Transoxanian Uzbek state. See A.N. Boldyrev, Zainaddin Vasifi (Stalinabad, 1957), p. 234. Its narrative begins with the Ṣafavid conquest of Herāt from Muḥammad Shībānī in 1510 and ends with the year 1531/2, the latest date given in the text (see Vāṣifī, Badāyi^c al-vaqāyi^c, 2: 1248). The time period actually covered is expanded, however, by means of a "flashback" technique by which the author relates incidents from his youth in Herāt during the latter part of the reign of Sulṭān Ḥusayn Bāyqarā (1469-1506) (For example, see Boldyrev, Vasifi, pp. 18, 22). Many non-autobiographical episodes which are related on the authority of eye-witnesses, who were members of the Tīmūrid court, refer to even earlier periods of Tīmūrid rule. See also A.N. Boldyrev, "Memuary Zain-ad-Dina Vosifi kak istochnik dlia izucheniia kul'turnoi zhizni Srednei Azii i Khorasana na rubezhe XV-XVI vekov," Trudy Otdela kul'tury i iskusstva vostoka (Gosudarstvennyi Ermitazh), 2 (1940), 203-270.

18 Boldyrev, Vasifi, pp. 17-18.

19 Ḥasan Nisārī Bukhārī, Muẕakkir-i aḥbāb, ed. Muḥammad Faẓlullāh (New Delhi, 1969), p. 204.

20 See, for example, chapters 13-17 for the cycle of stories about Navā'ī in Vāṣifī, Badāyi^c al-vaqāyi^c, 1: 484-632.

21 This would correspond to the date 1500/1, which was shortly before Navā'ī's death. See Boldyrev, Vasifi, p. 28.

22 The mu^cammā was a poetical form of one or two lines only. It was an enigma or word-puzzle, the object of which was to recognize hidden allusions contained in it to letters of the Arabic alphabet which, when assembled, spelled the solution (usually a proper name). For more on mu^cammā, see my article, "A Taste for the Intricate: The Persian Poetry of the Late Timurid Period," Zeitschrift der Deutschen Morgenländischen Gesellschaft (forthcoming 1985).

23 Ḥasan Nisārī, Muẕakkir-i aḥbāb, p. 205.

24 Vāṣifī, Badāyi^c al-vaqāyi^c, 1: 485-506.

25 Sayfī Bukhārā'ī (d. 1503/4) was a poet who belonged to the court circle of ^cAlī Shīr Navā'ī; see Maria E. Subtelny, "The Poetic Circle at the Court of the Timurid, Sultan Husain Baiqara, and its Political Significance" (Ph.D. diss., Harvard University, 1979), pp. 128-130. His treatise on mu^cammā is mentioned by ^cAlī Shīr Navā'ī in his Majālis al-nafā'is ed. ^cAlī Asghar Ḥikmat (Teheran 1323/1945), pp. 57, 230.

26 Ḥāfiẓ's remark seems to suggest that the possibility of Vāṣifī's mastering the mu^cammā is as remote as the connection between these disparate items.

27 Qur'ān, 55:60.

28 ^cAlī ibn Abī Ṭālib (d. 661), the cousin and son-in-law of the Prophet Muḥammad, is regarded in popular tradition as the originator of many esoteric phenomena, such as the invention of the mu^cammā.

29 Mu^cammās were so difficult to solve that the solution was usually provided ahead of time and the object became to demonstrate how it could be extracted.

30 Tangah--a gold coin.

31 Ṣāḥibdārā, whose full name was Faṣīḥ al-Dīn Ṣāḥibdārā Astarābādī, but who was known simply as Mawlānā Ṣāḥib (d. 1512), was a member of Navā'ī's intimate court circle of friends and advisers. He appears here in his capacity as a kind of talent scout for Navā'ī. See Subtelny, "The Poetic Circle," pp. 145-146.

32 Here follows the text of Ṣāḥibdārā's elegy on Navā'ī (pp. 493-497). It is also a chronogram in that the sum of the numerical values of the letters of the first hemistich of every line gives the year of Navā'ī's birth, while the sum of those of the second hemistich gives the year of his death.

33 For the term majlis, see below. Here it means a gathering of literati.

34 Qur'ān, 17:14.

35 Ḥusayn Nīshāpūrī, also known as Ḥusayn Mu^c^ammā'ī (d. 1498/9), was a member of Ḥusayn Bāyqarā's court circle of poets. He was an expert in mu^c^ammā and wrote a famous treatise on the subject. He is mentioned by Muḥammad Ḥaydar in his list of professional writers of mu^c^ammā of Ḥusayn Bāyqarā's time (see [Muḥammad Ḥaydar], "Iqtibās az Tārīkh-i rashīdī," Muḥammad Shafī^c^, ed. in Oriental College Magazine, 10 (1934), 161).

36 Muḥammad Badakhshī was for thirty years in the service of Navā'ī. He was a specialist in mu^c^ammā and is also mentioned by Muḥammad Ḥaydar in his list of professional mu^c^ammā writers of Ḥusayn Bāyqarā's time. See Muḥammad Ḥaydar, "Iqtibās," p. 161; also Subtelny, "The Poetic Circle," pp. 132-133.

37 For Majd al-Dīn Muḥammad, see Khvāndamīr, Dastūr al-vuzarā, ed. S. Nafīsī (Teheran, 1317/1939), pp. 400ff.

38 Vāṣifī, Badāyi^c^ al-vaqāyi^c^, 2: 529.

39 For Ṣāḥibdārā, see n. 30 above.

40 Vāṣifī, Badāyi^c^ al-vaqāyi^c^, 1: 523-528. The date of this majlis is given in the text (p. 531) as Friday, the first of Jumādà al-ākharah, 897 (= Saturday 31 March 1492).

41 An ancient mythical city mentioned in the Qur'ān.

42 Names of magnificent legendary palaces.

43 Qur'ān 3:27.

44 Names of rivers in paradise.

45 A concoction of hemp leaves and opium with syrup.

46 See Subtelny, "A Taste for the Intricate," n. 13.

47 See Hans Robert Roemer, Staatsschreiben der Timuridenzeit: Das Šaraf-nāmä des ^c^Abdallāh Marwārīd in kritischer Auswertung (Wiesbaden: Franz Steiner, 1952), pp. 22-24; also Subtelny, "The Poetic Circle," pp. 143-145.

48 Vāṣifī, Badāyi^c^ al-vaqāyi^c^, 1: 575.

49 Bābur, Bābar-nāma, fol. 175; Bābur, Bābur-nāma: Memoirs, p. 278.

50 The first excerpt is from Vāṣifī, Badāyi^c^ al-vaqāyi^c^, 2: 963-965, and the second--pp. 968-969.

51 Jāmī (d. 1492) was the outstanding Persian poet of the second half of the 15th century. He was a close friend of Navā'ī and was loosely associated with the court of Sulṭān Ḥusayn Bāyqarā. His poetry was very popular in Tīmūrid Herāt and was often imitated.

52 See Jami, Fatikhat ash-shabab (Fatihat al-shabab), ed. A. Afsakhzod (Moscow, 1978), p. 317, where the line reads: Khīz sāqī kaz furūgh'i subh shud khāvar safīd.

53 The radīf is the technical term for a word (or words) that follow the end-rhyme in a ghazal or qaṣīdah and that is repeated

throughout.

54 Āṣafī (d. 1515) was one of the poets of Ḥusayn Bāyqarā's court circle. He was in the service of ^{c}Alī Shīr Navā'ī and of Badī^{c} al-Zamān Mīrzā, one of Ḥusayn Bāyqarā's sons. See Subtelny, "The Poetic Circle," pp. 122-124.

55 See Āṣafī Haravī, Dīvān, ed. Hādī Arfa^{c} (Tehran, 1342/1964), p. 80.

56 Riyāẕī Turbatī (d. 1515/6) was a professional poet who probably belonged to the Tīmūrid court circle of poets. See Subtelny, "The Poetic Circle," p. 142.

57 Bābur, Bābar-nāma, fols. 179b-180, 182b; Bābur, Bābur-nāma: Memoirs, pp. 286-287, 292; see also Subtelny, "The Poetic Circle," pp. 124-128.

58 Khvāndamīr, Tārīkh-i Ḥabīb al-siyar, 4 vols. (Tehran, 1333s./1955), 4: 349.

59 Bābur uses the word muta^{c}arriẓ,(Bābar-nāma, fol. 180).

60 ^{c}Alī Shīr Navā'ī, Majālis al-nafā'is, pp. 60, 232.

61 For Navā'ī's background, see Maria E. Subtelny, "^{c}Alī Shīr Navā'ī: Bakhshī and Beg" in Eucharisterion: Essays Presented to Omeljan Pritsak on his Sixtieth Birthday, 2 vols. (= Harvard Ukrainian Studies, 3/4 (1979-1980)), vol. 2, pp. 799-800.

62 See A.N. Boldyrev, "Alisher Navoi v rasskazakh sovremennikov" in Alisher Navoi: Sbornik statei, ed. A.K. Borovkov (Moscow, 1946), p. 147; for a contradictory view which is in line with the Soviet theory emphasizing the historical "friendship" of the Uzbek and Tadzhik peoples, see Mirzoev, Binai, pp. 371-372.

63 See Subtelny, "The Poetic Circle," pp. 132-133.

64 Vāṣifī, Badāyi^{c} al-vaqāyi^{c}, 1: 614-615.

65 Binā'ī had been in the service of the Aq Qoyunlu ruler, Sulṭān Ya^{c}qūb Beğ (d. 1490/1) in Iraq.

66 For example, Khvāndamīr's panegyrical Makārim al-akhlāq, facs. ed. T. Gandjei (Cambridge: Gibb Memorial Trust, 1979) and even his Ḥabīb al-siyar.

67 See Subtelny, "^{c}Alī Shīr Navā'ī," pp. 798ff., where I attempt to rectify some of the misconceptions about him.

68 Bābur, Bābar-nāma, fol. 170b.

69 Muḥammad Ḥaidar, "Iqtibās," p. 157.

70 Vāṣifi, Badāyi^{c} al-vaqāyi^{c}, 1: 569.

71 Dawlatshāh, Taẕkirat al-shu^{c}arā, ed. Edward G. Browne (London: Luzac and Co., 1901), p. 496.

72 Vāṣifī, Badāyi^{c} al-vaqāyi^{c}, 1: 513-520.

73 For Faṣīḥ al-Dīn Ibrāhīm (who is called Faṣīḥ al-Dīn Muḥammad al-Niẓāmī in other sources), see Khvāndamīr, Ḥabīb al-siyar, 4: 352-353.

74 I.e., Ṣadr al-Dīn Yūnus became his son-in-law. For Ṣadr al-Dīn Yūnus, who was later to become the shaikh al-islām of Balkh, see Khvandamir, Ḥabīb al-siyar, 4: 352.

75 Literally, "son-in-law."

76 By "this cat" Navā'ī actually means Ṣadr al-Dīn Yūnus.

77 Ṣadr al-Dīn Yūnus thought that the letter kāf in the word "karīhī" was the so-called "kāf of comparison" in Arabic grammar, an utter impossibility in this case.

78 I omit Navā'ī's obscene story, with Ṣadr al-Dīn Yūnus intended, about a person who could not retain his urine.

79 A tārīkh consists of a word or set of words which provide a year in the Hijrah calendar when the numerical values of their letters are added together. It was a favorite verse form in the late Tīmūrid

period.

[80] See Vāṣifī, _Badāyi^c al-vaqāyi^c_, 1: 210. He indicates that one of these contains a _mu^cammā_ on the name of ^cAlī Shīr. For Ikhtiyār al-Dīn Ḥasan, see Khvāndamīr, _Ḥabīb al-siyar_, 4: 355-356.

[81] One, in Arabic, was inscribed on the north spandrel (_kitf_) of the main vaulted hall before the sanctuary (_ayvān-i maqsūrah_) and the other, in Persian, was written on the entrance portal (_pīshtāq-i ayvān_). See Vāṣifī, _Badāyi^c al-vaqāyi^c_, 1: 209. I am indebted to Lisa Golombek of the Royal Ontario Museum for clarifying the architectural terms.

[82] Other chronograms that have been preserved indicate the year only; see, for example, Khvāndamīr, _Faṣlī az Khulāsat al-akhbār_, ed. Gūyā I^ctimādī (Kabul, 1345/1966), p. 11; see also Lisa Golombek, "The Resilience of the Friday Mosque: The Case of Herat," _Muqarnas_, ed. Oleg Grabar (New Haven: Yale University Press), 1 (1983), p. 98.

[83] Dawlatshāh, _Tazkirat al-shu^carā_, p. 10; see also Maria E. Subtelny, "Art and Politics in Early 16th Century Central Asia," _Central Asiatic Journal_, 27 (1983), 124.

Part Three
Islamic Weltanschauungen

10

The Wines of Earth and Paradise: Qur'ānic Proscriptions and Promises

Jane D. McAuliffe
The University of Toronto

There are few things more widely known about Islam than its prohibition of intoxicants. Wine is the devil's work, proclaims the Qur'ān, so have nothing to do with it. The issue of temperance is one upon which Sunnī and Shīcī Islam, in its various legal manifestations, has achieved remarkable accord. The penalties mandated by classical jurisprudence for either drinking or trading in wine are severe. Its complete and life-long renunciation is demanded of every Muslim. Yet that renunciation need be no longer than life, for Muslims are promised a paradise whose rivers flow with wine. That which is forbidden on earth will be abundantly available in the Hereafter.

Certain verses in the Qur'ān provide the basis for both this earthly proscription and heavenly promise. I have selected the most important of these as the focus of this essay and will sketch their exegetical treatments in the works of two pre-eminent medieval commentators, al-Ṭabarī and al-Rāzī.

Sūra 2, verse 219 is the chief locus for the exegetical treatment of the Qur'ānic prohibition of wine. I have translated it as follows:

> They will ask you about wine and gambling, Say: There is great sin in them and (some) use for mankind but their sin is greater than their use.

Abū Jacfar Ibn Jarīr al-Ṭabarī begins his commentary on this verse with a word study of the term khamr. The root meaning for the verb from which this noun is derived is "to conceal, cover or veil." Therefore al-Ṭabarī's definition of khamr is "all drink which conceals (khammara) the intellect or veils it (satara-hu) or obscures it

---

Logos Islamikos: Studia Islamica in honorem Georgii Michaelis Wickens, ed. Roger M. Savory and Dionisius A. Agius, Papers in Mediaeval Studies 6 (Toronto: Pontifical Institute of Mediaeval Studies, 1984), pp. 159-174.

(ghaṭṭa ᶜalay-hi)."[1] He then amends this definition to include not only intoxicating beverages but even disease--in other words, anything which interferes with mental clarity.[2] He also notes another derivative of the root, khimār, the veil which covers the head and face of a woman.[3]

In examining the matter of wine as a "great sin," al-Ṭabarī reports two ḥadīth, one of which stresses the social and the other, the spiritual, consequences of wine-drinking. The first explains the sinfulness of wine by the fact that when a man drinks, he becomes drunk and hurts people. The second faults wine-drinking because it causes a decrease in religious observance (mā yanquṣu min al-dīni).[4] The exegete's own position blends these two explanations by stressing that intoxication so clouds the individual's mind that "awareness of his Lord slips away from him."[5]

This verse's description of wine as of some "use to people" prompts al-Ṭabarī's application of two poetical extracts as an interpretive device. The first of these highlights the different effect which wine has on the morning and evening imbiber: "Drinking it in the morning makes us bad-tempered and dejected, mindful of our anxieties while gulping down wine's ill-effects. But at supper it is a source of good humour and pleasure, so that inebriation is a great worldly benefit."[6] The second line of verse also offers a contrast between the possible psychological effects of wine, but one couched in more colourful imagery: "When we drink it, it leaves us feeling like kings and lions, yet it does not hold us back from suffering."[7] It is worth noting that in neither of these examples is wine depicted as an unalloyed benefit. Its possible advantages are fully balanced with its disadvantages.

The final phrase of this verse reaffirms the proper relationship between wine's sinfulness and its usefulness: "for its sin is greater than its use." Al-Ṭabarī mentions the morphological debate about whether the median letter of the comparative word is a bā' or a thā'. (The resultant difference is that between magnitude and pluralty.) He opts for the former because it parallels the verse's earlier use of that term to describe the word 'sin'.[8]

The sin, according to this exegete, which is associated with wine-drinking, on the basis of this revelation, is that of quarreling and fighting. It is not yet the sin of actually consuming the wine.

In other words, it is the effects of inebriation which are sinful not the consumption itself. This two-stage theory of human culpability can only be understood in light of the exegetical and jurisprudential theory about a sequential revelation on wine.

Most commentators and jurists maintain that God revealed His interdiction of intoxicants by degrees. Al-Ṭabarī agrees with this view and presents a series of eleven ḥadīth which sketch varying scenarios for this graduated revelation. The usual sequence charted places the initiation of prohibition within this particular verse, i.e., 2: 219, with 4: 43 as an intermediate stage and complete temperance mandated by 5: 90-91. Two of the ḥadīth reported by al-Ṭabarī include sufficient detail to flesh out this schema.

The first ḥadīth begins by mentioning that after the revelation of this verse some Muslims continued to drink wine until such time as two men got drunk and walked into the place of prayer. They started to shout out phrases incomprehensible to those in attendance--though presumably in an effort to follow the prayer--so God sent down 4: 43: "O you who believe, do not come near the prayer when you are drunk until you know what you are saying." Nevertheless, those who were wont to drink it continued to do so but took more care with regard to the prayer.

Then it happened that a man became drunk and started bemoaning those killed at the battle of Badr. News of this reached Muḥammad, which terrified the cowardly ranconteur. He grabbed the Prophet's cloak in a panic and pulled him to a stop. When the man looked at him, Muḥammad raised his hand to strike him and proclaimed "God forbid that you should anger God or His Messenger. I swear I will never taste it [wine]."[9] The account concludes with the statement that God then sent down 5: 90-91: "O you who believe, wine and gambling and stones and arrows are nothing less than an abomination, the work of Satan. So keep away from it that you may prosper. Satan only wants to cause enmity and hatred among you through wine and gambling and to hold you back from the remembrance of God and from prayer. Will you let yourselves be thus restrained?"

The second ḥadīth elaborates another set of circumstances and paints a more detailed picture of the Qur'ānic development on this issue. Concurring that the first two revelations about wine were 2: 219 and 4: 43, it goes on to describe the subsequent behaviour of some

Muslims: "It was permissible for them to drink from the prayer of dawn (al-fajr) until noon. Then, after sobering up, they took themselves off to the midday prayer (al-ẓuhr) and did not drink any more until the prayer of night fall (al-ᶜishā'). After that, however, they imbibed until the night was half over, only to sober up and head for the dawn prayer."[10] And so it continued until such time as Saᶜd ibn Abī Waqqāṣ, a hot-tempered, early follower of Muḥammad--he is credited with shedding the first blood and shooting the first arrow in Islam--held a party.[11] To this meal, for which he grilled the head of a camel, he invited some of the Prophet's Companions, including one of the anṣār (term used of the early converts in Medina). The ḥadīth concludes with this vignette: "Now when they had eaten and drunk wine, they became drunk and started chit chatting (akhadhū fī 'l-ḥadīth). Saᶜd said something which made the anṣār angry so he picked up the jawbone of the camel and smashed Saᶜd's nose with it. Therefore God sent down a revelation to abolish wine and declare it forbidden."[12] This final prohibition is 5: 90-91.

Fakhr al-Dīn al-Rāzī's commentary on this verse begins at the beginning--with the very first word, yas'alūna-ka. "They asked," this exegete is anxious to establish, "not just anything" about wine.[13] The questioning was not general and detached: the issue was wine's permissibility or prohibition. Al-Rāzī then details the sequence of revelation about wine. Unlike al-Ṭabarī, however, he postulates a four-verse sequence rather than one comprising only three.[14]

In Mecca, the commentator states, God sent down 16: 67: "Of the fruits of the palm-trees and the grapes, you will obtain intoxicants and good nourishment. Surely in that is a sign for a people who understand." At this point Muslims were drinking wine and this was considered permissible. Then, prompted by the concerns of some of his Companions who began to notice the problems caused by wine-drinking, Muḥammad sought a revelation and the verse under discussion, 2: 219, was revealed.[15] Yet, although others renounced it, some people continued to drink and an incident occurred which demanded further clarification. On this occasion a group of men who had been drinking stood to say the prayer with the rest of the community. They started to recite sūra 109 which begins "Say: O disbelievers, I do not worship what you worship." Unfortunately, in their inebriation, they omitted the negative so that what they actually said was: "Say, O disbelievers, I do worship what you worship."[16] As a result 4: 43 was revealed urging people not to come near the prayer unless sober.

The next stage in al-Rāzī's synopsis of the revelational sequence repeats the episode involving Saᶜd ibn Abī Waqqāṣ with some variation. In this version the eating and drinking led not to general conversation but to poetical vying, with Saᶜd ridiculing the anṣār in verse. For his efforts, he was rewarded not with a broken nose but a fractured skull. The outcome, however, was the same--the revelation of 5: 90-91 and the complete prohibition of wine.

As part of his explanation of the stages of this prohibition, al-Rāzī includes an interesting justification for the divine procedure in this matter: "The rationale for prohibition occurring according to this sequence is that God knew that people were in the habit of drinking wine and that they derived considerable profit from it. He knew that if He were to forbid them [to drink it] all at once, that would be oppressive for them. So, of course, He used this kind of gradualness (hādhā al-tadrīj) and this kind of considerateness (hādhā 'l-rifq) in declaring it forbidden."[17]

In keeping with his encyclopedic methodology and as a prelude to his own view, al-Rāzī includes the opinion of those who disavow this whole notion of a sequence of revelation about wine. This group holds that the complete prohibition of wine was effected by 2: 219. They, in turn, understand 4: 43 as a repetition and specification of this. By insisting that anyone who drinks is always to some degree, drunk, they conclude that a wine-drinker can never pray completely sober. According to this theory, 5: 90-91 is far more than a prohibition: "it is the strongest possible statement for 'temperance' (kānat fī ghāyati 'l-quwwati fī 'l-taḥrīmi)."[18]

This commentator then proceeds to a discussion of the key legal question: what beverges are included within the category of khamr? In response, he cites the decisions and supporting arguements of al-Shāfiᶜī and Abū Ḥanīfa, acknowledged founders of two of the four legal schools of Sunnī Islam. Al-Shāfiᶜī insists that khamr denotes every intoxicating drink. As proof of this al-Rāzī quotes a number of ḥadīth from the Sunan of Abū Dā'ūd. The first of these lists the five possible sources of intoxicants as grapes (al-ᶜinab), dates (al-tamr), wheat (al-ḥinta), barley (al-shaᶜīr) and durra (al-dhura).[19] The exegete's discussion of these particulars concludes with the observation that khamr is "anything which befuddles the mind" or "anything which takes possession of the intellect and changes it [for the worse] (kulluma khamarā al-ᶜaqla fa ghayyara-hu."[20]

In fact, to emphasize that the designation should not be restricted to the above-mentioned five items, al-Rāzī includes another listing which substitutes honey (al-ᶜasal) for durra and designates wheat by another term, al-burr. None of these lists is sacrosanct, he maintains; the individual items are mentioned only because use of them was customary in that period.[21]

As part of this discussion on the inclusive sense of khamr, al-Rāzī includes hadīth which answer another urgent question, i.e. is there any allowable amount of khamr? Is a little bit permitted? The response is, as might be expected, an emphatic "no". It is most dramatically expressed in a hadīth credited to ᶜĀ'isha, often referred to as Muḥammad's favorite wife: "She said: I heard the Messenger of God say: 'any intoxicant is forbidden, be it a firq [a large amount] or that which fills the palm of the hand.'"[22]

This exegete then moves into a whole other realm of argument for support of the connotation of khamr. This time he draws his ammunition not from the sayings of the Prophet and his Companions but from etymological analysis of the word khamr itself. As was noted in the tafsīr of al-Ṭabarī, the root meaning of KhMR is "to conceal, cover or hide." Al-Rāzī cites several derivatives from the root which display aspects of this root sense. One is al-khimār: the veil which covers a woman's head. Another is al-khamar: a natural place of concealment such as a covert of trees, a gorge or a hillock. In like manner, he contends, is khamr a veil or concealment, one which obscures the intellect. Inasmuch as all intoxicants act thus, all intoxicants must be considered khamr.[23]

Al-Rāzī then presents the views of the other renowned jurist, Abū Ḥanīfa, in abbreviated form and with a succinct rebuttal of each major point. Abū Ḥanīfa, unlike al-Shāfiᶜī, defines khamr as the "expressed juice of ripe grapes (al-ᶜinab al-shadīd) which throws up foam."[24] His main concern is the legal status of nabīdh, a drink made from dates or grapes and water. This, he maintains, is not khamr, a position for which he finds support in 16: 67 and in a story about the Prophet.

In 16: 67 it is the phrase "intoxicants and good nourishment" to which Abū Ḥanīfa turns in support of the permissibility of nabīdh--a position which al-Rāzī dismisses out of hand. The story about the Prophet is reported on the authority of Ibn ᶜAbbās, Muḥammad's cousin and one of the most celebrated of the Companions. The episode is set in the last years of the Prophet's life on an occasion when he asked Ibn ᶜAbbās for a drink. The latter hesitated before offering him a cup of nabīdh and was greatly chagrined when Muḥammad sniffed it, scowled and handed back the cup. He then requested a cup of spring water and said: "Since these drinks create violent passion in you (ightalamat ᶜalay-kum), cut their potency with water."[25] Abū Ḥanīfa concludes that the Prophet scowled not because of the drink itself but because of its intensity, allowing him to deduce that milder forms of this beverage are permissible.[26]

Al-Rāzī disagrees. In all likelihood, he contends, nabīdh was simply water into which dates had been pressed, thus changing its colour and making it a little sour. (In other words, there was no question of fermentation.) Muḥammad's constitution, this commentator maintains, "was so sensitive that he could not bear that taste; because of that he scowled."[27] In addition, water was added to his cup not to dilute the potency of a strong intoxicant but to eliminate this sour taste and odour.[28]

Having established that khamr includes all intoxicants, al-Rāzī ventures into another area of contention--whether or not this verse is in itself a prohibition of wine. His affirmative response separates him from most other exegetes and jurists, who adhere, as does al-Ṭabarī, to the theory of sequential revelation described above.[29] This exegete argues for his position on several levels. The first is by a conflation of this verse with 7: 33: "Say: my Lord only prohibits obscenities, those which are manifest and those which are hidden and sin (al-ithm) . . ." The reasoning process is syllogistic: 7: 33 states that sin is forbidden, 2: 219 states that wine is a sin, therefore wine must be forbidden.[30] Furthermore, this verse itself declares that wine's sin is greater than its usefulness, surely another proof, says al-Rāzī, of its being forbidden.[31]

He next examines the objections which may be raised against his view. The first is that which repeats al-Ṭabarī's position, i.e., that wine drinking is not itself sinful but that sin can be connected with it. In rebuttal al-Rāzī goes back to the exact words of the

Qur'ān-- "in it is sin." Given that God has called wine sinful, then that attribute is inseparable from it in all instances. "Therefore drinking wine is necessarily forbidden."[32]

Those who would counter that God also said that in khamr there is some use, are refuted with the statement that the fact that something is useful does not preclude its being forbidden.[33] A further objection which centers on the now-familiar sequence of revelations about wine is likewise summarily dismissed. In all probability, al-Rāzī comments, the Companions of the Prophet sought these further revelations out of a desire for additional confirmation.[34]

Although firmly convinced that wine is sinful because God has declared it to be so, this exegete proceeds to explain the gravity of the act, the reason why wine drinking is a "great sin (ithmun kabīrun)." As explanation he offers three different reasons. The first of these is that "the mind of man is the most noble of his attributes and wine is the enemy of the mind."[35] He continues his syllogism with the statements that "anything which is the enemy of the most noble is the most vile, so that it necessarily follows that drinking wine is the most despicable of acts."[36] Al-Rāzī then expands his argument with an interesting bit of etymological lore. The mind, he says, is so called by analogy to the hobble cord of a she-camel. When a man's natural disposition calls him to do something ignominious, the mind acts, as does the hobble cord, like a brake. But drinking wine obscures the intellect and nullifies its braking action. Al-Rāzī illustrates his point with a rather startling example. He cites the instance of "a drunk who urinated in his hand and rubbed his face with it in the manner of one performing the ritual ablution before prayer. While doing so he said 'Praise God who made Islam as a light and water as a cleanser.'"[37] To conclude this argument, he quotes the retorts of a pre-Islamic Arab who was asked why he did not drink wine, which gives one great courage: "I do not take into my hand and put into my belly something which makes me witless and I do not like to get up in the morning a leader among men and go to bed the stupidest of the lot."[38]

The second reason al-Rāzī offers for wine-drinking as a "great sin" is drawn directly from 5: 90-91. It is a repetition of the two-fold divine justification for its prohibition: it causes hatred and enmity and turns one away from the remembrance of God and from prayer.[38] The third and final reason is an interesting reflection on the psychology of sin. The distinction al-Rāzī draws is between those sinful acts which satisfy an evil inclination and those which do not. Most sins, he observes, are in the first category. When the object of desire is attained, the inclination toward it is removed. The example he gives is adultery: "when once the adulterer (al-zānī) has performed, his desire for the act abates."[40] Such is not the case with wine-drinking; the more one does it the more one wants to do it, to the point that "a man becomes immersed in bodily pleasures (al-ladhdhāt al-badaniyya), turning away from thought of the Hereafter and the life to come and becoming one who forgets God and is therefore forgotten by God."[41] Little wonder, concludes al-Rāzī, that the Prophet called wine "the mother of wickedness (umm al-khabā'ith)."[42]

Before closing his discussion of this verse this commentator feels compelled to provide some explanation for its characterization of wine as of "use to people (manāfiᶜu li-'l-nās)." He first acknowledges that wine was an item of trade and valued for its profits. He then, quite surprisingly, cites a long list of its benefits: "Among its uses are that it strengthens the weak, helps with the digestion of food, assists in sexual congress, consoles the grief-stricken, emboldens the coward, makes the miser generous, clears the complexion, raises the natural body heat and increases the ambition and desire for mastery."[43] (It is worth noting that the editor of this edition of al-Rāzī's commentary is appalled by his inclusion of such a list and inserts a special footnote to that effect. The editor's insertion begins: "Fakhr's, may God have mercy on him, statement about wine drinking--he then repeats the statement--is a remarkable declaration which would not stem from a reasonable man. If some of those advantages which he mentioned existed in it [wine] then why would God prohibit us from drinking it?"[44] Maintaining that God only forbids that which is bad for religion and for the body, the editor proceeds to rebut each item in al-Rāzī's list with a bald statement to the contrary.)

Al-Rāzī concludes his commentary on this verse with a discussion of the two variants, kabīr and kathīr, to which he adds nothing substantial to the analysis done by al-Ṭabarī.

How very different is the wine of Paradise! There are a number of vivid descriptions of the Hereafter included in the Qur'ān and several of them specify the celestial drink. The first to be considered is that in 37: 45-47, which details some of the delights in store for those who remain faithful:

> Circulating among them will be a
> cup of clear drink,
> White, a pleasure for the drinkers,
> There is no problem (ghawl) in it and they
> are not depleted in it.

Al-Ṭabarī's first concern is to define the means of circulation. Lest anyone visualize free-floating vessels, he specifies that servants (al-khadam) bring it around.[45] He also makes immediately clear that ka's, the word which I have translated as "cup," can only mean wine (khamr) when used in the Qur'ān. In fact, he says, "in Arabic usage ka's is a receptacle (inā') in which there is drink; if there is no drink in it, it is not a ka's but only a receptacle."[46] Since the adjective "white (bayḍā')" modifies ka's, it means that the wine is white.

To see wine described as "a pleasure for the drinkers" provokes no extended commentary from al-Ṭabarī. But for the phrase "there is no problem (ghawl) in it" he cites five shades of meaning. The first interpretation is that the wine of Paradise does not give one a headache, while the second is that this wine causes no physical damage (adhan) such as stomach irritation.[47] The third understanding stresses not corporeal consequences but mental ones by insisting that paradisiacal wine does not destroy the intellect. The final two interpretations are more general and inclusive: the fourth notes that there is no injury (adhan) or impropriety (makrūh) in it, while the fifth concludes that there is no sin (ithm) attached to it.[48] (The term used for "sin" is the same used in the above-discussed verses on the prohibition of wine.)

Al-Ṭabarī makes no attempt to choose among the five but rather considers all these meanings to be contained in the word (ghawl). God, therefore, intended that all the problems which this term connotes be excluded from the wine of Paradise. What should be understood, al-Ṭabarī insists, is that "there is no injury or impropriety, for the one who drinks it, in either mind or body or any other way."[49]

The chief concern with the final phrase of this verse is that there are two ways of reading the Arabic verb (yunzi(a)fūna), both of which are considered correct. By one reading the sense is that the wine drinkers of Paradise will not find that their intellects become drained through drink. However, by the other reading, the phrase means that the wine supply never dries up.[50] Again, al-Ṭabarī is content to let both connotations stand because, he says, both are true about the wine of heaven: it neither troubles the mind nor does it ever run dry.

Fakhr al-Dīn al-Rāzī repeats, of course, much of what is found in al-Ṭabarī's commentary. He adds nothing to the equation of the term ka's with wine, preferring to concentrate on the descriptive maᶜīn which I have translated as "clear drink." This commentator notes that the word means something which flows forth from a spring and is visible to the eye.[51] He, too, observes that the adjective "white (bayḍā')" refers to the wine and comments that "the wine of Paradise is an intense white, like milk."[52]

He spends more time than does al-Ṭabarī on the Arabic term for "pleasure (ladhdha)." His unexpressed question is why is the substantive used rather than the adjectival form (ladhīdh)? The use, he explains, corresponds to those instances when a man is described as "generosity" (itself) or "nobleness" (itself). On the other hand, perhaps "pleasure" is part of a phrase, one term of which, hādhā, has been suppressed, so that its full signification would be: "the pleasure of this is for the drinkers."[53] Al-Rāzī, who is frequently found to be uncomfortable with anything that verges on textual juggling, expressly prefers the first explanation.[54]

This exegete's discussion of the term (ghawl) is brief, as is his treatment of the concluding phrase of this verse. The point he wishes to stress is that since earthly wine-drinking is accompanied by a plethora of evils, God took extra pains to assure the faithful that heaven's wine would be free of all deleterious side-effects.[55] Sūra 56, verses 18 and 19 will be considered next because they so closely parallel the passage just analyzed. As part of a description of the delights to be enjoyed by the blessed in Paradise, there occurs the following:

With bowls and ewers and a cup
of clear drink
From it they have not headaches nor are
They depleted.

Al-Ṭabarī first determines the kinds of containers mentioned. To summarize the series of ḥadīths which he includes: bowls (akwāb) are broadmouthed drinking vessels, often made of silver, with neither handle nor spout. Ewers (abārīq) are narrow-mouthed pitchers with handles, used for constantly refilling the bowls.[56]

As the phrase "a cup of clear drink" duplicates 37: 45, this part of the commentary adds nothing new. The next section, "from it they have not headaches (lā yuṣaddaᶜūna)" is not a verbal repetion of sūra 37, but it carries much the same connotation. Al-Ṭabarī explains that this means that "their heads do not hurt from drinking it and they do not become intoxicated."[57] As the concluding phrase also duplicates sūra 37, al-Ṭabarī abbreviates his coverage of it. He does, however, repeat some of what he said earlier "so that no one would suppose that its meaning in this passage is inconsistent with its meaning in the former."[58]

Fakhr al-Dīn al-Rāzī, too, begins his treatment of this passage with a discussion of the various receptacles mentioned. A kūb, he says, is either a large drinking bowl or a small, handleless jug, while an ewer has both a handle and a spout. If questioned about the use of ka's in the singular when the other two containers are given in plural form, this exegete would answer that the reason is to be sought in the nature of drinking customs: "No one drinks from more than one cup at any one time, while the number of wine-containers used at one sitting can be multiple."[59] Another justification for the divine use of ka's in the singular and abārīq and akwāb in the plural is the distinction thus made between the vessel and what it contains. Inasmuch as ka's means a "filled cup," its use in the singular emphasizes that the drink is all of one sort. Whereas the use of abārīq, for example, in the plural casts emphasis on the containers, which are of great value, rather than on what is in them. Such is but another example, says al-Rāzī of "the fine style of the Qur'ān (balāghat al-Qur'ān)."[60]

An interesting sidelight is that he contradicts al-Ṭabarī on the way in which the heavenly drink circulates. Al-Rāzī's containers go around by themselves--they autoambulate. The attendant who accompanies them is there to show respect not to transport the containers.[61]

A final remark on the subject of containers reveals this exegete's delight in finding examples of divine patterning. Note, he says, how well these words are arranged; the order of their occurrence reflects the order of their use "for drink is poured from a large bowl (al-kūb) to an ewer (al-ibrīq) and from an ewer to a cup (al-ka's)."[62]

Up to this point al-Rāzī, unlike in his commentary on 37: 45-47, has not committed himself on the nature of the liquid in these three containers. In fact, he is quite willing to entertain the notion that the ewers (abārīq), which are evidently elaborately embellished, circulate empty as objects for aesthetic appreciation.[63] Such is not the case, however, with the cup (ka's) which is specified with the phrase min maᶜīn, meaning a liquid which flows freely. Such a descriptive, he comments, "if applied to water is certainly something praiseworthy; if it is applied to something other than water, then it is a wondrous matter not found in this world."[64]

The point which al-Rāzī hopes to make about the phrase "from it they have not headaches (lā yuṣaddaᶜūna ᶜan-hā)" is that it is a compliment to the drink not the drinkers. It is not the drinkers' superior constitutions which are being commended but the wine itself which is characterized as incapable of giving a headache. With the final phrase of this verse, al-Rāzī again immerses himself in matters of pattern and sequence. He tries out several combinations of the possible meanings attributed to this phrase and the one which precedes it. If the former phrase means "there is no headache from drinking wine" and the latter phrase means "there is no intoxication," then the sequence is good, for it moves from a minor side-effect to a major one.[65]

If the first phrase carries connotations of not being parted from wine and the second continues to connote lack of intoxication, this, too, is good. "The lack of intoxication combined with their continuous supply of drink is a marvel!"[66] The same rationale holds if the first phrase means that wine-drinking occasioned no headaches and the second phrase is understood to mean no depletion in supply. As al-Rāzī so aptly notes, there is nothing marvelous about the lack of headache "if their drink is but a little."[67]

The final verse to be considered is also a description of Paradise, but one worded quite differently than the two just treated:

> A parable of the Garden which is promised to the pious: In it are rivers of water which does not become brackish, and rivers of milk whose taste does not change, and rivers of wine (a pleasure for the drinkers), and rivers of honey which is clear . . . (47: 15).

Al-Ṭabarī's analysis of this verse is concise and straight-forward. His explanation of "rivers of wine (a pleasure for the drinkers) (anhāru min khamrin ladhdhatin li-'l-shāribīna)" cites the following curious ḥadīth. The wine is delicious because "the Majūs (Zoroastrians) have not poisoned it, Satan has not blown into it and the sun has not damaged it; it is yet fragrant."[68] Other than that, he has little to say about it.

Al-Rāzī expands on this treatment somewhat and does so by again finding evidence of divine patterning. The rivers, he notes, are of four kinds of drinks: two of them are drunk for their taste (honey and milk) and two are drunk for reasons other than taste (water and wine).[69] With respect to wine, he finds further support for this arrangement in the fact that wine is very unpleasant tasting (karīhatu 'l-ṭaᶜmi). What God does with these drinks when he offers them to the pious in Paradise is to rid each one of its earthly defect; thus, water never becomes brackish, milk never sours, wine tastes good and honey is filtered of waxpieces and other extraneous matter.[70]

In addition to praising these things on the basis of taste, God associated them with regard to frequency of use. In this respect "water which is not drunk for its taste but is the universal drink, He connected with milk which is drunk for its taste and is also a universal drink, as there is no one who has not drunk it."[71] Wine, by the same token, which is an unusual drink, not drunk for its flavour, is paired with another uncommon but flavourful drink, honey.

Al-Rāzī returns once again to the issue of wine's taste in his explanation of the phrase "a pleasure for the drinkers." Inasmuch as taste is idiosyncratic and because most people find the taste of wine repugnant, God had to specify that the wine He provides will taste delicious to everyone.[72]

What is most striking about the exegesis of this group of verses, taken as a whole, is the pattern of contrasts it displays and develops. While the commentators surveyed do not hesitate to catalogue wine's earthly evils, neither are they diffident about lauding its heavenly benefits. All the reasons for which they insist that wine is here forbidden will be reversed in Paradise. What is now a sin will be, for those who enter there, a pleasure.

Notes

[1] Abū Jaʿfar Muḥammad b. Jarīr al-Ṭabarī, Jāmiʿ 'l-Bayān ʿan Ta'wīl al-Qur'ān, eds. Maḥmūd Muḥammad Shākir and Aḥmad Muḥammad Shākir (Cairo: Dār al-Maʿārif, 1377/1954-), 4: 320. Because this edition is not yet complete, the commentary for verses after sūrat al-raʿd will be found in the edition cited in footnote 45.

[2] Ibid.

[3] Ibid., p. 321.

[4] Ibid., p. 325.

[5] Ibid., p. 326.

[6] Ibid.

[7] Ibid., p. 327.

[8] Ibid., pp. 328-329.

[9] Ibid., p. 334.

[10] Ibid., pp. 334-335.

[11] Muḥammad ibn Isḥāq, Sīrat rasūl Allāh, trans. A. Guillaume (London: Oxford University Press, 1955), pp. 118 and 281.

[12] Al-Ṭabarī, 4: 335.

[13] Muḥammad ibn ʿUmar Fakhr al-Dīn al-Rāzī, al-Tafsīr al-Kabīr (Cairo: al-Maṭbaʿa 'l-Bahiyya 'l-Miṣriyya, n.d.), 6: 42.

[14] Al-Ṭabarī does include one ḥadīth which speaks of a sequence of four verses. But unlike al-Rāzī's sequence of 16: 67, 2: 219, 4: 43 and 5: 90-91, this includes 2: 219, 16: 67 and counts 5: 90 and 5: 91 separately. (See al-Ṭabarī, 4: 334.) All the other ḥadīth which al-Ṭabarī cites mention only three--2: 219, 4: 43 and 5: 90-91.

[15] Al-Rāzī, 6: 42.

[16] Ibid.

[17] Ibid., p. 43.

[18] Ibid.

[19] Ibid.

[20] Ibid.

[21] Ibid.

[22] Ibid., p. 44.

[23] Ibid., p. 45.

[24] Ibid., p. 43.

[25] Ibid., p. 46.

[26] Ibid.

[27] Ibid.

[28] Ibid.

[29] For a comment on this, note A.J. Wensinck's statement in the article entitled "Khamr" which he wrote for the second edition of the Encyclopaedia of Islam: "This sequence of revelations regarding wine is the accepted one among the traditionists and commentators of the

Ḳur'ān." (Leiden: E.J. Brill, 1973), 4: 994, col. 2. Wensinck was apparently unaware of Fakhr al-Dīn al-Rāzī's rejection of such a theory of sequential revelation on wine.

30 Al-Rāzī, 6: 47.
31 Ibid.
32 Ibid.
33 Ibid.
34 Ibid.
35 Ibid., p. 49.
36 Ibid.
37 Ibid.
38 Ibid.
39 Ibid.
40 Ibid.
41 Ibid.
42 Ibid.
43 Ibid., pp. 49-50.
44 Ibid., p. 50, footnote 1.
45 Al-Ṭabarī, Jamiᶜ 'l-Bayān fī Tafsīr al-Qur'ān (Cairo: al-Maṭbaᶜa 'l-Yamaniyya, n.d.), 23: 31.
46 Ibid.
47 Ibid.
48 Ibid., p. 32.
49 Ibid.
50 Ibid.
51 Al-Rāzī, 26: 137.
52 Ibid.
53 Ibid.
54 Ibid.
55 Ibid., p. 138.
56 Al-Ṭabarī, 27: 90.
57 Ibid.
58 Ibid., p. 91.
59 Al-Rāzī, 29: 150.
60 Ibid.
61 Ibid.
62 Ibid.
63 Ibid., p. 151.
64 Ibid.
65 Ibid., p. 152.
66 Ibid.
67 Ibid.
68 Al-Ṭabarī, 26: 29.
69 Al-Rāzī, 28: 54. In this passage al-Rāzī divides taste into the following nine categories: bitter (al-murr), salty (al-malīḥ), pungent (al-ḥirrīf), sour (al-ḥamīd), sharp (al-ᶜafīṣ), astringent (al-qābiḍ), insipid (al-tafih), sweet (al-ḥulw) and fatty (al-dasim). The most delicious, according to al-Rāzī, are the sweet and the fatty while "the sweetest of things is honey."
70 Ibid.
71 Ibid.
72 Ibid., p. 55.

11

The Qur'ān's Doctrine of Prophecy

George Hourani †
The State University of New York at Buffalo

The prophetic career of Muḥammad has been the most significant single event in the life of all the Muslim peoples down to the present time, determining their religion and to a large extent their cultures and attitudes to life. Muslim theologians and philosophers have written extensively on the nature of Muḥammad's prophecy, in a wide variety of theories--theological (Sunnite and Shīᶜite), philosophical and mystical. But the framework which is expected to provide the structure and limits of all later theories is given by what the Qur'ān itself says about prophecy, in particular that of Muḥammad.

It is true, as the great Hungarian scholar Goldziher explained, that Islam did not spring up as a complete system of theology and law from the beginning.[1] But the Qur'ān does contain a good deal of reflection on itself and on prophets. Thus the most fundamental task of any study of theories of prophecy in Islam must be to study the theory which is explicit or implicit in the Qur'ān. Much has been written on this subject as parts of general studies of the Qur'ān. The most valuable study I have come across has been that of the late Arthur Jeffery in his classic lectures, "The Qur'ān as Scripture".[2]

I shall now present a simple account of the subject by seeking answers in the Qur'ān to some questions concerning prophecy and particularly that of Muḥammad:

What are the functions of a prophet?

What are his qualifications?

How does he operate?

What are the indications of his authenticity?

In answering these questions I shall generally avoid the temptation to refer to interpretations by later Muslim scholars of

Logos Islamikos: Studia Islamica in honorem Georgii Michaelis Wickens, ed. Roger M. Savory and Dionisius A. Agius, Papers in Mediaeval Studies 6 (Toronto: Pontifical Institute of Mediaeval Studies, 1984), pp. 175-181.

what the Qur'ān says about prophecy. I shall give my own interpretation, trying to keep as close as possible to the meaning and spirit of the Book.

I

The primary function of prophets is made very clear in the Qur'ān: it is to deliver a moral message from God to the world, and to the Arabs in particular. The message has two parts, corresponding to the two main purposes of ethics in the West, from Socrates to the present: (1) to provide the normative content (not merely a definition) of right living and thinking, (2) to provide motivation for such living and thinking--in the case of the Qur'ān through preaching rewards and punishments in this life and the next. This is the purpose of all the Biblical and Arabian stories, which illustrate how previous nations had ignored their prophets and come to grief for that. But more inward motives to virtue are also indicated.

A summary statement of these two messages is given in the opening verses of Sūra 2, the Cow (God addressing Muhammad):

> This is the Book, in which there is no doubt,
> guidance to the godfearing
> who believe in the Unseen and perform prayer
> and spend what We have provided them with,
> who believe in what has been sent down to you
> and what has been sent down before you,
> and have faith in the hereafter;
> those are upon guidance from their Lord,
> those are the ones who prosper. (2: 1-4).[3]

Then follow two corresponding verses on the unbelievers, with an added note of predestination: they are (2: 5-6) blinded, etc.

We notice that the message is written in a book, a scripture. A prophet may receive God's revelations audially; if so, as in Muḥammad's case, he has to write or dictate them soon afterwards, so that the messages will be preserved accurately.

This last point, accurate preservation of God's words in a scripture, is one that the Qur'ān insists on consciously. Indeed it provides one half of the justification for the Prophet Muḥammad's mission. This fact can best be explained from the Qur'ānic doctrine of its own relation to previous prophets and their scriptures. The same divine message had been given in different words to all the previous prophets. Twenty-four of them are named in the two longest lists (6: 84-89 and 21: 48-91), running from Noah to Jesus. There are also three Arabians, Hūd, Ṣāliḥ and Shu^{c}ayb.[4] They had all spoken truth, especially Abraham who had received the message in its purest form. But their peoples, the Jews and the Christians, had in course of time corrupted the texts of their scriptures. Thus their present texts are no longer wholly correct, although they contain much of the truth in religion; for this reason the Qur'ān allows a special status to "the People of the Book," (Jews and Christians), which would secure their toleration in Islamic countries.

The primary purpose of the Qur'ān, then, was to restore the pure, original religion of Abraham. It would of course come in different words and even in another language, but the message would be the same, a strict monotheism, a moral life, heaven and hell. And because it was being dictated immediately and accurately, its chances of preservation were better than the messages of the earlier prophets, and it would be the final revelation for mankind. This insistence on accuracy led in fact to the early, scholarly production of an official text about twenty years after Muḥammad's death, a text with very minor variations which has been standard ever since.

But there was a second justification for the new revelation. It was spoken and written in Arabic, so that the Arabs, who had previously lacked a scripture because they could not understand Hebrew or Greek, might have "a clear Arabic Qur'ān." They were, after all, the descendants of Abraham through Ishmael (Ismā'īl), and they deserved and needed a scripture as much as any other nation. This doctrine has a well-known parallel in some words of Mani, the founder of the Manichaean religion in the third century AD:

> Wisdom and mighty deeds have always been brought to mankind by messengers coming from time to time from God. So in one age they were brought to India by the messenger named Buddha, in another by Zarathustra to Persia, in another by Jesus to the West. So now this revelation has come down, this prophecy in this last age, through me, Mani, the messenger of the God of truth to Babylonia.[5]

Was the Qur'ān directed to the Arabs alone or to all mankind? Certainly it was directed specially to the Arabs, to give them a scripture in their own language. But also, I think, to all men, if we are to believe the Tradition the Muḥammad sent messengers to the four emperors of Byzantium, Iran, India and Ethiopia urging them to submit to Islam and take their nations with them. Other evidence of intended universality is found in the great sweep of Qur'ānic narratives going back to the ancient Egyptians, the Biblical Israelites and the Christians as well as the Arabians.

The Qur'ān's insistence that it was the final revelation has had definite consequences in the history of Islam. It has led Muslims not only to believe that all earlier religions were outdated, which is a normal reaction in followers of a new religion, but further, to resent strongly any attempt to create a new religion claiming divine inspiration. This attitude has been shown in the fierce hostility to the claims of ᶜAbd al-Bahā' and Bahā'uddīn, the nineteenth-century founders of the Bahā'ī religion, especially in Iran where it originated.

The doctrine of finality has also had a consequence for all later Muslim theorists of prophecy: that they have been concerned exclusively with a historical event of the past, and can never think about prophecy as an institution that might be revived in new forms for the further improvement of human life. This limitation is shared by the other historical religions.

Some prophets have a second function, which is illustrated in the historical roles of Muhammad and Moses: to act as political leaders of their people, in organizing, defending and expanding their new communities. This function is reflected in the Madīna sūras which state "Obey God and the Messenger." But it is recorded in detail in the Traditions, which narrate the history of the earliest Islamic state, led by the Prophet. The conception of religio-political leadership was to shape the whole of Islamic history until modern times, and has once more been put into practice in an extreme form in revolutionary Iran.

II

The qualifications of a prophet are not stressed in the Qur'ān, indeed the whole conception of "qualifications" as something needed by a genuine prophet may be alien to the thinking of the Book. The stress is rather on God's choice of a man as His messenger, al-muṣṭafà, "the chosen" according to His will. Prophets are mortal men, with no special powers or perfection.

Another qualification for a prophet is brought out in the stories of the prophets and in Muḥammad's own experience: the ability to stand firm against ridicule and threats.

III

How does a prophet operate in his major and essential role of delivering the message of God? The Qur'ān says many times to Muhammad, You are only a messenger, sent to deliver a message of guidance and warning to the people. Thus his role is a rather passive one, to receive God's message and transmit it faithfully, exactly as it is given to him. The mode of delivery is oral, from God or the angel Gabriel. Two words are used for revelation, tanzīl, "sending down" and waḥy, "inspiration." According to the contextual analysis of Jeffery, tanzīl connotes the sending of a message from an external source, waḥy the development of internal ideas.[6] But the two words are not consciously distinguished by the Qur'ān, no doubt because every message involves both transmission from God and an internal activity in the prophet's mind. The transitive verb awḥà is predicated of God: He "inspires" the messenger with the ideas that He wants them to transmit to the people.

The transmission is not completed until the messenger has repeated the message in public forms, through dictating it to a scribe and then having it recited aloud, in a mosque or a private meeting of Muslims. Muḥammad is urged by God not to be hasty in dictation as a consequence of his anxiety, but to wait until the message is clearly formed in his mind (20:114). This injunction implies an active role for the prophet in composing the message in Arabic.

But the Qur'ān contains no theory of prophetic psychology, such as was developed later by the philosophers Fārābī and Ibn Sīnā on the basis of Aristotelian psychology.

IV

Prophets who claimed a special relation with God were expected to give proof of the authenticity of this relation. This was an expectation of the Arabs of the Prophet's time, derived from their knowledge of history combined with a natural scepticism. Moses had proved himself by his magic, turning a rod into a snake which swallowed whatever Pharaoh's magicians produced, and by dividing the sea with another stroke of his rod, to save the Israelites and destroy the Egyptian army (26: 29ff). Jesus produced medical miracles, healing people by faith and reviving dead Lazarus.

So what miracle could Muḥammad perform as a sign (āya) of his authentic divine inspiration? Such a sign was urgently needed by him because from an early date of his mission he was accused by his opponents in Mecca of being an impostor and a liar. Three signs are mentioned in the Qur'ān.

One is the unique character of the Book; its opponents are challenged to produce a fragment like it (ten sūras), but of course they could not do so (11: 16). This claim was later elaborated by theologians as the miraculous literary style of the Qur'ān,[7] and by Ghazālī more profoundly as its miraculous moral message.[8] The Qur'ān admits that Muḥammad cannot produce the usual type of miracle, but it gives this impressive answer, that the message itself is the miracle. Ibn Rushd later expressed this point in a philosophical way, arguing that the miracle of Muḥammad is of the essence of his primary function, whereas the miracles of other prophets have been accidental, external acts which are irrelevant to their functions. Thus he proclaims the superiority of the "sign" of Islam to those of other religions.[9]

The second answer proving the divine origin of the Qur'ān is its harmony with the Bible. The Bible is said to contain forecasts of Muḥammad, and the Qur'ān confirms the messages of the Bible (3: 2, 10: 94, etc.).

A third sign of a divine origin is indicated in refutation of accusations by opponents that Muḥammad had copied bible stories that were read out to him by informants (25: 4-5). The answer is given in 16: 103--

> We know very well that they say,
> "Only a mortal is teaching him."
> The speech of him at whom they hint is foreign, (a^{c}jamī)
> And this is clear Arabic speech.

I think we must understand the "foreign speech" to refer to the written texts of the Bible in Hebrew and Greek. The argument then is that the Prophet produced his texts in Arabic without employing any Hebrew or Greek sources, so he could have derived them only from a revealed source, just as all the earlier prophets had done, from Abraham to Jesus.

Notes

1 I. Goldziher, Vorlesungen über den Islam (Heidelberg, 1910), pp. 33-36 seq.

2 Published: New York, 1952.

3 References are to the verse numbers of the standard Cairo edition. Quotations are from A.J. Arberry, The Koran Interpreted, 2 vols. (London, 1955), with minor stylistic modifications.

4 Adam is mentioned once as a prophet (3:33). Isaiah and the later Jewish prophets are not mentioned. The Arabians wrote no scriptures. Further details in Jeffery, pp. 37-38.

The probable existence of an Arabic Bible in Najrān, South Arabia, in the sixth century AD has been argued forcefully by I. Shahid on the basis of new evidence in a contemporary Syriac letter; see his The Martyrs of Najrān. New Documents (Brussels, 1971), pp. 242-250. But this Bible does not seem to have been known in Mecca or Medīna in the seventh century.

5 Quoted by Bīrūnī in his Chronology of Ancient Nations, trans. E. Sachau (London, 1879), p. 207; also in Jeffery, p. 43.

6 Jeffery, pp. 51 seq.

7 E.g., Muḥammad ibn al-Tayyib Bāqillānī, I^c^jāz al-Qur'ān.

8 Ghazālī, al-Munqidh min ad-Ḍalāl, in Istanbul, Şehid Ali Paša MS 1712, par. 117; trans. R.J. McCarthy, in al-Ghazālī, Freedom and Fulfillment (Boston, 1980), pp. 99-100.

9 Kitāb al-Kashf ^c^an Manāhij al-Adilla, ed. M.J. Müller (Munich, 1859), p. 103; Spanish trans. M. Alonso (Madrid-Grenada, 1947), pp. 319-320. This point ignores the centrality to Christianity of the miracle of the resurrection of Jesus; but a Muslim naturally thinks thus, since the Qur'ān denies the truth of the resurrection.

10 See A.T. Welch, "Ḳur'ān," in EI[2] 5: 402-404. I shall avoid the temptation to consider a third alternative, the use of Arabic intermediaries, either by oral transmission or written translation. This would lead to a long discussion, but any conclusion would not alter the statement of what the Qur'ān considers as proofs of authenticity, which is our subject. Nor shall I discuss the traditional interpretation of ummī as "illiterate," used in classical Islam to rule out Muḥammad as creative in any sense in the formation of the Book. As Welch says, "There is no basis in the Ḳur'ān for the traditional view that ummī means 'illiterate'" (ibid., p. 403). For evidence that he was literate, see Welch, ibid., and R. Blachère, Introduction au Koran (Paris, 1947), pp. 4-12.

The Significance of Kashshī's *Rijāl* in Understanding the Early Role of the Shī^{c}ite *Fuqahā'*

Abdulaziz A. Sachedina
The University of Virginia

Among the early Shī^{c}ite works on *rijāl* (biographical dictionaries) Abū ^{c}Amr Muḥammad ibn ^{c}Umar ibn ^{c}Abd al-^{c}Azīz al-Kashshī's (floruit in the first half of the fourth/tenth century) *Rijāl* is the earliest and different from the works of this genre. It is a collection of *ḥadīth*-reports about the doctrines and transmitters of the early Shī^{c}ah movement, each report being appended with the *isnād* (chain of transmission). Its value lies in its inclusion of contradictory narratives about the close associates of the Imāmite Imāms during the formative period of Shī^{c}ah thought (second/seventh-third/eighth centuries). Kashshī's inclusion of this material indicates that he was not compelled to provide a standard appraisal of the associate in question. It was this latter fact that led to the criticism of his methodology by a renowned Imāmite *rijāl* scholar, Aḥmad ibn ^{c}Alī ibn al-^{c}Abbās al-Najāshī (d. 450/1058-1059), who considered Kashshī's *Rijāl* informative but full of errors caused by incorporation of material related by "weak" transmitters (*al-ḍu^{c}afā'*).[1]

The original work of Kashshī was entitled *kitāb ma^{c}rifat al-nāqilīn ^{c}an al-a'immat al-ṣādiqīn* (Information on those who reported on the authority of the Truthful Imāms),[2] which was abridged and partly expurgated by Muḥammad ibn al-Ḥasan al-Ṭūsī (d. 460/1067), under the title of *Ikhtiyār ma^{c}rifat al-rijāl* (Select Information on the *rijāl*). It is this abridged version that has survived for posterity.

^{c}Ilm al-rijāl *and its centrality in the Imāmite Shī^{c}ism*

^{c}Ilm al-rijāl or *ma^{c}rifat al-rijāl* is a branch of the religious

Logos Islamikos: Studia Islamica in honorem Georgii Michaelis Wickens, ed. Roger M. Savory and Dionisius A. Agius, Papers in Mediaeval Studies 6 (Toronto: Pontifical Institute of Mediaeval Studies, 1984), pp. 183-206.

sciences dealing with the study of the transmitters (al-ruwāt) who figure in the isnāds that are appended to ḥadīth-reports. ᶜIlm al-rijāl, as such, is a discipline that studies the information about the rijāl (plural of rajul, literally "a man," technically "a prominent personage") critically, in order to determine the level of authenticity of an informant which directly affected the authenticity of a tradition reported by that person. Biographical information on each informant of a tradition was studied to gain insight into his character and to ascertain his moral probity and religious standing in order for him to be declared thiqah (reliable), or ḍaᶜīf (weak), or majhūl (unknown), or kadhūb (liar) and so on. It was on the basis of such examination that a ḥadīth-report was classified as ṣaḥīḥ (authentic), muwaththaq (reliable), ḥasan (fairly reliable), ḍaᶜīf (weak) and so on. Hence, the result of the investigations in ᶜilm al-rijāl was of great consequence for the religious practice of the Muslim community.[3]

In Imāmī Shīᶜism, from the early years of its history, ᶜilm al-rijāl has received much attention because of its preoccupation with the question of leadership (imāmah). The focal point of Shīᶜī religious belief system or cosmology is the Imām of the Age (imām al-zamān), representing the transcendental active God on earth. Thus, it is this basic religious focus on the leadership that orients the authoritative perspective or world-view of the faithful in Shīᶜite Islam. The concealment of the last Imām in 873-874 AD necessitated the assumption of the leadership by the prominent followers of the school, who, in addition, were the repositories of the Imāmite learning. Thus, there were two factors that decided the question of leadership among the Imāmite community: first, "sound belief" (īmān ṣaḥīḥ), that is, upholding the Imāmate of the twelve Imāms; and, second, "sound knowledge" (ᶜilm ṣaḥīḥ, that is, the learning acquired from the ahl al-bayt, i.e., the Imāms. These two factors had been held determinant for the Shīᶜī rijāl, at all times, to represent the Imāms among their adherents. Through this "sound belief" and "sound knowledge" one can discern a kind of continuity that is available in the isnāds of transmitted sciences (al-ᶜulūm al-naqliyya). The psychological reason for appending an isnād to a ḥadīth-report is to link a contemporary reporter to the past eminent figure who actually affords the necessary reliability of the reported text. In transmitted sciences (manqūlāt), each link in the isnād stands independently as well as dependently, because the requirement of "sound belief" and "sound knowledge" applies to each person mentioned in the chain individually, and to all collectively. It was probably for this reason that before accepting any part of the transmitted science, it was felt necessary to establish a chain of rijāl, who formed the links through whom that part of the knowledge became accessible, and to ascertain a continuity of the religious, reliable individuals who collectively afforded the authenticity of that knowledge. There is also a deeper reason for insisting on this kind of continuity, namely, the survival of the original ideology. In the intellectual environment of Madīnah, Kūfah or Baghdad, where the Imāmite rijāl could engage freely in discussion with their adversaries, there always remained the danger not only of compromise in regard to, but also of interpolation in, the original teachings of the Imāms. It is for this reason that in Imāmite jurisprudence only few associates of the early Imāms were accepted as forming a chain of people whose consensus of opinion (ijmā^c) in legal matters could be held legally binding.

There also seems to be a theological reason for the insistence on the proper isnād in the arena of transmitted religious sciences. The office of the Imāmate in Shī^cism was established through the process of al-naṣṣ al-ṣarīḥ (explicit designation). For any individual to claim the Imāmate without a proper designation was regarded as false claim. Hence, it was naṣṣ that provided the Imāmate with necessary legitimacy in assuming the leadership of the ummah. Moreover, naṣṣ, in the Shī^cī view, was the only guarantee that the Imām was infallible, since, according to the theory of Imāmate, only an infallible Imām could designate another infallible Imām. As a result, naṣṣ and ^ciṣma (infallibility) were made interdependent to ensure the succession of the rightful Imām. In the theory of the Imāmate, one can thus perceive the naṣṣ to be the chain (or more precisely, "chain of gold,", as described by ^cAlī al-Riḍā, the eighth Imāmite Imām), which links the Imāms to one another and to the actual source of divine authority, the Prophet. Without such a linkage in the Imāmate one cannot comprehend the insistence of the Imāmite theologians that a believer must either accept all the twelve or none of the Imāms, because it is a line of twelve Imāms, linked through the principle of naṣṣ for the assumption of the leadership of the ummah, that guarantees the preservation and protection of the Islamic message revealed to the Prophet.

The isnād in a ḥadīth-report consisted of a chain of transmitters who linked the tradition to the actual source from which it was acquired. Such a linkage was necessary in order to render the report sound. Furthermore, it created a sense of continuity in the religious leadership, because the rijāl had the confidence of the Imāms and, in certain cases, were properly designated as their trustworthy representatives among their followers with authority to disseminate their teachings. However, their proper designation by the infallible Imāms did not guarantee their immunity from becoming a cause of corruption; rather, it established their reliability and their righteousness. The latter trait of character is known as ᶜadālah in Imāmite jurisprudence. ᶜAdālah is a quality required of the ruwāt (the transmitters of the Imāms' teachings), in order to render their transmission "sound" (ṣaḥīḥ). Consequently isnād, like naṣṣ, was the process which provided the rijāl, who were also the ruwāt, with the required legitimacy is assuming the socio-religious leadership of the Imāmites, especially, during the occultation of the twelfth Imām. In the absence of a proper isnād going back to the original source of authority, the Imāms, no Imāmite jurist would have been able to establish the authenticity of the substance he was teaching, nor the place he was occupying. The meticulous study of the isnāds, from the early times, which is evident from the number of works on rijāl compiled in tenth and eleventh centuries, substantiates the point the isnāds were not only considered keys to authentic knowledge; they were also critical to authentic authority. Isnāds carried important information about the way a particular tradition was transmitted from person to person, giving names of a chain of persons who received the tradition from one another in succession. More importantly, it gave some idea about who studied under whom and who, possibly, had the permission (ijāzah) to cite on the authority of whom. It was knowledge, combined with the source of that knowledge, that gave a position of weight and influence to some of the prominent jurists and theologians of the Imāmite school, so that they were able to exercise their authority in that community. These early scholars saw themselves as forming part of the isnād going back to the infallible Imāms, and were acknowledged as such by later Imāmite scholars, who depended on their expositions and elaboration of the transmitted religious sciences.

The Authentication (tawthīq) of the Transmitted Sciences (manqūlāt)

In Imāmite Shīᶜism several methods of authentication of the manqūlāt have been recognized from the early days. One of the most basic methods has been to investigate whether one of the maᶜṣūmīn (the infallible personages, i.e., the Prophet or the Imāms) has left objective documentation in the form of a clear text (naṣṣ) to the effect that a certain transmitted report is related on their authority. Such an investigation would take a researcher through critical examination of the naṣṣ, so as to verify its authenticity in the light of historical and exegetical literature. At this point, rijāl-works like that of Kashshī provide material which is valuable for both historical as well as exegetical analysis. For instance, Kashshī in his biographical note ᶜImrān ibn ᶜAbd Allāh al-Qummī mentions two reports[4] in which the Imām Jaᶜfar al-Ṣādiq praises ᶜImrān and prays for him and his descendants. This naṣṣ from the infallible Imām establishes the reliability of ᶜImrān in regard to what he reports. However, on careful examination of the chain of transmission provided by Kashshī, one discovers that the isnād is defective because it includes "some [unknown] persons from Kūfah" whose reliability it is impossible to establish. As a result, what has been transmitted by ᶜImrān ibn ᶜAbd Allāh on the authority of al-Ṣādiq cannot be authenticated.

In Imāmite fiqh (jurisprudence) from the time of the "ancient" (al-mutaqaddimūn) fuqahā' (fourth/tenth century), the use of transmitted sciences by narrators whose reliability could not be established in the rijāl was problematic. The reliance on such information was regarded as having been derived from "biographical suppositions" (al-ẓunūn al-rijāliyyah). No legal judgement could become binding if derived from this kind of supposition. It is usually claimed that in Imāmite fiqh, al-ᶜaql (reasoning) plays a dominant role in the form of ijtihād (independent reasoning of a faqīh). But in actuality reasoning has a limited role, namely, to establish the intrinsicality (mulāzamah) between a ruling derived on the authority of revelation (al-sam^c) and that derived on the authority of reasoning (al-^caql). For instance, reasoning should be able to establish the intrinsicality between the prohibition regarding fasting on two particular days of festival (those following the fasting month of Ramaḍān and during the ḥajj) and the reason behind this prohibition. Consequently, in Imāmite fiqh, in order to derive a ruling in the sharī^cah, in most cases there is no other source than the ḥadīth reports related on the authority of the Prophet and the Imāms--the ma^cṣūmīn. These reports, before they can be used as a piece of evidence to support a legal ruling, have to be authenticated through study of the isnād. It is not without cause that one of the fundamental requirements for an Imāmite faqīh is that he should thoroughly equip himself with a knowledge of ^cilm al-rijāl, rather than with al-manṭiq (logic), as one might expect in the exercise of ijtihād.[5]

In addition to the objective documentation provided by the Imāms, the naṣṣ of the early, eminent Imāmite scholars has been regarded as equally authoritative in the authentication of the transmitted sciences. Thus, statements about the absolute or relative reliability and trustworthiness of the transmitters in what they transmitted in the works of Kashshī, Ibn Babūyah (d. 381/991-992), Mufīd (d. 414/1023), Najāshī, Ṭūsī (d. 460/1067) and others of their stature, are regarded as authenticating statements and hence, valid in deriving legal decisions. This inclusion of the Imāmite fuqahā' in the authentication process was the inevitable consequence of the end of the manifest Imāmate marked by the occultation of the last Imām. They, in fact, became part of the isnād, as discussed above.

However, this authentication of the rijāl by the fuqahā' was not always based on objective documentation; rather, it included their personal conjectures. As a result, accepting their statements in their entirety, without further investigation of the rijāl literature, was regarded as contributing to the "biographical suppositions." Undoubtedly, the fuqahā' in the later periods could not accept the documentation based on conjectural reliability of a transmitter provided by their predecessors. Nevertheless, the matter of authentication became crucial when the fuqahā' had to deal with contradictory traditions. In that situation verification of the reliability of the transmission, which depended directly on the verification of the transmitter, held the key for the use of the report as a proof in support of or against a legal or theological issue.

Further authentication of the transmitted sciences in Imāmī Shīʿism was provided, although in a limited way, by the later authors of the rijāl works, the notable among them being Muntajab al-Dīn Abū al-Ḥasan ʿAlī al-Qummī (floruit in the sixth/twelfth century) and Muḥammad ibn ʿAlī, known as Ibn Shahrāshūb (d. 588/1192). The time factor was an important consideration in regarding these works as forming a link with the classical fundamental works on rijāl. Much later works, by Aḥmad ibn Mūsā ibn Ṭāwūs (d. 673/1274-1275), Ḥasan ibn Yusūf ibn al-Muṭahhar al-Ḥillī, known as ʿAllāmah (d. 725/1325), and Ḥasan ibn ʿAlī ibn Dāwūd al-Ḥillī (d. 647/1249-1250), were not given a similar status in the authentication process. In fact, they were regarded as necessarily based on conjecture and personal judgement. It is safe to assume that the authentication provided by the "ancient" fuqahā', on which most of the subsequent research was based, remained the standard statement on the thorough or relative reliability of the rijāl and their transmission. Of these "ancient" fuqahā', Ṭūsī appears to be the most frequently cited authority in the ijāzahs (permissions) that were given to disseminate the transmitted sciences. The fact is that Ṭūsī's works form the link between the early authors of uṣūl works which consisted only of those traditions which had been heard directly from the Imāms and which became sources for the four major compilations of the Imāmite traditions,[7] and the later transmitters. Hence, for the latter group, in most cases, there was no other way of authenticating a transmitter or his transmitted information except through an investigation of Ṭūsī's works and the application of personal judgement and insight. This observation is corroborated by the fact that in the case of Kashshī, which is the earliest and principal work in this discipline, the original work has not been preserved except in the abridged version of Ṭūsī. Consequently, any reference to Kashshī in the writings of the post-Ṭūsī Imāmites was based on this abridgement.

In an elaborate ijāzah given by the ʿAllāmah to a group of Imāmite scholars to cite his transmitted works, the ʿAllāmah links his sources to the line of transmission (ṭarīq) of Ibn Babūyah, his father ʿAlī ibn al-Ḥusayn ibn Babūyah (d. 940-941), Mufīd, and al-Sharīf al-Murtaḍā (d. 1044-1045) and his brother al-Raḍī (d. 1029-1030). Then he mentions his various lines of transmission to the works by the Sunnites and their Ṣiḥāḥ (ḥadīth-compilations), and to the group of authors writing in the period subsequent to Ṭūsī. At this point he remarks that the books that were written during the period preceding Ṭūsī were recorded and authenticated by Ṭūsī in his two works al-Fihrist and Rijāl, respectively.[8] The ijāzahs which began promptly to be appended to the major works on Imāmite transmitted sciences during the later period,[9] demonstrate the significance of ṭuruq (lines of transmission) for the later Imāmite jurists, which gave the necessary credence to the communications transmitted by them. The ṭuruq which were based on authenticated isnāds, in manqūlāt took on a much wider meaning than was customarily understood by the Imāmite scholars. Since the Imāmate had formally been discontinued by the occurrence of the Complete Occultation (941 AD),[10] those among the contemporary rijāl who appeared in the isnād as the transmitters were bound to be looked upon as the authorities who afforded authenticity to the information transmitted. Thus, the proper isnād from the year 941 AD on, meant the continuation of the religious leadership among the Imāmites, which is reflected in the chronological link established between the "ancient" fuqahā' and a contemporary religious leader, e.g., the Āyat Allāh. This isnād also assured the Imāmites that the Imām's will was uninterruptedly and authoritatively transmitted to his Shīᶜah, thereby linking the Imāmite fuqahā' to one another and to the Imām, and, in turn, linking the community to them all. Such a linkage was the source of legitimacy for the Imāmite jurists, both in the early days as well as in the later centuries of the Complete Occultation, to assume the socio-religious leadership of the Imamite community.

The Leadership of the fuqahā' in Kashshi's Rijāl

The world-view of the faithful in Imāmī Shīᶜism is dominated by the question of the Imāmate, especially during the Occultation, when the Imām of the Age is not accessible. Who can orient the Shīᶜah toward the authoritative interpretation of the Islamic revelation? It was this question that gave rise to the search for the representatives of the Imām, the representatives who could generate a confidence among both lay and élite Shīᶜites to achieve the authoritative orientation in their religious belief system.

> The earth shall not remain except that there will always be a learned authority (ᶜālim) from among us, who will distinguish the truth from falsehood.[11]

This prophecy made by the Imām al-Ṣādiq was a clear assurance that through the presence of such a "learned authority" the religious leadership will continue to provide the necessary guidance in the absence of the infallible Imām.

Kashshī begins his Rijāl with such a conviction in the Imāmite world-view. It is important to remember that Kashshī was writing during the occultation of the twelfth Imām and, as a consequence, the historical understanding and interpretation of his Rijāl ought to take into consideration the context that generated the work. From what has been said above in connection with the significance of isnād among the Imāmites (the isnād that afforded necessary credence to the transmitted sciences), it is not difficult to construe a conception of continuous leadership emerging from the Rijāl of Kashshī, in so far as such a leadership forms a link with the divinely appointed Imāmate. Thus, Kashshī cites a tradition on the authority of the Prophet in which the latter declared that the religion of God will be carried on in every century by a righteous person who will refute the interpretations of vain interpreters and repudiate the deviations of extremists and the false claims of ignorant people "just as the bellows remove the dross from iron."[12] It will be the presence of such a righteous person or a learned authority in possession of a special kind of knowledge that will preserve the authoritative perspective of God's religion on earth. Consequently, the discrete components of Kashshī's Rijāl indicate the manner in which from the time of the Prophet onward, Shīᶜī cosmology survived historical vicissitudes, and the way in which the Shīᶜī rijāl have left their mark on the path to preserve the focal point of the Shīᶜī religious experience. What follows is an exercise in reconstruction of a coherent picture as that emerges from these discrete components dispersed throughout the biographical notes in order to understand the early role of the Imāmite fuqahā'.

The most important factor in determining the leadership during the occultation was the possession of a special kind of knowledge (al-ᶜilm). This is what we have designated as "sound knowledge" in the beginning of this study. This knowledge in the early days of Shīᶜism consisted of the exegesis of the Qur'ān and the ḥadīth. According to Kashshī, it is related on the authority of the fifth Imām Muḥammad al-Bāqir (d. 113/731-732) that true knowledge (i.e., the authoritative interpretation of the Islamic revelation) could not be obtained either in the east or in the west; rather, it could be acquired only from the ahl al-bayt, the family of the Prophet, i.e., the Imāms in this context.[13] This ḥadīth implies that in order to ascertain the veracity of any knowledge, one has to ascertain its source. Hence, one can discern Kashshī's assertion that it was the close associates of the ahl al-bayt who received the true knowledge and because of this fact, only these devotees of the Imāms were in possession of necessary knowledge to protect the religion of God from corruptive innovations. This assertion by Kashshī finds support in the declaration of the Imāms that such of their adherents belong to the ahl al-bayt, which meant that they had partially inherited the ᶜilm (special kind of knowledge, sometimes esoteric) which the Imāms had inherited from the Prophet as his rightful successors.[14]

The rijāl were the prominent followers of the Imāms whose status, as Kashshī informs us, was to be reckoned in accordance with the number of communications related by them. Al-Ṣādiq is reported to have said, "Acknowledge the status of the rijāl among us in accordance with the number of riwāyāt (communications) reported on our authority."[15] Moreover, their influence and prestige among the followers of the Imāms was to be measured in proportion to their ability to transmit the Imām's opinion with great clarity on various legal as well as theological problems. As a consequence, these early rijāl were also the fuqahā' (theologians-cum-jurists). A person, according to Kashshī who quotes al-Ṣādiq's tradition here, could not become a faqīh until he was a muḥaddath, that is, a veracious person with true opinion, who reports a thing as he was told, with sagacity.[16] The rijāl were then the thorough jurists who were trained by the Imāms to represent them in matters pertaining to the faith, and as such, they were the indirect deputies of the Imāms in that sphere of their function.

In Shīᶜite Islam matters pertaining to the faith evolved gradually. These, as discerned from Kashshī's chronological arrangement of his biographical items, included anything from support of the ᶜAlid cause to the question about God's knowledge and practical issues covering canonical obligations imposed by the Islamic revelation. It is significant to note on the basis of Kashshī's Rijāl that since the political aspect of the Imāmate ended with ᶜAlī, in the subsequent period more attention was given to the religious leadership of the Imāms; whereas their temporal role was confined to the theory of the Imāmate. It is for this reason that in Shīᶜism, as it appears from the study of the Rijāl, it is almost impossible to comprehend the theory of political leadership without the study of the intellectual superstructure which sustains and organizes the concept of religious leadership. It was the latter kind of Imāmate that was historically available to the Imāms. Although early disciples of the Imāms did not conceive the Shīᶜī Imāmate in two spheres, temporal and religious, with the former being postponed for the future, gradually this fact became obvious to them during the Imāmate of the fifth and the sixth Imāms, al-Bāqir and al-Sādiq. It was probably during this period that the Shīᶜites were made aware of the futility of insisting upon their Imāms assuming their full responsibility as the leaders of the community. However, with the re-orientation of the Shīᶜites toward a more politically quietistic posture, by postponing the establishment of the true Islamic government to the future, the Imāmate became more or less a spiritual office with the potential of assuming temporal authority when the time came for such an undertaking.

Such a re-orientation of the Shīᶜites could not have come about without resistance from among the overly zealous disciples of the Imāms. These disciples are characterized as ghulāt, extremists, by Kashshī. Here, again, ᶜilm was a crucial factor in giving credence to the claims made by the ghulāt associates of the Imām. Their ghuluww, extremism, lay in their claim to the ᶜilm al-balāyā wa al-manaya,[17], esoteric knowledge about future events which was believed to have been taught by the Imāms to their special associates. That this knowledge had something to do with the establishment of the just government by over-throwing the wicked rule of the caliphs is confirmed by the fact that those of the Shīᶜah who claimed such knowledge were killed mercilessly by the government forces.[18] Furthermore, such claim by the disciples necessitated attribution of divine qualities to the Imāms who were declared as the actual source of the ᶜilm al-balāyā wa al-manāyā. The Imāms clearly sensed the danger of such attributions to them. The danger lay in the disruption of the peaceful relationship between the Imāms and the government authorities who suspected them of instigating political opposition to the ruling house. This danger was felt early on during the Imāmate of al-Bāqir and al-Ṣādiq in Kūfah, which was the nucleus of Shīᶜah activity in the eighth century. Moreover, the ghulāt had threatened the survival of the Shīᶜāh community within the larger Muslim community. By ascribing to the Imāms reports that exempted the Shīᶜah from performing the religiously prescribed duties, such as ṣalāt, if they acknowledged the Imām of the Age, the ghulāt endangered the acceptance of the Shīᶜah as part of the tolerated deviation of the ummah.[19]

Kashshī provides a striking example of such attribution in his note on al-Mufaḍḍal ibn ᶜUmar, who was among the ghulāt followers of Imām al-Ṣādiq and who later joined the extremist Shīᶜite faction of the Khaṭṭābiyyah. A man by the name of Yaḥyā ibn ᶜAbd al-Ḥamīd al-Ḥammānī, according to Kashshī, recounts the following incident in his book entitled: Fī ithbāt imāmat amīr al-mu'minīn (the Proof of the Imāmate of the Amīr of the Believers [ᶜAlī ibn Abī Ṭālib]):

> I told Sharīk [ibn al-Aᶜwar al-Ḥārithī] that a group of people maintain Jaᶜfar ibn Muḥammad [al-Ṣādiq] was weak in ḥadīth. He said: "Let me explain to you the true state of affairs. Jaᶜfar ibn Muḥammad was a pious Muslim, and fearful of God. A group of ignorant persons surrounded him, visiting him frequently and saying that 'Jaᶜfar ibn Muḥammad said such and such.' They related traditions which were all objectionable, fabricated and falsely attributed to Jaᶜfar. They did this in order to make money out of it from the people. Hence, they performed all that was objectionable on the basis of these traditions. The masses heard all these. Some followed them and destroyed themselves; while others refused to accept such (traditions). Among the former were al-Mufaḍḍal ibn ᶜUmar, Bayān, ᶜAmr al-Nabṭī and others. They were the ones who reported that Jaᶜfar [al-Ṣādiq] had told them that acknowledgement (maᶜrifah) of the Imams suffices and exempts a person from fasting and praying. They also reported on the authority of his father (i.e., al-Bāqir), and his grandfather (i.e., ᶜAlī ibn al-Ḥusayn), and that the latter had informed them concerning the events preceding the Day of Judgement . . . Indeed, Jaᶜfar [al-Ṣādiq] never said anything of this sort and he was surely above these utterances."[20]

The above citation evidently proves the point that in the process of disciplining of the ghulāt element, as in the development of the

Shīᶜah school of thought in general, the rijāl were destined to play a major role. The Imāms, from the early days, had seen the possibility of continuing their teaching by training these associates and had taken steps to realize this end. With the growing political turmoil and the atrocities committed against the family of the Prophet, the Imāms were unable to maintain normal contacts with their followers. Hence, the close associates were deputized to represent them in relations with their followers and thus was created the institution of the deputyship (niyābah) of the Imām in the early days of the Shīᶜah history.

The Deputyship of the rijāl during the Imāmate of al-Bāqir and al-Ṣādiq

The Imām, according to the Shīᶜī belief, is the leader of the Muslim community, and as such, the only legitimate authority who could and would establish the Islamic rule of justice on earth. But, in view of the inability of the Imāms to assume political leadership, the entire question of their establishing the ideal Islamic rule was postponed. Nevertheless, this postponement applied only to the Imām's temporal authority, because they continued to exercise their religious authority as the descendants and true heirs of the Prophet. They had from time to time delegated their religious-juridical authority to their close, trusted associates, who acted as their deputies or agents in places like Kūfah, Rayy and Qumm. The deputyship of the Imāms was a necessary and gradual process in order to provide guidance to the growing Shīᶜah community in far-flung areas. The idea of the Imām delegating his religious authority and functioning through his personal representatives, from among the rijāl, must be attributed to the political atmosphere in the eighth-ninth centuries, when the Imāms were for the greater part of their lives kept under surveillance or imprisoned as politically suspect by the caliphal authorities.

Kashshī tells us about the appointment of the personal representative of the Imām in the early days which was done indirectly, following a request from the Shīᶜah in distant lands for a religious guide who could teach the Imām's opinion authentically. In his long note on a prominent disciple of the Imāms al-Bāqir and al-Ṣādiq, Kashshī relates that ᶜAbd Allāh ibn Abī Yaᶜfūr, another disciple of both the Imāms from Kūfah, once came to visit Imām al-Ṣādiq in Madīnah. During this visit he told the Imām that it was not possible for him to meet him at all times; and that many times a Shīᶜī would come and ask him about a matter and he would have no answer. The Imām said: "What stops you from asking Muḥammad ibn Muslim al-Thaqafī, who heard (ḥadīth) from my father and was highly esteemed by him?"[21] It was in this manner that al-Thaqafī was indirectly appointed by the Imām to represent the Imāmite views and spread the teaching of the school among the Shīᶜah in Kūfah.

From several biographical notes on the prominent associates of the Imāms al-Bāqir and al-Ṣādiq provided by Kashshī, it is evident that the main qualification of these indirectly appointed deputies of the Imāms, who happened to be quite a few in various parts of the empire, was their comprehension of the teachings of the Imāms, the extent of which was determined by the fact of their close association with the Imām. It was the latter fact that was decisive in their being held high in esteem by the Imāms. That these prominent associates were carefully selected on the basis of their knowledge ("sound knowledge," of course) and loyalty to the Imāms ("sound belief") is attested by the oft-quoted tradition of the Imām al-Ṣādiq that among his numerous disciples four were the trusted ones of his father and himself, namely, Burayd ibn Muᶜāwiya al-ᶜIjlī, Abū Baṣīr Layth ibn al-Bākhtarī al-Murādī, Muḥammad ibn Muslim al-Thaqafī and Zurārah ibn Aᶜyān. They were, according to al-Ṣādiq, the noble and trusted ones of God on matters of His injunctions concerning that which is lawful and unlawful. "Had it not been for them, the Prophetic traditions would have been disrupted and obliterated."[22] It is obvious that the continuation of these disciples was significant in spreading the Shīᶜī ideology as taught by the Imāms and this fact was recognized repeatedly by the Imāms who depended on these rijāl to be trained as the fuqahā', to carry on the function of guiding the religious lives of the Shīᶜah.

The matter of trust and thorough reliability in the disciple was of prime importance for the Imāms, who were faced with the problem of the overzealous among their disciples, the ghulāt, who did not hesitate to interpolate in the teaching of the Imāms and announce their agency and deputyship in the esoteric knowledge, which in theory was confined to the Prophet and the Imāms. Such a claim was important for these disciples because it was the claim to have received the special knowledge from the Imām that helped them organize a social upheaval under their own leadership. Abū al-Khaṭṭāb Muḥammad ibn Abī Zaynab Miqlās al-Asadī, the founder of the extremist Shīᶜite faction of the Khaṭṭābiyyah, was a close associate of al-Ṣādiq, who presumably held a significant position as a <u>dāᶜī</u> (missionary) of this Imām in Kūfah.[23] Abū al-Khaṭṭāb, according to Kashshī, was accused by the Imām of divergences from the ritual law, which points to the fact that questions concerning law were referred to him in his capacity as one of the chief agents of this Imām in Kūfah. Furthermore, Abū al-Khaṭṭāb had asserted that al-Ṣādiq had transferred his authority to him by designating him as his <u>waṣī</u> and <u>qayyim</u> (deputy or executor of his will) and entrusting him the <u>ism al-aᶜẓam</u> (the Greatest Name) which was supposed to empower its possessor with extraordinary power in conceiving hidden matters.[24] This assertion was decisive in giving special recognition to him in Kūfah.

The whole episode of the execution of Abū al-Khaṭṭāb in Kūfah in 138/755-756 shows the extent to which any shrewd and ambitious disciple of the Imām could manipulate the genuine religious devotions of the Shīᶜah in the name of the Imām, no matter how emphatically the latter might deny any designation of the disciple as his <u>waṣī</u> or his possession of the hidden knowledge.[25] Nevertheless, the position of deputy of the Imām, however indirect and limited, inherently possessed the potential of becoming an influential office in the Imāmite community, even more so when the Imāms could not maintain regular contact with their Shīᶜah at all times. Most probably, it was during al-Ṣādiq's Imāmate that the leadership of some of these trusted transmitters of the Imāms' teachings -- the <u>ruwāt</u>, was becoming noticeable. Both Muhammad ibn Muslim al-Thaqafī and Zurārah ibn Aᶜyān had gained widespread recognition among the Shīᶜites in Kūfah as the agents of the Imāms as well as their reliable representatives in matters pertaining to the Law. Some disciples, like Zurārah and Abū Baṣīr al-Murādī, had remained the students of more than one Imām, and hence, had found themselves in an advantageous position to comment on the insight and depth of the knowledge of the living Imām of the Age. The growing authority of the transmitters of the Imām's teaching, the <u>ruwāt</u>, is symbolized by Zurārah ibn Aᶜyān's position among the disciples of the two Ṣādiqs, al-Bāqir and al-Ṣādiq.

Zurārah ibn A^cyān: A Symbol of the Power of the Early Disciples

His full name was ^cAbd Rabbih Zurārah ibn A^cyān (d. 150/767). Kashshī mentions a tradition which is reported on the authority of al-Ṣādiq, who said: "Had it not been for Zurārah, I think, the traditions of my father would have disappeared."[26] with this and other good reports about him, Kashshī recounts other traditions which show that Zurārah had on some important issues contradicted al-Ṣādiq, having reported something different on the authority of the fifth Imām al-Bāqir.

The long section dealing with the relationship between Zurārah and the Imām al-Ṣādiq in Kashshī's Rijāl raises the question of the extent to which Tusi had expurgated the early version of this work. From what has been preserved in the abridged version there is far too much material that has been considered objectionable by later authors on rijāl works,[27] especially in the section dealing with Zurārah, as will be discussed below. Although most of the traditions in criticism and rebuke of Zurārah have been discredited by later Imāmite scholars on the grounds that their isnād is weak or that they were uttered by the Imam under taqiyyah (dissimulation),[28] the fact remains that such utterances regarding Zurārah would not have been considered improbable either by Kashshī or later on by Ṭūsī. Ṭūsī abridged the Rijāl, and did not expurgate these reports on Zurārah.

These disparaging traditions about Zurarah, however, did not become obstructive in his being authenticated as a thoroughly reliable transmitter of the Imāmite traditions. As a matter of fact, he is included in the ahl al-ijmā^c, that is those who had participated with the infallible Imām in reaching a legally authoritative consensus.[29] In the later days the process of isnād, as seen above linked the contemporary Imāmite leaders to the ahl al-ijmā^c. In a sense, then, the jurist was also an imām, recognized by the will of the Imāmite community. Zurārah was acknowledged as the most renowned faqīh among the close associates of the Imāms. His legal opinions, cited on the authority of al-Bāqir, were regarded as authentic and even binding. Both Zurārah and al-Ṣādiq had remained al-Bāqir's disciples and as such Zurārah's transmission of the latter's opinion was considered to be equally authoritative as al-Ṣādiq's relating of the same. However, as Kashshī reports, on some occasion, it was necessary for al-Ṣādiq to remind Zurārah of the difference between his own authority as the Imām of the Shīᶜah, and Zurārah's position, no matter how eminent, as the close associate of the Imām. This point is explicitly made in a long tradition in which al-Ṣādiq sent a message to Zurārah through the latter's son, ᶜAbd Allāh. Al-Ṣādiq said:

> Give your father [Zurārah] my regards and tell him [this]: "I find faults in you [O Zurārah] so as to defend you from my direction [because my finding faults in you will endear you to your enemies]. Assuredly, the people [in general,] and the enemies [in particular,] hasten [to seek out] anyone whom we have taken as an associate and whose position we have praised. [They do this] so as to harm anyone whom we love and whom we have taken as an associate. [Moreover,] people reproach such a person because of our love for him, and they see it appropriate to harm him and even kill him. [On the other hand,] they praise all those with whom we find fault. Thus, we criticize you because you are a person who is well-known because of [your relationship with] us and your devotion to us. In the eyes of the people you are for this reason blameworthy, and not deserving praise because of your love and devotion for us. Hence, I desired that I should find fault with you in order for them to praise your authority in religion, in spite of [my criticism of] your shortcoming and imperfection. We are in this way, repelling their evil from you. [What we are doing in your case resembles that which is revealed in the Qur'ān in the story of Moses and Ezra]. It is as God has said in the Qur'ān: "As for the ship, it belonged to poor people working on the sea, and I wished to mar it, for there was a king behind them who was taking every (good) ship by force." [18:79] This is the revelation from God. I solemnly declare that the ship was marred in order for it to be saved from the king. This was in no way to destroy it with His aid. Indeed, the ship was perfect and it was not easy to swallow the fault in it. Praise be to God. Do understand this allegory [as I have explained it to you], and may God have mercy on you, for you are to me, by God, the most beloved of the people. And I love my father, [al-Bāqir's] associates, living or dead. Surely, you are the most excellent of the ships in this deep, exuberant ocean. But, behind you is an oppressive, usurping ruler watching the passing of every solid ship which passes through the ocean of guidance, [i.e., the Imām,] in order to seize it by force and then take illegal possession of it and its occupants. God's mercy be on you while you live and his mercy and pleasure be on you when you die. Your sons, al-Ḥasan and al-Ḥusayn, have brought your letter to me. Any may God protect them both . . .
>
> "Do not let things that my father and I have ordered [you to do] annoy you. And Abū Baṣīr [al-Murādī] came to you [and reported to you] against what we had instructed him to do. By God, we have not ordered you or him to do anything that was not within our and your ability to

> shoulder. For all that [we have asked you to carry out] we possess variants (taṣārīf) and explanations, in accordance with the truth. If we are allowed, we will indeed teach you that the truth is in what we have commanded you to do. So return the authority to us and hand it over to us intact; and, then, wait for our injunctions and be satisfied with them. The one who scatters you [like a shepherd does in order to save his flock] is your protector [i.e., the Imam], towards whom God attracts His creatures . . .
>
> "It is your obligation to submit and refer to us and await [the realization of] our and your matter and our and your deliverance. Even when our Qā'im rises and our spokesman speaks and commences the teaching of the Qur'ān and the ordinances of the religion, the injunctions and the obligations as God revealed them upon Muḥammad (peace be upon him and his progeny), that day those who are with deep insights (ahl al-baṣā'ir) among you will begin to object [to his teaching]. This [objection] will be an outright disavowal . . ."[30]

This report, cited at length, indicates that al-Ṣādiq was faced with a grave problem of limiting the authority of the ruwāt in the elucidation of the religious precepts. Further evidence of this situation is provided by al-Ṣādiq's disavowal of the traditions that were reported on the authority of his father by Zurārah, who was probably challenging the Imām's authority in this matter. A frequent statement made by al-Ṣādiq when he heard something communicated on his father's authority by Zurārah, which was in contradiction to what he had related, was to declare that which was communicated as being "neither my father's religion nor mine."[31] In some instances, as related by Kashshī, Zurārah was in direct opposition to the views expressed by al-Ṣādiq. Thus, on one occasion Zurārah came to al-Ṣādiq and told him that al-Ḥakam ibn ʿUtaybah, a disciple of al-Bāqir, had heard the latter relate the ḥadīth about the evening prayer (al-maghrib) which was to be performed before reaching al-Muzdalifah, during the annual pilgrimage. This ruling is contrary to the generally held opinion about the evening prayer which has to be performed in al-Muzdalifah. Al-Ṣādiq said, "I thought about this tradition. My father never said this. Al-Ḥakam has falsely attributed it to him." Zurārah left the presence of the Imām, saying to himself, "I have not seen al-Ḥakam attributing falsehood to his father [al-Bāqir]."[32]

On another occasion, Ziyād ibn Abī Hilāl, an associate of the Imām from Kūfah, went to al-Ṣādiq in Madīnah and recounted what he had heard on the authority of Zurārah regarding the question of istiṭāᶜah (human capacity to perform an act), so as to seek confirmation from the Imām as to its being his opinion. The Imām denied the explanation offered by Zurārah as being his own and cursed him for spreading distorted views. Ziyād asked the Imām's permission if he could inform Zurārah about this, which the Imām did. On his return to Kūfah Ziyād went to visit Zurārah and related to him the Imām's actual opinion on istiṭāᶜah, without mentioning the curse. Hearing that, Zurārah said, "Indeed he has presented to me [his definition of] istiṭāᶜah, whereas he himself does not know. This master of yours (i.e., the Imām) does not have insight into the speech of the rijāl (the eminent transmitters of the teachings of the Imāms)."[33]

The implications of these reports are momentous. On the one hand, it shows that the disciples like Zurārah were looked upon by the Shīᶜah as the spokemen, who could inform them of the authoritatively binding opinion of the Imām on a given problem, whether legal or theological; on the other, Zurārah's comment about the insight of the Imām, explicitly shows that the associates, who were in close contact with more than one Imām, found themselves in the sensitive position of validifying the authenticity of the Imāms' utterances. Furthermore, the function of guiding the adherents of the Imāms in religious matters, especially in Kūfah, was becoming even more central due to the systematization of the sources of the Law at somewhat the same time. As a matter of fact, according to Kashshī, Zurārah and Muḥammad ibn Muslim al-Thaqafī used to hold discussion on some legal as well as theological issues with Abū Ḥanīfah, the founder of the Ḥanafī school of Law.[34]

It is plausible to maintain that persons like Zurārah symbolized the growing authority of the transmitters of the teachings of the Imāms, the so-called rijāl, who had the advantage of learning from several Imāms. However, their authority was, at the most, partial because the Imāms were still living. This is substantiated by occasional refutation of their transmission by the Imām al-Ṣādiq, who was informed about the conflicting statements made by the most prominent among them like Zurārah and al-Thaqafī.[35] However, these occasional statements in refutation of their transmission were balanced with abundant statements of confidence in them by the Imāms who, in most cases, appointed them as their deputies upon requests made by the Shīᶜah in distant regions like Kūfah. This early deputyship of the close associates of the Imāms evolved more fully in the period subsequent to the Imāmate of al-Bāqir and that of al-Ṣādiq, following the re-orientation of the Shīᶜah towards political acquiescence in the face of frequent failure of the Shīᶜah leaders to establish their political power. Consequently, their appointment to this kind of leadership had a twofold purpose: first, it was to guide the Shīᶜah in their religious lives; and second, it was to maintain a peaceful relationship with the Muslim community at large, so as to provide a necessary continuity in the teachings of the Imāms from Madīnah. However, after al-Ṣādiq's death in 148/765, Madīnah as the intellectual center was weakened by the ᶜAbbāsid caliphs who, realizing the potential challenge to their authority from that direction, forced all the succeeding Imāms to remain incarcerated in the prisons or under strict surveillance in their own capital in Iraq. However, it is important to bear in mind that the ᶜAbbāsid weakening of Madīnah's influence was not, of course, aimed at the Shīᶜah only. It was part of a much larger policy the discussion of which is beyond the limits set for this study.

The Deputyship of the rijāl) under the Successors of al-Ṣādiq

The death of Imām al-Ṣādiq in the year 148/765 can be marked as the period in which occurred decentralization of the Shīᶜite religious authority. No less than three sons of al-Ṣādiq were proclaimed as Imāms by different groups. However, the majority of the Shīᶜah acknowledged the younger son of al-Ṣādiq, Mūsā al-Kāẓim as the Imām. It is significant that the rijāl were greatly responsible in bringing about the acclamation of the Imām al-Kāẓim as the only true successor of al-Ṣādiq.[36] It was probably from this time on that the close associates of the Imāms were destined to play a crucial role in the acknowledgement of the Imām of the Age, because, evidently, after al-Ṣādiq's Imāmate no Imām seems to have been recognized as the single leader of all the Shīᶜites. Most of the time there appears to have been more than one contender for the Imām's position, in the absence of one centrally recognized leader of the ᶜAlids. Moreover, in certain cases, like that of the ninth and tenth Imāmite Imāms, who had become

Imāms at the age of eight and nine, it was the influential leadership of the rijāl that became instrumental in the allegiance being paid to them.

The Imāmate of Mūsā al-Kāẓim coincided with a turbulent period in the early ᶜAbbāsid period. The early caliphs of this dynasty were occupied with the internal problem of establishing their authority, more so, in the absence of well-defined rules of succession, following the revolution based largely on the Shīᶜī ideology, which had actually brought them to power. The latter fact was also the reason why they felt insecure in their claim to be the legitimate successors of the Prophet, when there were ᶜAlid leaders with far more numerous followers, who could and did challenge their claim to legitimacy. It was mainly because of such a challenge from the direction of the Imāms that the ᶜAbbāsid caliphs adopted an inflexible and intolerant attitude towards them, especially following the death of al-Ṣādiq. Under these circumstances, the sole responsibility of guiding the Shīᶜah was delegated to the close associates of the Imāms. One additional function that was carried out by these associates, and which is mentioned more frequently from this time on, was the collection of the khums, a tax intended for pious purposes and particularly for descendants of the Prophet, to be administered by the Imām. The khums was given to the Imāms by their followers at different times. In distant lands the agents of the Imāms were responsible for collecting these and bringing them to the Imāms. The revenue from khums seems to have been a significant source of income for the Imāms who were not, according to the Law, entitled to receive other forms of benevolent charity, such as ṣadaqāt (alms). It was also a mark of their strength and that of their followers.

In his account of the Wāqifite conception of the messianism and occultation of al-Kāẓim, Kashshī reports that at the time when this Imām was imprisoned by the ᶜAbbāsid Hārūn al-Rashīd, an amount of thirty thousand dinars for khums had been deposited with his two agents in Kūfah. One of these agents was Ḥayyān al-Sarrāj who, together with the other agent, had spent this amount in buying houses and trading, and had made a considerable profit. When al-Kāẓim died and the news reached them, they denied his death and spread the story that the Imām had not died, and could not die, because he was the promised Mahdī, and he had disappeared.[37] It emerges from this story that the idea of the occultation of al-Kāẓim may possibly have been utilised by those agents who wanted to benefit from the material wealth which could have been claimed by the succeeding Imam.

Kashshī's Rijāl does not include information on the close associates of the last Imāmite Imāms in Sāmarrā. In fact, it ends with the rijāl of the eighth Imām ᶜAlī al-Riḍā (d. 202/817-818). The major part of Kashshī's work, approximately half, is devoted to the rijāl of the fifth and sixth Imāms. This fact points to the large number of the disciples who had transmitted communications on the authority of these two Imāms. That the Shīᶜī transmitters and compilers of ḥadīth had increased in numbers during the Imāmate of the two Ṣādiqs is corroborated by the testimony of al-Ḥasan ibn ᶜAlī al-Washshā' who related that he met nine hundred masters of ḥadīth in the mosque of Kūfah, who used to say, "It was related to us by Jaᶜfar ibn Muḥammad al-Ṣādiq that so and so."[38] Consequently, in our attempt to reconstruct the Imāmite world-view, we have depended heavily on this section of the Rijāl. Kashshī's treatment of his material makes his work indispensable in order to comprehend the relationship between the Imāms and their close associates, on the one hand; and the development of the role of these associates as the deputies of the Imāms, on the other. Through the delineation of the textual facts we have been able to demonstrate the significance of Kashshī's Rijāl for the reconstruction of the early history of Imāmite Shīᶜism, especially its central doctrine of the Imāmate.

Following the Imāmate of al-Bāqir and that of al-Ṣādiq and his successors, the central organization of the deputyship was the only way through which the Imāms could foresee the continuation of their teaching regarding the leadership of the community with all its implications in the realm of religion and politics. The institution of the deputyship of the prominent rijāl also prepared the ground for the eminent scholars of Imāmite Shīᶜism, the mujtahids, to assume the religious leadership of the Shīᶜites in the absence of the manifest Imāmate.

Notes

[1] Amhad ibn ᶜAlī ibn al-ᶜAbbās al-Najāshī, Fihrist asmā' musannifī al-shiᶜah, known as Rijāl (n.p., n.d.), p. 263. See also B. Scarcia Amoretti, "ᶜIlm al-ridjāl," EI[2], 3: 1150-1152, and W. Madelung, "al-Kashshī," ibid., 4: 711-712.

[2] Muḥammad ibn ᶜAlī ibn Shahrāshūb, Maᶜālim al-ᶜulamā' (Najaf, 1961), p. 101.

[3] Āqā Buzurg al-Tihrani, al-Dhariᶜah ila tasanif al-shiᶜah (Tehran, 1968), 10: 80.

[4] Abū ᶜAmr ᶜUmar ibn ᶜAbd al-ᶜAzīz al-Kashshī, Ikhtiyār maᶜrifat al-rijāl (Mashhad, 1348 sh./1964), 331-332/606, 608 (the first number refers to page and the second to item).

[5] This point is well discussed by the present marjaᶜ al-taqlīd of the majority of the Imāmite Shīᶜites, Āyat Allāh Abū al-Qāsim al-Mūsawī al-Khū'ī in his lectures on usūl al-fiqh entitled al-Tanqīh fī sharḥ al-ᶜurwat al-wuthqā, compiled by al-Mīrzā ᶜAlī al-Gharawī al-Tabrīzī, 4 vols. (Najaf, 1386 AH/1966-1967), especially volume 1. In his main work on rijāl--Muᶜjam rijāl al-ḥadīth, 18 vols. (Najaf, 1970)--he summarizes his position on the sunnah as a source in the uṣūl al-fiqh in the first volume, which constitutes an introduction to his work.

[6] Khū'ī, Muᶜjam, 1: 57.

[7] These are (1) al-Kāfī fī ᶜilm al-dīn, by Muḥammad ibn Yaᶜqūb al-Kulaynī; (2) Man la yaḥḍuruh al-faqīh, by Muḥammad ibn ᶜAlī ibn Bābūya; (3) Tahdhīb al-aḥkām; and (4) al-Istibsār fī mā ikhtalafa min al-akhbār, by Muḥammad ibn al-Ḥasan al-Ṭūsī.

[8] Khū'ī, Muᶜjam, 1: 57.

[9] Ṭihrānī, al-Dharīᶜah, 1: 123.

[10] For a detailed study on the Occultation and its implications in Imāmite history see A.A. Sachedina, Islamic Messianism: The Idea of Mahdi in Twelver Shi'ism (Albany, 1981).

[11] Muḥammad ibn al-Ḥasan al-Hurr al-ᶜĀmilī, Wasā'il al-shīᶜah ilā tahsīl masā'il-sharᶜiyyah (Beirut, 1381 AH/1971-1972), 11: 483, H # 2.

[12] Kashshī, al-Rijāl, 4/5.

[13] Ibid., 206/369.

[14] Ibid., 12/25 where al-Ṣādiq says regarding Salmān al-Fārisī that he possessed both "ancient" and "modern" learning, and that he belonged to the ahl al-bayt. He is also mentioned among the only three associates of the Prophet who did not apostatize after the latter's death by paying allegiance to Abū Bakr. The other two persons were al-Miqdād ibn al-Aswad and Abū Dharr al-Ghifārī. See ibid., 6/12 and 15; and also 331/605 and 607 where al-Ṣādiq declares ᶜUmar ibn Yazīd Bayyāᶜ al-Ṣābirī and ᶜĪsā ibn ᶜAbd Allāh as belonging to the ahl al-bayt, with similar implications.

[15] Ibid., 3/1.

[16] Ibid., 3/2. See also E.W. Lane, Arabic-English Lexicon, bk. 1, pt. 2, p. 529 for the lexical explanation of the term muhaddath which conforms with the signification of this term in Imāmite ḥadīth in Kulaynī, Kāfī, Kitāb al-ḥujjah, bāb 54, H # 3.

[17] Kashshī, al-Rijāl, 76/131 and 84/139.

[18] Ibid. In a note on Maytham al-Tammār (767/131), Kashshī reports that he claimed such esoteric knowledge and he was put to death. Similar treatment was suffered by Rashīd al-Hujrī, who, according to Kashshī, was taught ᶜilm al-balāyā by ᶜAlī.

[19] Ibid., 224/401-225/402.

[20] Ibid., 324/588.

[21] Ibid., 161/273. In still another place (171/291) Kashshī reports a similar request made by another disciple and the Imam referred him to Abū Baṣīr al-Murādī.

[22] Ibid., 170/286.

[23] Ibid., 290f./511f. See also my article, "Abū al-Kaṯṯāb," in Encyclopaedia Iranica, 1: 329-330.

[24] Kashshī, al-Rijāl, 291-292/515.

[25] Ibid.

[26] Ibid., 133/210. Zurārah was his title. Aᶜyān, his father, was a slave from Byzantium and belonged to a person from the Banū Shaybān. His master taught him the Qur'ān and then freed him and offered to accept him as one of his family. But Aᶜyān preferred to remain his friend. Aᶜyān's father was a monk in Byzantium. Zurārah had many sons and brothers, who formed the large and well-known family of Banū Zurārah. They were all reporters of several traditions and the authors of various original works and compilers. Zurārah reported from the fourth, fifth and sixth Imāms. Najāshī, Rijāl, pp. 132f. sums up his note on Zurārah saying, ". . . he was a reciter [of the Qur'ān], a jurisprudent (Faqīh), a theologian, a poet and a man of letters. In him were combined excellence of character, piety and truthfulness in what he reported."

[27] See for instance, al-Sayyid Muḥammad al-Mahdī Baḥr al-ᶜUlūm, al-Fawā'id al-rijāliyyah, 3 vols. (Najaf, 1965), where he discusses in different places the reason why preponderance should be given to the Rijāl of Najāshī among the classical works. In some cases, preference should be given to the latter work even in comparison with Ṭūsī's works on the same subject. Baḥr al-ᶜUlūm supports his conclusions by reference to the earlier works on isnād criticism like that of the renowned Imāmite jurist al-Shahīd al-Thānī, Sharḥ al-istibṣar, in which the author discusses the chains of transmission in the process of explicating the traditions. See Baḥr al-ᶜUlūm's comments (2: 46-50) in connection with Najāshī's Rijāl as compared with Ṭūsī's works.

[28] Khū'ī, Muᶜjam, 7: 231 f.

[29] Kashshī, al-Rijāl, 238/431, 375/705 and 556/1050. In all, Kashshi counts eighteen among the prominent disciples of the Imāms who formed the ashāb al-ijmāᶜ.

[30] Ibid., 138-139/221.

[31] Ibid., 160/269.

[32] Ibid., 158/262.

[33] Ibid., 147/234.

[34] Ibid., 145/231.

[35] Ibid., 162-163/275.

[36] Muḥammad ibn Muḥammad al-Nuᶜmān al-Mufīd, al-Irshād (Tehran, 1351 sh./1972), pp. 560, 565-567.

[37] Ṭihrānī, al-Dharīᶜah, 1: 17, citing al-Dhahabī's biographical note on Ābān ibn Taghlib.

13

ᶜAbd al-Jabbār on the Imāmate

Erwin I. J. Rosenthal
The University of Cambridge

To Michael Wickens in friendship

The qāḍī 'l-quḍāt ᶜAbd al-Jabbār's al-Mughnī in its Egyptian edition of a Ṣanᶜā' manuscript in the 1960's has as part XX a polemical discussion Fī 'l-Imāma in two parts. It is not an original contribution by a late Muᶜtazilī thinker (d. 415/1024-1025) to a subject much written about because of its importance as an Islamic institution, but a comprehensive statement on the origin, meaning and purpose of the imāma as the most significant religious and political institution in Islam, Sunnī as well as Shīᶜī. Fī 'l-Imāma can only be fully understood and appreciated as an integral part of the whole Mughī, a digest of Islamic theology in the widest sense of the term rather than a Summa of such outstanding distinction, significance and clarity as that of Thomas Aquinas. Naturally, the question of the imāma is intertwined with that of the imām, his nature and functions. ᶜAbd al-Jabbār furnishes much detail referring to other parts of his Mughī and other of his works no less than to his predecessors among the Muᶜtazila from al-Jāḥiẓ, the first and foremost Muᶜtazilī political thinker, to his contemporaries, in particular, however, to his teachers Abū ᶜAlī b. Jubbāᶜī and his son Abū Hāshim whose works have not yet come to light. Their views are frequently quoted and often accepted, especially those of Abū ᶜAlī. To my mind ᶜAbd al-Jabbār's importance where his Fī 'l-Imāma is concerned mainly rests in making known the views of his teachers and establishing them as the missing link in the chain of Muᶜtazilī authorities on the imāma. We learn from his text that Abū ᶜAlī wrote a Kitāb al-Imāma (239). A no less important source for our treatise is the radd of the Imāmī

Logos Islamikos: Studia Islamica in honorem Georgii Michaelis Wickens, ed. Roger M. Savory and Dionisius A. Agius, Papers in Mediaeval Studies 6 (Toronto: Pontifical Institute of Mediaeval Studies, 1984), pp. 207-218.

al-Sharīf al-Murtaḍā (d. 436/1044-1045) under the title al-Shāfī. His radd was obviously provoked by ᶜAbd al-Jabbār's openly anti-Shīᶜī (or, more correctly, anti-Imāmī/Shīᶜī) tendency and polemic. This feature of ᶜAbd al-Jabbār's treatise caused al-Sharīf al-Murtaḍā to quote large parts of Fī 'l-Imāma in order deftly to demolish their argument on behalf of his sect. He seems to have had a better text than we are presented with in the Egyptian edition which enables us to arrive at a better understanding of ᶜAbd al-Jabbār's often faulty, unintelligible text, making full allowance for a probably deliberate vagueness and ambiguity in kalām-inspired theological argument. Both authors use dialectical argument: Murtaḍā mostly at the expense of ᶜAbd al-Jabbār. ᶜAql, reason, rather belongs to the realm of dialectic than of logic. Yet, despite its obvious deficiences the Fī 'l-Imāma not only explains the Muᶜtazilī position on the imāma and the imām fully and usefully; it also shows that the discussion of imāma and imām was by no means a theoretical, academic exercise, but very much a live issue in the various sects themselves and between all shades of Sunnī and Shīᶜī opinion. ᶜAbd al-Jabbār stresses that Muᶜtazila, Zaydiyya and a small group of Imāmīs have much in common despite fundamental differences. Moreover, ᶜAbd al-Jabbār clearly distinguishes between Baṣrīs and Baghdādīs individually and collectively. We thus learn that at least where opinions on imāma and imām are concerned there was more variety in one sect than there were sects in existence: another indication of how much imāma and imām agitated the minds of theologians and jurists. This concern covers the whole history of Islam under the Umayyads and ᶜAbbāsids, but especially in the time of active, effective rule of the Buyid dynasty which favoured the Muᶜtazila, particularly in the time of ᶜAbd al-Jabbār's teachers.[1] The Buyids started as Zaydīs, veered between Shīᶜīs and Sunnīs with whom they eventually sided for political reasons. ᶜAbd al-Jabbār counted prominent Zaydīs among his pupils, among them the Zaydī Imām Al-Mu'ayyad. His brother an-Nātiq bi-l-haqq who succeeded him as Imām quotes ᶜAbd al-Jabbār and became a Muᶜtazilī.[2] This shows that at that time the distinctions between the various sects had not yet hardened, especially between Zaydīs and Muᶜtazilīs. We are here only concerned with their different attitudes to the Imāmate and the Imām as seen in ᶜAbd al-Jabbār's polemic. As far as one can see he has not much new to offer for his period when the various positions were final and static. As already stated, his importance lies in summing up the opposing views on whether the Imāmate was necessary or not. There is -- apart from the Khārijīs who reject the need for an Imām -- no doubt about the necessity of the Imāmate, as is well known. The question only is where this necessity is derived from (16). For the Muᶜtazila as for Sunnīs generally the Imāmate is a divine institution demanded by revelation (samᶜ): Qur'ān, Sunna and tawātur traditions -- in certain cases a khabar wāḥid -- furnish the source for the establishment of the imāma. Tawātur is understood to be a continuous, uninterrupted, authoritative tradition which ultimately goes back to the prophet or one of his companions. Khabar wāḥid means in the context an isolated but well-attested tradition, acceptable in special circumstances.

The other derivation of the necessity of the Imāmate is reason. ᶜAbd al-Jabbār says that he will bring proof for its establishment through samᶜ. This proof consists in his argument against the requirement of reason which would require taklīf[3] (responsibility, responsible fulfilment of the religious commandments) which plays a significant role in ᶜAbd al-Jabbār. Yet, taklīf rests on tamkīn (establishment or investiture): bayān, and luṭf. Tamkīn is excluded by ᶜAbd al-Jabbār since the mukallaf as a responsible commandments-fulfilling Muslim believer does not need the existence of the Imām, but according to the Imāmīs bayān and luṭf are necessary. Since ᶜAbd al-Jabbār denies reason (and bayān rests on reason) as necessitating the Imāmate bayān is not the function of the Imām. The mukallaf does not need a prophet, let alone an Imam: hence he does not need a ḥujja from God who is -- according to the Shīᶜa -- the Imām. ᶜAbd al-Jabbār holds that there is not only a rational taklīf, but also necessarily a religious-legal (sharᶜī, a few lines later called samᶜī) one. This may be interpreted in the sense that the mukallaf practising taklīf neither needs the institution nor its representative to live in accordance with the dictates of the sharīᶜa, setting himself outside the opposing sects and groups within them (20-24). Imāmate and Imām are, therefore, necessary for the general run of the ummah, which needs guidance and warning which can be provided by the Imām. In the case of Sunnīs, guidance, and especially warning, may also be provided by the ᶜulamā'. Shīᶜīs, however, concentrate both guidance and warning in the Imām alone. To assign this task to the ᶜulama' is an opinion contrary to Imāmī doctrine.

Al-Sharīf al-Murtaḍā insists on the infallible Imām as the preserver of the sharīᶜa, excluding, as we have seen, the umma from any share in this preservation, whereas ᶜAbd al-Jabbār associates the umma with it through tawātur, ijtihād, confirmed by qiyās -- on the role of which he wavers and contradicts himself in other passages -- and khabar wāḥid. Al-Murtaḍā admits tawātur after the death of the prophet only in the matter of ṣalāt as part of the sharᶜ, hence ᶜAbd al-Jabbār asks whether the belief in the Imām is the most important matter of the sharīᶜa and answers "No," for tawātur legitimizes the Imām after he was set up. Since there is, thus, no need for an Imām as far as ṣalāt as part of the sharīᶜa is concerned, there is also no need of him in any other constituent element of the sharīᶜa. This is hardly convincing, and we are not surprised that al-Sharīf al-Murtaḍā shifts his ground away from tawātur and makes ᶜaql (reason) the criterion for the existence and the qualities of the Imām. For him, the Imām is necessary for tawātur since its transmission may be faulty, taking up a point made earlier. It should, in Murtaḍā's reasoning, be unnecessary anyhow! In fact, ᶜAbd al-Jabbār restricted the range of tawātur by stating (72) that the whole of the sharᶜ is not preserved by tawātur, for there is also what the umma has agreed upon and transmitted (72). He does not say whether the whole umma or its representatives, the ahl al-ḥall wa 'l-ᶜaqd or the ᶜulamā'. Though more cogent in argument, and hence more convincing, Murtaḍā, too, is certainly not free from contradictions. For, does he not, in common with the Shīᶜa as a whole, stipulate that naṣṣ is the bedrock of the establishment of the Imām no matter how great a part reason or rational argument play, as they do with the Muᶜtazila only, as far as the imāma is concerned much more determinedly and significantly.[2] We need only recall ikhtiyār, ijtihād, ijmāᶜ and, when appropriate, qiyās. For ᶜAbd al-Jabbār as for his predecessors among the Muᶜtazila revelation is the source and method of appointing an Imām as necessary for the umma. It appears from the context of a given passage and argument that the expressions ahl al-maᶜrifa, the ahl al-ḥāll wa 'l-ᶜaqd and other combinations like ahl al-siyar wa 'l-ṣalāḥ wa 'l-ᶜilm (256) -- all apparently synonymous -- refer to those who elect the new Imām. Since they are usually found in arguments or proofs taken from Abū ᶜAlī or Abū Hāshim they may well belong to them. When the Imam makes a mistake the culama' of the umma help him in the sense of assuming responsibility on his behalf (76). At present there is no Imam in the opinion of cAbd al-Jabbar, hence the hudud cannot be applied. It would, therefore, be better to have a fallible Imam who makes mistakes, but carries out the hudud. In his view, the Imamate is a matter of controversy among the Muctazila (77). He, therefore, relies on Abu cAli and Abu Hashim. He reports of the former that the Imam can be salah in religion and lutf; for if he attains the truth (haqq) he falls into place (?), if he is at fault God lets take somebody else his place . . . the hudud are being executed for him. Even if he is at fault he does not lead to corruption (fasad). If he is right he brings benefit to religion, if he is wrong he may be replaced. Abu Hashim says the Imam is only concerned with worldly matters. If he is right there will result worldly advantage, if wrong there will be no corruption in religion because of it. This contrasting description of his two teachers' views is not free from contradiction and rather doubtful since both are Muctazilis and make the Imam responsible for din wa dunya and the masalih al-dunya.

cAbd al-Jabbar is strongly influenced by his two teachers in the very detailed treatment he accords to Abu Bakr, cUthman and cAli. He stresses that unlike the prophet-messenger the Imam is not a warner; this role falls to the culama' and enhances their importance, especially in the time of a weak Imam whom they help. For the Shica the hujja warns and guides; thus, al-Murtada does not recognize the role of the culama'. Corroborating evidence for the right way of appointing a suitable person -- from the Quraysh, if possible -- is the fact that the Imam is on a par with the Amir and in the same category as the qadi, though to a different degree. At the same time this parity underlines the difference between the prophet and the Imam: in the case of the latter there is neither nass nor hujja, for he is elected by ikhtiyar and ijtihad.

That cAbd al-Jabbar deals at length with afdal and mafdul is to be expected, so is the fact that he does not differ therein from the jurists.[4] There is only the additional aspect of his use about the permissibility to elect the mafdul, not only in the absence of an afdal, but even if those who exercised ikhtiyar and ijtihad knew that an afdal existed, yet circumstances required the establishment of the mafdul. He applies the distinction with all it implies in particular to Abū Bakr and ^{c}Alī, and this must be briefly touched upon. He says that the Imāmiyya hold that the prophet appointed ^{c}Alī as his successor, while all others stress that ^{c}Alī paid homage to the Imāms preceding him and only claimed *bay^{c}a*, e.g., from Ṭalḥa and al-Zubayr (125-6). That according to him the Shī^{c}a as a *madhhab* is of recent date proves nothing unless he thinks the *naṣṣ* claimed for ^{c}Alī is a recent invention.

He points to Abū Bakr's Imāmate as confirmed by *ijmā^{c}* which is to be set as a *ḥujja* in opposition to the shī^{c}ī claims of ^{c}Alī's declared right. *Ijmā^{c}* is only applicable to suitable persons in respect of the Imāmate: hence Abū Bakr has a valid claim, but not Mu^{c}āwiya because he had no *^{c}ilm* nor *faḍl* and was a sinner. *Ikhtiyār* is more important and more necessary than *bay^{c}a*. Our author is at pains to vindicate the four *khulafā' rāshidūn*, especially ^{c}Uthmān and ^{c}Alī, but his elaborate argument is very much on the defensive, e.g., in the case of ^{c}Uthmān's *ḥadath* and ^{c}Alī's fighting Ṭalḥa, al-Zubayr and ^{c}Ā'isha. That he (^{c}Alī) received their *bay^{c}a* proves that his Imamate was valid. A little earlier, we saw that *ikhtiyār* is more important than *bay^{c}a*! Yet, in the case of ^{c}Alī *bay^{c}a* obviously outweighs fighting those who had sworn their allegiance to him in the mosque of the prophet in Medinah. ^{c}Abd al-Jabbār's attitude to ^{c}Alī, like that of the Mu^{c}tazila in general, is as positive as that of the Shī^{c}a, although he opposes *naṣṣ* and *^{c}iṣma*. ^{c}Alī's status was nobler than that of the Imāmate, but he was not a prophet (172). As the prophet's deputy in Medinah he was next to Muḥammad in excellence and according to some Mu^{c}tazilīs he was *al-afdal* after the prophet. Yet, Abū ^{c}Alī rejects measuring others by the *faḍl* of the prophet. The succession of ^{c}Alī to the prophet -- a Shī^{c}ī doctrine -- led the Mu^{c}tazilīs to stress that the fact that ^{c}Alī was appointed by the prophet his deputy in Medinah during his absence does not mean that he should succeed him after his death. No *naṣṣ* of this kind could be deduced from the deputyship. ^{c}Abd al-Jabbār dilates over many pages on the relationship of Moses and Aaron, the latter being -- like his brother Moses -- a prophet, his deputy and, had he not died, his successor no doubt. To compare the relationship between Muḥammad and ^{c}Alī to that between Moses and Aaron would be wrong, since ^{c}Alī was not a prophet (158-175). That he was *afḍal* was no necessary quality in an Imām, only in a prophet. Most Baṣrians and a group of Baghdādīs attribute the contract (ᶜaqd) with Abū Bakr to his faḍl; Abū ᶜAlī and Abū Hāshim say that the ᶜaqd went to Abū Bakr because, if he was not afḍal, he was like al-afḍal (215f.). Sometimes, a contract is made with a mafḍūl, despite the existence of an afḍal, because he has knowledge of fiqh and siyāsa (228). A mafḍūl from the Quraysh has precedence over an afḍal not stemming from the Quraysh. To guarantee the maṣlaḥa of the people is decisive (229f.). If there is danger of fitna on the death of an Imām the mafḍūl is to be appointed. The Imām needs ᶜilm (religious knowledge), maᶜrifa and siyāsāt (232). There should be one Imām at a time; only if their countries are widely separated, two Imāms may be tolerated (243f.). All this is good orthodox doctrine of the jurists.[5] The combination of religious, "secular" knowledge and the know-how of politics is reminiscent of al-Fārābī who, in his Iḥṣā' al-ᶜUlūm, Chapter 5, treats of theology, jurisprudence and politics together. On the point of combinations, we mentioned earlier on various combinations of ahl as apparently synonymous and we may add for good measure nass and ᶜisma over and against ikhtiyār and ijtihād or ikhtiyār and ijmāᶜ. It is most likely that our author took these pairs and combinations over from Imāmīs and earlier Muᶜtazilīs. As far as his own shaykhs are concerned he was of course helped by Ibn al-Murtaḍā's Ṭabaqāt al-Muᶜtazila. We saw earlier on that for him the Shīᶜa is of recent date and we must add that according to him the claim to naṣṣ on ᶜAlī goes back to Abū ᶜĪsā 'l-Warrāq[6] and al-Rawandī -- both apostates and heretics (mulḥidūn) (273)!

What matters to ᶜAbd al-Jabbār is the obligation on the Imām to apply the ḥudūd and implement the laws and judgements (aḥkām), a point he stresses again and again in his capacity as a jurist. The Imām also has to attest the witnesses and defend the territory of Islam, as we know from any Fiqh-book on Constitutional Law such as al-Māwardī's (Aḥkām al-sulṭāniyya).

A significant aspect of his book is his sympathy with much of Zaydī teaching, quite apart from the above mentioned personal contact with two of its Imāms. But he wavers as to khurūj (rebellion) leading to the Imāmate. He only accepts khurūj against oppression (275). Rebellion, forceful seizure of the Imāmate are against the sharᶜ. Nor does he go along with the Zaydīs who only acknowledge ᶜAlī, Ḥasan and Ḥusayn as legitimate Imāms.

In the second part of his book ^{c}Abd al-Jabbar discusses at great length the four *khulafā' rāshidūn*. He often repeats earlier statements from Part One, is not always consistent (who is?) and not infrequently contradicts or calls in doubt an earlier view. The principal question is the legitimacy of their Imāmate. He also discusses the various divergent views on their sequence. A few examples may illustrate his tendency and method. Anti-Shī^{c}a polemic is uppermost, hence al-Sharīf al-Murtaḍā's *radd*.

Leaving out ^{c}Umar we note that ^{c}Abd al-Jabbār's defence of ^{c}Uthmān is at first straightforward and direct, but later somewhat qualified and strongly on the defensive. Thus, he recognizes his legitimacy without reservation until he comes to his *ḥadaths* (pl. *aḥdāth*). For he was properly elected through *ijmā^{c}* and *bay^{c}a*. An Imam, he says, who is established by *sam^{c}* must be retained even if he later commits a *ḥadath*, provided the *ḥadath* was *ḥasan* and not *qabīḥ*, i.e., moderate and not repugnant (2: 33). But later on ^{c}Abd al-Jabbār qualifies his acceptance of ^{c}Uthmān, sees a contradiction between his religiosity, generosity and honourable behaviour on the one side and on the other he has doubts about his *ḥadaths*. Yet, he allows for the removal of the Imam only if there is clear evidence of *ḥadath* (i.e., *qabīḥ*), supported by *sam^{c}* and *tawātur* traditions or on evidence from reliable persons (2: 35f.). Then action must be taken against the Imām. Allegations must be refuted or confirmed by statements of the *rasūl*, or, in their absence, by rational argument, just as reason can determine the external meaning of the Qur'ān. This use of reason is extended to the Imām who must employ *ijtihād* on the basis of *ghālib al-ẓann wa 'l-ra'y* (probability and [his own] opinion) for the benefit of the *maṣāliḥ al-dīn wa 'l-dunyā* (2: 44). On this basis, he defends (or, rather, thinks he defends) ^{c}Uthmān to the hilt: his mistakes were mostly rectified later if it became clear that a wrong appointment had been made. ^{c}Uthmān's enemies used his "mistakes" (*ḥadaths* are meant) only as a pretext for killing him; they had no right to do so. He goes on to say that some supported ^{c}Uthmān, thus not everyone deserted him. In the wake of his two teachers (Abū ^{c}Alī and Abū Hāshim) he does not consider it a fault when the caliph judges with his own *^{c}ilm* (2: 50-54). It is a moot point whether such a defence is defence in the strict sense of the term or simply white-washing. Moreover, it must always be borne in mind that the primary purpose of the book is anti-Shīᶜī polemic, therefore all four *khulafā' rāshidūn* are legitimate and must be recognized as such, and not only ᶜAlī. To repeat, in the case of ᶜUthmān our author was greatly helped by Abū ᶜAlī who gave ᶜUthmān the benefit of the doubt: he was properly elected, hence there was no justification for a suspension of judgement; to desert him was wrong and to kill him was a crime (2: 59).

As for ᶜAlī our author repeats the two methods of establishing an Imām: *naṣṣ* and *ᶜiṣma* or *ikhtiyār*. He discusses at length al-Aṣamm's claim that there was no *ijmāᶜ* on ᶜAlī. Yet, ᶜAlī fulfilled the same conditions as Abū Bakr and ᶜUthmān, was most accomplished in *faḍl*, *ᶜilm*, *siyar*, *siyāsa* and *shajāᶜa* (courage), in other words he was a true Imām capable to look after the *umma*, its worldly welfare as well as the welfare of religion, to wage *jihād* with courage (2: 60ff.). Only his *bayᶜa* was different: after the people had gone to the mosque of the prophet in Medinah and acclaimed him there (i.e., gave their consent) *bayᶜa* was given him afterwards outside the mosque. (This was mentioned earlier on, p. 8.) ᶜAbd al-Jabbār quotes Abū ᶜAlī in support of *ijmāᶜ* and on ᶜAlī generally. We have already mentioned the affair with Ṭalḥa, al-Zubayr and ᶜĀ'isha and need only add here that they repented of their hostility to ᶜAlī to whom they gave *bayᶜa*, but refused to fight the *ahl al-ṣalāt* on his behalf (2: 87). Their acceptance of ᶜAlī enabled him to keep the Imāmate intact, which is the means of keeping the affairs of the *umma* on the straight path. Their repentance confirmed his legitimacy as Imām, and his actions were right. Again following Abū ᶜAlī he castigates indecision of the early Muᶜtazilīs as damaging to the Imām who must apply himself to two matters simultaneously: *dīn wa dunyā* (2: 97). The Imām personifies the unity of religion and politics, as we would say. Next, he defends ᶜAlī's killing of the Syrians because of the danger their doings posed to the Imāmate and to *siyāsa*. This seems to imply that ᶜAbd al-Jabbār was motivated by political considerations as much as by religious concerns. He defends ᶜAlī's consent to arbitration because the people did not want to fight. Yet, it was a consent from necessity, not from choice.

In a full discussion of *afḍal* ᶜAbd al-Jabbār quotes al-Jāḥiẓ and his *risālat al-khaṭṭābiyya* (2: 113),[7] assigning the predicate *al-afḍal* to ᶜUmar b. al-Khaṭṭāb. The order of *afḍal* in the four *khulafā'* rāshidūn differs in several Muᶜtazilī writers from Baṣra and Baghdād: for, Baṣran al-Naẓẓam and al-Jāḥiẓ follow this order: Abū Bakr, ᶜUmar, ᶜUthmān, ᶜAlī whom they consider less afḍal than Abū Bakr who surpassed him in zuhd, ᶜibāda, ᶜilm and fiqh. Most Baghdādī Muᶜtazilīs opt for ᶜAlī as afḍal. For them ᶜAlī is more afḍal than Abū Bakr from the point of view of dīn, not of ᶜamal, meaning that God made him ᶜafḍal. Faḍl is only known by samᶜ, whereas ᶜamal through tradition (2: 131). He refers to Ṭabari's tafsīr for the view that ᶜAlī's primacy in faḍl was decided by the Qur'ān.

The discussion of the Imāmate is rounded off with recording the opinions of the various Imāmī factions and of the Zaydīs. The position of the bāghī (rebel) no doubt has, in the first place, the Zaydīs in view: we mentioned earlier ᶜAbd al-Jabbār's opposition to khurūj as a means of obtaining the Imāmate. The text here is very difficult, though it is mainly based on Abū ᶜAlī and Abū Hāshim, yet it is generally important for the relevance of an unsullied Imāmate. Needless to say, the view only exists in theory. It tries to show that the Imāmate, properly constituted, has precedence over forceful seizure. The Sunnī jurists often wrote and acted from expediency and tolerated the usurper of the Imāmate because he was stronger than the reigning Imām. ᶜAbd al-Jabbār asks the question what of his authority the Imām can delegate to the rebel?

These are questions which have occupied the jurists, and a close comparison between ᶜAbd al-Jabbār's Fī 'l-Imāma and their treatises on constitutional law is necessary to determine his own position which, to repeat, is largely conditioned by his two teachers.

It is not possible to go into more detail, desirable as this is, at this stage. Enough has been reported to get an idea of ᶜAbd al-Jabbār's treatise, and we return to the beginning and conclude that a close comparative study of our treatise with other parts of the Mughnī, his other independent writings and the writings on the Imāmate of the jurists is necessary in order to arrive at a fair assessment of his significance. So much is certain that we have in his Fī 'l-Imāma an extensive summary of the opinions of the Muᶜtazilīs within the Sunnī camp and of the Imāmīs. Together with al-Sharīf al-Murtaḍā's al-Shāfī they will throw light on the development of the argument about the most important religious and political institution of Islam. ᶜAbd al-Jabbār seems to me -- at this stage of my work -- outstanding in that he writes as a theologian with real religious commitment on the Imāmate, the purpose of which is in his own words *tadbīr* and *siyāsa* (2: 169). His treatise is a classical example of the religious and political unity of Islam whether he shows much or little originality.

Notes

That I can present here a preliminary, provisional assessment of ʿAbd al-Jabbār's *Fī 'l-Imāma* I owe in the first place to the Leverhulme Trust which awarded me an Emeritus Research Fellowship in 1974 for two years to enable me to prepare a comprehensive study, "The Political Thought of the Muʿtazila: ʿAbd al-Jabbār's Treatise on the Imāmate." I am happy to take this opportunity to express my thanks and appreciation to the Leverhulme Trust. Circumstances over which I had no control delayed publication, and I was only recently able to take up this difficult task again. During my tenure of the Emeritus Fellowship I enjoyed the active assistance of Dr. Ian K. Howard, now of Edinburgh University, in the translation of the *Fī 'l-Imāma* and of al-Sharīf al-Murtaḍā's *al-Shāfī* and in discussion and argument for which I wish to thank him here as well.

The text of ʿAbd al-Jabbār's *Mughnī* used is that published in 1966(?) by the Egyptian Company for Authorship and Translation in the series, "Our Heritage." I am indebted to the British Library for a photostat of Murtaḍā's *al-Shāfī*. The manuscript of the *Mughnī* is in Ṣanʿā' in Yemen; regrettably, I have so far been unable to acquire a photostat of it.

There is an excellent introduction to the work and life of ʿAbd al-Jabbār in Arabic: ʿAbd al-Karīm ʿUthmān, *Qāḍī 'l-quḍāt* (Beirut, 1967[?]).

It was not possible to pay any attention to the peculiar form in which *Fī 'l-Imāma* is written: question and answer; objections raised and refuted; errors and their corrections, etc. Naturally, the form suits the polemical nature of the treatise.

Figures in parentheses in this essay refer the reader to ʿAbd al-Jabbār's text.

[1] Cf. H. Busse, *Chalif und Grosskönig. Die Bujjiden im Iraq* (Beirut, 1969), pp. 405ff., 417-420, 431, 437f, 441.

[2] Cf. W. Madelung, *Der Imām al-Qāsim b. Ibrahīm und die Glaubenslehre der Zaiditen*, Beiheft der Islam N.F. 1 (Berlin, 1965), pp. 127, 141, 178, 181-188. On p. 214 he states that Qāḍī Jaʿfar was both Muʿtazilī and Zaydī and wrote a refutation of the doctrine of the Imāmate of ʿAbd al-Jabbār. Madelung also points to Ibn al-Murtaḍā's *Ṭabaqāt* as a source for ʿAbd al-Jabbār. Cf. also J. van Ess, *Frühe muʿtazilitische Häresiographie* (Beirut, 1971), p. 41, who mentions as a further source for our author Abū 'l-Qāsim al-Kaʿbī's *Kitāb al-Maqālāt. Die Erkenntnislehre des ʿAdudaddin Al-Içi* (Wiesbaden, 1966), pp. 16-25.

[3] Cf. R. Brunschwig, "Devoir et Pouvoir," Studia Islamica, 20 (1964), 5-46, for taklīf -- an important study; also idem, "Rationalité et Tradition dans l'analogie juridico-religieuse chez le Muᶜtazilite ᶜAbd al-Ǧabbār," Arabica, 19 (1972), 213-221.

[4] Cf. J. van Ess in Der Islam, 44 (1968), 3 and especially p. 48 on imāmat al-fāḍil and imāmat al-mafḍūl.

[5] Cf. my Political Thought in Medieval Islam, 3rd ed. (Cambridge, 1968), ch. 2, "The Caliphate: Theory and Function."

[6] W. Madelung quotes Abū ᶜĪsā 'l-Warrāq's Kitāb al-Imāma in Der Islam, 43 (1967), 47f.

[7] This treatise is absent from C. Pellat's "Essai d'inventaire de l'oeuvre ǧāḥiẓienne," Arabica 3.2 (1956), 147-180. Pellat's "L'imamat dans la doctrine de Ǧāḥiẓ," Studia Islamica, 15 (1961), 23-52, is indispensable.

14

Avicenna on Primary Concepts in the *Metaphysics* of his *al-Shifā'*

Michael E. Marmura
The University of Toronto

A. Introduction

"The ideas of 'the existent', 'the thing', and 'the necessary'," writes Avicenna (Ibn Sīnā) (d. 428/1036-1037), initiating the pivotal Chapter 5 of Book 1 of the Metaphysics of his al-Shifā', "are impressed in the soul in a primary way, this impression not requiring better known things to bring it about." Just as in the category of propositions, he then explains, "there are first principles, in themselves found to be true, causing [in turn] assent to the truth of other [propositions], . . . similarly in conceptual matters, there are things which are principles for conception that are conceived in themselves."[1]

It is not difficult to identify Avicenna's first principles in the realm of propositions or judgments. These are none other than the self-evident logical truths which the human mind apprehends directly, without any need for perceptual experience of the external world. In his psychological writings, Avicenna refers to them as "the primary intelligibles" (al-ma^c^qūlāt al-ūlà) which he distinguishes from "the secondary intelligibles" (al-ma^c^qūlāt al-thāniya).[2] The latter include syllogistic inferences dependent on the primary intelligibles. They also include those universal concepts that are normally "acquired" (muktasaba). By this, Avicenna means that, with the exception of their being revealed to prophets,[3] these concepts are not directly apprehended by the human intellect. They require for their apprehension (a) the presence in the mind of the primary intelligibles, and (b) certain preparatory activities of the human soul on the sensory, mnemonic and imaginative levels that include

Logos Islamikos: Studia Islamica in honorem Georgii Michaelis Wickens, ed. Roger M. Savory and Dionisius A. Agius, Papers in Mediaeval Studies 6 (Toronto: Pontifical Institute of Mediaeval Studies, 1984), pp. 219-239.

cogitation, that is, thinking in terms of particular images.[4]

But what about the primary intelligibles, needed for the apprehension of the acquired concepts? Does Avicenna in his psychological writings include with them the primary concepts? There is nothing explicit to indicate such inclusion.[5] In these writings he simply identifies the primary intelligibles with the self-evident logical truths. There is no mention of such primary concepts as those of "the existent," "the thing," and "the necessary." Hence the opening declaration of Metaphysics 1.5, that there are these primary concepts and that they are needed for the apprehension of the acquired, less general, concepts is quite unexpected. In a work like the al-Shifā', which is singularly prosaic, this announcement carries with it a touch of the dramatic.

Thus according to Avicenna, there are "primary concepts" -- concepts of the widest generality that are epistemologically prior to the "acquired" concepts, forming a necessary condition for the latter's acquisition. They are, moreover, "rational," not only by the very fact that they are concepts, but in that they do not require for their apprehension perception of the material world. This, as we have indicated elsewhere,[6] is quite basic for a proper understanding of the ultra rationalism of his philosophical system. In this chapter, however, Avicenna does not discuss the implications of his theory of primary concepts to his rationalist world view taken as a whole, his main concern being with establishing that there are these concepts and with analysing the terms that express them.

His analysis of these terms serves another purpose. This is to criticize views held by the Mu^c^tazilite school of Islamic speculative theology (kalām). There are two related doctrines that receive the brunt of his criticism. The first is that non-existence (al-^c^adam) in the absolute sense, that is, both mentally and extramentally, is a "thing" (shay'). The second is that the resurrection, that is the bringing back to existence something that has ceased to exist, is possible. According to the Mu^c^tazila, what is brought back to existence is not a mere replica of what had existed, but the very thing. Their explanation for this rests on their doctrine that the non-existent is a "thing" or "an essence" (dhāt) to which existence is a state that occurs. Thus a non-existent, A, will acquire the state of existence at time 1, cease to have this state at time 2, and resume having it at time 3. A remains A before and throughout all these states.[7] In rejecting these doctrines, it should be added, Avicenna does not refer to the Mu^{c}tazilite school or any of its members by name. But the ideas he criticizes are Mu^{c}tazilite through and through.

The content of the Chapter can be divided into the following subjects:

1. The parallel between primary concepts and self-evident logical truths (p. 29, l. 13 - p. 30, l. 2);

2. The primacy of the concepts of "the existent" and "the thing" (p. 30, l. 3 - p. 31, l. 2);

3. The distinction between "affirmative" and "proper" existence (p. 31, l. 2 - p. 32, l. 15);

4. The relation of "the thing" to non-existence (p. 32, l. 6 - p. 34, l. 14);

5. Existence as the object of one science (p. 34, l. 15 - p. 35, l. 1);

6. The problem of determining which modal concept is logically prior (p. 35, l. 13 - p. 36, l. 6);

7. Refuting the doctrine that what has ceased to exist can be brought back into existence (p. 31, ll. 6-20).

Avicenna's style in this chapter is at times deceptively casual. Although the themes treated are all closely related, this is not always immediately apparent. Furthermore, his wording can be involved. Thus, the second sentence in the chapter (p. 29, ll. 7-14) is one of the longest and structurally most complex encountered in his writings. He can also be cryptic -- the passage at the end of the chapter forming part of his attack on the Mu^{c}tazilite view of the resurrecting of what has ceased to exist (p. 31, ll. 6-11) is a case in point.

In what follows we offer a translation of Avicenna's Metaphysics, 1.5, with a commentary.

B. Translation and Commentary

Chapter: On Indicating the Existent, the Thing and their First Division, Wherewith Attention is Directed on the Objective Sought [The Primary Concepts and Self-Evident Truths]

> We say: the ideas[8] of "the existent," "the thing," and "the necessary" are impressed in the soul in a primary way, this impression not requiring better known things to bring it about (p. 29, ll. 5-6).

As we have indicated in the Introduction, this opening statement is not found in Avicenna's psychological writings. The sense in which these concepts are "impressed" (tartasim) in the soul is not explained. If their analogy with the logical self-evident truths is pressed, these in the final analysis would have to be direct emanations from the Active Intellect, the last of the series of intelligences emanating from God.[9] We also notice here that "the necessary" is included among the concepts impressed "in a primary way." The question of which of the modal concepts, the necessary, the possible and the impossible has the greater claim to priority, is discussed later on in the chapter. As we shall see, Avicenna opts for the priority of "the necessary."

The opening statement is followed by the chapter's very long and involved sentence. For the sake of clarity, we have broken it into shorter sequences, giving in a footnote (n. 10) a version that follows closely the structure of the original.

> This is similar[10] to what obtains in the category of judgment[s] where there are primary principles, in themselves found to be true, causing [in turn] assent to the truth of other [propositions]. If these [primary principles][11] do not come to mind or if the expression designating them is not understood, then it would be impossible to know whatever is known through them -- [this], even though the informative act striving to bring them to mind or to explain the expressions designating them is not engaged in an endeavor to impart knowledge not [already] present in the natural intelligence, but is merely drawing attention to a comprehension of what the speaker intends and upholds. This may occur through things which in themselves are less evident than the things intended to be made known, but which for some cause or for some expression have become better known.
>
> Similarly, in conceptual matters, there are things which are principles for conception that are conceived in themselves. If one desires to indicate them, [such

> indication] would not in reality constitute making an unknown thing known, but would merely consist in drawing attention to them or to bringing them to mind through the use of a sign which in itself may be less known than [the principle], but which for some cause or circumstance happens to be more obvious in its signification.
>
> When such a sign is used, the soul becomes aware that such a meaning is being brought to mind, in [the sense] that it is the [meaning] intended and not something else, the sign in reality having given no knowledge of it.
>
> If every conception requires a prior conception, then such a state of affairs would lead either to infinite regression or to circularity (p. 29, l. 7 – 30, l. 2).

In the above, there are two key terms, al-taṣawwur and al-taṣdīq, translated as "conception" and "judgement," respectively.[12] Concepts are conveyed in language by nouns and terms; judgments refer to propositions for which the values, true and false, are applicable. In the above passages, Avicenna does not give examples of self-evident truths. Elsewhere quite frequently he gives as his example the geometrical axiom, the whole is greater than the part.[13]

Avicenna tells us that this primary knowledge, whether in the realm of taṣawwur or taṣdīq, resides in "the natural intelligence."[14] Often, however, we are unaware that we have it. It is evoked by some expression or sign which in reality is less known than the primary knowledge, but for some reason appears to be better known. These expressions or signs do not impart new knowledge, but simply draw attention to knowledge already there.

The last paragraph of the text above constitutes part of the argument for the existence of primary concepts: if every concept requires for its apprehension a prior concept this would lead either to infinite regression or circularity. An infinity of coexisting ordered concepts is impossible for Avicenna.[15] But even if this infinite regression is possible it would not constitute an explanation: nor would circularity. The argument, however, rests on the premise that the apprehension of the acquired concepts needs prior more general concepts, a point to which we will return.

[The Primacy of "the Existent" and "the Thing"]

> The things that have the highest claim to be conceived in themselves are those common to all matters, as for example, "the existent" and "the one thing"[16] and so on. For this reason, none of these things can be shown by a

> proof totally devoid of circularity or by the exposition of better known things.
>
> Hence, whoever attempts to place in them something as a [defining] constitutent falters. An example of this is the person who says: "It is of the existent's true nature[17] to be either active or passive." This, while inescapably the case, belongs to the divisions of the existent, the existent being better known than the active and the passive. The masses conceive the reality of the existent without knowing at all that it must be either active or passive. For my part, up to this point, this has only been evident to me through nothing less than a syllogism. How then would it be with the person who strives to define the state of the evident thing in terms of some quality belonging to it which [to begin with] requires proof to establish that it exists for that thing?
>
> The case is similar with someone's statement: "The thing is that which an informative statement is correct."[18] For "is correct" is less known than "thing" and [similarly] "informative statement" is less known than "thing." How then can this be the definition of the thing? Indeed, "is correct" and "information" are only known after one uses in explaining what they are [terms] indicating that each is either a "thing" a "matter" a "whatever" or "a that which"[19]: all of these being synonyms to the word, "thing."
>
> How then can the thing be truly defined in terms of that which is only known through it? Yes, in this and similar things there may be some act of directing attention; but in reality, if you say, "the thing is that about which an informative statement is correct," it is as if you have said, "the thing is the thing about which an informative statement is correct," because the meaning of "whatever," "that which," and "thing" is one and the same. You would thus have included "thing" in the definition of "thing."
>
> Still, we do not deny that through this [statement] and its like, despite its vitiating starting point, there occurs in some manner a directing of attention to the thing (p. 30, l. 3 – 31, l. 2).

In the above section, Avicenna argues (through illustration) for the premise that in order to apprehend a less general concept one must apprehend first a more general one.[20] This leads to concepts of the widest generality that do not require prior concepts. These are conceived "in themselves."

The two primary concepts discussed are "the existent" and "the thing." He points out by way of illustration, that while it is true to maintain that every existent must be either active or passive, being active or passive cannot be used to define the existent. For the existent is better known than both. Again, although admittedly the thing is that about which a correct informative statement is made, this cannot constitute a definition of "the thing." This is because "the thing" is the better known concept. It is a concept used in defining "correct" and "informative" statement. (His statement about the definition of "the thing" is a first indication that he is concerned with Mu^ctazilite doctrine, a concern to which we will shortly return.)

Avicenna's argument here is clear. It can also be interpreted in terms of our use of language. He seems to be saying, in effect, that unless to begin with we understand the meaning of "the existent" and "the thing" discourse would be impossible. As he tells us in the paragraph immediately following, terms like "the existent," "the established" and "the realized" are synonyms. There is no doubt, he adds, "that their meaning has been realized in the soul of whoever is reading this book." Such concepts, he seems to be saying are the starting point of all thought and discourse.

["The Thing" and Existence]

> We say, moreover: the meaning of "existence" and of "thing" are conceived in the soul and are two meanings, while[21] "the existent," "the established" and "the realized" are synonyms. We do not doubt that their meaning has been realized in the soul of whoever reads this book (p. 31, ll. 2-4).

Here Avicenna tells us that both "existence" and "the thing" are conceived by the mind, but that they are not identical. As we shall shortly see, however, although distinct, they remain related. Existence, whether mental, extramental or both, is a necessary concomitant of "the thing." This is significant for his criticism of Mu^ctazilism. The non-existent, in the absolute sense, that is, that which exists neither extramentally nor mentally, cannot be a thing. By contrast such terms as "the existent" (al-mawjūd), "the established" (al-muthbat) and "the realized" (al-muḥaṣṣal) are synonyms. This again is rejection of the Mu^ctazilite identification of the non-existent with the established or affirmed and the realized. In this connection, it should be remarked that the Ash^carite school of speculative theology identifies "thing-ness" (al-shay'iyya) with existence (al-wujūd),[22] a position closer to that of Avicenna, though not identical with it.

> "The thing" or its equivalent may be used in all languages to indicate some other meaning. For to every thing there is a reality[23] by virtue of which it is what it is. Thus the triangle has a reality in that it is a triangle and whiteness has a reality in that it is a whiteness. It is that which we should perhaps call "proper existence," not intending by this the meaning given to affirmative existence; for the expression, "existence," is also used to denote many meanings, one of which is the reality a thing happens to have. Thus, [the reality] a thing happens to have is, as it were, its proper existence.
>
> To resume: It is evident that each thing has a reality proper to it, namely its quiddity. It is known that the reality proper to each thing is something other than the existence corresponding to what is affirmed (p. 21, ll. 5-11).

Here Avicenna singles out two meanings of "existence": "affirmative" and "proper." The first is the common usage of the term when we say that something exists either in the external world or mentally. "Proper existence" (al-wujūd al-khāṣṣ), the esse proprium of the medieval Latin translation of Avicenna, as far as the above text indicates, seems to be identical with a thing's quiddity or essence. This is supported by other texts. For example, in the Isagoge of the al-Shifā', after stating that quiddities exist either in external reality or in the mind, but that they have a consideration simply in themselves, where the question of existence if not relevant, he goes on to state in a later chapter that "the triangle has as a necessary concomitant that the sum of its three angles should equal to two right angles, not by reason of the two [kinds] of existence [i.e., mental and extramental], but [simply] because it is a triangle."[24] Hence the distinction between affirmative existence and proper existence appears to be another way of expressing the distinction between quiddity and existence, or between essence and existence, so central to Avicenna's system.

That there are these two different meanings of existence, namely "affirmative" and "proper," the latter being equated with a thing's quiddity or "reality," is shown, Avicenna maintains, when we are able to affirm the existence of such a reality, that is, either mentally or extramentally, without involving ourselves in uttering sheer tautaulogy. He states this and elaborates on it:

> This is because if you said, "the reality of such thing exists either in the concrete, in the soul, or

> absolutely, being common to both," this would have a meaning, realized and understood. Whereas, if you said, "the reality of such a thing is the reality of such a thing," of that "the reality of such a thing is a reality," this would be superfluous useless talk. Again, if you said, "the reality of such a thing is a thing," this too would not be a statement imparting knowledge of what is not known. Even less useful than this is for you to say, "reality is a thing," unless by "thing" you mean "the existent": for then it is as though you have said, "the reality of such a thing is an existing reality." On the other hand, if you said, "the reality of A is something and the reality of B is another thing," this would be sound, imparting knowledge, because, [in saying this], you make the reservation within yourself that the former is something specific differing from the latter. This would be as if you have said, "[this] is the reality of A and the reality of B is another reality." If it were not for both this reservation [you make within yourself] and this conjunction, [the statement] would not impart knowledge.
>
> This, then, is the meaning intended by "thing." Nor does the necessary concomitance of the meaning of existence separate at all from the meaning of [the thing]; rather, the meaning of existence is permanently concomitant with it because the thing exists either in the concrete or in the estimation and intellect. If it were not so, it would not be a thing (p. 21, l. 11 - 32, l. 5).

In the concluding paragraph, Avicenna makes the statement that existence (and here he must mean "affirmative" existence) is a necessary concomitant of a thing. He had stated earlier that "the thing" and existence are two meanings. Here he is stating that existence, whether mental, extramental or both, must accompany the thing. In other words, we cannot speak meaningfully of "the thing" without relating it either to mental or extramental existence. This view underlies Avicenna's analysis of the relation of the thing to non-existence which follows immediately, as well as the argument at the conclusion of the chapter that what has ceased to exist cannot be brought back into existence.

["The Thing" and Non-Existence]

> Regarding the statement, "the thing is that about which information is given," it is true. But when in addition to this it is said, "the thing may be absolutely non-existent," this is a matter that calls for study. If by the non-existent is meant the non-existent in external reality, this would be possible; for it is possible for a thing to be existing in the mind, not existing in external things. But if other than this is meant, then this would be

> false. There would be no information about it at all. It would not be known except only as conceived in the soul. [To the notion] that [the non-existent] could be conceived in the soul as a concept referring to something external, [we say], "certainly not" (p. 32, ll. 6-11).

When Avicenna maintains at the beginning of this passage that the statement, "thing is that about which information is given," is true, he is not contradicting what he said earlier. He only denied that this is a definition of "the thing." Throughout this section Avicenna is criticizing the view held by Muᶜtazilites that non-existence is "a thing." A first indication of this is the very statement about that "the thing is that about which information is given." For we have a report that the Muᶜtazilite theologian Abū ᶜAlī al-Jubbā'ī (d. ca. 303/915) argued that we can refer to God as a "thing" because "the thing is that about which information is given."[25]

The thrust of Avicenna's argument is that "the thing" cannot be the absolutely non-existent. It may not exist in external reality, but then it would have to exist in the mind. As we have indicated earlier, existence whether mental or extramental, is a necessary concomitant of "the thing." What follows, including the argument that we cannot describe or predicate anything of what, in the absolute sense, does not exist, that, that does not exist mentally or extramentally.

Referring back to the statement that "the thing is that about which information is given," Avicenna writes:

> Regarding the informative statement, the above analysis is correct because information is always about something realized in the mind. [Now] the absolutely non-existent is not given information in the affirmative. But if, moreover, information is given about it in the negative then some form of existence would have been given in the mind. This is so because our saying, "it," entails some reference; and reference to the non-existent that has no concept in any manner whatsoever in the mind is impossible. For how can anything affirmative be said about the non-existent when the meaning of our statement, "the non-existent is such," is that the description "such" is realized for the existent, there being no difference between the realized and the existent? It would be as though we have said, "this description exists for the non-existent" (p. 32, ll. 12-18).

What immediately follows is an argument to demonstrate the utter absurdity of maintaining that a description exists for the non-existent:

> Indeed we say:
>
> "That which describes the non-existent and is predicated of it either exists for the non-existent and is realized for it or does not exist nor is realized for it.
>
> "If it exists and is realized for the non-existent, then it must in itself be either existent or non-existent.
>
> "If existent, then the non-existent would have an existing description. But if the description exists, then that which is described by it necessarily exists. The non-existent would then be an existent; and this is impossible.
>
> "If, [on the other hand], the description is non-existent, then how can that which in itself is non-existent exist for something? For that which in itself does not exist cannot exist for the thing. Yes, a thing may exist in itself without existing for some other thing, [but this is a different matter].
>
> "[Now], if the description did not exist for the non-existent, this would be tantamount to the denial of the description for the non-existent; for if it were not the denial of the description for the non-existent, then if we were to deny this description, we would obtain the opposite of this, the existence of the description for it. And all this is absurd" (p. 33, ll. 1-11).

In this argument it must be remembered that Avicenna is speaking of the non-existent in the absolute sense. He is not, in other words, speaking about mythical beasts, or what concerns him most, past no longer existing events and future not yet existing events. For all these have a conception or some reference in the soul. The continuation of the argument brings home this point.

> Rather, we only say that we have knowledge of the non-existent because when the meaning occurs only in the soul and no reference to the external world is made by it, what is known is only that very thing in the soul. The judgment occurring in terms of the two parts of what is conceived consists in [affirming] that it is possible in the nature of the thing known that a relation belonging to it, conceived with respect to what is external, should occur; at the present time, however, there being no such relation. Thus at present, it is the only thing known (p. 33, ll. 12-15).

"The judgment occurring in terms of the two parts of what is conceived" (beginning of second sentence of above translation), is an interpretation of the Arabic, wa 'l-taṣdīq al-wāqi[c] bayn al-mutaṣawwar min juz'ayni. Judgment pertains to propositions consisting of subjects with their predicates. The reference to the "two parts of what is conceived" seems to be to the parts that render what is conceived a proposition having a subject and predicate, the predicate being the possibility of relating what is conceived in the mind to external existence. This seems to be borne out by what follows. But the wording and idiom is difficult to fathom.

> According to those who uphold the view [rejected above], what is reported and knowable includes matters that in [the state of] non-existence have no "thing-ness." Whoever desires acquaintance with their doctrine should turn to what they rave about in their statements -- [statements] that hardly deserve preoccupation with (p. 33, ll. 16-18).

Here again Avicenna is reiterating his rejection of the view that the non-existent in the absolute sense, that is, the non-existent both mentally and extramentally can be conceived. To speak meaningfully about the non-existent, there must be a "thing-ness" (shay'iyya) to which one refers, at least in the mind. As the continuation of the argument indicates, Avicenna has in mind some of the Mu[c]tazilite theologians. One of the questions they discussed (and of which they held different views) was whether or not God has knowledge of what he knows will not exist.[26] This also raised the question of knowing future not-yet existing events, as well as events that have ceased to exist.

> These people have fallen into their error because of their ignorance [of the fact] that giving information is about ideas existing in the soul, even though these may be non-existent in external things, where the meaning of giving information about these ideas is that they have some relation to external things. Thus, for example, if you said, "the resurrection will be," you would have understood "resurrection" and would have understood "will be." You would have predicated "will be," which is in the soul, of "resurrection," which is in the soul, in the sense that this meaning, with respect to another meaning also conceived, namely one conceived of a future time, would be characterized by a third meaning, namely the concept of existence.
>
> This pattern of reasoning applies correspondingly to matters relating to the past. It is thus clear that that about which information is given must have some kind of existence in the soul. Information, in truth, is about what

> exists in the soul; accidentally about what exists externally.
>
> Hence, you have understood now the way in which "the thing" differs from what is understood by "the existent" and "the realized," and that, despite this difference, they are necessary concomitants (p. 34, ll. 1-10).

Avicenna's analysis of how we can make informative (and hence meaningful) statements about future and past events is closely connected with his concept of the relative which he discusses both in the Categories of the Logic and the Metaphysics of the al-Shifā'.[27] The problem for him is how to relate something existing with something that does not as yet exist (or something that has ceased to exist). His resolution of this problem is to maintain that in this case the relation is between two contemporaneous existing mental events. (The relation here is entirely mental.) It is between a concept that at present has an existing counterpart in external reality and a concept that at present does not, a concept of something that will be, both concepts, however, coexisting in the mind.

The last paragraph refers to the difference between "the existent" and "the thing," and the identity of "the existent" and "the realized." The distinction between "the existent" and "the thing" is not as clear as Avicenna assumes. If we understand him correctly, he seems to be saying something as follow:

When we speak of the "existent," or its equivalent, "the realized," we are affirming directly and explicitly that what we are referring to exists either mentally or extramentally. When referring to "the thing" on the other hand, the primary intention is not with its "existence," but with a "something" that can be considered in itself without reference to existence. Nonetheless, existence is a necessary concomitant of this something since it must exist at least in the mind. (What seems implicit here is the distinction between a quiddity which when considered in itself excludes the idea of existence and this same quiddity having existence as a necessary concomitant.)[28]

> Yet, it has reached me that some people say that what is realized is realized without being an existent; that the description of a thing can be something neither existing nor non-existing; and that the [expressions], "that which" and "whichever," denote something other than what [the expression], "thing," denotes. Such people lie outside the

> pale of the discerning; if challenged to distinguish between these terms according to their meaning, they would be exposed (p. 34, ll. 11-14).

Those who "lie outside the pale of the discerning" again are Mu^c^tazilite theologians. This is also indicated by the statement that such people held the absurd view that the "description of a thing can be something neither existing nor non-existing." This view is encountered in a special context, in the attempt of the Mu^c^tazilite Abū Hāshim al-Jubbā'ī (d. ca. 321/933) to resolve the problem of how to attribute to God such characteristics as power and knowledge without violating His unicity. He formulated a doctrine of "states" or "conditions" (<u>al-aḥwāl</u>), according to which when one, for example, describes God as a knower, what is being affirmed is simply a state or a condition that differentiates him from a non-knower. This state of condition can only be understood in terms of the essence to which it relates, but is not an ontological entity attached, as it were, to the divine essence. In fact, it is improper to speak of it as either existing or non-existing.[29]

[<u>Existence as the Proper Object of One Science</u>]

> We now say: although the existent, as you have known, is not a genus and is not predicated equally of what is beneath it, yet it has a meaning agreed upon with respect to priority and posteriority. The first thing to which it belongs is the quiddity which is substance, and then to what comes after it. Since it has one meaning, in the manner to which we have alluded, there adheres to it accidental matters proper to it, as we have shown earlier. For this reason, it is taken care of by one [field of] knowledge in the same way that anything pertaining to health has one science (p. 34, l. 15 - 35, l. 2).

This brief paragraph is an interlude reminding us of the definition of metaphysics. The subject matter of metaphysics is the existent inasmuch as it exists, just as medicine has matters pertaining to health as its subject. The existent is not a genus, but relates to things beneath it in terms of priority and posteriority. The passage harkens back to what Avicenna had said earlier in <u>metaphysics</u> Book I, Chapter 2 (p. 13, lines 13-17): "The primary subject of this science [i.e., metaphysics], is the existent inasmuch as it exists. The questions sought in it are the things that follow it simply inasmuch as it exists, without further condition. Some of these things belong to it as though they are species, for example, substance, quantity, and quality . . ."

[Determining which Modal Concept is Prior]

In the opening statement of his chapter, Avicenna had included among the primary concepts, the necessary. But thus far he has said nothing about it. In this section he discusses it but within the context of a problem. The necessary, the possible and the impossible are all primitive concepts. Which of them has then the greatest claim to be prior? The problem arises because each of the three modal concepts is definable in terms of the other. Avicenna's presentation of this problem is clear:

> It may also prove difficult for us to make known the state of the necessary, the possible and the impossible through ascertained definition [and would have to make this known] only by way of a sign. Almost all of what has reached you of the sayings of the ancients [purporting] to define these involves circular reasoning.
>
> This is because, as you have come across in the various parts of the Logic, whenever they want to define the possible, they include in its definition either the necessary or the impossible, there being no other way save this. And when they want to define the necessary, they include in its definition either the possible or the impossible; [likewise], when they want to define the impossible, they include in its definition either the necessary or the possible.
>
> Thus, for example, if they define the possible, they would at one time say that it is that which is not necessary, or [at another], that it is the presently non-existent whose existence at any supposed moment in the future is not possible. [Again], if they find that there is a need to define the necessary, they would either say that it is that which is not possible to suppose as non-existent, or that which is impossible to suppose other than it is. Thus at one time they include the possible in its definition, at another, the impossible.
>
> Regarding the possible, they would have already included in its definition either the necessary or the impossible.
>
> Again, when they wish to define the impossible, they either include the necessary in its definition by saying, "the impossible is that whose non-existence is necessary," or the possible, by saying, "it is that which it is not possible for it to exist," or some other expression equivalent to these two.
>
> The case is similar with such statements as: the

> impossible is that whose existence is not possible, or that whose non-existence is necessary; the necessary is that whose non-existence is not allowable and impossible, or that which is not possible for it not to exist; the possible is that which it is not impossible for it to exist or not to exist, or that which it is not necessary for it to exist or not to exist. All this, as you see, is clearly circular. A fuller exposure of this is something you have come across in the Analytics[30] (p. 35, l. 3 - 36, l. 3).

In this section, Avicenna has perhaps already given us a hint of his own position, namely that the necessary is the most basic of these concepts when he writes (third paragraph above): "[Again], if they find that there is need to define the necessary . . .," implying that there may not be such a need. However, his preference is given quite explicitly in what follows.

> Nonetheless, of these three, the one with the highest claim to be first conceived is the necessary. This is because the necessary points to the assuredness of existence (ta'akkud al-wujūd), existence being better known than non-existence because existence is known in itself while non-existence is, in some manner or another, known through existence (p. 36, ll. 4-6).

The first point Avicenna makes favoring the priority of the concept of the necessary over the concepts of the possible and the impossible is that the former points to the "assuredness of existence." The necessary for him is not applicable only to propositions, but to existence. Avicenna's "necessity" is both logical and ontological. The second point he makes is that existence is better known than non-existence. Apart from the significance of this to his criticism of the Muᶜtazilites, this assertion sums up his metaphysical stance. There is no room for uncertainty and doubt as regards existence. The problem for the philosopher is not doubt, as with Descartes. Rather, we are faced with the brute fact of existence, as it were; how then do we explain it? This concern manifests itself in Avicenna's argument that whatever exists (other than God) is necessitated by another. For such an existent in itself is possible: it can exist or not exist. Yet in fact it exists. This requires an explanation which must be sought outside the contigent's own nature or quiddity, this being the cause that necessitates it.[31]

Avicenna, however, does not expand on this aspect of his

doctrine of existence in this section. His argument for the priority of the necessary over the other two modal concepts and of the existent over non-existence leads him to a refutation of the view that what has existed in the past, but ceased to exist, can be brought back into existence.

[The Resurrection of Past Existents]

Avicenna devotes this concluding section of the chapter to a refutation of the belief that what has ceased to exist can be brought back into existence. It is part of his denial of bodily resurrection and his doctrine that only the immaterial soul is immortal. The refutation, however, is directed against Mu^{c}tazilite arguments for the resurrection. Again, there are no direct references here either to Mu^{c}tazilism or to the theory of the soul's immortality.

His argument divides into two parts, the first of which is presented in condensed language and is not easy to follow.

> From our explaining[32] these things, it will become clear to you that it is false for someone to say:
>
> "The non-existent can be brought back into existence because it is the first thing about which information is given in terms of existence.
>
> "This is because if the non-existent were to be brought back into existence, then there would necessarily be a difference between it and that which is similar to it, if it were to exist in its place.
>
> "If [only] similar, it would not be identical with it because it is not the thing that had ceased to exist, this latter, in its state of non-existence, being other than the former."
>
> [But if one argues in this way], the non-existent becomes an existent in the manner we have alluded to previously (p. 36, ll. 6-11).

When in reporting his opponent's argument (the Mu^{c}tazilite), Avicenna's statement in the first sentence above in quotation that the non-existent "is the first thing about which information is given in terms of existence," can be interpreted in one of two ways. Avicenna may simply be referring specifically to something that had existed, ceased to exist, and now exists again. Unlike a replica of it that is created anew but which had no previous existence, the former, since it existed once, "is the first," of the two, "about which information is given in terms of existence." On the other hand, he may be referring more generally to the Muᶜtazilite theory that the non-existent is "a something" to which existence is a state that occurs, and as such is the thing about which information as regards the possibility of existence is given first.

The second sentence between quotation marks, "This is because . . ." to the rest of the argument between quotation marks, at first sight appears to be Avicenna's own refutation of the first sentence. The Arabic lends itself to this interpretation. But a closer look at the text in conjunction with the more detailed (and also quite difficult) exposition of Avicenna's position in his Kitāb al-Mubāḥathāt,[33] shows that this is not the case. Avicenna's position is that what the Muᶜtazilites regard as bringing what has ceased to exist back into existence can only represent a replica of the first, not what is identical. He rejects as self-contradictory the Muᶜtazilite idea that in its state of non-existence it continues to be something affirmable, an essence (dhāt), to which existence can attach again.

In the second part of his refutation, Avicenna introduces the idea of the temporal period in which a thing endures, al-waqt, which for the sake of convenience we will translate as "time." This temporal period, he argues, is a property of an existent. A thing that has existed in the past will have its waqt as one of its properties. If after ceasing to exist such an existent were to be brought back into existence, then its waqt would have also to be brought back with it. But then how can there be two times, past and present?

> Moreover, if the non-existent were to be brought back into existence, then this would require that all of its special properties in terms of which it was what it was, should also be brought into existence. But these properties include the time in which it existed. But if this time is brought back, then the thing would not have been brought back into existence, because that which is brought back into existence is that which would be existing in another time.
>
> Now, if it is allowed that the non-existent could return into existence with all the non-existing properties previously existing with it, time being considered either as having real existence that has ceased to be or, according to what is known of their doctrine, as one of the accidents having correspondence with an existent,[34] then we would be allowing that time and [temporal] states could return into existence. But then there would not be [one period] of time and another and hence no return of the non-existent to

> existence.
>
> The mind, however, rejects the notion that there are no different periods of time in a manner that renders exposition unnecessary; all that is said concerning this is deviation from peripatetic teaching (p. 36, ll. 12-19).

With this criticism of the Mu^c^tazila that includes reference to their theory of time as an accident, Avicenna's chapter ends. His criticism is premised on his theory of primary concepts, whose implications to his metaphysics taken as a whole, are far reaching. But as we have indicated earlier, he does not discuss these implications in this chapter, his concern being to establish that there are these primary concepts, to explain their function in the human act of knowing, to analyse the terms expressing them, and to use all this for a critique of Mu^c^tazilite ontology.

Notes

1 Ibn Sīnā (Avicenna), al-Shifā' (Healing): al-Ilāhiyyāt (Metaphysics), ed. G. C. Anawati, S. Dunya, M. Y. Musa and S. Zayid, 2 vols. (Cairo, 1960), p. 29, ll. 5-14. The chapter to be translated and commented on consists of pp. 29-36 of this text. References to the text will be abbreviated, Ilāhiyyāt, in the notes.

2 Avicenna's De Anima, edited by F. Rahman (London, 1959), pp. 49, 209; Ibn Sīnā (Avicenna), al-Najāt (Cairo, 1939), p. 167; Fī Ithbāt al-Nubuwwāt (On the Proof of Prophecies), ed. M. E. Marmura (Beirut, 1968), pp. 43-44.

3 See English Introduction to Fī Ithbāt al-Nubuwwāt, pp. xi-xviii, also, the author's, "Avicenna's Psychological Proof of Prophecy," Journal of Near Eastern Studies, 22.1 (1963), 49-56, and "Avicenna's Theory of Prophecy in the Light of Ash^c^arite Theology," in The Seed of Wisdom, ed. W. S. McCullough (Toronto, 1965), pp. 159-178.

4 Avicenna's De Anima, p. 235; Fī Ithbāt al-Nubuwwāt, p. 44.

5 Avicenna's De Anima, p. 209, ll. 7-8, speaks of "the primary premises and 'what accompanies them' (wa mā yajrī ma^c^ahā)." Avicenna here may be hinting at the primary concepts. As we shall shortly see, he states that the self-evident truths represent knowledge that belongs to the natural intelligence. In the Ta^c^līqāt, comments Avicenna dictated to his student Bahminyār which probably contain expansions by the latter, we find a passage in which certain types of existents are known "naturally" to the human soul. Here the reference is not to self-evident truths, but in fact, to the soul's awareness of itself. The passage translates something as follows:

"The human soul is [so constituted that] it is by its very nature aware of existents. It is aware of some naturally, with others it gains the power to become aware of them by acquisition. That which is realized for it naturally is always actual. Thus its awareness of itself is by nature, this being a constituent of it and hence belongs to it always and in actuality. Its awareness that it is aware of itself, however, is through acquisition." Ibn Sīnā, *al-Ta^{c}līqāt*, ed. A. R. Badawi (Cairo, 1973), p. 30.

One should perhaps also add that in a work attributed to al-Fārābī, but whose language is suggestive of Avicennian authorship, namely, *^{c}Uyūn al-Masā'il*, the concepts of necessity, existence and possibility are given as examples of concepts that do not require prior concepts for their apprehension. F. Dieterici, *Alfārābī's philosophische Abhandlungen* [Arabic Text] (Leiden, 1890), p. 56.

6 See the author's, "Avicenna's Proof from Contingency in the *Metaphysics* of the *Shifā'*," *Mediaeval Studies*, 42 (1980), 337-352.

7 For a succinct statement of the Mu^{c}tazilite position, see al-Ghazālī, *Tahāfut al-Falāsifa* , ed. M. Bouyges (Beirut, 1927, p. 358.

8 *Ma^{c}ānī*, the plural of *ma^{c}nà* (the *intentio* of the medieval Latin translations of Avicenna), "meaning," "idea," "notion," "signification," "concept," depending on context.

9 Ibn Sīnā, *Fī Ithbāt al-Nubuwwāt*, p. 44; *Avicenna's De Anima*, p. 235.

10 Strictly, "For just as . . ." Here we have a sequence beginning with "For just as . . .," complemented by "Similarly . . ." A translation that follows the original structure would read something as follows:

"For just as in the category of judgement[s] there are primary principles, in themselves found to be true, causing [in turn] assent to other [propositions; principles of such a nature that], if they do not come to mind or if the expression designating them is not understood, it would be impossible to know whatever is known through them -- [this], even though the informative act striving to bring them to mind or to explain the expressions designating them is not engaged in any endeavor to impart knowledge not [already] present in the natural intelligence, but is merely drawing attention to a comprehension of what the speaker intends or upholds (something that may occur through things which in themselves are less evident than the things intended to be made known but which for some cause or some expression have become better known) --; similarly, in conceptual matters, there are things which are the principles of conception that are conceived in themselves."

11 Reading *takhtur* in the feminine, instead of *yakhtur* in the masculine, as given in the text. This reading is supported by lines 9-10, *wa in lam yakun al-ta^{c}rīf al-ladhī yuhāwil ikhtāraha bi-'l-bāl*, "even though the informative act striving to bring them to mind," where the bringing to mind refers to the proposition, not the expressions designating them.

Read in the masculine, the protasis of the sentence would translate either as: "If [the assent to their truth] does not occur to the mind or the expression designating them is not understood"; or, "If the expression designating them does not occur to the mind or is understood."

12 For a discussion of these terms, see H. A. Wolfson, "The Terms Taṣawwur and Taṣdīq in Arabic Philosophy and their Greek, Latin and Hebrew Equivalents," *The Moslem World*, 33 (1943), 1-15.

13 *Avicenna's De Anima*, p. 49; *al-Najāt*, p. 167.

14 *Fī 'l-gharīza*. See also reference to the *Ta^{c}līqāt*, 5 above.

15 See "Avicenna's Proof from Contingency in the *Metaphysics* of

the *Shifā'*," pp. 348-349.

16 Reading *al-Shay' al-wāhid* as given in the text, not, *al-shay' wa 'l-wāḥid*, "the thing and the one."

17 *Min ḥaqīqat al-mawjūd*.

18 *Inna 'l-shay' huwa 'l-ladhī yaṣiḥḥ ^{c}anhu 'l-khabar. Al-khabar*, has the ordinary meaning of "information," "report," "news"; in Arabic grammar, "the enunciative" of a nominal sentence.

19 *Annahu shay' aw annahu amr aw annahu mā aw annahu al-ladhī*.

20 In *^{c}Uyūn al-Masā'il*, p. 56, the conception of "body" is given as an example. One cannot conceive body unless one first conceives length, width and depth.

21 Reading *wa 'l-mawjūd*, as given in one manuscript, instead of *fa 'l-mawjūd*.

22 Al-Shahrastānī, *Nihāyat al-Iqdām fī ^{c}Ilm al-Kalām*, ed. A. Guillaume (London, 1934), p. 151.

23 *Ḥaqīqa*, "reality," "true nature."

24 Ibn Sīnā (Avicenna) *al-Shifā': Isagoge (al-Madkhal)*, ed. M. Khudayri, G. Anawati and A. F. Ahwani (Cairo, 1953), p. 34.

25 Al-Ash^{c}arī, *Maqālāt al-Islamiyyīn*, ed. H. Ritter (Istanbul, 1930), p. 519; see also pp. 161, 522-523. The Mu^{c}tazilite theologian credited with initiating the doctrine that the non-existent is a thing is al-Shaḥḥām (d. ca. 231/845); al-Sharastānī, *Nihāyat al-Iqdām*, p. 151. For an account of the Mu^{c}tazilite position, see also Fakhr al-Dīn al-Rāzī, *Muḥaṣṣal Afkār al-Mutaqaddimīn wa 'l-Muta'akhkhirīn* (Cairo, 1323 A. H.), pp. 34-41.

26 Ash^{c}arī, *Maqālāt*, pp. 158ff.

27 See the author's, "Avicenna's Chapter, 'On the Relative', in the *Metaphysics* of the *Shifā'*," in *Essays on Islamic Philosophy and Science*, ed. G. F. Hourani (Albany, New York, 1975), pp. 95-97.

28 See the author's, "Avicenna's Chapter on Universals in the *Isagoge* of his *Shifā'*," in *Islamic Past Influence and Present Challenge*, ed. A. T. Welch and P. Cachia (Edinburgh, 1979), p. 42. The reference is to Avicenna's concept of logical genus.

29 Al-Shahrastānī, *Nihāyat al-Iqdām*, pp. 131ff.

30 Ibn Sīnā, *al-Shifā': al-Mantiq (Logic), al-Qiyās (The Syllogism)*, ed. S. Zayed (Cairo, 1964), pp. 16-170.

31 *Ilāhiyyāt*, pp. 38-39; see also the author's, "Avicenna on Causal Priority," in *Islamic Philosophy and Mysticism*, ed. P. Morewedge (Delmar, New York, 1981), p. 69.

32 Reading *tafhīminā*, as given by two manuscript variants, instead of *tafahhuminā*.

33 In A. R. Badawi, *Aristu ^{c}Inda 'l-^{c}Arab* (Cairo, 1947), pp. 131-32.

34 *Aw muwāfaqat mawjūd li-^{c}araḍ min al-a^{c}rāḍ*. Again, the wording is awkward and at first sight one is apt to understand Avicenna as saying, "as having correspondence with an existent by reason of some accident or another." In the *Ta^{c}līqāt*, p. 132, Avicenna refers to the Mu^{c}tazilite doctrine that time is "nothing but an accident."

15

The College in Medieval Islam

George Makdisi
The University of Pennsylvania

In modern usage, madrasa is the name of an institution of learning where the Islamic sciences are taught; in mediaeval usage, from the tenth and eleventh centuries and up to a period as yet undetermined, it was a college of law in which the other Islamic sciences of the cirriculum, including the literary arts, were ancillary subjects. In what follows, this institution will be treated in its origins and development, as well as in its relations with other educational institutions of Islam in the middle ages.

More than half a century has elapsed since the appearance of Johann Pedersen's monographic article entitled "masjid," published in the first edition of the Encyclopaedia of Islam, in which he treated the mosque in its various aspects including that of institution of learning. In the meantime, other data have come to light on institutions of learning, methods of instruction and institutional staff, in source materials much of which was unavailable to him (ca. 1930). Nevertheless, Pedersen's article remains authoritative in a great many of its essentials, and the reader is urged to refer to it. The present article is therefore meant to be a supplement to that of Pedersen, supplementing and updating it. It relates particularly to Sections F ("The Mosque as an Educational Centre"), G ("The Administration of the Mosque"), and H ("The Personnel of the Mosque"). Section F alone, considerably modified, not as to its essentials, mainly by a shortening and rearrangement of some of its parts, was first published in the Handwörterbuch des Islam,[1] and then in the Shorter Encyclopaedia of Islam.[2] Pedersen saw no difference between the mosque and the madrasa; he therefore treated the latter institution, under the general heading of the former one. And

---

Logos Islamikos: Studia Islamica in honorem Georgii Michaelis Wickens, ed. Roger M. Savory and Dionisius A. Agius, Papers in Mediaeval Studies 6 (Toronto: Pontifical Institute of Mediaeval Studies, 1984), pp. 241-257.

although the article in the German Handwörterbuch and its later English edition was entitled "madrasa", seemingly indicating an awareness of an institutional difference between madrasa and masjid, no evidence of such awareness appears in the body of the article.

The present article deals with the original Section F of Pedersen's study, except for part nine of that section, "Recent Reforms in Education," as well as with Sections G and H, not included in the shorter version of HWB and SEI, cited above.

A. Institutions

The madrasa is the product of three stages in the development of the college in Islam. The masjid, particularly in its designation as the non-Friday mosque, was the first stage and functioned as an instructional centre; the second was the masjid-khān complex, the khān used as lodging for out-of-town students; and the third was the madrasa, combining the functions of masjid and khān in one waqf deed.

The masjid appears early in Islam as a centre of learning. The most important subjects of study were the sacred scriptures: the Qur'ān and the ḥadīth. It was from the study of the scripture that a science of jurisprudence began to develop, since the principles which were to be followed by the faithful did not always come ready-made from the mere reading of scripture. Although the early religious scholars, the ᶜulamā' (sing. ᶜālim), were usually the experts on the Qur'ān and were called al-qurrā' (sing. qāri'), on the ḥadīth, and were called al-muḥaddithūn (sing. muḥaddith), and on Qur'ānic exegesis and were called al-mufassirūn (sing. mufassir), yet the first century of Islam saw the development of the jurisconsult-doctor of the law, the muftī-faqīh. The turn of the century was later commemorated as "the Year of the Jurisconsults," sanat al-fuqahā', because of a number, generally considered to be seven, who died in and around that time.[3]

At this early period the masjid was used for the teaching of one or more of the Islamic fields of knowledge. It was the first institution of learning in Islam, and the first term used to describe the locus of learning within the masjid was majlis. This term is an ism makān (nomen loci) of the verb jalasa, which means to sit up, in contradistinction to the synonymous verb qaᶜada, which means to sit *down*. Learning took place in the *masjid*, a place of worship, specifically a place of prostration (from the verb *sajada*, to prostrate oneself) in prayer before God. From the prostrate position of the prayer, the teacher and his students would then *sit up*, and the class, or *majlis*, would begin. (From the synonymous verb *qa^{c}ada*, the *ism makān*, *maq^{c}ad*, is a bench, upon which one sits from a *standing* position.)

The *masjid* continued to be used for the teaching of one or more of the Islamic sciences or their ancillaries among the literary arts, well into the third century of Islam. The turning-point in its use came after the *miḥna*, or Great Inquisition. Begun in the last year of al-Ma'mūn's caliphate, 218/833, the *miḥna* extended across the caliphates of al-Mu^{c}tasim and al-Wāthiq, to the second year of al-Mutawakkil's caliphate, 234/848, a period of fifteen years. The upshot of the *miḥna* was the political bankruptcy of its authors, the rationalist forces represented by the philosophical theologians, and the correlative triumph of the traditionalist forces, its victims, the doctors of the law, a triumph due in great measure to the heroic endurance of Aḥmad ibn Ḥanbal.

After the *miḥna*, more and more *masjids* came to be founded for legal studies, as colleges of law. Since the *masjid* could not serve as a lodging place for teaching staff and students -- the exceptions being the wayfarer (*ibn al-sabīl*) and ascetic pious men who had given up all worldly goods (*zuhhād*, sing. *zāhid*) -- *khāns* were founded next to the *masjids* to serve as lodging for students from out-of-town. The outstanding example of this type of arrangement was the extensive network of *masjid-khān* complexes founded in the lands of the Eastern Caliphate during the fourth/tenth century by Badr ibn Ḥasanawayh (d. 405/1014), governor of several provinces under the Buwayhids. Such men of power and influence needed the good offices of the *^{c}ulamā'*, their sole sure link with the masses of the faithful. To establish this connection such men founded for the *^{c}ulamā'* institutions wherein they could teach the Islamic sciences. Besides currying the favor of the *^{c}ulamā'*, the powerful founders were performing highly meritorious acts of charity endearing them to the masses and the *^{c}ulamā'* alike.

The terminology for legal studies developed before the flourishing of the *madrasa* in the eleventh century. It derived from the radicals *drs*. The second form of the verb, *darrasa*, used without a complement, meant to teach law; tadrīs, its infinitive noun (maṣdar), meant the teaching of law, the function as well as the post of professor of law; the plural, tadārīs, or professorships of law, was of later development, when the holding of several professorships by one doctor of the law became a practice of common occurrence. The term dars, meant a lesson or lecture on law; mudarris, the active participle, meant the professor of law. It must be kept in mind that these terms had these significations in reference to law especially when used in the absolute, without a complement. The verb faqqaha is of rare occurrence, and was not commonly used to designate the teaching of law. The term faqīh was used in the sense of doctor of the law, or student of law, particularly a graduate student, in contradistinction to mutafaqqih, used to designate the undergraduate. The accomplished faqīh was eligible to become a mudarris and a muftī; for as faqīh who has successfully defended his theses in disputations (munāẓara) he obtained his licence to teach and to issue legal opinions (ijāza bi-'l-tadrīs wa 'l-iftā'.

The college of law therefore began as a masjid, and was soon joined by the khān, inn, for out-of-town students. The lodging place next to the masjid was especially necessary for the student of law as distinguished, for instance, from the student of the ḥadīth. Jurisprudence was by now a science whose rudiments had to be learned in a period of years, usually four, and that, usually under the direction of one master. After this basic undergraduate training, if he was successful and chosen by his master as a ṣāḥib, fellow, he went on to graduate studies that lasted an indefinite period of time, some fellows working as repetitors (mu^{c}īd) under their masters for as many as twenty years before acquiring their own professorial chair. In contrast, the student of ḥadīth traveled from one place to another, acquiring rare ḥadīths, and collections of ḥadīths, from ḥadīth-masters who often were the last link in the chain of transmitters, holding alone the authorization to pass on their collections authoritatively to others. The ḥadīth student traveled therefore from place to place and collected as many authorizations, ijāzas, as possible from as many masters as he could reach. The law student was interested in an authorization covering a field of knowledge, that of law, in one ijāza: the licence to teach law and issue legal opinions, ijāzat al-tadrīs wa 'l-fatwā, which he obtained from one master-jurisconsult. The khan, founded near the masjid, was therefore necessary as a lodging place for law students away from home.

Already in the fourth/tenth century there were a number of madrasas, outside of Baghdad, cultural center of the Muslim world. But the flourishing of the madrasa took place in the following century. The outstanding example of this type of college was the network of madrasas founded by the second wazir of the great Saljuks, Niẓām al-Mulk. The madrasa, combining the functions of the masjid and its nearby khān in one architectural unit, brought nothing new to legal studies as such. Nor was the student-body more numerous in the madrasa than it was in its predecessor; the number in either type of college of law was usually twenty. Nor did the new madrasa put an end to the masjid as a college; these continued to be established as charitable foundations. Indeed, many ᶜulamā' deplored the innovation of the madrasa which provided for all the needs of the student, including room and board, and encouraged, according to the complaints of the ᶜulamā', the worthy and unworthy alike to pursue knowledge for the wrong kind of motivation, a parasitic life of ease, instead of learning for the greater glory of God. Thus the masjid-khān type of college continued to be founded and many professors of law continued to teach there; as for instance, the Ḥanbalī madhhab whose first madrasa was founded only in the first part of the sixth/twelfth century. This lingering preference for the masjid is not surprising given the place of the mosque in the Muslim community, and the encouragement of the faithful to build mosques.[4]

The legal status of the madrasa allowed the founder to retain complete control over the administrative and instructional staff of the institution, and therefore the retention of the power of patronage. For government officials, such as a wazīr, it permitted him to attract the support of the rank and file through their religious leaders employed by the founder. For these men as well as for men of lesser power the law of waqf permitted them to place their wealth where it could be secured against confiscation.

Another aspect of the madrasa, which at first blush may be cause for surprise, is that it developed in the Eastern caliphate, outside of the cultural center of the Muslim world at the time; that is, outside of Baghdad. This fact has been taken as indicative of a cultural swing away from Arab Baghdad towards Persian Khurāsān, especially Nīsābūr, a misreading of cultural history due to anachronistic nationalist sentiment. Since there was no change in the curriculum, or in the teaching staff or students, and since the final product of the two types of colleges was exactly the same, that is, the muftī-faqīh, the reason for the change in institutional typology must be sought elsewhere and may be found in the legal status of the two institutions concerned.

Both the masjid and the madrasa were charitable foundations based on waqf. The founder, wāqif, was free to found the one or the other type of institution. He could, in his deed of foundation, make any stipulations he wished regarding any aspect of his foundation, whether it be a masjid or a madrasa, with only one limitation to his freedom of choice: none of his stipulations were to contravene the tenets of Islam. Legally speaking he could not appoint the imām of the masjid. If the masjid had a professor, in addition to the imām, the founder could appoint the professor. The imām, or the professor-imām, was appointed by the caliph alone, or by the caliph with the consent of the people of the quarter where the masjid was located. A madrasa, as such, had no imām, unless the foundation was a complex including a madrasa and masjid. The fundamental difference between the two institutions was that the masjid, once the waqf deed was signed, became a waqf taḥrīr; that is to say, a foundation whose legal status is assimilated to the manumission of a slave. As the master, once he freed his slave, had not further rights over him, the founder, once the deed of his masjid was signed, had no further rights over it, other than those legally valid stipulations in his deed pertaining to the instructional aspects of his foundation.

Thus between the two great patrons of learning mentioned previously, Badr and Niẓām al-Mulk, the difference is that while the former founded masjids over which he had limited control, the latter founded madrasas over which his control was complete. Niẓām al-Mulk retained for himself and his progeny complete control over his network of madrasas. In Baghdad, where professorial tenure was usually for life in the masjid-college of law, Niẓām al-Mulk's stipulations allowed him and his successors to hire and fire professors, some after a tenure of a month, and even a simple day. The introduction of madrasas in Baghdad may therefore be viewed as an incroachment upon the patronage of the caliph, whose control over masjid-and jāmi^{c}-mosques did not extend to the madrasa.

After the masjid and madrasa other institutions came into existence, especially the dār al-ḥadīth, the first of which was founded by Nūr al-Dīn Zankī in Damascus. In this institution the muḥaddith was raised to the level of the mudarris in the madrasa. The madrasa founded for one madhhab tended to be divisive, since only those students who chose to belong to that madhhab were admitted for the study of law and the ancillary sciences. The dār al-ḥadīth served to bring together students of all madhhabs, and may thus be seen as a further manifestation of the triumph of traditionalism over the forces of rationalism represented by the dār al-^{c}ilm institutions which soon disappeared from the scene. The dār al-ḥadīth must not be confused with either dār al-tadrīs or dār al-sunna, occasional terms that referred not to the study of ḥadīth but of fiqh, and were used as terms of traditionalism opposing the rationalism of dār al-^{c}ilm.

Education in Islam was religious in nature and an obligation incumbent upon the ^{c}ulamā', the men of religious science. The Caliph as the successor to the Prophet made it possible for teachers to teach in the Friday mosques where ḥalqas, study-circles, provided instruction in the various religious sciences and their ancillaries. Private individuals endowed institutions of learning, masjids and madrasas, which they specified for one or the other of the madhhabs as they chose. Muslim institutions of learning, based on the law of waqf, were endowments made by individual Muslims, of their own free will, without interference from the governing power. Even when the founder was a caliph, a sulṭān, a wazīr, or other official, he endowed his foundation as a Muslim individual, instituting his own private property as waqf for a public purpose. These institutions were not public in the sense that anyone was entitled to attend them. They were set aside for restricted use in accordance with the waqf stipulations of the founder, restricting admission to one or the other madhhab.

Founded at first for only one madhhab, madrasas were later founded for more than one. In the latter case, the students of each madhhab were taught separately. The system was as individualistic as the law itself: one madrasa, one madhhab. There were double, triple and quadruple madrasas, meaning that two, three or four madhhabs were involved; but the students of each madrasa within the compound were kept separate, each student-body following the madhhab of its choice.

Madrasas were usually Ḥanafī, Shāfiʿī or Ḥanbalī, with very few for the Mālikīs. Spain, predominantly Mālikī, had no madrasas, as late as the seventh/thirteenth centuries; the earliest madrasa, said to be that of Granada, was founded in 750/1349. Their penury throughout the Islamic world can be explained by the Mālikī law of waqf which prohibits Mālikī founders to retain control of the trusteeship of their institution. This discouraged founders from foundling madrasas as a means of sheltering their wealth against confiscation, by retaining control of their institution for themselves and their progeny to the end of their line. Mālikī madrasas were generally founded in North Africa and Spain by the sovereigns whose motives differed from those of private individuals. They were motivated by the prestige brought by their foundations to themselves and to their realms.

Besides the jāmiʿ and its study-circles, the masjid, the madrasa, the dār al-ḥadīth, there were also the dār al-Qur'ān, the ribāṭ and other monasteries (khānqāh, zāwiya) in which learning took place in the Islamic sciences. There were also institutions of learning consisting of a combination of two or three of the institutions mentioned; as, for instance, a madrasa ribāṭ dār al-ḥadīth.

Learning took place in the hospitals (māristān, from the Persian bīmāristān) which were also used as schools of medicine, as well as in the private homes of scholars and elsewhere.

B. Instruction

Knowledge was classified under three divisions in mediaeval Islam: the Islamic sciences, the sciences of the Ancients, meaning the non-Arabs, especially the Greeks, and the Arabic, or literary arts; they were designated, respectively, al-ʿulūm al-sharʿiyya (al-ʿulūm al-mutasharriʿa), al-ʿulūm al-qadīma (ʿilm [ʿulūm] al-awā'il), and al-ʿArabiyya (al-ʿulūm al-ʿArabiyya, ʿilm al-adab). The literary arts were propaedeutic to the other two divisions.

Memory was highly cultivated, especially with regard to the learning of ḥadīth. With the advent of legal studies, emphasis came to be placed also on understanding (this is the lexical meaning of the term fiqh, which means technically positive law). This shift of emphasis to both memory and comprehension is illustrated by the saying that "learning is a city one of whose gates is memory, and the other, understanding" (al-ᶜilmu madīnatun aḥadu bābayhā 'l-riwāya, wa 'l-ukhrā 'l-dirāya).

Repetition was cultivated especially in connection with the study of law. Jurisconsults were quoted as saying that in their student days they used to repeat each law lecture fifty times or more in order to imbed it in the memory. A school exercise was developed, whereby students quizzed one another, as an aid to learning their lessons, and as a contest to see who knew more than the other. The term used for the exercise was mudhākara (a calling something to mind with another, conferring with another).

But the most important method developed for legal studies was the method of disputation (munāẓara, ṭarīqat al-naẓar), the legal-school exercise par excellence. It consisted of (1) a thorough knowledge of khilāf, that is, the divergent legal opinions of jurisconsults, (2) a thorough knowledge of jadal, dialectic, and (3) munāẓara, disputation. The disputant had to know by heart as extensive a list as possible of the disputed questions of law (al-masā'il al-khilāfiyya) and have ready answers for them. It was his skill at disputation which earned for him the licence to teach law and issue legal opinions (ijāzat al-tadrīs wa 'l-fatwā). This licence he obtained after a long period of study, usually four years of basic studies of law, followed by an indeterminate period of fellowship (ṣuḥba) during which he apprenticed as muᶜīd (repetitor) of his master or otherwise made himself useful to the younger students, sometimes called mufīd (one who imparts useful knowledge) and holding the post of ifāda.

During the ṣuḥba stage of his learning, the graduate student wrote a taᶜlīqa, which was a compilation of notes from the lectures of his master, often including notes taken from the latter's writings. When such a compilation was original in nature, as to its arrangement and the treatment of the subject-matter, it came to be known by the name of its compiler. The term taᶜlīqa is also applied to a compilation of the master, a syllabus on law, from which the master taught his disciples. Some of these taᶜlīqas consisted of many volumes, as many as fifty in one case. Masters who had no taᶜlīqas used those of others.

C. The Scholastic Community

It has been said that in Islamic education there was no "distinction between teachers and taught," a remark that could be applied only to fields where the authoritative transmission of a text is involved. This occurs especially in ḥadīth. In this field one remained, in a sense, a student all his life, collecting authorizations (ijāza) for the transmission of one or more ḥadīths. There were many instances where an accomplished scholar of ḥadīth would seek the authoritative transmission of a collection of ḥadīths, or even of a single ḥadīth, from one many years younger than he but who had the ijāza, authorization, to transmit the ḥadīth(s), and was, most likely, the last to receive that authority from its last holder. This situation was due to the oral character of authoritative transmission. The perennial preoccupation of the conscientious ḥadīth scholar was to travel in search of those rare ḥadīths, whose rarity was due to the ever decreasing number of transmitters duly authorized to transmit them. Biographical notices sometimes tell of the authorized transmitter who had made a collection of such ḥadīths and waited until he had survived all other authorized transmitters before making them available; at which time he could exact his own price for them. This practice was, of course, condemned. There are well-known ḥadīths not only encouraging the gathering and spreading of knowledge, but also the condemnation of those who would gather and conceal it.

On the other hand, the distinction between teacher and taught in the field of law was quite clear. To obtain the licence to teach law one had to study many years under a professor of law, become proficient in the scholastic method of disputation, and build up as vast a repertoire of disputed questions of law as possible, together with solutions to these questions, then successfully defend his thesis or theses against the adversary, often his own master. This long process could take place under one master alone; but it sometimes took place under two, one for the basic four years, another for the graduate, apprentice, period. More rarely a law student could study under as many as five professors, but the process was always the same, the defense of a thesis or theses which earned him the licence to teach and issue legal opinions, a licence attesting to his competence in the law as a field of knowledge.

It has often been said that teachers were organized into a guild. And the usual argument advanced for this assertion is an anecdote cited in Yāqūt, Udabā' 1: 246 sq., according to which al-Khaṭīb al-Baghdādī (d. 463/1070) had to have the permission of naqīb al-nuqabā' in order to teach ḥadīths in Baghdad's Mosque of al-Manṣūr. The functions of the naqīb al-nuqabā' were also confused with the term ra'īs, further adding to the concept of a head of a guild of masters. No one has claimed to know how the guild worked, which is no surprise, since there was none. The naqīb was the marshall of the nobility, the ashrāf. His function was to investigate all claims to descendancy from the Prophet's family, and to keep rolls of legitimate descendants of the Prophet, for they were entitled to a lifetime pension. There were two naqībs: one for the Sunnīs, naqīb al-hāshimiyyīn; and one for the Shīᶜīs, naqīb al-ṭālibiyyīn.

The above mentioned anecdote has to do with naqīb al-hāshimiyyīn. The Mosque of al-Manṣūr was located in the quarter of Bāb al-Baṣra, on the west side of the city, stronghold of the constituency of the naqīb. This constituency was made up of traditionalist ashrāf, and an overwhelming majority of Ḥanbalīs. Al-Baghdādī had been a Ḥanbalī, had changed over to the Shāfiᶜī school of law, but was suspected of Ashᶜarism, to which theological movement the Ḥanbalīs were highly hostile. Al-Baghdādī asked the Caliph's permission to lecture in the Mosque, for it was his declared lifelong ambition to do so, the Mosque being known as the institution with the highest reputation for the science of ḥadīth. The Caliph, aware of the hostility of the Bābaṣrians to the lecturer, called on the naqīb, as the Marshall of the Sharīfs of the Bāb al-Baṣra quarter, to see to it that the event would not produce a riot. The naqīb agreed to do so, but reluctantly, since he felt that he did not have enough men to control the assembly if it got out of hand. An incident did occur, bricks were thrown at the speaker, and turbans were snatched, but the naqīb succeeded in limiting the damage.

Thus permission to lecture in the Great Mosque was sought from the Caliph who alone made appointments to the teaching posts, the ḥalqas, of the great mosques (there were, at the time, six of these) in Baghdad. The *naqib* was not the head of a guild of masters, such as the *universitas magistrorum* of the Latin West; there was no such guild in mediaeval Islam.

The term *ra'īs* was applied to any scholar who had reached the summit of his field in his locality. It was used especially in the field of law; biographical notices often express it by saying that "leadership in the school of law ended up with him" (*intahat ilayhi riyāsatu 'l-madhhab*). The terminology used in these notices is indicative of the competition that existed among the jurisconsults: *baraʿa fī 'l-fiqh* (he excelled in the field of law); *lā yushaqqu ghubāruh* (his dust cannot be penetrated -- comparing the legal scholar to a thoroughbred so swift that other horses in the race fail to keep him in sight, the dust of his hoofs having settled by the time they get to where he was); *kāna qāṭiʿa 'l-nuẓarā'* (he was the annihilator of his peers); etc. The titulature is also indicative of this competition to gain the heights, not only in learning but also in the military and in government: *amīr al-umarā'* (prince of princes), *malik al-mulūk* (king of kings), *sulṭān al-salāṭīn* (sultan of sultans), *qāḍī 'l-quḍāt* (judge of judges), *ʿālim al-ʿulamā'* (scholar of scholars), and even of the term *ra'īs* itself, *ra'īs al-ru'asā'* (leader of leaders).

In places where the term *ra'īs* designated a post, as for instance in Nīsābūr, where there was also a *nā'ib-ra'īs*, a substitute-leader, or deputy-leader, the post appears as one requiring, besides the qualification of leadership, that of non-partisanship, someone capable of acting as peace-maker, a moderator between opposing factions among the scholars. This, however, was not the head of a guild of masters. Such an organization was unlikely in a system highly individualistic in character. The concept of a guild, or corporation, based on juristic personality was unknown to Mediaeval Islam where juristic personality belonged to the natural physical person alone.

Islamic law is individualistic; this may be seen in the function of the *qāḍī*, the *muftī*, and the *mudarris*, or professor of law, as well as in the *madrasa*, the college of law. The *qāḍī* was alone responsible for his legal decision; the *muftī* was alone responsible for his legal opinion, based on *ijtihād*, an individual personal activity of research in the sources of the law. Likewise, every *madrasa* represented one madhhab; a double madrasa represented two madhhabs where students were kept separate; so also with the triple, and quadruple madrasa; and every madhhab was represented by one professor of law, who may have under his direction one or several muᶜīds and mufīds. Some instances in history illustrate this unicity of the professorial chair in the college of law. In 483/1090, a few months after the appointment of Abū ᶜAbd Allāh al-Ṭabarī to the Niẓāmiyya's chair of law in Baghdad, Abū Muḥammad al-Fāmī arrived with orders to occupy the chair. Both professors were made to share the chair, and taught law according to an alternating schedule, one teaching one day, the other, the next. A variety of this solution later became standard procedure in some colleges of Damascus, where the professorial chair was assigned to two, three and four professors of law, each retaining half (niṣf), third (thulth), or fourth (rubᶜ) of the post and being paid accordingly.

The Muslim system of education in the middle ages was based on the waqf, which, in all institutions except the masjid, as already mentioned, gives the founder a free hand in determining the course of his foundation, as long as his stipulations were in keeping with the tenets of Islam. The historian must be circumspect about generalizing for one institution on the basis of the particulars of another. The history of Muslim education must therefore be written on the basis of the deeds of waqf, of which few are extant (and those, mostly late in date), as well as on the basis of biographical literature and the chapters on waqf in the fatwā-works. These are the main sources to be consulted for the history of institutionalized education; that is, that education which took place in the jāmiᶜ, the masjid, the madrasa, the dār al-ḥadīth, the dār al-Qur'ān, the ribāṭ, the khānqāh, the zāwiya, and the various combinations of these.

As for the "ancient sciences," that is, the philosophical and the natural sciences, their history is more elusive. Medicine, taught in the hospitals (māristān, bīmāristān), was the Trojan horse par excellence for the teaching of the ancient sciences, an activity which usually took place discreetly, or in complete secrecy, according to the times and places. Ḥadīth was another venerable science that was used as a Trojan horse for philosophical kalām-theology; and where kalām was tolerated when taught discreetly in homes and shops it was used as a Trojan horse for philosophical studies. The sources for the non-institutionalized fields of the "ancient sciences" are chiefly the biographical works and the waqf deeds of the libraries, institutions designated by one of these terms, dār, khizāna, bayt, followed by one of these terms, al-ᶜilm, al-ḥikma, al-kutub, occurring in all the possible nine combinations. It is indeed noteworthy that, although the Islamic waqf did not tolerate anything in its foundations that was inimical to the tenets of Islam, the libraries often contained books of all fields of law including the "ancient sciences" which were not tolerated in institutionalized learning. This apparent inconsistency is explained by the essential authoritative character of Muslim institutionalized education, which is based on oral transmission from the authorized master to the disciple who became in turn licensed to transmit authoritatively. Books on philosophy could be read in private, they could even be discussed, but they were not eligible for oral transmission through religiously recognized authoritative channels. Libraries could contain books on philosophy, which could be discreetly read, copied and discussed, but no religiously recognized authoritative teaching took place in the libraries. The waqf as such could be used to preserve books on the ancient sciences, whose subject matter was tolerated and condoned, or prohibited and condemned, according to time and place; which explains how so many books on the "ancient sciences" were preserved and transmitted from place to place throughout the Muslim world.[5]

The general designation for master was shaykh. When used with a complement the term designated the master of various fields; as, for instance, shaykh al-ḥadīth, shaykh al-qirā'a, for the professor of ḥadīth and the professor of Qur'ānic studies respectively. On the other hand, the professor of law had a designation all his own, a term used without a complement: mudarris. He was not referred to a "shaykh al-fiqh." The term mudarris with a complement was sometimes used to designate other professors. Shaykh al-ribāṭ was used to designate the director, or abbot, of a monastery. The mudarris, like the qāḍī, was entitled to have a deputy, a nā'ib-mudarris, who taught during his absence. The mudarris could, in fact, have several nā'ibs. This happened when the professor of law held several posts (tadrīs, pl. tadārīs); he would teach in one or the other of these posts, and hire deputies to teach in the others. Thus, as the chair for the professorship of law could be divisible, the professorships could be multiple.

The professor of law could also be the professor-trustee of the madrasa, designated by the term mutawallī, or nāẓir, both terms deriving from the original designation, al-nāẓir al-mutawallī. In large foundations there could be a mutawallī as well as one or more nāẓirs, a mushrif and a qayyim, and their functions could differ somewhat from one foundation to another, with legal opinions (fatwā) solicited in order to determine the division of administrative functions in a particular case.

The professor of law assisted by the "repetitor", muʿīd, who, as drill-master, "repeated" the lecture of the professor to the latter's students. The professor of law was also assisted by the mufīd, a sort of "scholar in residence" who imparted "useful information," fā'ida, pl. fawā'id, to the students of the institution. The post of mufīd was also used in the field of ḥadīth, for the same general purpose. The counterpart of the muʿīd, in law, was the mustamlī, in ḥadīth, whose function it was to repeat the ḥadīth dictated by the professor of ḥadīth to a class that could often run into the hundreds of thousands. In the case of such large classes, several mustamlīs relayed the ḥadīth to those who were not within earshot of the professor.

Other posts in the various institutions included the grammarian, naḥwī, who taught grammar and the other literary arts generally; the various preachers: al-khaṭīb -- who preached the Friday sermon in the jāmiʿ; al-wāʿiẓ -- who preached the academic sermon and taught the art of the sermon; and the popular preachers called al-qāṣṣ and qāri' 'l-kursī; al-imām, who led the five daily prayers in the mosques; the elementary school teacher of the maktab and kuttāb, called variously al-muʿallim, al-muʿaddib and al-faqīh (colloquially, in Egypt esp., al-fiqī); the monitors, al-ʿarīf, kātib al-ghayba; the copyists of manuscripts, al-nāsikh and al-warrāq, the latter term was also used for the bookseller; (it would seem that the warrāq copied books for sale and hired the nāsikh [pl. nussākh] to copy for him); the corrector of copied manuscripts, al-muṣaḥḥiḥ; the collator of copied manuscripts, al-muqābil, al-muʿāriḍ; the servitor, al-khādim, a man-servant who worked for a professor or a rich student while pursuing his own studies. Most of these functions were performed by students working their way through college.

For the relation between Muslim institutions of learning and those of the mediaeval Latin West, see some of the articles in the following bibliography, and especially the last book cited.

Bibliography

A. S. Tritton, Materials on Muslim Education in the Middle Ages (London: Luzac, 1957) and the bibliography cited there on pp. ix-xii; for libraries, Y. Eche, Les Bibliothèques arabes publiques et semi-publiques en Mésopotamie, en Syrie et en Egypte au moyen âge (Damascus: PIFD, 1967), published posthumously; G. Makdisi, "Madrasa and University in the Middle Ages," Studia Islamica (Memorial dedicated to J. Schacht), 32 (1970), 255-264; idem, "Madrasa as a Charitable Trust and the University as a Corporation in the Middle Ages" in Correspondence d'Orient, No. 11, Actes du Ve Congres International d'Arabisants et d'Islamisants (Bruxelles, 1970), pp. 329-337; idem, "Law and Traditionalism in the Institutions of Learning of Mediaeval Islam," in Theology and Law in Islam, edited by G.E. von Grunebaum (Wiesbaden: Otto Harrassowitz, 1971), pp. 75-88; idem, "The Madrasa in Spain: Some Remarks," in Revue de l'Occident Musulman et de la Méditerranée, Extrait des Mélanges le Tourneau (Aix-en-Provence: 1973), pp. 153-158; idem, "The Scholastic Method in Mediaeval Education: An Inquiry Into Its Origins in Law and Theology," Speculum, 49 (1974), 640-661; idem, "Interaction Between Islam and the West," in Mediaeval Education in Islam and the West, edited by George Makdisi, Dominique Sourdel and Janine Sourdel-Thomine, The International Colloquia of La Napoule, 1 (Paris: Paul Geuthner, 1977), pp. 287-309; idem, "Ṣuḥba et Riyāsa dans l'enseignement médiéval," in Recherches d'Islamologie: Recueil d'articles offert à Georges C. Anawati et Louis Gardet par leurs collègues et amis (Louvain--Louvain-La-Neuve: Peeters-Institut Supérieur de Philosophie, 1978), pp. 207-221; idem, "An Islamic Element in the Early Spanish University," in Islam: Past Influence and Present Challenge, edited by A. T. Welch and P. Cachia (Edinburgh: University Press, 1979), pp. 126-137; idem, "On the Origin of the College in Islam and the West," in Islam and the

Mediaeval West: Aspects of Intercultural Relations, edited by K. I. H. Semaan (Albany, N.Y.: SUNY Press, 1980), pp. 26–49; idem, *The Rise of Colleges: Institutions of Learning in Islam and the West* (Edinburgh: University Press, 1981).

Notes

[1] Edited by A. J. Wensinck and J. H. Kramers (Leiden: E. J. Brill, 1941).

[2] Edited by H. A. R. Gibb and J. H. Kramers (Leiden: E. J. Brill, 1953).

[3] G. Makdisi, *The Rise of Colleges*, (Edinburgh, 1981) p. 145 and note 367.

[4] "The Apostle of God ordered . . . that *masjids* be built" ("*amara rasūlu 'illāhi. . .bi-binā'i 'l-masājid*," Abū Dāwūd, *Sunan*, *ṣalāt* 13; Tirmidhī, *Jāmi*^{c}, *jumu'a* 65; see also Muslimk, *Ṣaḥīḥ*, *masājid* 288; Tirmidhī, *Jāmi*^{c}, *da*^{c}*wāt* 82; Dārimī, *Sunan*, *salāt* 60).

[5] Cf. F. Sezgin, *Geschichte des arabischen Schrifttums*, 7 vols. (Leiden: E. J. Brill, 1967–1979).

16

Usurpers and Tyrants: Notes on Some Islamic Political Terms

Bernard Lewis
Princeton University and
the Institute for Advanced Study

The *sharī^{c}ah*, the holy law of Islam posits a divinely ordained community, the *ummah*, ruled by a divinely ordained sovereign, the *imām*. To comply with the law, the *imām* must meet certain requirements:

1. He must be qualified, that is to say he must be one of a group of people possessing certain necessary minimal qualifications. These are differently defined by Sunnī, Shī^{c}ite and Khārijite Muslims, but all agree that there are qualifications and that the *imām* must meet them.

2. He must become *imām* by a legally recognized and approved procedure. Here again there is a difference between the Sunnis and the Shī^{c}a, the first prescribing election, the second hereditary succession within the House of the Prophet. Both of them however, and even the Khārijites, agree that succession must be in accordance with the holy law as defined and interpreted by them.

3. He must govern justly.

Granted the existence and acceptance of these rules, it follows that any ruler who fails to meet either the first or second requirement is not legitimate, i.e., is a usurper; any who violates the third is unjust, i.e., a tyrant. These categories may, but do not necessarily, coincide.

The different schools agree that obedience to the *imām* is a religious obligation, prescribed by holy law. From this it follows that disobedience is a sin as well as a crime. But in principle such obedience is owed only to a legitimate and just ruler. It may be withheld from an illegitimate or unjust ruler. Some go even further and argue that in such a case the duty of obedience not only lapses but is replaced by a right or rather duty of disobedience.

Logos Islamikos: Studia Islamica in honorem Georgii Michaelis Wickens, ed. Roger M. Savory and Dionisius A. Agius, Papers in Mediaeval Studies 6 (Toronto: Pontifical Institute of Mediaeval Studies, 1984), pp. 259-267.

From the beginning, Islamic history, tradition and law embrace two distinct and indeed contradictory principles, one activist, the other quietist.[1] The advent of Islam was in itself a revolutionary challenge to the old leadership and the old order, both of which were overthrown and supplanted, the one by the Prophet and his companions, the other by Islam. This radical tradition was continued with what later historians have usually called conquests but what the Muslim tradition calls futūḥ, literally openings. These were seen not as conquests in the vulgar sense of territorial acquisitions, but as the overthrow of impious regimes and illegitimate hierarchies and the opening of their people to the new revelation and dispensation. The notion of the superseded old order is vividly expressed in the invocation of an ultimatum said to have been sent by the Muslim commander Khālid ibn al-Walīd to the princes of Persia: "Praise be to God who has dissolved your order (ḥalla niẓāmakum), frustrated your evil designs, and sundered your unity."[2] The use of the root fataḥ is thus not unlike the twentieth century use of the verb "liberate," and is indeed sometimes replaced by the latter verb (ḥarrar) in modern Arabic writing. The Arabic verb ghalab, conquer, with a connotation of overwhelming with superior force, may be used of the Muslim conquests, in the context of actual military operations. It is normally used of the conquest or reconquest of Muslim lands by the non-Muslim armies.

This underlying concept of the essential rightfulness of the Muslim advance tallies with the doctrine, expressed in a well-known ḥadīth, that every infant has an inborn predisposition to be a Muslim, but his parents make him a Jew or a Christian or a Zoroastrian. It is thus an opening, or a liberation, to give free vent to this divinely ordained propensity.[3] This spirit of activism is expressed many times in Islamic literature, notably in Qur'ānic injunctions not to obey wilful and intemperate rulers who bring corruption to the world, or in the traditions to the effect that there is no obedience in sin—i.e., that the duty of obedience lapses when the orders of the sovereign conflict with God's commandments.[4] If the first clearly refers to non-Muslim rulers, the second would seem to be directed against erring Muslim holders of authority.

The quietist tradition is also firmly based in the same Qur'ānic and traditional sources. The verse "Obey God, obey His Prophet and obey those in authority over you" is supported by numerous *ḥadīths*[5] enjoining the duty of obedience to legitimate authority, and was reinforced by the authoritarian traditions of the older societies which had flourished in the Middle East and became the political and cultural centres of the House of Islam.

In the course of the early Islamic centuries, there were significant changes in the definitions of legitimacy and justice and consequently in the definitions of usurpation and tyranny. The first and second requirements--legitimacy in terms of qualifications and manner of accession--were progressively reduced to the point when in effect only two conditions remained--power and Islam. As long as the ruler possessed the necessary authority to seize and hold power and as long as he was a Muslim, however minimal and however nominal, that sufficed.[6] Some were even willing to go a step further and admit the rule of a non-Muslim, but this was exceptional and in classical times was not generally admitted. The other qualification, that of ruling justly, was also whittled down though never finally eliminated. It was in fact reduced to one basic requirement--the public, though not necessarily the private, recognition and enforcement of the social and ritual prescriptions of the *sharīʿah*.

In time the concepts of usurper and tyrant, previously distinct, begin to overlap and even coincide. Muslim writers on the related subjects of religion, law and history developed a rich vocabulary of technical terms to denote different kinds of rule and ruler. The evolution and specialization of the terms applied to rulers not recognized and, so to speak, not validated by the holy law help to document the history of political institutions and ideas.

The prototype of the non-*sharīʿah* ruler is of course the infidel, particularly--but not exclusively--when he oppresses the apostles of God and their faithful. Such were Pharaoh, Haman, and other figures portrayed in the Qur'ān; such too were the pagan chiefs and rulers whom the Prophet Muḥammad ousted or converted in Arabia. The Christian kings whom the Muslims encountered outside Arabia, being followers of a revealed religion, have a somewhat better status, and are referred to by neutral or even respectful terms (*Ṣāḥib*, *ʿAẓīm*) or by their own titles (*Najāshī*, *Qayṣar*). The term most commonly applied to non-Muslim rulers, whether before Muhammad or outside the world of Islam, is *malik*, king, a term already sufficiently negative in its connotation in early Islam to be suitable for this purpose.

Later, when the title malik acquired a certain legitimacy within the Islamic world through its adoption by a succession of Muslim rulers, the practice grew of using other, less flattering terms for infidels. Some of these terms were also used for Muslim rulers who were seen as failing to meet the requirements.

One sometimes used was ṭāghiya, from a root frequently used in the Qur'ān both of rulers and of peoples. it carries a connotation of insolence and overweening pride, of disregard for God's law and hostility to His apostles--in a word, a kind of Muslim equivalent of the Greek notion of hubris. In the Qur'ān it is used of Pharaoh and other pagans who defied the will of God and were duly punished. In Islamic times it remained in use for rulers whose title to authority was not recognized. Thus, the ᶜAlid Muḥammad al-Nafs al-Zakiyyah, in a khutba delivered in Medīna in 145/762, applied it to his successful rival the ᶜAbbāsid Caliph al-Manṣūr, whom he denounced as hādhā al-ṭāghiyah ᶜaduww Allāh--"this tyrant the enemy of God."[8] It was used by Shīᶜa of Sunnī government[9] and by many Muslim writers of the Byzantine Emperors. Later, it was applied in North Africa to the Christian kings of Europe, while eastern writers continued to use the term malik for this purpose.

The rulers of the Christian states established by the Crusaders in Muslim territory do not qualify even for this title. They are not malik, king, but mutamallik, pseudo-king. Kings who came from Europe were called malik, e.g., Richard Coeur de Lion, Malik al-Inkitār, but the King of Cyprus, as Qalqashandī explains, was called mutamallik "because the Muslims had taken (fataḥ) Cyprus and then the Christians had conquered (taghallab) the island and ruled it. That is why the one who prevails over it is called mutamallik and is not called malik." The same title was used, for the same reason, of the Armenian king of Sīs and the Georgian king of Tiflīs, both cities conquered by the Muslims and then recaptured by the Christians.[10]

In principle, even a Muslim ruler who does not possess the necessary qualifications of descent and capacity or is not chosen or appointed according to the law, is a usurper. Among the Shīᶜa this remained a crucial question, and all Sunnī rulers, not being of the line of ᶜAlī and not being nominated and appointed by an ᶜAlid predecessor, are usurpers. Among Sunnī Muslims, as has been already noted, effective power became a sufficient qualification. In a phrase used by Mālikī jurists, man ishtaddat waṭ'atuh wajabat ṭā^c^atuhu – "whose power prevails must be obeyed."[11] The ruler need no longer be of the tribe of Quraysh, nor even an Arab. He need no longer possess the legally prescribed qualifications of rectitude, judgment, physical soundness, wisdom and courage. It is sufficient if he can stay in power and keep order. The Khārijites, the Mu^c^tazilah and a minority among Sunnī jurists go a little further, and demand that the ruler be guilty neither of blameful innovation (bid^c^ah) nor of major sin (fisq). According to Baqillānī, for example, the imām forfeits his imāmate if he falls into this category and thus ceases to be legally qualified. The same applies if he becomes senile or otherwise physically incompetent.[12] The majority Sunnī view was that the imām, even if he is a sinner (fāsiq), must be obeyed, though some authorities conceded that this might not apply to the imām's agents who are fasaqa.

In general, such limitations are either explicitly dropped or tacitly abandoned. Only one requirement survives the rest--that he rule justly. The notion of usurper has thus lost its meaning; that of tyrant remains. In other words, when a ruler is challenged on religious grounds, the challenge is based not on the manner in which he gained power but on the manner in which he exercises it--not usurpation, but tyranny.

Tyranny--it is generally agreed--is a great evil. But it is not the greatest evil. The dictum that "Tyranny is better than strife" is cited to defend a doctrine of quietism, of submission even to an evildoing and tyrannical authority, if the alternative is the collapse of all authority, and a situation in which the unity of the Islamic community would be disrupted and the legally valid execution of normal legal acts such as court judgments, the contracting of marriages, the division of inheritances, would cease to be possible.[13]

Anarchy was not the only alternative which was worse than tyranny. Another, according to some jurists, was the rule of an infidel monarch over Muslims. The advance of the Christian reconquest in Sicily and Spain gave this question a growing urgency. While some jurists were willing to concede a certain legitimacy to a Christian ruler who permitted his Muslim subjects to live according to Muslim law, others took the opposite view, and insisted that if a Muslim country falls under infidel rule, its Muslim inhabitants must follow the scriptural precedent of the Prophet and leave their homes, to migrate to a Muslim land. In a famous fatwā on the question whether Muslims might remain in Christian Spain, the Moroccan jurist al-Wansharīsī insists that they must leave, even if the new Christian regime is tolerant and just, and the Muslim regime to which they go is neither. A tolerant infidel is a greater threat to their faith, and therefore even Muslim tyranny is better than Christian justice.[14]

The terms used for tyranny, their synonyms and their antonyms, give some indication of how tyranny was perceived and defined. The commonest term is ẓulm, which occurs very frequently in the Qur'ān, where it appears to have the broad, general meaning of misdeed, wrongdoing, and hence injustice and tyranny. In post-Qur'ānic usage it is increasingly specialized in the latter sense, and is sometimes coupled with jawr, a word the primary meaning of which is deviation, straying from the path, whence also the developed meaning of wrongful or unjust treatment. One of the most commonly cited messianic traditions speaks of a mahdī, a divinely guided one, who will come and "fill the earth with ᶜadl and qisṭ as it is now filled with ẓulm and jawr."[15] ᶜAdl and qisṭ, usually translated justice and equity, express the converse of tyranny. The basic meaning of ẓulm is the absence of ᶜadl, and its political content changes as does that of ᶜadl.

Another word occurring frequently in the Qur'ān, with the meaning of an insolent and overbearing figure, is jabbār, sometimes coupled with mutakabbir, arrogant, self-important, ᶜanīd, willful, shaqī, fractious, and ᶜāṣī, rebellious, sinful. It is the converse of taqī (God-fearing) and barr (pious), and is no doubt related to the hebrew gibbōr, which however has a positive and not a negative connotation. Jabbār, in the plural form jabābira, appears in a famous ḥadīth enumerating the stages of deterioration in the Islamic institution of sovereignty: "The Prophet said: After me there will be caliphs, and after the caliphs amīrs, and after the amīrs kings, and after the kings oppressors (jabābira), and then a man of my family will arise who will fill the world with justice (ᶜadl) as it is now filled with tyranny (ẓulm)."[16] The jabābira obviously represent the final stage of wickedness, before the advent of the messianic age.

In general, the term jabbār is not much used in Islamic political literature, possibly because of its adoption as one of the divine names. Two other terms however gained some currency to denote oppressive or unauthorized rule.

The first is *istibdād*, which may be translated colloquially as doing it alone. As used in medieval texts, it carries a connotation of arbitrary and capricious rather than tyrannical or illegitimate rule. It is used of a ruler who decides and acts on his own, without due consultation of his religious and other advisors, and it is contrasted with *naṣīḥah* or *mushāwarah*, as *ẓulm* is contrasted with *ʿadl*.[17] In the nineteenth and twentieth centuries *istibdād* came to be the term commonly used by liberal democrats in both Turkish and Arabic, to characterize the autocratic rulers whom they wished either to limit or to remove.

In modern Arabic *zaʿīm* means leader, especially political leader. It was used as a military title in Mamlūk Egypt, and seems to have first come into use in the modern sense in the nineteenth century. It has usually been a positive term, which political leaders were happy to adopt. It was not always so. One of the meanings of the root is pretence or false claim, and the term *zaʿīm* was sometimes used in medieval Islamic documents for leaders or rulers whose title was for one reason or another invalid or at least unrecognized. It was thus used of the chiefs of the Ismāʿīlīs in Persia and Syria, of the head of the Jewish community in Baghdad, and of certain Muslim rulers, such as the Zaydīs in the Yemen and the Almohades in North Africa, who claimed to be caliphs and whose claim was not admitted.[18] The modern expression *mazʿūm*, so-called, pretended, *soi-disant*, retains this connotation.

Ottoman usage retained the classical Islamic terminology, with some variants. Thus Christian kings were not called *malik* but *kiral*, a word of European origin. The Ottomans were very reluctant to apply any Islamic title, even those of Persian or Turkish origin, to non-Muslims, and only conceded this under pressure. The preferred term was *kiral* (feminine *kiralice*), sometimes followed, in accordance with a common Ottoman practice, by an abusive jingle--*kiral bedfiʿāl*--evildoing king.

In modern Arabic most of these Qur'ānic and other classical terms can still be used, but have become somewhat archaic. Some others have taken their place. *Ghāsib*, which in classical usage usually refers to the forcible and illegal seizure or misappropriation of property, is given the political meaning of usurper. Among many synonyms for repressive or oppressive government, *idtihād*, is probably the most common. A loan word of European origin, *diktātūr* and *diktatūrī*, is also widely used of regimes in other countries.

Notes

[1] For a brief but interesting recent discussion of these traditions, see R. Stephen Humphreys, "The political values of traditional Islam and their role in twentieth-century Egypt," in *Self-views in Historical Perspective in Egypt and Israel*, ed. Shimon Shamir (Tel-Aviv, 1981), pp. 25-32.

[2] Ṭabarī, *Ta'rīkh*, 1: 2053; cf. ibid., 1: 2020; Abū Yūsuf, *Kitāb al-Kharāj* (Cairo, 1382/1962-1963), p. 85; Abū ᶜUbayd al-Qāsim ibn Sallām, *Kitāb al-Amwāl*, ed. Muḥammad Ḥāmid al-Fīqī (Cairo, 1353/1934), p. 34. Similar expressions occur in other early letters ascribed to Muslim leaders. See for example the texts collected by Muḥammad Ḥamīdullah, *Majmūᶜat al-wathā'iq al-siyāsīya* (Cairo, 1376/1956), especially pp. 295ff.

[3] References in A. J. Wensinck, *A Handbook of early Muhammadan Tradition* (Leiden, 1921), p. 43 and idem, *Concordance*, 5: 179-180. See further D. B. Madonald, *The Religious Attitude and Life in Islam* (Chicago, 1909), p. 243; idem, "Fitra," *EI²*, 2: 931-932.

[4] Qur'ān, 18: 28 and 26: 150-152; cf. 28: 3/4-5/6, 34: 33/34-37/38, and 59: 7. For traditions, see A. J. Wensinck, *Concordance*, svv. *maᶜṣiya*, *ẓulm*, etc.

[5] Qur'ān, 4: 59, Traditions in al-Muttaqi, *Kanz al-ᶜummāl* (Hyderabad, 1312), 3: 197 ff. Further examples in Wensinck, *Concordance*, svv. *imām*, *amīr*, *wālī*, etc.

[6] This development was first traced and analysed by A. von Kremer (*Geschichte der herrschenden des Ideen Islams* [Leipzig, 1868], pp. 413ff. and *Culturgeschichte des Orients unter der Chalifen* [Vienna, 1875], 1: 380ff) and presented in exemplary form by David Santillana, *Istituzioni di diritto musulmano malichita con riguardo anche al sistema sciafiita* (Rome, 1926), vol. 1 especially pp. 12-24, where the major Arabic sources are cited. See further H. A. R. Gibb, *Studies on the Civilization of Islam* (London, 1962), pp. 141 ff; idem, "Constitutional Organization," in *Law in the Middle East*, ed. Majid Khadduri and Herbert J. Liebesny (Washington, DC, 1955), 1: 3-27. The whole question has recently been thoroughly and comprehensively reexamined by Ann K. S. Lambton in a major work, *State and Government in Medieval Islam* (London, 1981).

[7] On this and other terms used in the Qur'ān, see Toshihiko Izutsu, *Ethico-religious concepts in the Qur'ān* (Montreal, 1966).

[8] Ṭabarī, *Ta'rīkh*, 3: 197.

[9] E. g., Kulīnī, *Uṣūl*, pp. 4, 63.

[10] Qalqashandī, *Ṣubḥ al-aᶜshā* (Cairo, 1334/1915), 8: 29 and 51-52; Shihāb al-Dīn al-ᶜUmarī, *Al-Taᶜrīf bi-'l-muṣṭalaḥ al-sharīf* (Cairo, 1312), pp. 55-56. Maqrīzī, in the *Khiṭaṭ* (ed. Wiet; 3: 297) refers to the Christian ruler of Nubia as *matamallik*, but elsewhere

(e.g., Sulūk, 1: 611) discussing the same episode, follows the normal practice of according this old established monarchy the title malik.

[11] Santillana, 1: 24.

[12] Lambton, pp. 74ff.

[13] See, for example, al-Ghazālī, Al-Iqtiṣād fī 'l-iᶜtiqād (Cairo, n.d.), pp. 102-108: "We do not concede this voluntarily, but necessity may make licit that which is forbidden. Thus, we know that to eat carrion is forbidden, but to starve to death is worse." In the same way, Ghazālī argues, a tyrannical ruler who validates the law and thus maintains the life of the community is better than none at all and the resulting communal death.

[14] Wansharīsī's fatwā was included in his al-Miᶜyār al-Mughrib (Fez, 1896-1897), 2: 90-106 and published in a critical edition by Ḥusayn Mu'nis, "Asnā 'l-matājir fī bayān man ghalaba ᶜalā waṭanihi 'l-Naṣārà wa-lam yuhājir," in Revista del Instituto de Estudios Islamicos en Madrid, 5 (1957), Arabic section pp. 129-191, summary in Spanish section pp. 273-275. On the problem of emigration from Muslim lands conquered by non-Muslims, see in general Santillana, 1: 69-72, where other sources are cited.

[15] Ibn Mājah, Sunan (Cairo, 1372/1952), 2: 1366-1367.

[16] Ibn al-Athīr, Usd al-ghāba (Cairo, 1285-1287/1869-1871), 5: 155.

[17] E.g., Ibn Sīdah, al-Mukhaṣṣaṣ (Cairo, 1316-1321), 12: 250.

[18] Abū Shāmah, Tarājim rijāl al-qarnayn al-sādis wa-'l-sābiᶜ, ed. Muḥummad Zāhid al-Kawtharī (Cairo, 1366/1947), p. 81; ibn al-ᶜAdīm, "Biography of Rāsid al-Dīn Sinān," ed. B. Lewis, in Arabica, 13 (1966), 266; Ibn al-Fuwaṭī, Al-Ḥawādith al-jāmiᶜa, ed. Muṣṭafà Jawād (Baghdad, 1951), p. 218; Qalqashandī, Ṣubḥ, 6: 513. See further Ḥasan al-Bāshā, Al-Alqāb al-Islāmīyah (Cairo, 1957), pp. 310-311.

17

The Delay of Maghrib: A Study in Comparative Polemics

Steven M. Wasserstrom
The University of Toronto

Disputes between Sunnīs and Shīᶜites over points of ritual proliferated throughout the first centuries of Islam. The times of the five daily prayer periods were becoming fixed in the traditions even as anathemas were being cast at Umayyad leaders, ghulāt and Jews for delaying the prayers beyond these now fixed starting points. A study of the various curses and conflicts concerning the delay of the evening prayer (maghrib) shows that this controversy mirrored the respective concerns of groups who were dissociating themselves from a suspect practice. In this paper I will first discuss the Sunnī and the Shīᶜite variations of this accusation and I will then examine the case of the Khaṭṭābiyya. Although the deviation of Abū 'l-Khaṭṭāb is well-recorded in the Shīᶜite biographical and jurisprudential collections, the question of his ritual innovation has not been systematically examined by modern scholarship. In concluding my paper with such an examination I will thereby try to show that not only did all the diverse groups who were accused of delaying their evening prayers actually do so, but also that this superficially similar practice arose out of distinct religious and historical contexts, with which circumstances the polemicists were largely unconcerned.

The earliest prooftexts in Muslim tradition for the time of the sunset prayer are found not in the Qur'ān, which contains no explicit statement on this question which could usefully serve as example for the community, but in ḥadīth.[1] Ḥadīth concerning the time of the maghrib prayer emphasize that Muḥammad's own practice was to perform this service after the sun set, but before the end of dusk. "Rāfiᶜ ibn Khadīj said 'We used to observe the sunset prayer with God's messenger, then one of us would go away when it was still possible to

Logos Islamikos: Studia Islamica in honorem Georgii Michaelis Wickens, ed. Roger M. Savory and Dionisius A. Agius, Papers in Mediaeval Studies 6 (Toronto: Pontifical Institute of Mediaeval Studies, 1984), pp. 269-286.

see the distance of a bowshot (i.e., still twilight).'"[2] In Ṣaḥīḥ Muslim other variants are given which agree that the time of the evening prayer begins with the setting of the disc of the sun and lasts "as long as the spreading appearance of the redness above the horizon after the sunset does not sink down."[3]

Many traditions in the classical ḥadīth collections stress that prayers should not be delayed beyond their prescribed periods. "Umm Farwa said that when asked what act was most excellent, the Prophet replied that it was prayer at the beginning of the proper period for it . . . ᶜĀ'isha said that God's Messenger did not pray any prayer at the last possible moment except on two occasions during his whole life."[4] All the major ḥadīth collections contain the definitive statement of Muḥammad's, with various wordings, that "My people will continue to prosper (or he said, to follow Islam) as long as they do not postpone the sunset prayer till the stars are out in abundance," "My people will continue in their proper state (fiṭra) as long as they do not postpone evening prayer till the stars shine brightly."[5] These ḥadīth, it would seem, "presciently" anticipate the controversy that was growing over this issue at the time of the writing of ḥadīth.

This controversy can be roughly dated, for it must certainly postdate those Umayyad rulers who are explicitly condemned for just this bidᶜa. At least one Umayyad leader, Ḥajjāj ibn Yūsuf, is specifically accused of this transgression in the Ṣaḥīḥ Muslim, and other evidence indicates that it was at the time of his governorship of Iraq that the prayers were delayed. Thus in Ṣaḥīḥ Muslim, "Muḥammad ibn ᶜAmr al-Ḥasan ibn ᶜAlī reported, 'Ḥajjāj used to delay the prayers . . .'"[6] In the middle of the ninth century the quasi-Muᶜtazilite litterateur al-Jāḥiẓ (d. 255/868) angrily reiterates this inculpation in one of his polemical tracts:

> ᶜAbd al-Malik ibn Marwān, his son al-Walīd, their governor al-Hajjāj ibn Yūsuf and his freedman Yazīd ibn ᶜAlī Abī Muslim . . . destroyed the holy house, invaded the sanctity of Mecca, demolished the Kaᶜba, looted the holy places, changed the qibla to Wāsiṭ and delayed the Friday prayer to sunset. If a man said to any one of the, "Fear God for you have delayed the prayer beyond its proper time!" he killed him for these words . . .[7]

A generation after al-Jāḥiẓ, Ibn ᶜAbd Rabbihi quotes a tradition of al-Shaᶜbī which accuses both Jews and Shīᶜites of delaying the beginning of evening prayers. In his *ᶜIqd al-Farīd*, Ibn ᶜAbd Rabbihi (d. 328/939), the earliest great Arabic-language belle-lettrist of al-Andalus, gives a list of parallels between the Rāfiḍa and the Jews.[8] The list is cited in a quotation attributed to the Kufan ᶜĀmir ibn Sharāhil ibn ᶜAbd al-Shaᶜbī (103/721-722), an authoritative reporter of *Maghāzī* and a well-respected *ḥadīth* tradent.[9] While the discussion of these parallels by al-Shaᶜbī is almost certainly spuriously placed in the mouth of this reliable transmitter -- the issues involved and the neatly symmetrical equations indicate an authorship dating from at least several decades after Shaᶜbī's death, when these "heretical" positions and the polemics against them had become well-defined -- there were in fact some disputes over the evening prayer in the days of Shaᶜbī.[10] Shaᶜbī had a well-recorded on-again off-again relationship with the imperious al-Ḥajjāj, who, as seen in the passages from al-Jāḥiẓ, and from *ḥadīth*, is held culpable of delaying prayers. Even if we assume that Shaᶜbī and Ḥajjāj are used here as metaphorical representatives of two broadly-drawn opposing positions, this choice may still be evidence for that opposition existing in their day, or shortly thereafter.

Shaᶜbī prefaces his catalog of damning linkages by saying "Beware of these misleading beliefs; the worst of them are the Rāfiḍa's, for they are the Jews of this community, and they loathe Islam, as Jews despise Christianity . . ."[11] There follows a succinct list of nine reprehensible beliefs and practices ostensibly shared by the Jews and the Rāfiḍa.

The device of linking the Jews and the Rāfiḍa was to become a standard feature of Sunnī polemical historiography.[12] That this device was an element in the Ashᶜarite *kalām* presentation can be seen by the inclusion of this list of equations in Abū Yaᶜla's *Kitāb al-Muᶜtamad* and in *Tabṣīr fī 'l-Dīn* of al-Isfarā'inī, who repeats a number of Shaᶜbī's equations when he introduces his discussion of the Hishāmiyya.[13] The list of Shaᶜbī, variously repeated by Ibn ᶜAbd Rabbihi, Abū Yaᶜla and al-Isfarā'inī, is then considerably amplified in Ibn Taymiyya's *Minhāj al-Sunna*.[14] While the list in *Minhāj al-Sunna* in all likelihood incorporates his own (and/or other later) accretions, it does certainly incorporate the earlier polemical motifs, while amplifying their number and clarifying their wording. On the issue at hand, he says

> The Jews postpone the evening prayer till the stars shine, as do the Rāfiḍa, who postpone the maghrib till the stars shine. There is a hadith that the Prophet said "My people will continue in their proper state so long as they do not postpone the evening prayer till the stars shine brightly."[15]

The reiterated lists of parallels between Rāfiḍa and the Jews show that the Muslim community's well-known initial efforts to disengage itself from Jewish practices -- the primordiality of the concern is reflected in the choice of early first-century Shaᶜbī as tradent -- becomes conflated with criticisms of the reprehensible Shīᶜite ritual practices with which Jewish customs are literally equated. Whether or not any of the other positions on the list ascribed to either group has any historical basis, the accusation of the delay of the evening prayers is not inaccurate in connection with Jews and Shīᶜites.

Jewish tradition has commemorated its own conflict over the time of the recitation of the Shema in the evening with a certain pride of place. The first line of the first tractate (Berakhot) of the first order (Zeraᶜim) of the Mishnah is "From what time do they begin to recite the Shema in the evening?"[16] The various tannaitic disagreements over the mandating of the time of this recitation are then recorded in Rabbinic tradition.[17] After centuries of debate over the content of the evening service -- evidence from the Cairo Geniza shows that in the twelfth century a variety of texts were still being used -- the rabbinic traditions concerning its timing were consolidated to confirm a specified, binding practice (but with continuing variations according to exigence and national custom).[18] This is recorded in the first great liturgical manual, the mid-ninth century Seder Rab Amran.[19] After stating that the Shema of the evening service is to be recited only after the appearance of the stars -- "(if) any man recites (the Shema) before the prescribed time, he has not fulfilled his obligation" -- the siddur adduces the Talmudic prooftexts for the exact time:

> And how many stars should appear for it to be night? There is a Baraitha: R. Nathan says: (As long as only) one star (is visible) it is daytime, (as long as only) two (are visible) it is twilight, (when there are) three it is night. And R. Jose ben Abin said: Nor the great stars which

appear by day nor the small stars which appear in the night, but the average stars.[20]

We can assume that from the earliest years of Islam close proximity to Jewish communities, Jewish conversion to Islam and direct consultation with Jewish scholars must all have sustained the Iraqi Muslim scholars' awareness that the Jewish practice was to wait till the stars were out before beginning the evening service. Perhaps it is due to this awareness that the Prophet's prognosticating the right path, the norm (fiṭra) for Muslim practice becomes modified in some collections with a phrase specifying the wrong path: the Jewish practice. "The Prophet said 'My people will stay on the right path only so long as they do not postpone the maghrib in waiting for the advent of darkness, as do the Jews . . ."[21] "My people will remain adhering (to Islam) so long as they do not . . . postpone the maghrib prayer till darkness, as in Judaism . . ."[22]

As we have seen, Sunnī tradition explicitly condemns the delay of the maghrib as a kind of Judaizing practice, and also condemns certain leaders who allegedly tried to lead the community in such a practice. In lists of linkages with other practices this practice was later also condemned as "Rāfiḍī" practice. Imāmī fiqh, in fact, also establishes the same timing of the evening prayer as do the Sunnīs.[23] It is therefore not entirely surprising to discover that Shīᶜite sources also consider this practice unacceptable and also curse those held responsible for proposing it. But these culprits, according to the Imāms, are neither Jews nor Umayyad leaders, but rather are certain "extremists" (ghulāt) from the "proto-Shiite activist period" (the periodization is that of Watt).

According to authoritative Shīᶜite traditions, the delay of the evening prayer was enjoined upon the people of Kūfa by Abū 'l-Khaṭṭāb (d. ca. 143/760), eponymous "founder" of the Khaṭṭābiyya, sometimes listed in the heresiographies as among the ghulāt, sometimes among the Rāfiḍa.[24] The bulk of the reports on Abū 'l-Khaṭṭāb in the biographical dictionaries deal with his falling-out and excommunication by Jaᶜfar al-Ṣādiq, the sixth Imām, but one of his practices is always singled out for stricture: the delay of the evening prayer.[25] The Fāṭimid Ismāᶜīlī jurist Qāḍī al-Nuᶜmān gives the most complete single report on the conflict between these two over this issue:

> It is related that the Prophet said "When night come from this side, and he pointed with his hand toward the East (then is the time to begin the prayer)." Abū 'l-Khaṭṭāb, God's curse be upon him, was listening to Ja^{c}far as he was saying "If the redness has fallen below this point -- and pointed with his hand to the East -- then is the time of sunset prayer." Whereas Abū 'l-Khaṭṭāb said to his companions, when he brought the major deviation which he brought (i.e., his deification of Ja^{c}far), "The time of the prayer at sunset is the disappearance of the redness from the western horizon; therefore, do not pray maghrib till the stars shine brightly." They brought this to Ja^{c}far's attention, at which he cursed Abū 'l-Khaṭṭāb for it, and cursed Abū 'l-Khaṭṭāb saying "He who intentionally leaves off saying the evening prayer till the stars shine brightly, I will have nothing to do with him."[26]

This is clearly an attempt to portray Abū l-Khaṭṭāb as slavishly extending Ja^{c}far's refinement of Muhammad's practice.

It was perhaps after Ja^{c}far had been informed of Abū 'l-Khaṭṭāb's heretical teaching that the Imām was forced personally to direct the extremist in the proper procedure. "Ja^{c}far ordered Abu 'l-Khaṭṭāb to pray maghrib only at the time of the disappearance of the redness at the time of the sun's beginning to set, for he thus located (in the western horizon) the redness which is before the actual sunset, and would accordingly pray so at the time of the disappearance of that twilight."[27] But, just as the extremist claimed a divinity for the sixth Imām which Ja^{c}far repudiated, so did Abū 'l-Khaṭṭāb -- according to the "official" version -- claim that Ja^{c}far had commanded this innovative practice. "Ja^{c}far said, 'As for Abū 'l-Khaṭṭāb, he lied about me, saying that I commanded him and his followers not to pray maghrib till they see stars in the sky.'"[28]

As believers came to the Imām perplexed over the variations in practice, he gave them reasons for his own teaching. "A man said to Ja^{c}far, 'Shall I postpone the maghrib till the stars shine?' He replied, 'Are you (one of) the Khaṭṭābiyya? For Gabriel came down to the Prophet at the time when the disc of the sun was sinking below the horizon' (i.e., that time was good enough for Gabriel . . .)."[29] There are many Sunnī and Shī^{c}ite legends about Gabriel concerning his angelic pedagogy in teaching the practices of worship to the Prophet.[30]

There must have been many such ^{c}Alid loyalists in the Kūfa of the 750s, for Ibn Ḥazm -- a fanatic ghulāt-hater, but also a frequently reliable historian -- tells us that the Khaṭṭābiyya numbered in the thousands.[31] Ithnā ᶜAsharī traditions also record an apparently wide acceptance among the Kūfans: "Abū 'l-Khaṭṭāb corrupted the ᶜāmma of Kūfa (in this case ᶜāmma many connote not "the common folk" but the Sunni majority, a usage of the term commonly found in the Shīᶜite jurists in such contexts) so that they began not praying the maghrib till the disappearance of twilight, though this is acceptable practice only for travellers and the ill, and for those waiting for an appointment with an important man. A man asked Imām Riḍā, 'How could Jaᶜfar say what he said about Abū 'l-Khaṭṭāb (i.e., his earlier approval of him) and then proclaim his disavowal of him?' He replied, 'Is it for Jaᶜfar to install someone and not to displace him?'"[32]

Once Jaᶜfar had deposed Abū 'l-Khaṭṭāb, for reasons of theology as well as ritual, the breakaway leader and his low-status followers were summarily dismissed by the Imām: "Beware of these lowlife (safala) and watch out for those lowlife, for I have proscribed Abū 'l-Khaṭṭāb because he did not submit to my command."[33]

Imāmite tradition has forever vilified Abū 'l-Khaṭṭāb for his divergence from the example of the sixth Imām. In a canonical Twelver collection from the tenth century, Man Lā Yahduruhu al-Faqīh by Ibn Bābūya, Jaᶜfar apodictically pronounces his position against Abū 'l-Khaṭṭāb. "Jaᶜfar al-Ṣādiq said, 'Accursed, accursed (malᶜūn, malᶜūn) is the one who postpones the evening prayer in seeking to accrue virtue from doing so.' It was said to him that the people of Iraq postpone the evening prayer till the shining of the stars, to which he replied, 'This is this practice of Abū 'l-Khaṭṭāb, the enemy of God.'"[34] Similarly, in the Tahdhīb al-Aḥkām of Muḥammad ibn al-Ḥasan al-Ṭūsī we read "There are people of the companions of Abū 'l-Khaṭṭāb who postpone the evening prayer till the stars shine brightly: I ask God to protect me from anyone who does this intentionally."[35]

I have tried to show so far in this paper that the calculation of the time of the evening prayer, which had been a source of dispute between Jewish Rabbis of pre-Islamic times, was also a highly charged issue in early Islamic history. The delay of prayers is one of the stock accusations of impiety against the Umayyad Caliphs, and the sixth Imām, Ja^c^far al-Ṣādiq, beleaguered by those same Caliphs, reacted sharply to this same innovation when it cropped up among his own followers.[36] By early ^c^Abbāsid times, it appears that prooftexts have been fabricated to curse those who delayed the evening prayers. Thus, some Sunnī ḥadīths state that it is a Judaizing heresy, while other Sunnī traditions attack it as a Rāfiḍī (=Shī'ite) heresy which is like that of the Jews. The Shī^c^ites themselves in fact possess essentially the same laws about the calculation as do the Sunnīs and themselves sharply denounce the Khaṭṭābiyya for this same bid^c^a.[37] This accusation, therefore, played a continuing role in Sunni anti-Umayyad, anti-Jewish and anti-Shi^c^ite polemics, and in Shī^c^ite anti-ghulāt polemics.

The polemical positions taken by the Sunnī traditionalists, as I have tried to indicate, developed in reaction to actual practices. It is not hard to see why the Sunnī authors would attempt to dissociate themselves from the practice of the Jews, who waited till dark for the evening prayer. The linkage with "Rāfiḍī" practice was most likely a response to the Imāmite practice of combining the evening and night prayers, and praying the two together later than the time otherwise set by Imāmite tradition for the performance of maghrib.[38] As for the delay of maghrib among the Umayyads, whom the traditionalists vehemently denounce for impiety and illegitimacy, this may simply have been a question of ignorance; for, as Goldziher points out, "At the time of Ḥajjāj and ^c^Umar II, people had no idea of the proper times for prayer, and the most pious Muslims were unsure of the quite elementary rules."[39]

The deviation of Abū 'l-Khaṭṭāb, however, remains to be explained. While the innovation of Abū 'l-Khaṭṭāb is the best documented of all those so accused in the sources, it has not yet been analyzed as such by modern scholarship. If some of his motivations and possible self-justifications can be found, then the polemics against him can also be understood in their context. If I can suggest some of these motives, then all of the variations of this accusation can be explained as having been reactions to actual practices, practices which are themselves explicable within their own historical contexts. In order to do this, I will try and put the controversies over ṣalāt into perspective, and then I will suggest some possible explanations for the divergence in practice initiated by Abū 'l-Khaṭṭāb.

One factor contributing to the continuation of this controversy might well have been the absence of an incontrovertible legal opinion on the matter. For at least two centuries after Muḥammad's hijra the calculation of the maghrib prayer was not finally canonized in the Sunnī legal codes. We know this quite clearly from the law manual of al-Shāfiᶜī (d. 204/819-820): his continuator al-Nawāwī thus summarizes the great legist's position on the timing of the maghrib (to which he devotes twice as much space as to any of the other prayers): "In his first period Shāfiᶜī admitted that the legal time for this duty extends until the red color of the sky has disappeared; but in his second period he contended that it lasts not longer than is necessary for performing ablution, dressing suitably, listening to the first and second call and accomplishing the five rakᶜas that form the act of devotion."[40] Eventually, the scientific genius of Islamicate Civilization applied itself to this problem and developed instrumentation for the exact calculation of the five daily prayers.[41] And any doubt left by even these sophisticated tools seems to have been removed by today's computers which, as recently announced, now have a new program which calculates the precise times of prayer anywhere in the world.[42]

But in these first centuries, when no uniform system had been accepted, when the uniformity of ritual was just then being consolidated for the cohesion of community, variations in practice accordingly bore the threat of schism. Ṣalāt, despite, or perhaps because of the variations in practice, early played an essential role in the institutionalization of Islam. The stipulated timing and precise unison of the five daily prayers, once these were established by a faction or a community, became, in the famous phrase given currency by Hitti, "the first drillground of Islam."[43] Not only for the masses, but for the leadership as well, for much of the early "religio-political" conflicts involved the legitimacy of the right to lead prayers, particularly the question of whether or not the prayers performed behind a prayer-leader who was an illegitimate ruler could be considered valid.[44] Ṣalāt was an essential requirement of membership in the umma and the legitimate leadership of that community carried with it the right to lead prayers.

The "minor issue" of calculating the time of the evening prayer cannot therefore be judged a priori absurd. Issues of significance for the whole community were involved in the still disputed ritual. Indeed, the very self-definition of Islam was involved in a debate that implicated not only legists, generals, Caliphs, Imams and sectarians but also the believers at large.

Nor is the choice of Abū 'l-Khaṭṭāb by the Shi^c^ite polemicists random or merely obsessive. The Shī^c^ite traditions, as did the Sunni, could well have chosen the Umayyad leaders as target for the accusation of the delay of prayers. As Goldziher points out, "Nothing is more common in ^c^Alid circles than to refer to 'the tree cursed in the Koran' (17:22, al-shajara 'l-mal^c^ūna fī 'l-Qur'ān) to the Umayyad house"; and yet, in the instance of this deviation, of which the Umayyad house was accused by Sunnī traditionalists, the Shi^c^ite curses are flung at Abū 'l-Khaṭṭāb.[45] It is therefore necessary to examine more closely the one group described in detail in Shī^c^ite sources as delayers of the evening prayer, the Khaṭṭābiyya.

Although the ghulāt are castigated in the heresiographies for abandoning the obligations of worship, in fact one aspect of their excess (ghuluww) was to increase the ritual requirements. This is also true of the Jewish "extremists" of the period, whose movements betray many striking similarities to those of the contemporary ghulāt.[46] Conflicts over the innovations in prayer rituals were marked in this period not only as a point of controversy between Muslim factions, but among the "extremists" of Judaism and Zoroastrianism as well.[47] These groups shared many common features of their metaphysics, as they did of their other "innovations." At the time of the fall of the Umayyads Bihāfarīd, "The Pseudo-Prophet," ordained seven prayers on his followers.[48] The Kūfan Khārijite ^c^Abdallāh ibn Ḥārith "imposed seventeen prayers every day and night, each prayer having fifteen bows."[49] Abū ^c^Īsā al-Iṣfahānī, according to Qirqisānī, established seven prayers for his Jewish followers, or, according to Shahristani, ten prayers.[50] The continuators of Abū ^c^Īsā, the Yudghāniyya, further increased the numbers of prayers.[51] Such pietist increases among the sects indicate that they were concerned to amplify the legal requirements incumbent upon the believer. It was their extremism in regard to ritual, it seems, as much as their "wild" metaphysics, which drew down the wrath of later heresiographers, both Jewish and Muslim.

In contradiction to the accusations of antinomianism common to the heresiologists' polemical presentations of the ghulāt positions, therefore, there is some evidence that the Khaṭṭābiyya "went too far" in their zeal over worship. Ivanow, who first pointed out the issue of evening prayer in connection with this group, adduced as evidence to refute the heresiographers' charge of antinomianism against the Khaṭṭābiyya the fact that this sect was devoted to prayer and was apprehended and massacred in the mosque of Kūfa.[52] Another tradition shows Iblīs appearing to Abū 'l-Khaṭṭāb by the wall of the mosque, which image suggests his "evil" activities in that place.[53] Hodgson's thorough reevaluation of the charges of antinomianism, in his classic study of the ghulāt, concludes that in fact the attitude to the Law among these groups seems rather to have been "that there is a hidden truth hidden in the Law . . . so that points of ceremony, at least, are dispensed with when what they symbolically represent is followed instead [or that] whoever is devoted to the imām will be forgiven his transgressions to the Law -- though not actually exempted from it."[54] I believe that Hodgson is correct here, and that the Khaṭṭābiyya attitude to the Law was not mere rejection or willful distortion, but rather a radical bāṭinī revaluation of the place of the worshipper in regard to that Law.

It is in the context of this sectarian revisionism, particularly their bāṭinī hermeneutics of ritual, that the few scattered reports concerning the Khaṭṭābiyya attitude toward worship may be understood. Abū 'l-Khaṭṭāb's teaching of the inner, spiritual meaning behind the "exterior" duties extended to prayer as well. Ibn al-Athīr says that "he taught that the acts of worship had a hidden meaning, and that the externals were not binding on those who knew the Imāms."[55] The followers of Bazīgh ibn Mūsā, the weaver, who are grouped with the Khaṭṭābiyya, asserted that "they would not die but be raised up to heaven when their worship reached perfection."[56] Here again there is no evidence of teaching the mere abandonment of fixed prayer, especially for the unenlightened "masses," but rather a perfecting of it, towards the deeper revealing of its "hidden meaning."

We possess only a few clues as to what, specifically, that hermeneutical signification of the evening prayer may have been for the Khaṭṭābiyya. Massignon argued that "The putting in relation of the Five of the Mubāhala to the five daily awqāt al-ṣalāt dates at lest from Abū 'l-Khaṭṭāb."[57] Daylamī, Kashshī, and others also describe other parallelisms of pentads and other linkages of symbolic sets taught by the ghulāt.[58] These would indicate that each prayer period carried with it a certain symbolic association.

But linkages of sets of fives, or even the symbolization of each prayer period, would not seem to be sufficient reason for a change in ritual. Another hint about the evening prayer time itself is found in Ashᶜarī and Shahristānī, about which Hodgson comments: "There must have been some sort of search for spiritual experience back of the report that one group pretended to see their fellows, who had passed on, morning and evening."[59] Muṭahhar ibn Ṭāhir al-Maqdīsī tells us that another group of Kūfan ghulāt, the Ṭayyāra of the Sabā'iyya believed that "death is a flying of their souls in the nighttime."[60] It may be that the pentadic symbology, homologized to the times of prayer, held a particular significance for the ushering in of night, when the dead were thought to be in some way more capable of contact with the living.

This possibility seems to be borne out by some later evidence. The time from the setting of the disc of the sun below the horizon until the unequivocal emergence of the stars apparently continued to carry a certain eschatological signification in Ithnā ᶜAsharī ritual. A Twelver ḥadīth says of the Qā'im, the Twelver Messianic Imām, that "He will come out from Mecca in the month of Muḥarram, on the day of ᶜĀshūrā', after evening prayers in the year two hundred after one thousand."[61] Ibn Baṭṭūṭa describes a ceremony among the Shīᶜites of Hilla in which the occultated Twelfth Imām is called upon at the end of every day, before the recitation of the maghrib prayer. This ceremony begins "every evening after the afternoon prayer [and lasts] until the evening prayer."[62] Ibn Khaldūn describes the same ceremony, but gives a slightly different time. The ceremony he describes apparently begins later than that described by Ibn Baṭṭūṭa: "Each night after the evening prayer they bring a mount and stand at the entrance to the cellar where (the Mahdī is 'removed'). They call his name and ask him to come forth openly. They do so until all the stars are out."[63] These rituals suggest that a survival of Shīᶜite beliefs in the particular significance of the twilight as a time propitious for the return of souls became conflated with the very return (rajᶜa) of the Hidden Twelfth Imām, "The Expected One."

This apparent Ithnā ᶜAsharī conviction that the eschaton will arrive at twilight may perhaps also be connected with one of the most frequently cited signs of the approach of the Hour. "The rising of the sun in its place of setting" is found in both Sunnī and Twelver traditions along with the emergence of Dajjāl and the descent of ᶜĪsā from the heavens as one of the major signs of the advent of the Endtime.[64] Can the rising up of the Mahdī at the time the sun sets be an echo of this tradition? Such a happening is a cosmic reversal signifying God's absolute determination of events and also (as if the sun's setting is itself an act of ritual prostration) a propitiation of His absolute might. This is suggested by a ḥadīth from the section of Fitan in Tirmidhī: "Abū Dharr said, 'I entered the mosque when the sun was setting. The Prophet was sitting there, and he said to me, 'O Abū Dharr, do you know to where the sun goes?' I replied, 'God and His Messenger know best.' He said, 'It goes to ask permission to make prostration (before God), and it will be permitted it. It is as though it has been said to the sun, Rise up from the place in which you set, and it would rise up from its place of setting.'"[65]

In the absence of conclusive evidence, however, we are on firm ground only in the certainty that Abū 'l-Khaṭṭāb's innovative teachings about the evening prayer, what ever their theological, mythological or spiritual legitimation, were repeatedly singled out for special calumniation by Shīᶜite traditionists. It is also certain that Sunnī polemicists were themselves factually accurate in their analogy that the delay of evening prayer was "like the Jews do" and "like the Rāfiḍīs do" just as the Shīᶜite theologians were correct in saying that it was "as the Khaṭṭābiyya do." For each instance of this polemical topos, then, we may conclude that one real practice of an opposing party was considered, in a kind of metonymy with the group itself, to be threatening enough to warrant repeated vilification and stricture.

In the case of the delay of maghrib, we find that even when the time of its performance is the same for both opposing parties, the opponent can still be condemned. Thus, even when the delay of maghrib became accepted in Twelver practice and the time of twilight retained an important eschatological valorization which was daily evoked in Twelver ritual, the Imāmite theologians could still attack Abū 'l-Khaṭṭāb for his innovation. Ritual invariability, as this case shows, can reveal considerable institutional variation, for it is by the fixed point of ritual that the opposing parties aimed their polemical weapons.

Notes

[1] See S. D. Goitein, "Prayer in Islam," in *Studies in Islamic History and Institutions* (Leiden, 1966), pp. 73–89. See Qur'ān, 11:116, 17:80, 50:38 and 76:26 which indicate three prayers, and Qur'ān 20:130 which indicates five prayers; and the more general observations of Robert Brunschvig, "Le Culte de le temps dans l'Islam classique," in *Études d'Islamologie* (Paris, 1976), 1: 167–177, and of Louis Massignon, "Time in Islamic Thought," in *Man and Time*, ed. Joseph Campbell (New York, 1957), pp. 108–114.

[2] *Mishkat al-Masabih*, trans. J. Robson (Lahore, 1963), 1:122; and the same in *Sahih Muslim*, trans. A. H. Siddiqi (Lahore, 1973), 1: 308, no. 1328.

[3] *Sahih Muslim*, 1: 299–301, nos. 1273, 1275–1276, and 1278–1281.

[4] *Mishkāt al-Maṣābīḥ*, 1: 123–124. And see, for example, *Ṣaḥīḥ Muslim*, chapter 133, 1: 313 ff.: "Disapproval of delaying the prayer from its prescribed time; What one who is led in prayer should do when the Imām delays it." See also Al-Ghazālī, *The Mysteries of Worship in Islam*, translation of the chapter on *ṣalāt* from the *Ihyā' ^{c}Ulūm al-Dīn* by E. E. Calverley (Lahore, 1977), p. 130 where Al-Ghazālī says, "The most liked thing is to lose no time in performing the Worship of sunset especially. If you delay and perform the Worship before the disappearance of the red after-glow, it would be a payment of the worship in the prescribed time, but it is disliked. ^{c}Umar delayed the Worship of sunset one night until the stars appeared, so he freed one slave. Ibn ^{c}Umar delayed it until two stars appeared, so he freed two slaves."

[5] See the variants found in Mālik ibn Anas, Ibn Māja, al-Tirmidhī et al., as collected in ^{c}Alī ibn ^{c}Abd al-Malik al-Mutaqqī, *Kanz al-^{c}Ummāl fī sunan al-aqwāl wa 'l-af^{c}āl* (Aleppo, 1387/1969), 7: 177–178. And see, for a penetrating short discussion of these traditions, I. Goldziher, "Usages juifs d'après la littérature religieuse des musulmans," *REJ*, 28 (1894), 84-85.

[6] *Ṣaḥīḥ Muslim*, 1: 312, nos. 1348–1349.

[7] Translation by Bernard Lewis in *Islam* (New York, 1974), 2: 56–57. The tract is also translated and discussed by C. Pellat, "Un document important pour l'histoire politico-religieuse de l'Islam: la 'Nābita' de Djāḥiẓ," *AIEO* 10 (Alger, 1952), 319. See too M. J. Kister, "On 'Concessions' and Conduct. A Study in Early Hadīth," in *Studies on the First Century of Islamic Society*, ed. G. H. A. Juynboll (Carbondale, Ill., 1982), pp. 106 f. on many accusations against the Umayyad Caliphs of *bid^{c}a*.

[8] Aḥmad ibn Muḥammad ibn ^{c}Abd Rabbihi, *Kitāb al-^{c}Iqd al-Farīd* (Cairo, 1321 H), 1: 409–410. On the term "Rāfiḍa" and its various usages, see W. M. Watt, "The Rāfiḍites; A Preliminary Study," *Oriens*, 16 (1963), 110-121; idem, *The Formative Period of Islamic Thought* (Edinburgh, 1973), pp. 157 ff., where he gives five different

meanings and some sense of their contemporary context; B. Lewis, "Some Observations on the Significance of Heresy in the History of Islam," SI, 1 (1953), 46-63, for a useful general discussion of opprobrious terminology; and the recent erudite article by Etan Kohlberg, "The Term 'Rāfiḍa' in Imāmī Shī^{c}ī Usage," JAOS, 99 (1979), 677-679, where he describes the intra-Imami development of a self-image as Rāfiḍa, metahistorically linked to the Banū Isrā'īl.

9 On al-Sha^{c}bī, see M. M. Azmi, Studies in Early Hadīth Literature (Beirut, 1968), pp. 63-64; Watt, Formative Period, pp. 73-74 on his politics; and Shiv Rai Chowdhry, Al-Ḥajjāj ibn Yūsuf (New Delhi, 1972), pp. 205-206 on his forgiving al-Sha^{c}bī.

10 Kohlberg, "The Term 'Rāfiḍa'," shows that the term did not come into use until some decades after al-Sha^{c}bī's death. Watt also doubts, in another context, the use of rafḍ by al-Sha^{c}bī (see Formative Period, p. 333 n. 18) as does I. Friedlander in "Heterodoxies of the Shiites According to Ibn Hazm," JAOS, 29 (1908), 86: "The utterances put into his mouth are no doubt spurious."

11 Kitāb al-^{c}Iqd, 1: 409. See also H. Laoust, La Profession de foi d'Ibn Batta (Damascus, 1958), p. 49 n. 1: "Abū Muḥammad al-Tamīmī rapelle que, selon ibn Ḥanbal, les 'Qadariyya etaient les Zoroastriens de cette communauté comme les Rāfiḍa en sont les Juifs.'"

12 Shāhfūr ibn Ṭāhir al-Isfarā'inī also repeats, "The Rawāfiḍ are the Jews of this community," in al-Tabṣīr fī 'l-Dīn (Baghdad, 1374/1955), p. 133. And a Sunnī theologian of the Seljuk period, writing in Persian, also says, "The Rāfiḍites resemble the Jews in saying, 'We will go to paradise and the others won't'"; cited in J. Calmard, "Le Chiisme Imamite en Iran a l'Epoque Seldjoukide, d'apres le Kitab al-Naqd," in Le Monde Iranien et l'Islam (Geneva and Paris, 1971), 1: 51 n. 32.

13 Abū Ya^{c}la ibn al-Farrā', Kitāb al-Mu^{c}tamid fi ^{c}Uṣūl al-Dīn, ed. Wadi Haddad (Beirut, 1974), p. 260, fasl 466; and al-Isfarā'inī, al-Tabṣīr, pp. 43-44.

14 Ibn Taymiyya, Kitāb Minhāj al-Sunna al-Nabawiyyah fī Naqd al-Kalām al-Shī^{c}a wa 'l-Qadariyya (Cairo, 1321), pp. 6-9.

15 Ibid.

16 Berakhot, 1: 1. See Philip Blackman, Mishnayoth (New York, 1965).

17 This resulted in the deposal of Rabban Gamaliel II; see Berakhot (Bavli), 27b-28a. The Karaites, who pray two times daily, also varied in the setting of the times of prayer; see Percy Goldberg, Karaite Liturgy and Its Relation to Synagogue Worship (Manchester, 1957), pp. 1-5; see p. 4 n. 3 where he notes that "from the time of Aaron ben Joseph (second half of the thirteenth century), however, the Karaites held that the evening prayer (arav) can only be recited between sunset and darkness . . ."

18 Stefan Reif describes some of the textual variations in the evening service in "Liturgical Difficulties and Geniza Manuscripts," in Studies in Judaism and Islam, ed. S. Morag, I. Ben-Ami and N. A. Stillman (Jerusalem, 1981), pp. 116-117. And see J. Mann, "Genizah Fragments of the Palestinian Order of Service," in Contributions to the Scientific Study of Jewish Liturgy, ed. J. Mann, "Genizah Fragments of the Palestinian Order of Service," in Contributions to the Scientific Study of Jewish Liturgy, ed. J. Petuchowski (New York, 1970), pp. 412 ff.

19 Seder Rab Amran Gaon, ed. and trans. D. Hedegard (Lund, 1951).

20 Ibid., p. 162. See also Leo Levi, "On the Astronomical

Aspects of Twilight in Halakha," in ᶜAteret Tzvi, Jubilee Volume for Rabbi Joseph Breur (New York, 1962), pp. 251-263.

21 Al-Zurkānī, Sharh Muwaṭṭa' (Cairo, 1310), 1: 32.

22 See al-Mutaqqī, Kanz al-ᶜUmmāl, 7: 277-278, where all the variations are collected.

23 Muḥammad ibn al-Ḥasan al-Ṭūsī, Tahdhīb al-Aḥkām (Najaf, 1378/1959), 2: 27-35.

24 Ibn Qutayba lists the Ghāliya and the Khaṭṭābiya among the Rāfiḍa; see Watt, Formative Period, pp. 61-62. Al-Nawbakhtī includes the Khaṭṭābiya as among the Ghulāt; see al-Nawbakhtī, Firaq al-Shīᶜah, French trans. M. J. Mashkur, in RHR, 154 (1958), 73-78, 148-150.

25 See V. Ivanow, who discusses this controversy in The Alleged Founder of Ismailism (Bombay, 1946), p. 137; and Farouk Omar, "Some Aspects of the ᶜAbbāsid-Ḥusaynid Relations During the Early ᶜAbbāsid Period," Arabica, 22 (1975), 176.

26 Al-Nuᶜmān ibn Muḥammad Abū Ḥanīfa, Dā'im al-Islām, ed. A. A. Fyzee (Cairo, 1951), 1: 168; repeated in Muḥammad Bāqir al-Majlisi, Biḥār al-Anwār (Tehran, 1956), 83: 70, no. 44.

27 Biḥār, 83: 56, no. 8.

28 Muḥammad Taqī al-Tustarī, Qāmūs al-Rijāl (Tehran, 1379), 8: 402.

29 One of the more frequently cited traditions on this conflict; see Abū ᶜAmr al-Kashshī, Rijāl al-Kashshī (Karbalā, 1962, p. 247; al-Tūsī, Tahdhīb, 2: 32, no. 98, 49; al-Majlisī, Biḥār, p. 65, no. 29.

30 See "Djibrā'īl" in EI[2]

31 I. Friedlander, "Heterodoxies of the Shiites," p. 69.

32 Al-Kashshī, Rijāl, p. 249; repeated with slight variations in al-Ṭūsī, loc. cit.; and Biḥār, loc. cit., which repeats al-Kashshī's version.

33 Al-Kashshī, Rijāl, p. 250.

34 Muḥammad ibn ᶜAlī ibn Bābūya, Man Lā Yaḥḍuruh al-Faqīh (Tehran, 1390), 1: 142, no. 660, 15.

35 Al-Ṭūsī, Tahdhīb, p. 33, no. 102.

36 See M. G. S. Hodgson, "How Did the Early Shīᶜa Become Sectarian?" JAOS, 75 (1955) 1-13, and idem, Venture of Islam (Chicago, 1974), 1: 262 n. 7 where he modifies his earlier position: "I would suspect, now, that the disciplining of the notions of the ghulāt begun by Jaᶜfar came chiefly in response to the anti-Shīᶜī reaction under al-Manṣūr."

37 See al-Ṭūsī, Tahdhīb, pp. 27-35 for a listing of the regulations on this issue.

38 The Ithnā ᶜAshariyya, in practice, combined the evening and night prayers and recited that combined service later in the evening. See ibid.

39 Muslim Studies, trans. S. M. Stern and C. R. Barber (London, 1971), 2: 40 n. 2, citing al-Nasa'i.

40 Minhāj at-Ṭālibīn, trans. E. C. Howard (London, 1914), book 2, chapter 1, section 1.

41 E. S. Kennedy, "Al-Bīrūnī on the Muslim Times of Prayer," in The Scholar and the Saint, ed. Peter Chelkowski (New York, 1975), pp. 83-94.

42 The Globe and Mail (Toronto, 23 April 1983) reported that one Saᶜīd Bakāzī has now developed such a program.

43 Philip Hitti, History of the Arabs (London, 1964), p. 132.

44 The question of legitimate leadership involved many parties struggling over this central issue: "The main preoccupation of the

constitutional theorists in the first and second centuries of Islam was over the question of the election and deposition of the Imām, and reflects the struggles between the Sunnīs, Khārijīs and the Shī^cīs, and the conflicts between the Mu^ctazila and the other schools." A. K. S. Lambton, "Islamic Political Thought," in The Legacy of Islam, ed. J. Schacht and C. Bosworth (Oxford, 1979), p. 406.

[45] Goldziher, Muslim Studies, p. 111.

[46] See the article by I. Friedlander, still the only study of this subject: "Jewish-Arabic Studies," JQR, n.s. 1 (1910-1911), 183-215; 2 (1911-1912), 481-516; 3 (1912-1913), 235-300.

[47] As, for example, pointed out by R. N. Frye in The Golden Age of Persia (London, 1975), p. 132: "When one compares the beliefs of the extremist Shī^cites (ghulāt) with their ideas of the reincarnation of an Imām in his successor, with similar beliefs of the 'Zoroastrian' rebels, there is little to choose between them."

[48] Abū Rayḥān al-Bīrūnī, Chronology of Ancient Nations, trans. C. E. Sachau (London, 1879), pp. 193-194; and Friedlander, "Jewish-Arabic Studies," 3: 299.

[49] Friedlander, "Heterodoxies," p. 71.

[50] Al-Qirqisānī in the translations of L. Nemoy, "Al-Qirqisānī's Account of the Jewish Sects and Christianity," HUCA, 7 (1930), 382. Al-Shahristānī, al-Milal wa 'l-Nihal (Cairo, 1367/1948), 1: 23-25. And see Friedlander's discussion in "Jewish-Arabic Studies," 3: 298-300.

[51] Al-Shahristānī, pp. 25-26; al-Qirqisānī, p. 383.

[52] Ivanow, p. 137.

[53] Al-Tustarī, Qāmūs al-Rijāl, 8: 400.

[54] Hodgson, "Early Shī^ca", p. 7.

[55] A. S. Tritton, Muslim Theology (London, 1947), p. 27, citing Ibn Athīr.

[56] W. Madelung, "Khaṭṭābiya," in EI², p. 1132.

[57] Louis Massignon, Salman Pak and the Spiritual Beginnings of Iranian Islam (Bombay, 1955), p. 28 n. 154.

[58] See Muḥammad ibn al-Ḥasan al-Daylamī, Die Geheimlehre der Batiniten, nach der Apologie Dogmatik des Hauses Muhammad, ed. R. Strothmann (Istanbul, 1939), pp. 45-46; al-Shahristānī, 1: 302; and the examples cited by H. Corbin in "Ritual Sabeean et exégèse ismaelienne du ritual," Eranos Jahrbuch (1950), 232.

[59] Hodgson, "Early Shī^ca," p. 8 n. 44, citing al-Ash^carī, Maqālāt al-Islāmīyīn, ed. H. Ritter (Istanbul, 1929), 1: 12; and al-Shahristānī, 1: 302. In a Christian-Arabic apocalypse found in St. Catherine's Monastery at Mt. Sinai, dated to the ninth century but incorporating earlier materials, seven prayers are designated for "ascetics, monks and solitaries." The prayer at twilight is described in this way: "And a prayer at the hour of the coming of the night, because in that hour the heavens resound with the voices of the glorifications and sanctifications of the myriads of angels and the myriads of the squadrons of those beings that are near (to God) and of the heads of the Cherubim, who in different musical tunes and modulations inspire with awe all the corners of the abodes of the heavenly beings. If a man makes his devotions at that moment his prayers will be accepted by God." Apocalypse of Peter, trans. A. Mingana, Woodbrooke Studies 3 (Cambridge, 1931), p. 118.

[60] Cited in Tritton, Muslim Theology, p. 27, citing Mutahhar ibn Ṭāhir al-Maqdīsī, Kitāb al-Badā wa 'l Ta'rīkh, ed., trans. Cl. Huart (Paris, 1899-1919), 5: 129.

[61] Quoted in A. A. Sachedina, Islamic Messianism (Albany, 1981), p. 208 n. 71. Sachedina found this ḥadīth in al-Mutaqqī al-Hindī,

Talkhīs al-Bayān fi ᶜAlāmāt mahdī Ākhir al-Zamān, fl. 4 -- Mecca, Library of the Haram, MS 34 (microfilm in Najaf, Amīr al-Mu'minīn Library).

62 Selections from the Travels of Ibn Baṭṭūṭa, trans. H. A. R. Gibb (London, 1929), pp. 98-99.

63 Ibn Khaldūn, The Muqaddimah, trans. F. Rosenthal (Princeton, 1958), 1: 408.

64 The "sun rising in the west" is often listed as one of the ᶜalāmāt al-sā'ah, "Greater Signs": see J. I. Smith and Y. Y. Haddad, The Islamic Understanding of Death and Resurrection (Albany, 1981), pp. 69 and 128. And see Hava Lazarus-Yafeh, Some Religious Aspects of Islam (Leiden, 1981), p. 147 n. 26.

65 Muḥammad ibn ᶜĪsà al-Tirmidhī, Sunan al-Tirmidhī (Ḥoms, 1385/1965), 5-6: 348, no. 22, 2187.

18

Islam and Christianity: The Opposition of Similarities

Charles J. Adams
McGill University

The purpose of this paper is to suggest a comparison of the two religious orientations in the very broadest of terms in the hope that thereby we may set into relief some aspects of their reality that seem often to escape the attention of students of Comparative Religions. In what follows we shall suggest something of the prevading spirit of these two great historic religious communities, to view them, as it were, from a great distance, so that only their broad outlines and their most distinctive features meet the eye. The effort will be to show that despite a host of similarities and close relationships between the two, ranging from doctrinal stands to genetic affinities, the view from a distance reveals two religious entities of quite different outlines, characters, and structures.

I

Even the casual observer of Islam and Christianity must be struck with the many similarities between the two faiths. Both acknowledge a common line of spiritual descent from Abraham and the line of the past prophets, and both in consequence admit to kinship with the other; Islam does so most explicitly and strongly, while Christianity, as the elder brother, does so only with some reluctance and condescension but in the end acknowledges its Islamic cousin as a relative, though one of dubious blood lines. Because each sees itself as a phase in God's evolving relationship with the world and his intercourse with the human race, they share many of the same heroes and lay importance upon many of the same symbols. Personages of the Biblical tradition play an important role in each as formative figures of their past history,

Logos Islamikos: Studia Islamica in honorem Georgii Michaelis Wickens, ed. Roger M. Savory and Dionisius A. Agius, Papers in Mediaeval Studies 6 (Toronto: Pontifical Institute of Mediaeval Studies, 1984), pp. 287-306. © P.I.M.S. 1984.

and each gives a place of first importance to the concepts of prophecy, revelation, and Scripture as God's historic means of communication with men. Both are uncompromisingly monotheistic, insisting upon the uniqueness and the sovereignty of the Divine Being who is the Lord of History. To push the matter even further, it may be suggested that in their respective wrestling with the difficulty of expressing the nature of the Divine Being in language that is both redolent of faith and acceptable to reason they face the same fundamental problem and find themselves ultimately confronted with the same dilemma that is posed by the inadequacy of language. In their formal aspect, in terms of what is truly at issue, and in the conclusions which they reached, the Islamic discussions about the relations of God's attributes to His essence and the Christian controversies over the Trinity are not so unlike as polemics between the two communities might lead one to believe. Further, the two religious communities share many elements of a common philosophy of history. Both see the world as the creation of the Sovereign Deity who acted at a decisive moment to bring the universe into being. The world thus has a beginning; it also has a developing linear history that is marked by God's control and his intervention in the affairs of men. Finally, it will have a definitive end, a great climactic and culminating event in which the sovereignty of history's Lord will be indisputably asserted. As part of these last events both speak of the Resurrection from the dead, of the Judgment before God, and of everlasting reward and punishment for men according to their merits.

Since the two faiths share so much together, it might seem that Islam and Christianity would experience little difficulty in entering sympathetically into the world view of one another. Yet, such has not been the case historically, nor is it true today in spite of the existence in both symbolic lexicons of concepts and understandings so numerous and so fundamental as those just passed in quick review and many others that might be mentioned as well. For most of their history the two communities have exhibited a greater or lesser degree of outright hostility towards one another. There has seldom enough been even the effort to understand the viewpoint of the other, not to speak of success in doing so. While political and other factors must be taken into account, this situation would suggest that the many evident similarities between the two faiths may not be of the importance that a quick comparison might seem to indicate, for they lead to expectations that have not, in fact, been fulfilled.

Part of the purpose of this paper is to suggest that comparisons of doctrines and symbols may not only fail to be helpful but may actually serve to mislead the student of Comparative Religions in his thinking about Islam and Christianity. The kind of thinking that contents itself with considering, for example, the role of prophecy or some other shared doctrine in each tradition, even with all the variations that are exhibited in each context, is likely to miss something of great importance. For even a foundational concept such a prophecy must be considered, not in isolation and for itself alone, but in the setting of the total group of concepts of which it is but one element. The factor which gives flavour or character to Islam or Christianity in general is the way in which the various symbols and expressions and ideas fit together to form a whole. One must ask not only about the occurrence of the concept and symbol of prophecy in each of the two religions we are considering, but also about the role which the concept and the symbol play in the integrated outlook of each. If one fails to take this additional step towards understanding, the existence of similar ideas in the two communities may actually prevent one from seeing the far more important matter of the thrust and the direction of the whole. The isolated details may render the outline of the whole so obscure that it escapes perception, and, furthermore, they constitute a constant temptation to read into the understanding of the other one's own insights and preferences. To establish the existence within two religious communities of concepts and symbols that have similar origins and that bear apparently similar meanings is not to establish an equivalence between the concepts nor to establish an identity of experiential content between the two communities. On the contrary, this very similarity may make it all the harder to see that one and same symbol can play different roles in the structure and thought and experience of different communities. The similarity can well thus render the task of appreciating the peculiar and unique character of each religious orientation more difficult. When one is perfectly familiar with a religious symbol from one's own tradition and personal experience, and when one finds that symbol in another tradition, more rather than less effort will be required to penetrate behind the face of the symbol to grasp what it means for the other. Our contention is, then, that the symbols of prophecy, revelation, Scripture, the Last Judgment, etc., though apparently very much alike in the thinking of the two communities, have in fact quite different meanings and especially so when considered in the light of their mutual inter-relationships and the whole religious complex which they serve to form.

If I may be allowed a parenthetical remark, I believe that apparent similarities among Judaism, Islam and Christianity hold the explanation for much of the indifference towards Islam that may be observed in religious studies in North American universities and among Western students generally. Students who come from a background that is saturated with Judaeo-Christian ideas find little at the outset to excite them about the study of Islamics. All seems familiar, perhaps drearily so -- the often repeated story of peoples who believe in the advent of prophets, in revelation, and Scripture and final Judgment. What is there here to capture the imagination or to open new vistas to the understanding? What is there that has not been rehearsed before? To venture into the study of Islam is like setting out on a well worn path where all the landmarks are well known and there are no surprises. This very familiarity, though it is illusory and rapidly fades away with any effort to penetrate beneath the surface of matters, breeds disinterest. It is not surprising that students flock to follow courses in the more exotic traditions of India and the Far East where they hope to find something that breaks the established pattern of their own and their society's thinking. Because of its apparent similarities with their own religious backgrounds or, if they are not religious people, with the religious heritage that is most common in the West, Islam seems to hold out little that is novel or stimulating. In such circumstances attention is likely to be turned elsewhere. Similarity thus obstructs understanding or in this case short-circuits the very desire for it.

Our purpose then is to attempt a view of Christianity and Islam that ignores the specifics of similar doctrines, symbols, and expressions in favor of a broader view. In the space that remains we shall endeavour to paint a large and highly general picture of the two faiths we wish to compare. We want to mark out only the grand outlines without regard to nuances, to subtleties, or to the internal changes that have occurred in the two communities. Our search is for the spirit of Islam and of Christianity in comparative juxtaposition; or in other words the attempt will be to sketch the ethos of two faiths in the sense of their most general views of man and the world. In following this procedure we shall be violating a principle that is fundamental to historical and philological scholarship, for in the final analysis the intellectual validity of such broad pictures must be radically called into question. The procedure followed here requires that too many exceptions be ignored and too many details be passed over. In its historical reality religiousness is always the experience and response of particular individuals in particular situations and not something that can be abstracted from the flow and the uniqueness of historical development. As abstract entities there is no Islam and no Christianity, only the faith and the expressions of that faith on the part of millions of devotees. The reality is highly nuanced and differentiated, as diverse in its concrete embodiments as is the myriad swarm of human existence itself. The defence for proceeding as we shall lies in the belief that a worthy purpose will be served by doing so, that a possibility will be created for demonstrating something about Islam and Christianity that may help in comprehending their mutual relationship.

II

In order to get at the ethos or broad and general picture that we aim for we may pose three questions and attempt to answer them from first a Christian and then an Islamic perspective. The questions to be posed are fundamental in any religious point of view and are raised in one form or the other by every one at least of the higher religions, if not by all religious systems whatsoever. As students of theology will recognize, the questions are precisely those which are framed in connection with the understanding and assessment of any soteriological system. The questions are these: (1) What is the human problem or the human situation that calls the religious response into existence and to which the religious man is seeking an answer? This question is equivalent to asking what is the nature of man, what is the character of human existence in the world, and what is the destiny that men may ultimately expect? (2) By what means is the human problem solved? In the situation of difficulty, unfulfillment or danger, etc., in which men naturally find themselves as a result of their very humanness, what appears as the solution which obviates the difficulty or evades the danger? How is man given the possibility of a fuller existence than his own unaided nature permits? (3) To what kind of state does the solution of the problem lead? As the result of the application of the solution to the problem, where does man find himself? In soteriological terms one could ask (1) salvation from what? (2) salvation by what means? and (3) salvation to what? Adequate answers to these queries, if we are able to derive them, should show us the inner logic of Islam and Christianity and reveal to us the issues that are really at stake in the inner counsels of each community. To put the matter in simple, even colloquial terms, the answers should tell us what Islam and Christianity are truly all about.

III

Let us then begin with Christianity, putting ourselves the three questions that we have posed. In the most basic and straightforward terms what is it that Christians perceive as the problem that all men face, as the characteristic of human existence which is so integral that it becomes the defining condition of our humanness? The question may be answered in a single word, "sin." The element that gives rise to all else in the formidable arsenal of Christian belief and practice is man's experience of his own sinfulness. there is a profound awareness in Christian experience of inadequacy, of failure, of shortcoming, or in the terms of the traditional myth, of stubborn self-assertion and rejection of what is known to be the standard and the ideal for human life. There is no question for Christians of not knowing what is required of them; the issue is rather that they know but do not act in accord with their knowledge. One of the most pervasive and fundamental of Christian perceptions is expressed in the words of the traditional Anglican prayer of confession: "We have done those things which we ought not to have done, and we have left undone those things which we ought to have done, and there is not health in us." Men are not what they should be, and they are both aware of this fact and are oppressed by it. The result is a split within ourselves, a kind of turning against ourselves or alienation, the keen sense of obligation towards a level of human conduct that realizes the deepest spiritual potentialities along with a constantly present vivid consciousness of not approaching that ideal. The sense of sin is made all the stronger because it is cumulative and because there is nothing within the power of the individual or the race to arrest the continuing process of self-betrayal and alienation. To the burden of his past rebellion, failure and shortcoming that still weighs upon him the Christian every day adds new and fresh transgressions until, for the religiously and morally sensitive mind, their weight crushes the very meaning from life. This sinfulness is not a matter of inevitability; otherwise, its consequences would be relatively easy to accept. It is rather a matter of established patterns of behavior, of human nature in the sense of the cumulative experience of the race as a whole, of a recurrent and, to us, in some way preferable infringement against the way in which human life ought to be lived. Men know that they have always been sinful and despite their determination and their best efforts they always will be so; in the face of their own makeup and their long history they are powerless to be otherwise. This awareness is borne in and the situation dramatized by the awesome command of Jesus to his followers: "Be ye perfect even as your Father in Heaven is perfect." This saying of Jesus has often been forgotten or interpreted in a way to lessen its impact. Any attempt to blunt the absoluteness of this command, however, would miss the point. In the Christian understanding men should be like God, perfect, but in fact they are far from being so and will never attain that magnificent ideal. Instead they are condemned to live with the consciousness of their sin and their alienation.

The most important aspect of the Christian sense of alienation, however, is not the separation from one's ideal self or the betrayal of one's ultimate possibility that is experienced within the personality of the individual, but rather the separation from the creator and source of value itself, i.e., the separation from God. The result of one's own sin is to cut one off from the ground of reality, to put attainment of meaning, of sharing what is real and true and good, beyond one's grasp because one's own actions and responses have made one incapable to approach it. Sin is a species of corruption that spreads of itself and that leads ultimately to meaninglessness and destruction because it eats away the connection between human existence and the life-giving and sustaining forces of the universe.

The predicament in which every man finds himself is that of being cut off from God by the gulf that he has dug by his own sin without hope of being able to bridge that fatal and always growing chasm. In short, he is in need of salvation, and that in turn cannot be achieved without the agency of a saviour, since he is himself unable either to overcome the effects of his cumulative burden of sinfulness or even to cease from adding to it. Thus, it follows that "salvation" and "saviour" are also key words in the Christian religious vocabulary as concomitants of the key notion of "sin," that is, as implications of the fundamental perception of the human situation. Such is not the case with Islam, whose starting point in its instinctive grasp of the human situation is quite different from that of Christianity, and for which, therefore, the notion of "sin" does not provide the fulcrum upon which the religious system turns. As a consequence, the notion of salvation, or more properly redemption, and the need for it are also not to be found among the basic religious ideas of Islam, and the concept of the saviour is not to be discovered there at all. To be sure there is a word used by Muslim thinkers that is commonly translated as "salvation," but it seems to refer to the state of eternal reward that good Muslims may expect and is not in any case one of the basic terms and conceptions at the heart of the Islamic religious outlook.

In psychological terms the attitude that accompanies the perception of sinfulness as the universal human condition and problem is that of guilt. Not only is a burden of guilt something that is characteristic of the believing and committed Christian; it is a legacy that the Judaeo-Christian tradition has passed on to the whole of Western civilization including those persons who have long since repudiated any connection with a Christian or Jewish heritage. I have a Muslim friend who once remarked to me, half in jest and half in earnest, "The trouble with you Christians is that you are all peccatists." He was referring to the agonizing the depths of the soul that is inseparable from Christian piety, the brooding over wrong-doing, the striving to be what it is impossible to be, the eternal moralizing, the constantly pricking conscience which makes itself felt in the innermost counsels of the spirit whether its existence be outwardly acknowledged or not. All of this amounts almost to a preoccupation with sin, at least as others see Christians, and it elevates guilt to a status of being the primary mark of a serious Christian.

As part of the same complex of perceptions and ideas we must also call attention to the Christian concern with confession and the seeking of forgiveness. Neither is comprehensible except in the light of awareness of our sinfulness, and both therefore form part of a complex of ideas which have their origin and their centre in this awareness. Much the same thing might also be said of such other familiar Christian theological conceptions as "grace" or atonement or justification. Grace is that supernatural balm which in the form of the sacraments serves to eliminate or neutralize the corruption of sin and for at least a time to restore what sin has corroded away. Atonement is atonement for sin, and justification is the making right or balancing of what sin has made wrong or sent awry. In all of these cases we have to do with a complex of conceptions that are intimately linked to one another and to the notion of sin. They have an integral character as a whole. To separate any one of them from this matrix would distort its sense and perhaps make it incomprehensible altogether.

So that the point may be clear let us set out the Muslim attitude as a contrast to this sometimes gloomy and forbidding Christian dwelling upon sin. I remember a discussion of this subject some years ago in a seminar. The seminar leader, an eminent scholar and person of strong religious sensibilities, repeated to the group for perhaps the twentieth time that Christian men look upon themselves as sinners. One of the Muslim participants, who apparently registered the import of this assertion for the first time, sat upright in his seat and demanded, "Professor, do you mean that you are a sinner?" The seminar leader with the great earnestness characteristic of him replied, "Yes, I must confess that I am a sinner;" thereupon, the Muslim participant broke out in a loud guffaw. The attitude being expressed was not only alien but outright ridiculous to the mind of this Muslim who, it must be emphasized, was a serious and learned man. For him to have made such a confession would have been a shocking and indecent thing, something all but inconceivable, with the most dire psychological and even social consequences. Not only did the idea awaken no immediate response, but even on sober reflection it touched no chord of sympathy in the Muslim soul that would vibrate in harmony with the Christian experience.

I should like also to underline that we speak here, not simply of abstract ideas or mental constructions, but of the very taste of life. Christian theology, like Muslim theology and any other that is worth the trouble to talk about, has its basis in certain profound human experiences and is but the systematic verbal expression of those experiences and their implications. Christians speak of the sinfulness of man because they know from their own lives that human existence is so; they have themselves experienced the recurrent tendency of their own natures towards what they know they should not do. The centrality of man's predicament as a sinner does not derive from logical considerations nor even from the authority of revelation but from the quality of life. If Christians speak of themselves as sinners, this is so because they feel themselves to be such. Similarly, Muslims who do not find it important to give first priority in their religious lexicon to "sin" can by-pass the concept because it does not correspond to or express something essential in their perception of themselves. To be sure Muslims have a sense of sin and of the need for forgiveness; one need go no farther than the Qur'ānic emphasis on God's quality as forgiver or than the moving devotional materials collected by Constance Padwick from Ṣūfī prayer manuals to discover abundant evidence of these sentiments. What is at issue, however, is the role which these religious perceptions play in the structure of the Islamic outlook as a whole, and as we shall demonstrate shortly, that role is by no means so central or so vital as for Christianity.

The religiously important thing about the human situation and <u>the</u> human problem of problems for Christians, then, is man's sinfulness. Now, what is the solution to this problem, how is it to be dealt with? Here the story of Christian experience becomes more convoluted. Because men cannot command the perfection which alone would allow them to supply what they have lost, to restore what their own contumaciousness and willfulness have destroyed, the initiative must lie with the Divine Being to restore the broken connection and to bridge the gulf that separates Him from his creatures. An agency other than human effort must be the means of saving men from their sinfulness and its consequences, for they themselves can only flounder hopelessly under their burden of transgression and guilt. Hence the need for a saviour, for one who will do what sinful men cannot do, the need for one who embodies the perfection which men have marred.

The saviour is, of course, none other than God Himself who in a supernatural drama that defies understanding takes on human form in order to come and live a human life among men. The Incarnation, no less than the other concepts we have mentioned, is bound up integrally into a complex whole that we call Christianity. For the notion of Incarnation derives from what might be called a second pole of Christian experience, of which the perception of man's sinfulness is the first pole. That second pole, or to put it in the terms used before, the second fundamental perception of Christianity, is the reality of redemptive love. The Incarnate God, who is nonetheless fully and wholly God, took on human form in order to experience what men experience and in doing so to overcome sin and its great consequence, death. To accomplish so great a victory it was necessary that the Divine Being plunge into every aspect of human experience, its pettiness, its temptation, and most of all, its suffering. The cosmic act which answers the problem of human sin and leads the race out of its dilemma is an act of self-sacrificial love, the Incarnate God giving Himself over to the humiliation and pain of crucifixion and submitting Himself even to the ultimate evil, death, so that his salvation of the human state might be complete. The good news, the Gospel, is that of Christ crucified and risen from the dead. This act of self-immolating love which paradoxically culminates in victory is the revelation of the nature of ultimate reality. It is no accident that the fundamental Christian symbol is the Cross, the grisly reminder of a death by slow torture, for it is in an ultimate kind of suffering that Christian experiences the highest meaning.

No one can say quite how it happens -- and the Church has disagreed on the precise mechanisms -- but somehow in this self sacrifice of the cosmic creator, through His suffering, degradation into death, and eventual resurrection, a power is released that can atone for the sinfulness of men and supply the element required to restore the perfection which they have lost. "All we like sheep have gone astray, and the Lord hath laid on him the iniquity of us all." The divine love and the manner of its expression in the Incarnation and the Atonement are a mystery, and the Christian church has frankly said so. Nevertheless, it is in the event of the dying and rising

Christ that the reality of release from the burden of sin and guilt has been felt by the Christian heart. Here the burden is taken away, and the problem is solved; and here the possibility of communication with the divine is once again opened. All that needs must happen from the human side is to lay hold or appropriate the power of salvation that Christ's death and resurrection have provided. There is none of this cosmic drama, however, in the case of Islam and no involvement of the divine in suffering and the horrors of death -- far be He above that! as Muslims would say -- and this fact marks an essential difference between the two faiths in spite of any number of apparent similarities.

To what state then is the Christian led when he avails himself of the divine initiative to overcome sin and death? Basically the state is one of restored spiritual soundness or health, one in which the sinfulness that caused his separation from God has been wiped away or treated as though it had never occurred at all. The fellowship with God, the immediacy of sharing in the real and ultimate truth, becomes once again possible. The man whom sin had plunged into meaninglessness and subjected to the dissolution of death acquires an eternal horizon, an eternal life; he is redeemed. Although his past transgression is still a fact, it no longer weighs upon the consciousness as a split in the personality, as a fundamental betrayal of what man, who is made in the image of God, should be; for it has somehow been made right and its evil consequences counterbalanced by an outpouring of self-sacrificing divine love. There is no change in human nature and no disappearance of the confirmed tendency towards sinfulness. All men, even Christian men, continue to act wrongly and to insult the majesty and purity of God. The prayer of confession, after all, is a prayer recited by confirmed Christians in the course of their normal worship, not a liturgy intended only the for the newly converted to the community. Men are thus in need of the continued outpouring of divine grace or love so that the breach between themselves and God that they create with each new act of contumaciousness may always be bridged. Thus, imperfect sinful men find salvation in the sense that they live in a state of grace, in circumstances where the divine outreach towards men in love is constantly renewed and constantly reappropriated. In the final analysis the state of salvation is mystical, for it has to do with the possibility of fellowship between the Creator and His creatures. Apart from God man is nothing, but in the intimate association with the Creator implied by faith there is life, joy, and eternal significance.

IV

We must now turn to Islam and raise the same three questions that we have attempted to answer for Christianity. If from an Islamic perspective we ask "What is the human problem?" the answer comes in terms of man's creaturehood, not of his sinfulness or his flawed nature. Like every other aspect of the universe around us, we men are brought into being by the power who is sovereign over everything, and like all other creatures we stand in a vastly inferior position relative to the Sovereign Lord. We were made to exist at a certain plane in the great hierarchy of being, and in terms of the level of reality for which we are intended there is no natural defect in our makeup nor is there any expectation that we should rise above what we naturally are. Creaturehood, in other words, implies limitation, a specification of capabilities that opens certain possibilities to the human race but not others. Some of the limitations upon human nature are evident and obvious; even relative to the animals we have certain disabilities. We possess neither the strength of the elephant, the speed of the antelope, nor the agility of the monkey. More important, however, is the limitation upon the spiritual dimension of our makeup, for we do not possess the capacity through our unaided intellectual or other powers to find out the ultimate truth or things or, what is more fundamental to practical life, even to discover the difference between right and wrong. As a consequence, left in our natural state we would be condemned to flounder about, first in this direction and then in that, without orientation until we ultimately end in disaster. Since we do not know and cannot readily find out what is the proper goal of life or the way that leads to it, we are unlikely ever to get there. The great difficulty that human creaturehood and its attendant limitation pose for the race is that we do not know the right way in which to live in order to realize our full human potential and to avoid coming into conflict with the creative force of the universe. In contrast with the Christian who knows what he ought to do but cannot and will not do it, the Muslim as mere human finds his basic difficulty to be that he does not know what to do. Left to his own devices, he will go astray and make an utter mess of his life -- and, indeed, what else could be his fate? Such has been the recurrent human tendency throughout history even though God has intervened on numerous occasions through His prophets and Books to provide the signs and guideposts that are needed. To put the matter in other terms, the fundamental human situation is that of ignorance, ignorance of the mystery of the universe, of the principles of its order, which results in ignorance as well of the pathway of *sharī^{c}ah* in which men should direct their feet.

In such an understanding of human nature, there is no element of guilt or blame that attaches to men. We should think it ridiculous to hold a cow at fault for being unable to fly or to penalize a snake because it cannot jump fences. No more should, or does, anyone think men guilty because of the limitation which their nature inherently imposes upon them. The problem that all men face does not stem from their own actions nor from some defect that has become entrenched in the character through continual reinforcement. The ignorance that limited human nature entails is morally and spiritually neutral, but it is nonetheless a most real problem that must somehow be overcome for the race to achieve felicity here and hereafter.

In the religious vocabulary of traditional Islam what men lack and most desperately need is guidance -- not salvation or redemption -- but guidance. There is no more basic concept in the Islamic order things than the notion of guidance, for it is this which can supply the need that poses the fundamental dilemma. Men require to be told how to live, to be given specific directions about what is right and proper and about what is wrong and detestable. If this information is supplied in a form that makes it accessible and so that men can understand it, then Muslims have every confidence in their ability to do what is asked. The key to a good and successful life and the secret of eternal felicity is to know in what a good life consists, and this is precisely what men have to find out.

Guidance is what the Muslim most wants and most expects from his religion, specific guidance for a whole host of situations, indeed, for every kind of situation that life might present. To understand this is also to grasp the reasons why considerations of law play such an important part in Islamic life and history. Islam has often been characterized as a religion of law. This description has much to justify it, for concern with spelling out the detailed rules of belief and conduct is _the_ Islamic religious activity _par excellence_. The whole business of Islamic law is nothing more than the attempt to make the guidance proferred initially in the Qur'an, the prophetic life, and the experience of the community always more specific and always more clear. Jurisprudence is the science of elaborating divine guidance in a systemic way so that in no area of human concern need men be without firm principles for their behavior. Our point is that there is something in the fundamental nature of the Islamic experience of man's situation in the world and in its experience of the character of ultimate reality to which the activity of law corresponds and which that activity expresses. There is a clear connection between the idea of guidance and those of Islam (commitment to follow the guidance given by God), _sharīcah_ (pathway), the general name for the normative pattern ordained by the divine will, and _fiqh_, the name of the jurisprudential process that contributes to forming a complex of integrated notions such as we saw emerge in the case of Christianity.

If lack of guidance or ignorance be the problem of men, how is that problem solved in the Muslim religious dispensation? Quite simply it is dealt with by the needed guidance being supplied. Guidance is proferred as an act of mercy through the agency of revelation which in turn is actualized by the institution of prophecy and the Books that God has sent down through His various prophets. There is no compulsion acting upon God to rescue men from the predicament caused by their ignorance of the straight path. Had He chosen to allow us to live according to our own best insights, He could well have done so, just as He has done with the lesser orders of beings. But because of His compassion for the creatures He has made, God has chosen to supply sufficient guidance for men to be able to live successfully on earth and to attain reward in the Hereafter. This guidance He gave to the very first man, Adam, the father of us all, whom He chose as a prophet. He made known to Adam a sufficient portion of the content of the Heavenly Book which is the embodiment of God's eternal will that our first forefather and his descendants were enabled to order their lives with assurance and confidence. Adam as the messenger of God passed down this vital life-giving information to his offspring who could, thus, continue in the path that had been marked out. When in the course of time later generations of men had forgotten the guidance, ignored it, or even distorted it, divine compassion sent another prophet to renew what had originally been given and to set the straying feet of men again upon the straight path. To some prophets, such as Moses, David, Jesus, and Muḥammad, He gave books that He "sent down," i.e., revealed to them. To others He gave no books but made them warners and reminders to men of the power of God and of the revelation sent in previous time for the benefit of the race. This cycle of prophecy has continued throughout the whole of human history which can be seen as a series of fallings away from the divine pattern and returns to it through a new expression of divine compassion and the sending of another prophet to restore and reaffirm the guidance. For every people in every place at some time there has been a prophet speaking in their own language so that men have never had to live in the darkness of their ignorance without the benefit of the guidance they require. With the advent of Muḥammad this cycle of prophecy was brought to its fulfillment, culmination and climax by the bestowal of guidance in such sufficiency that this time uniquely it will not again require to be renewed.

The revelation thus is a revelation of guidance; indeed, it is difficult to distinguish a real difference of meaning between the two ideas. The prophets and the Scriptures are the means by which the guidance or the revelation has been conveyed. If one asks what it is that was revealed, the answer does not come in the form of the nature of the Divine Being but rather in terms of the divine will. What the Qur'ān gives to us men is information about how we ought to live, a set of propositions in the form of prescriptions and prohibitions, principles as well as information, all of which tell us how God wishes us to react and to behave. The revelation conveys information in God's own words. In this instance the idea of guidance provides the pivot point round which an entire set of related religious ideas turns. With guidance being the profound need of men, it becomes clear why the historic mode of divine communication with the world has been the sending of Books. For Books preserve and convey information in permanent and accessible form as few other agencies can. This also explains why religious authority for Muslims is focussed so sharply upon the Scripture and the exposition of its precise meanings. The Scripture is not the sole source of guidance, to be sure, but it is the primary one, and the others that are associated with it, the example of the prophet and the cumulative experience of the community, are but further expressions of the same thing, i.e., ways to make known, specific and clear what the will of God may be for those who are His devotees.

In our situation of helpless ignorance we men are proferred guidance which opens up to us a life that is otherwise inconceivable. In such circumstances only one response is appropriate, that of grateful and joyful submission to the guidance, for it confers a great benefit upon all who receive and accept it. One who responds to the message that comes through the Prophet and the Book with grateful obedience is called a Muslim, i.e., one who submits to or one who commits himself to follow what God has ordained for him. In our normal language we use the word "Islam" as the name of a religion, but to do so robs the word of much of its meaning and raises many problems. More properly "Islam" is submission to or commitment to follow the expressed will of God. Now, "the expressed will of God" is only another phrase that can be used to convey the notion of guidance. Islam, the correct relationship of men to their Sovereign Lord, consists in grateful, joyful, continuing commitment to observe the guidance that men have received. At once the most foolish and the most heinous thing of which we are capable is to refuse the guidance and to turn aside in ingratitude from the mercy so freely offered us. Refusal to be heedful of the guidance is kufr whose essential meaning, as recent philological studies have shown us, is not disbelief in a set of doctrines but rather ingratitude for God's mercy in making the right way of life known to men. The point to be made in covering this familiar territory is that the choice of the term Islam as the designation of the correct relationship with God is not accidental or arbitrary. Rather there is a logic in both its use and its linguistic sense that derives from the structure of Islamic piety and expression as a whole. Muslims accept the word as expressing their most fundamental values because it corresponds to something basic in their perception of man's situation in the world and their perception of the nature of God's relation to His creatures. The most solemn and most consequence-filled duty of man is to give himself fully, without reservation, and joyfully into the hands of his sovereign creator and Lord. This self-giving or Islam is at once an inner state, an attitude of the heart, an orientation of the spirit (īmān or faith) and the outward expression of the inward surrender in the form of the observance of the rites and obligations established in the Muslim community. Christians do not speak primarily in terms of guidance but of salvation or redemption; and as we have tried to suggest, they do so because the foundations of their religious outlook rest upon different bases.

The final question that we must ask concerns the state of the Muslim who in all earnestness accepts and endeavours to follow the guidance that God has given. The characteristic of the faithful Muslim that perhaps stands out in greatest contrast to Christian piety is the Muslim's optimism and his affirmative attitude towards self. This attitude, so sharply distinct from Christian peccatism, derives from several considerations. The first is the fact that the divine guidance does not impose an impossible task upon men or set and ideal that we cannot attain. In a significant verse of the Qur'ān God addresses men telling us that he lays no burden upon us that is too difficult. The things which a Muslim must do in order to satisfy the divine will are both well known and perfectly within our ability to accomplish. Man is a creature, and nothing in the Islamic perspective compels us to struggle futilely to become something else. His duty is first in sincerity to commit himself and then to observe certain restraints and perform certain acts that have been clearly laid down in much detail in either the revelation itself or the books of law that have expounded the implications of the revelation. Thus, the Muslim may expect in the course of his earthly life actually to fulfill what is required of him. He can be what he ought to be with nothing left over to nag at the conscience or create guilt. For most Muslims the feeling of being essentially good men is apparently the normal state of affairs. So long as one performs his religious duties and does not transgress the limits God has laid down, his state is one of health and soundness. Both the psychological and the social consequences of this conviction are enormous in the Islamic societies. There is a feeling of assurance and confidence about the rectitude of life, no profound spiritual ground for disquiet or agony of the soul, but conviction that one has set one's feet upon the single path of truth. At the level of the political community this important religious attitude goes far towards explaining the historical Islamic view of rival communities. Just as individual men have an affirmation of the rightness of their lives, so also does the community as a whole. As a community whose task is to apply the will of God in the social sphere, the Islamic ummah is manifestly superior to those which do not commit themselves to walk in the ordained pathway. There is a buoyancy that is noticeable is Islamic life, an expectancy, a positive sense of assurance and confidence, all of which come in large degree from the sense that one has done what he ought. Man is, indeed, limited but not in respect to his capability of being what a man should be. Not only does the Muslim live in the reassuring knowledge that he can achieve all that is expected with some exertion of his will, but a great many persons in addition enjoy the incalculable satisfaction of feeling they have actually done the full duty of man in this world.

Hand in hand with the sense of confidence in life that comes from knowing one's duty lies within one's grasp is another consideration that contributes to the characteristic optimism of Islam. This consideration is the expectation of success, not only the felicity of the world to come, but on the stage of present history as well. Muslims have set themselves as individuals and as a community to act in accord with the creative principle that brought our universe into being and that sustains it. God's will concerning the moral and religious behavior of men has its counterpart in the natural realm in the form of the laws of physical nature. One who acts in accord with physical laws can be effective in changing the physical realm or in using it to his advantage because he acts in the same direction in which the controlling forces of the universe are moving. Similarly, to live as God has ordained is also to co-operate with the force that governs the universe, and how can such co-operation eventuate in anything except success? Historically the Islamic community has experienced a success and glory that numbers it among the great civilizations mankind has known. In the Muslim mind there is the closest of connections between the magnificence, power, wealth, and accomplishment that Muslims once displayed as bearers of the world's leading civilization and Islam, or the community's subservience to a divine pattern. It is inconceivable that those who walk in the straight path should not be favoured in the world that God has created and that He controls. History is on the side of Islam and must inevitably be so because Islam is but submission to the rule of history's Lord. There may be puzzlement, even dismay, that history has betrayed Muslim expectations, as is certainly the case in the modern era, but confidence that the truth and rightness of the Islamic life will be vindicated even in the vicissitudes of earthly life is strong and flourishing in the Muslim heart. One has to look no farther than the resurgent Islamic movements of our time with their messianic hopes to find abundant evidence of such as positive view of history.

It is hoped that enough has now been said to support a general statement of the conclusion that we have been striving to justify. We have seen that at one level Christianity and Islam have much in common in their allegiance to specific doctrines and in the terms that are fundamental to their religious vocabularies. In spite of this similarity we have also seen that in other more important respects there is a profound contrast between the two. They begin, as it were, with different estimates of the religious situation of mankind, offer different solutions to the problem that all men face, and issue in states and attitudes that are also marked by contrast rather than similarity. What this simple analysis has attempted to show is that the two communities differ radically concerning the structure of the religious life. Indeed, they appear to be addressing themselves to entirely different problems, not so much contesting one another's insights as talking about quite different things. To the extent that similar doctrines or positions prevent us from seeing the more far-reaching differences inherent in the way in which doctrines and concepts combine into an integrated whole to form a perception of man, of God and of their relations with one another -- to precisely this extent -- such similarities obstruct understanding. The matter of importance is the thrust of the whole, its distinctive character. Here the difference is so great that one may well ask whether in truth there is any hope of Christian-Muslim dialogue ever progressing beyond the stage of registering the differences with one another.

Meeting of Opposites: Islam and Hinduism

R. Morton Smith
The University of Toronto

Not being among the very few who command both Sanskrit and Islamic languages, I might be regarded as rather an interloper in this volume, but I do hope the following may have both sense and interest for my colleagues.

On the higher level, Islam and Hinduism (which includes its heresies like Jainism and (earlier) Buddhism), are well made for mutual non-appreciation. In the religious sphere, therefore, the impact of Islam is to be expected on the emotional theism, and not on the intellectual philosophy of the thinking class, the brahmans, though by this late stage in Indian history theism has made inroads also into that class.

The Muslim differed from previous invaders of India. While some like the Śaka or Kushan of the 1st centuries BC and AD may have come to stay, they could not resist assimilation because of their small numbers, which could not be replenished, and their only effectual distinction was racial/linguistic. The Muslim had an inexhaustible fund of reinforcements from the very real unity of the Muslim world; any adventurer from Morocco to Loulan, from East Africa to Farghānah could come to carve out for himself a political or military fortune under his co-religionist in India, who racially a foreigner, was always likely to be glad of the reinforcement, since his position always depended on military superiority. There was a real sense in which an Islamic ruler could not be legitimate in a Hindu society; and even a Hindu _cakravar-tin_, universal ruler, could not hold that position legitimately, i.e., by personal right, whatever place might be in the system for such a position. But the adventurer's loyalty is primarily to himself, hence the chronic history of political

Logos Islamikos: Studia Islamica in honorem Georgii Michaelis Wickens, ed. Roger M. Savory and Dionisius A. Agius, Papers in Mediaeval Studies 6 (Toronto: Pontifical Institute of Mediaeval Studies, 1984), pp. 307-323.

turbulence. The great majority of immigrating adventurers was likely to be male, which would in itself reinforce the fighting rather than the thinking nature of the Muslim population. But the main difference was that the Muslims came with a religion to impose, which previous invaders like the Greeks or Persians did not. Zoroastrianism would seem to have become the family religion of the Achaemenids, and the Greeks equated gods and did not suppress them. Moreover, the theory of transmigration and karma, based on the atomic theory of Prakudha Kātyāyana, gave brahmin or Buddhist a far more complete and self-consistent explanation of life than was available elsewhere at that time. The Muslims had a unifying religion with a history of expansion by conquest, whose superiority thus proved justified its imposition by further conquests; this bond of a foreign religion could unite the invaders, as that of an Indian religion, Buddhism, could not bind Iranians together against Indians. And Islam could draw strength from its converts, since they could not go back. The Portuguese, coming before the Reformation and later rejecting it, were also willing to convert their subjects, even forcibly. They, like Islam, retained the heritage of the Roman Empire -- the Christian/Muslim must live in a Christian/Muslim society of unitary belief (reduced finally by Europe and Iran to the principle cuius regio (not mundus) eius religio, and to establish that society entails conversion. By the time the English, French or Dutch came, the social unity of Christendom had broken up, and religion was highly individual; there was therefore no call to convert the native society. Moreover, these nationals to the end expected to return to their native lands to more comfort than they had left.

It seems that in the first invasions (of Sindh, 711/2, and by Maḥmūd, 1000-1030) the brahmans were either wiped out or retreated to cleaner parts of India. Apart from the simplicity of the Islamic creed carrying its own appeal, it is also true that the natives thus remaining to be converted were not of the thinking class; and it is very significant that despite the Indian predilection to philosophy, for a major figure of Indian origin in the Islamic world we have to wait till Shāh Walī Allāh in the 18th century (and one might reasonably ask in the Indian society how Indian was his ancestry? -- that of Amīr Khusraw was Central Asian). But conversion does not of itself change the mentality, and we find that when the natives take to religion, they often do it in the old brahman way; they become ascetic, the pīr or faqīr, just as the unqualified demanded equal opportunity for austerities in Buddha's day. In the Hindu society -- and there had been a resurgence of Hinduism in the North-West after the Hunnish invasions -- saintliness can not be separated from some asceticism. The brahman mentality remained impressed on the non-thinking classes, so that the prestige of the religious remains under Islam, and it is impressive to find the old Buddhist attitude to killing animals living strongly in a Bengal Muslim of today, or in the Indian-Muslim historian, political scientist or economist who really wants to write on Muslim mystics, i.e., to deal with permanent truth like the old brahmin. I would not share Prof. Schimmel's scepticism on the importance of Abū ᶜAlī al-Sindhī on the development of Bāyazīd Bisṭāmī's idea of fanā', annihilation of the individual; such annihilation is commonplace in Indian thought, and we find the old message of Quit duality reappearing in Niᶜmat Allāh writing of ca. 1400. But the annihilation is now Muslim, with positive content. Niᶜmat Allāh says; "Thou art I and I am Thou"; The Upanisad said, "Thou art that," impersonal. Islam in removing the primacy of philosophy, would make devotion, bhakti, of the unthinking class respectable, and this does not call for the rejection of asceticism, but it is modified to rational form, avoiding the extremes of India, and cut off from its magical/sexual origins.

That the direct influence of India on Islam of the early centuries was important, I would not believe; but I am willing to suggest that Indian influence was important in the Syrian/Iranian background, on Gnosticism, Manichaeism, even Neo-Platonic thought, and not all asceticism or distrust of the flesh is ultimately Pythagorean. Nor did all asceticism arise from distrust of the flesh; as providing magical power it goes back to the Indo-European tradition and the shamanism of Inner Asia, whence it may also descend into Iranian and Turkish mysticism. Buddhism had a strong connection with the merchants, and some of its ideas might well be disseminated along the trade routes from Bactria and Transoxania to the West, where Islam enters on the heritage of Sāsānid and Byzantine.

It might be well to explain why Islam had so little appeal to the thought of traditional India. Its great message is the unity, uniqueness, power and mercy of God: Hinduism is unsympathetic to all of these. The brahman might tolerate Allāh as an ethnic Brahma, but Allāh was not to continue as a monopoly of the invaders, and even if he should so continue by the suspension of conversion, Allāh is active and arbitrary -- the very continuance of the world is an exhibition of his power. Brahma however is neither active nor arbitrary, for even if the next cycle of emanation could be different, karma has taken hold on this. Allāh cares, Brahma exists. Allāh is a personal and ethical God, just and merciful; damnation is not far away, and Allāh could rightly damn, but he is merciful. But Hindu damnation is more life, not destruction.

Hindu Atman might be unique like Allāh, but it is not unique as a personality, but as a definition, a pantheos, of unqualified being. As it is the only real existing thing, its uniqueness is meaningless, because everything different is equally unique as partaking of Atman, and that is its only value. The uniqueness is a meaningful necessity for Islam as a protest against the polytheistic environment where the pagan gods were as many, varied and real personalities as they had been from ancient Babylonia down to pagan Rome, and often as unedifying. The Mediterranean world had had to fight polytheism; real powers were real enemies; their power followed from their existence, which had therefore to be disproved or denied. India never had to fight polytheism, because Brahma was the self: a spiritual social conscience was unnecessary -- only Mahayana Buddhism protested -- since one is fulfilled by being, and the doctrine of karma rationalizes its futility by declaring desert. One can be but not love the qualityless absolute. Life, like other rituals, is to be performed, not improved.

A moral polytheism is very difficult to produce -- Socrates got into trouble for trying. Such gods spring from the old pre-ethical and power-magical past, and their myths cannot be wholly purged of the unethical, the improper or the infantile. It is not easy to raise polytheism above the level of humanity unless the gods are static and inactive -- the cult of the saints in Catholicism might be considered in this light; the saints have no independent initiative or responsibilities beyond intercession; otherwise questions of relationship, spheres of power and interest of individual gods always arise. If we believe in the reality of the world, and if polytheism is going to be sustained, its gods must have real personalities, and the unity of the godhead becomes impossible -- here Islam objects to the Christian Trinity -- as the human intellect's natural drive is to unity, thus explaining a maximum by a minimum. It is against such real polytheism that the western world has waged implacable war from the time of the Hebrew prophets till the end of the 4th century AD, the reign of Theodosius I marking the official triumph. Unity is final, and understandable. India preserved polytheism by unreality; yet men do not like their idol unreal, and we may note the Indian struggle for divine reality and unity and personality in the growth of the godheads of Śiva and Viṣṇu, that ends in the brahman-imposed stalemate of the Hindu trinity, Brahma added with little worship.

Muḥammad had a similar real war on his hands in Arabia; hence Islam was not well prepared for tolerant understanding of Hindu polytheism with its relativity and impersonal self or being, as a hidden underlying and rather disinterested reality. The tolerance and slow conversion of subject populations are the outcome of political and social realities -- religion is not an individual matter in India's impersonal society -- but it is not to be believed that the only missionaries of Islam were those with the sword; rice-Muslims like rice-Christians may be an undeniable phenomenon, but in the West we are lamentably ignorant of the real missionaries.

The idol is immemorial in the Near East. The suppression of idolatry is also a blow against polytheism; the loss of the idol will to some degree cut the tradition, quite as much as the suppression of the scriptures which only a few can read. The destruction of idols has therefore a propaganda purpose as well as being a blow against error and falsehood; it is an easy way to merit in the assertion of truth even by those who do not understand it, commanded by the absolutism of the new faith.

This absolutism may copy the political absolutisms of the leading powers of Muḥammad's time. The Hebrew heritage, especially as known in its post-exilic militant and pharisaic form, not to mention the Christian intolerances of Byzantium, contribute to the absolutism of command or veto. God remained jealous, and the decisiveness of his authority may also reflect the necessary strictness of the patriarchal tribal rule, a rule that may also be military discipline, in a land of harsh physical environment with sharp boundaries between the good land and the desert, sharp and extreme contrasts of light and shade, heat and cold. This absolutism may also be some emotional compensation for the impotence of man. But there is also the factor that Islam, like Christianity and Zoroastrianism, is deadly serious about life; as creatures we have but one life in which to find salvation, be justified to our maker whose grace we cannot compel. This seriousness can neither be understood nor attained by a discipline of relativity. This urgency Hinduism with its mathematical kalpas of millions of years and constant transmigration cannot feel or appreciate. But to us life comes with a duty not of our choosing, for which we must be prepared, and for which truth is a necessity. If the West revolts against obedience today, we must remember that there was no egalitarianism to resent it in the past, and while the ethical religions might have equality of men before God, (which Hinduism did not have), they would despise the idea of equality with God.

Fertility goddesses are not separable from their flesh or their sex. Ritual prostitution, essentially a (degraded) form of (degraded) magic, was known in Arabia. Muḥammad reacted with a fiery puritanism, sublimated (with a deferred compensation?) in the decidedly earthly paradise awaiting the faithful, which though supremely enjoyable, will be eminently decent. But whatever the souls of the just, who are surely of no immoderate sensuality, will enjoy, God is irrevocably immaterial, and the conjunction of flesh and sensual enjoyment with the divine is blasphemy. Islam, while denouncing idolatry, is revolted by it in a sexual form, as was the Victorian; and since crops come from the omnipotence of God and his mercy, cannot even consider the fertility magic theoretically underlying. Those who can indulge sexuality as religion are not merely different, but inferior -- we may see how the current Western religion of sex has discredited us in Islamic lands. Christian incarnation is bad enough, but that gods should indulge is vile. Thus the Muslims found in India much of what was for all purposes the old heathendom, no more admirable, of the days before knowledge in Arabia. The divine to Islam as to Christianity is inseparable from moral sanctity, and is primarily transcendent.

We may concede too much to modern relativity (which derives much from humanism on the rejection of immediate God), in saying that Islam cannot understand idolatry or religious sexuality, because there are occasions when we must reject because we do understand, and the polite phrase is that we have no sympathy for the rejected; the lack is not of understanding but of motivation to accept it. The early god is the power-god, and power is amoral; so then is the power-god. Muḥammad knew such gods and rejected them. Nor has such a power-god any reason to claim uniqueness. Islam's one God has all power and is ethical; power outside him may be supernatural but is devilish, not divine, nor final. Nor can the Godhead be symbolized by the material; the body is no symbol, and God does not need one; he is not the world; immanent and transcendent, he has no identity with it, did not evolve into it, hence he is no multiplicity to be represented. Polytheism is not tenable as a relative truth. God made the world and made souls, and while like Atman he is unchanging, it is not because he has no qualities, but because his qualities are perfect. Pantheism or Atman, self, can be amoral, but Allāh, having arbitrarily created, like a father retains responsibility for (and power over) his children.

It is said that there is little evidence of strong rejection of Hinduism by Muslims. This may be true; conquerors tend to be secularized by success -- the Spanish Christianization of America is a counter-example. But besides that what is obviously wrong has not normally been held to demand refutal, Islam need never be on the defensive in India. In the core lands people of the Book were ubiquitous, and by no means passive, and have coreligionists without; they must be converted or refuted, and neither their creeds or arguments are puerile. But in India there is no counter-attack; the brahmin can not proselytize, having no equality to offer, nor is the Purānic mythology defensible to the Western mind, which had long rejected such with paganism. Nor can the unthinking classes be expected to put Islam on the defensive. One of the great attractions of India was as a source of wealth, which does not spiritualize.

God is merciful and just. Now it is quite clear that only a sinner or "other"/opponent needs God's mercy; the brahman, since he is essentially Atman, is not other, and equally therefore he cannot be a sinner. No brahman needs salvation: he may hope for release, but this involves a disengagement, not a change or purification of his nature -- nor has he a psychological basis for a sense of sin, since he has begun his life with the correct choice of being male. Insofar as the word "saved" is applicable, he was saved in essence when he first attained knowledge (which is acquiring, not giving). No one has power over him. But to the Muslim God has the absolute patria potestas and as perfect, the perfect power; and in this respect Islam avoids the controversy of faith versus works; works do not compel God -- indeed the Ash^{c}arites attribute their effective existence to him.

The brahman's perfection does not need paradise, and the materialism or sensualism of the Islamic would have no appeal -- he can always get ten thousand years in Indra's sensual paradise if he wants. The brahman is beyond desire, but in the Islamic, desires fulfilled remove the roots of evil. God in his mercy accepts the faithful without a preparation of purgatory, and life continues in paradise without the evils of this world, much as was the case for Zoroaster. The patriarchal family remains relevant; as on earth being born into it as a basic virtue, God will protect his family of the faithful. But the brahman as Atman has escaped the relevance of family tie or obligation.

Power implies will, mercy implies love, and justice implies discrimination. These are personal qualities/acts such as cannot be possessed by an impersonal God. Nothing is juster than Atman, but it is the justice of a law of nature, not of one who could choose otherwise. And even if owing to God's perfect nature such an other course is inconceivable, he is consciously just and delights in that justice. *Karma* is utterly just, and completely merciless. No amount of goodness removes a bad *karma*; it is inhuman. Yet by the nature of the case, since the crime as often as not took place in a previous existence, it is hard to conceive what crime the punishment fits. The consequences one hears in fiction are usually quite incommensurate with the offence -- as they have to be for the hero/heroine to retain their necessary perfection: this is true of rewards also, especially hagiographical, for actions which call for no great effort, like giving a bowl of rice to an ascetic who happens to be the right one. Here we have the logical extreme of assertion in an intellectual culture; but Islam, which arose and spread in civilized lands remains influenced by rationalistic Hellenism.

Action and reaction are equal and opposite; man cannot love the unloving, at least long -- e.g., the spiritual disillusion with Marxism where it has been experienced. Man wants to love, and therefore the mercy of God is a necessity. But with the Atman/brahma there is no place for mercy, since one cannot be merciful to one's self, and at any rate there is no sin, at worst an error of judgment. Nor has Atman power, for there is no other reality over which to exert it; any amount of māyā, delusion, can be projected, but if it is, karma takes control. Yet in the contemplation of God's nature and person what impresses Muḥammad is God's power; the great difficulty of Muslim theology is to reconcile God's power with his justice, which involves the relation of man's will to God's. This is a problem that cannot arise in India, since Atman has no will, manas; will is through manas, an action, karma, and the absolute is beyond anything, pure existence, not active, being, not action. When the Vedantist Šankara admits that the world is Brahma's play/whim, he is asserting as much as Sartre the absurdity of existence, which he does not believe, since he is sure man must strive to return to pure Atman by knowledge. But to the Muslim, life is not a callous imposition; it too is part of God's mercy.

Hinduism and Islam are both social religions, but in very different ways. Islam is one community socially purposive to bring God's justice among men (which implies some individual value). Hinduism and its heresies are intellectually antisocial with monasticism and Atman; they are social in caste and ritual, but rather for the continuation than improvement of society, where the individual has no value for his own sake.

It will be seen that on all these matters there is no common ground between Islam and Hinduism, and the Indian/Buddhist content of Iranian mysticism (which is not to attribute it all to India), remained somewhat indigestible in Islam. But if the Muslim was not qualified to give a just estimate of Hinduism, the brahman does not understand the Muslim to this day; he cannot see why he cannot be content to be a Muslim Hindu (or Sikh Hindu for that matter) and keep quiet. Brahma may subsume all by māyā, unreality, but Allāh is not to be subsumed; a personality and a non-personality are contradictory, and the values that flow from them are also irreconcilable. A personal God, unique and eternal, can be no relative truth even if it can be a falsehood, and is at least meaningful and related to experience in a way an Existence beyond being and not-being, (a contradiction in terms), consciousness and non-consciousness, action and non-action, good and evil, is not.

The Muslim needs and relies on God's mercy, while the brahman cannot conceive that he is a sinner in need of redemption or forgiveness. But if the brahman is not a sinner, he sets the tone for the lower ranks of society, so that they are not sinners either, however unclean by caste. Hence the slowness and even absence of appeal by Islam (or Christianity) to people whom one would have thought had an immediate great lot to gain from it. For even if "redeem" is not the right word for Islam, spiritual equality does free: but freedom may not be easily intelligible in a collective society.

Islam comes from that Western world whose ideology is stamped by the fighting class. But the brahman caste is not for fighting or ruling; the caste system aims to divide, not concentrate and increase power. The power-god has an inevitable appeal to some strands in human nature, but they are those of which the brahman disapproves, not perhaps forgetting that power is ill to share, and he is himself a god, by _tapas_, austerity, a power-god, and need bow to none. The power-god in India must then turn to the devotion of the non-thinking classes. But while Allāh is far more powerful, he is not a god of miracles, which are always more popular with the cultural proletariat, and it is significant (and advanced) that Muḥammad did not claim to perform miracles. God's miracle is creation; but whatever be the admiration for the miracle on the popular level, Allāh is so transcendent that to assert power miracles of him (as opposed to his capacity for them), would almost be to commit the blasphemy of allying him with matter. And while the world to the Indian is evil, that evil is pain; flesh is a mistake, not a sin. But what God made cannot be evil, but he cannot be contained in his own creation; hence to the Muslim whatever flesh may be in itself for us, it has a Manichaean connotation in relation to God, who could only suffer diminution from its limitation (as is accepted that he did in Christianity -- he humbled himself). The unhuman mythology of the Purāna of mediaeval (into modern) Hinduism is therefore repugnant to Islam (not even poetically usable as was the classical in Europe); and while the constant danger to the gods from the _asuras_ is contrary to the omnipotence of God, incarnation of God in the unclean pig or the man-animal mixture is doubly degrading -- bad enough in man. Here Buddhism would not come off any better than orthodoxy, for Buddha had been an animal often enough in the Jatakas, there were Buddhist idols, and much Buddhism was tantric by 1000 AD. Islam retained the Greek/Hebrew opposition of man and animal, which however paradoxically, remains a force towards man's progress and refinement to mercy.

The influence of Islam in India is immediately apparent in the matter of idolatry. After Muslim control the idol has to retreat into the temple, and is not, emphatically not in its sexual form of activity, displayed outside -- witness the difference between the Govind Dev temple at Brindaban of ca. 1500, where the whole ornamentation is in moldings, and the erotic sculptures of Khajurao. Islam caused a reduction in the status of the idol at least in the eyes of the thinkers, to that of a symbol. Considering the formlessness of Atman, the charge of idolatry hit home, wounding the brahman's prestige in his own eyes; idolatry was unprogressive, intellectually untenable; the days before Islam were of ignorance because of it; hence the intellectual brahman cannot afford to be accused of ignorance and childishness (in Sanskrit a synonym for folly). To be retarded, therefore inferior, is a hard blow to the brahman's prestige in his own eyes, the deepest wound possible for the living deity; hence to save this prestige, his dearest possession, the brahman had to do something about his idols, even if he could not reject them, not only owing to the authority of the past, but also because of his "parishioners," as it were. The ignorant of the depressed and unthinking classes had not been prepared for the single abstract God. For on abstraction unity must follow. The reduction to symbols rather than being magical tools or abodes of real deities was as much as the brahman could concede. He might decide not to need the symbol himself, but he must permit it for the common man who always does in the absence of education.

The Muslim is especially contemptuous of the sexuality of Indian religion. Islam greatly increased the shame of nakedness and sex to the brahman, so that sublimation is necessary. This results in a great strengthening of (emotional) deism of a monotheistical nature, tending, one would expect, to the abstract. Leadership in this deism often comes from the lower and non-thinking classes/castes. As before, the brahman with his sincerity may join in, and he tends to provide the more intellectual of the saints; the tailor or merchant drew their philosophy (when they have it), rather from the popular levels, which would be accessible in the Sāmkhya of the MahāBhārata.

This devotion, again under Islamic influence, ignores caste, though quite often the saints were fiercely opposed or even persecuted by the "ministry," the brahman caste. It seems to be a movement of the village and the small town, and the brahmin opposition usually breaks down on the brahman's sincerity; little though he likes it, he finds that he must admit and respect the saintliness. This devotional movement accordingly adds humility to virtue; the nearer the sexual, the farther from humility -- it is irrelevant to Caitanya -- as to our pornographers.

The Muslim was always humble, if not always to man: the sense of his weakness against the unutterable power of God enforced the virtue of humility -- indeed what might be called the Muslim sense of sin seems to spring rather from impotence than guilt. There was no possibility of compelling God to reward one with heaven; let one be humbly resigned to God's will. The brahman as god without a sense of sin did not need humility, and could not feel it, but with a more Islamic conception of monotheism, finding that God is no respecter of persons in caste, he finds that there is no escape from humility, and that humility deepens love. This is new, for the Indian male never seems to need worry about his unworthiness of his lady, however doubtful his success. Humility is a peaceable virtue, and also, what the traditional brahman cannot understand, a happy and liberating one; by freeing us from self-consciousness it makes devotion easy and happy.

The more interesting theistic devotional group are the Mahratta saints, living in a district where Jainism, Buddhism and Hinduism are all in the tradition, though Buddhism had predeceased Islamic rule. They were saints as it were for themselves, in Buddhist terms pratyekabuddha, and accepting pupils on the old brahmanic lines, did not try to found a community or sect (as did the Sikhs). There was Chokhā the untouchable; he went to the temple and received the garland of the god. The worshippers ask, "How?" and beat him, saying that he had polluted God. Chokhā asserts the sugar cane may be crooked, but the juice is not; the bow may be crooked, but the arrow is not. Take refuge in, contemplate the name of God, and you have nought to fear. God had come to his house to partake of dinner with him, and his wife tells God that even though the food is unworthy of him, he may be gracious to partake.

There was Samvatā the gardener. He found that God pervaded all his garden. He prays to God to relieve him from samsāra, to bereave him of all his progeny (i.e., either to remove his karma, or it might be the submission of unworthiness). He is glad that he has not attained greatness, and very content that he was born in a low caste. Once Jñānadeva and Nāmadeva, great saints, but brahmins, were passing his garden when his eyes were wide open, his arms outstretched and his heart full of humility; but God came into Samvatā's garden, laid his hand on him and embraced him. By the power of God's name one may cease to fear, and strike a blow on the head of death; by this name one may bring God from heaven to earth and dance and sing his praise. Samvatā wants God, not nirvāna, and though the name may bring the God as in the Veda, he is to be served, not serve.

There is also another change that is Islamic, resignation to the will of God, not karma. This is not the popular Western image of the impassive slavish East, but a continuous act of trust in God's mercy and goodness and justice, and as such, a source of happiness. The traditional resignation to karma can make no joy, since that persecutor cannot be loved; but Samvatā's resignation is a source of joy.

The emphasis on the name of God may come from Islam. There are 99 names of God, and the camel knows the hundredth. God taught his names to Adam, and therefore, the Ṣūfī says, man is superior to other beings, including angels (which superiority we might compare to that of men over gods in India where only men, not gods can attain mokṣa, release/nirvāna). There is in Hinduism the tradition of many names of the deity as far back as the MahāBhārata, e.g., the thousand names of Viṣṇu in the (late) AnuŝāsanaParvan, and in the Purāna, early mediaeval or tantric, and there are magical tantric syllables for repetition. But with the Mahratta saints we have one name for one God, not many for devotion by flattery. Even the outcaste Kanhopatrā, the courtesan, a woman, daughter of a dancing woman, has been lifted up by the name of God. Happy was she that she had seen his feet, the feet of the image of Viṭṭhala (even if he was originally the brahmin's form of Viṣṇu).

Just as the ŝūdra or the goldsmith, women too may take part in this movement of devotion and personality. There was also Janabāi, maidservant of Nāmadeva, and most famous, Muktabāi. She too is a devotee, and like the others well aware of grace. While the conception of grace is apt to occur in Hindu theism from its early days, it is most insistent with the Mahratta saints. Humility in its new status must confess grace, which is not merely a kindness -- which it is -- but also a strength.

The greatest of these saints is Tukārām. He has a very Islamic message, but is wholly Hindu. The personal is superior to the impersonal. He who says he has become God is a fool, and the service of God's feet is superior to the identification with the monist absolute, advaita. Reincarnation is better than release if one can praise God. All things depend on God, the universal power, who can make even one leaf of a tree move. Since God is omnipotent, what is lacking to him that man should beg of anyone else? Nobody can withstand the will of God; he gives according to our deserts. Evil is a mystery we must respect; fire may ward off cold, but you cannot gather it in your lap; saints and sinners are both men, but we cannot respect both alike. God loves his saints, and will never leave them uncared for. There is a mystical pantheism, and the saints are God and he them by grace. Tukārām knew that he was a sinner, and his sins stand between God and him; but God must save (i.e., he must love): "Do not fail in they compassionate duty, O God."

While those Mahratta saints, whose general message is the prayer of the publican, seek God for their own sakes and his in the humbler walks of society, others in North India see the miseries of the continuous wars, occasionally religious if they can be so called, and of the probably more frequent if unrecorded Hindu-Muslim riots that were a substitute for Saturday sport. However pleasing to God, those riots were viewed with more regret by the government, causing as they did loss of life, order and revenue, and being always liable to blossom into an unforeseen political revolt.

One by-product of Islamic rule was the loss of prestige by Sanskrit, today being recovered somewhat under the aegis of nationalism and Comparative Philology. The brahman's Sanskrit had always been the language of culture and the court. The presence of two other prestigious languages, visible if not legible in Islamic inscriptions, Arabic the language of God and Persian of the conquerors, must have lessened the prestige of Sanskrit (and with that the credibility of the pretensions of its owners, the brahmans), so that the popular languages could more easily become audible and articulate. The brahman with threatened supremacy has again to depend on other classes, and will need their languages as his own Sanskrit gets more remote. The vernaculars are used by the devotional movements, bhakti, which may well be encouraged by the democracy of Islam. We find oftener caste being ignored in the religious sphere.

However, Hinduism like Islam finds that it must reject union, and so the chief offshoot of Kabīr's teaching, the pupils of Nanak, the Sikhs, become virtually a new caste, despite their claim to be a religion. One might say that sects rising under foreign influence under Hindu rule or majority can be kept within the fold of Hinduism, while those rising under foreign rule have to be put out. So the Mahratta saints and the Lingayat Śaivas, in whom Muslim influence is usually seen, remain Hindu, perhaps more readily so since they failed to produce a philosophy -- surprising in the case of the Lingayats, whose founder was a brahman.

Conversion to Islam was not assisted by the politics of northern India. After the conquest by Muḥammad of Ghūr one could not call the wars religious and the armies of the contenders for power, or further invaders, were Muslim, or at least under Muslim command, and to the harried peasant were no advertisement for the religion. However sympathetic to Muslim doctrines Nanak or Kabīr could not therefore be Muslim. There may indeed also be a deliberate rejection of Islam in the erotic and antinomian cults, some of whose greatest excesses are post-Islamic. But while the puritanism of Islam may be chosen for defiance, it would seem that the caste society is also becoming a burden with its ever greater rigidity, aggravated by the progress to totality of wars with their scorched earths, mercenaries, rebellions of governors, etc., all ultimately paid for by the peasantry. Indeed one influence of Islam in India is the greater ravage of war; this is due to the tradition of the Iranian absolute monarchy. In traditional India wars had not been against the populations of territories to be conquered, even if the progress of enormous armies could be like a visitation of locusts. Islam had a more Roman/Byzantine view of the state, but in India society was unchanged by war, and only suzerainty acknowledged; taxes were redirected, not increased.

Islam from its ultimately Hellenistic background wants

consistency -- philosophy is needed to attain it. Hinduism never was a unity, and it is not the duty of philosophy to coordinate. So in Sikhism Muslim ideas may be imposed in an Indian way on an Indian premise; for example, Nanak retains karma and samsāra, but God does the judging and rewarding. Nanak is very insistent on the unity of God and his uniqueness, and forbids the worship of idols and symbols. Kabīr, his teacher, had forbidden mantras/spells and rites; Nanak had no use for outward signs of religion like garments, asceticism, pilgrimages (doubtless in reaction from the all too common fraudulent sādhus, a traditional burden on Indian economy). God prefers a pure and upright heart to all temples -- that at Amritsar was first built in the reign of Akbar under the fourth guru. Nanak followed Islam in asserting the right of everyone to seek God, and also in his rejection of celibate austerities. The ideal is to seek saintliness living as a member of society. This is an Islamic idea, and involves emphasis on practical virtue. Virtue tended in the Hindu way, as it may in Islam, to quietism until the militarization of the sect in face of Awrangzīb's persecution.

As in its founder, so too in the further development of Sikhism Hindu and Muslim elements contend and combine. The book, the Adi Granth, gets the place of the Qur'ān. The will of God is quite clear, but God made māyā, delusion, by his power -- what is the reality of this world? Absorption and paradise are both offered as reward of the blessed. In some respects these contradictions may be paralleled with the distrust and even resentment of theology of the ordinary man, suspicious of intellectualism that may create an élite when he has just won equality. The creativity of orthodoxy had transferred itself to epistemology and language, no more to the taste of the masses then than now: the non-thinking classes want a guide to life, which is more easily found in the love of God than in epistemology.

Islam is usually credited with the final elimination of Buddhism from India, especially owing to the destruction of the Buddhist university of Nalanda. I am not myself so sure of this: Buddhism survived no better in the south, where there was not yet Muslim rule, and in Afghanistan/Gandhara Hinduism had made great inroads in the eighth to tenth centuries. At Ellora Buddhism seems to decay in the ninth and tenth, and I suspect that the chief factor was the growth of the magical tantrism, which had no valid religious/philosophical distinction from Hinduism -- Avalokitšvara was already Šiva. While we may expect an initial destruction of available idols, Buddhism was not eliminated by persecution.

Technical effects of the Islamic conquest seem to be long delayed; technology is not a brahman interest. In some things India was the teacher, e.g., in medicine, astronomy, mathematics; but Indian thought influenced Islam rather as part of Persian, whither its export was pre-Sāsānid, and in the translation from the ethos of the thinking to the fighting class it is not likely to be unchanged, e.g., the assertion of the self as the universe, static in India, must be dynamic outside, hence personalized. We should remember that Buddhism was in Iranian lands for 800 years before Islam, and even if not institutionalized in the west, it should not be expected to have had no effect. We suggest Ṣūfism owes something in this way, and it may be that the dervish does Šiva's cosmic dance unknowing. But Islam did not come to India to learn, nor can it be said that the brahman was ever eager to teach outsiders his secret lore: his high philosophy was for the very few; the popular philosophy of the Epic/MahāBhārata might have been more accessible to invaders, but it is not particularly impressive. The ordinary Muslim had no reason to be dissatisfied with his own religion, or therefore to learn -- the idea that everyone else is as good as ourselves if not better is one of our modern Western advances. But the teaching impulse seems to have been early exhausted, and certainly did not find a willing pupil in the brahman. He or his substitute, the heretic monk, has no reason to want to learn about a world he has transcended, and indeed he never has learned from another culture without having to (as today Western science is a necessity), e.g., there is no trace of influence from East Asia despite all the pilgrims of Buddhism, including many very intelligent men. Of social effects of Islam the most important were the introduction of purdah, and a more secular system of taxation -- the Muslim ruler was not bound to observe the rules of Manu in this matter. Where Islam does influence the Indian feeling, its triumph is incomplete, e.g., the basic inequality of man remains untouched, even if Lingayat Šaivas theoretically hold men and women equal; the idol remains, and there is no thought of a Muslim India.

Bibliography

The Publications of G. M. Wickens 1949-1984

Eleazar Birnbaum
The University of Toronto

In gratitude for twenty years of friendship,
and in appreciation of his wit and skill

Dūstī bā mardum-i hunarmand
va nīk-ᶜahd va nīk-maḥżar dār.
Qābūsnāmah, chapter 28.

A. BOOKS

Including books edited and translated.

1. Avicenna: Scientist and Philosopher. A millenary symposium. Edited by G. M. Wickens. London: Luzac, 1952. 128 p.

[For his chapter in this work, see below, no. 15.]

2. Book List on Asia, including parts of Africa, for Canadians. Edited by G. M. Wickens. Ottawa: Canadian National Commission for UNESCO, in association with the University of Toronto Library, 1961./ Liste de livres sur l'Asie et certaines parties de l'Afrique, à l'intention des Canadiens. Editée par G. M. Wickens. Ottawa: La Commission nationale canadienne pour l'UNESCO avec le councours de la Bibliothèque de l'Université de Toronto, 1961. 46 p.

3. First Readings in Classical Arabic. Edited by G. M. Wickens. [Toronto]: University of Toronto Press, 1961. 36 p.;
----------. Edited by G. M. Wickens and M. E. Marmura. [2nd edition] enlarged and reprinted. [Toronto]: University of Toronto Press, 1963. 44 p.

4. Naṣīr ad-Dīn Ṭūsī. The Nasirean Ethics. Translated from the Persian by G. M. Wickens. UNESCO Collection of Representative Works, Persian Series. London: George Allen and Unwin, 1964. 352. p.

5. Persia in Islamic Times: A Practical Bibliography of its History, Culture and Language. Compiled by G. M. Wickens and R. M. Savory, edited by W. J. Watson. Montreal: Institute of Islamic Studies, McGill University, 1964. v, 57 p.

Logos Islamikos: Studia Islamica in honorem Georgii Michaelis Wickens, ed. Roger M. Savory and Dionisius A. Agius, Papers in Mediaeval Studies 6 (Toronto: Pontifical Institute of Mediaeval Studies, 1984), pp. 325-338.

6. *Morals Pointed and Tales Adorned: The Būstān of Sa^c^dī.* Translated by G. M. Wickens. Toronto, Buffalo: University of Toronto Press, 1974 [released 1975].

7. *Introduction to Islamic Civilisation.* Edited by R. M. Savory; editorial committee: E. Birnbaum, L. M. Kenny, M. E. Marmura, R. M. Savory, G. M. Wickens. Cambridge, London, New York: Cambridge University press, 1976. viii, 204 p. Reprinted [with minor corrections] 1977, 1979, 1980; reprinted, New Delhi: Vikas, 1980.

[For Wickens' chapters see below, "Articles," nos. 91-95.]

8. Sādeq Hedāyat. *Hājī Āghā: Portrait of an Iranian Confidence Man.* Translated by G. M. Wickens. Middle East Monographs, 6. Austin, Texas: Center for Middle Eastern Studies, University of Texas at Austin, 1979 [released 1980]. xxxvii, 130 p.

9. *Arabic Grammar: A First Workbook.* By G. M. Wickens. Cambridge, London, New York: Cambridge University Press, 1980. viii, 171 p.

B. BOOKS IN PREPARATION

10. *Zād al-musāfirīn*, by Nāṣir-i Khusraw. [Translation from the Persian with introduction and notes.]

11. *Vor der Sturm*, by Theodor Fontane. [An historical novel. Translation from the German with introduction and notes.]

C. ARTICLES

In Periodicals, Festschriften and Other Collective Works.

12. "The Wahhābis in Western Arabia in 1803-4 A.D." [By] R. B. Serjeant [and] G. M. Wickens. *IC*, vol. 23, no. 4 (October 1949), pp. 308-311.

13. "The Islamic Renascence and 'The West'." *IL*, [vol.] 2, no. 4 (April 1950), pp. 413-415 (pp. 5-7).

14. "The Mysticism of Islam." *LOTS*, vol. 5, no. 64 (1951), pp. 143-149.

15. "Some aspects of Avicenna's work." Chapter 3 in *Avicenna: Scientist and Philosopher*, edited by G. M. Wickens, pp. 49-65. London, Luzac, 1953. [See above, no. 1.]

16. "The Persian Concept of Artistic Unity in Poetry and its Implications in Other Fields." *BSOAS*, vol. 14, pt. 2 (1952), pp. 239-243.

17. "An Analysis of Primary and Secondary Significations in the Third *Ghazal* of Ḥāfiẓ." *BSOAS*, vol. 14, pt. 3 (1952), pp. 627-638.

18. "A University-Handbook of the Islamic Eighth Century." IL, vol. 4, no. 10 (October 1952), pp. 567-572 (pp. 31-36).

19. "Arabic Literature." Chapter 2 in Literature of the East, an Appreciation, edited by Eric B. Ceadel, pp. 22-49. Wisdom of the East Series. London: John Murray, 1953. Republished, (Evergreen E167) New York: Grove Press, 1959.

20. "Religion." Chapter 6 in The Legacy of Persia, edited by A. J. Arberry, pp. 148-173. The Legacy Series. Oxford: Clarendon Press, 1953; reprinted 1963 [etc.].

21. "The Transliteration of Arabic: An Approach in the Light of Current Problems of Printing and Publication." JNES, vol. 12, no. 4 (October 1953), pp. 253-256.

22. "Communication from Mr. G. M. Wickens." BSOAS, vol. 16, no. 2 (1954), p. 389.

[Draws attention to his rebuttal of "an article written in a kind of informal collaboration with Prof. [W. B. H.] Henning" by N. E. M. Boyce, published in BSOAS, vol. 15, pp. 279-288, which had criticized the two articles numbered 16 and 17 above. The rebuttal, a 15-page stencilled typescript headed "Intiqāḍ al-Iᶜtirāḍ," was circulated privately.]

23. "The Saᶜādatnāmeh attributed to Nāṣir-i Khusrau." IQ, vol. 2, no. 2 (July 1955), pp. 117-132; vol. 2, no. 3 (October 1955), pp. 206-221.

[English translation of the Persian text, with an introduction and notes.]

24. "The 'Persian Letters' attributed to al-Ghazālī." IQ, vol. 3, no. 2 (July 1956), pp. 109-116.

25. "Al-Jarsīfī on the Ḥisba." IQ, vol. 3, nos. 3-4 (October 1956 and January 1957), pp. 176-187.

[English translation, with introduction and notes, of a risālah by al-Jarsīfī.]

26. "The Chronology of Nāsir-i Khusrau's Safarnāma." IQ, vol. 4, nos. 1-2 (April and July 1957), pp. 66-77.

27. "Saᶜdi's Pandnāma. A New English Version with Notes." AOR, vol. 13—Centenary Number (1957), [Arabic, Persian and Urdu section] pp. 1-26.

28. "Bozorg Alavi's Portmanteau." UTQ, vol. 28, no. 2 (January 1959), pp. 116-133.

29. "Developing an Academic Tradition." In Proceedings: The National Conference of Canadian Universities and Colleges, 1959. 35th meeting . . . June, 1959, pp. 62-69. Ottawa:

[National Conference of Canadian Universities and Colleges], 1959. Reprinted in Asian Studies and the Canadian Universities. A contribution to UNESCO's East-West Major Project. Papers read at the National Conference of Canadian Universities and Colleges, Saskatoon, Canada, June 9, 1959, pp. 9-16. Ottawa: Canadian National Commission for UNESCO [1959?].

30. "Poetry in Modern Persia." UTQ, vol. 29, no. 2 (January 1960), pp. 262-281. Reprinted in The Islamic Near East, edited by Douglas Grant, pp. 262-281. University of Toronto Quarterly, Supplements, 4. [Toronto:] University of Toronto Press, 1960.

[Note by the editor, D. Grant, p. 165: "I have had to rely entirely in the matter of this Supplement [The Islamic Near East, pp. 163-296] on the advice and far-reaching assistance of my colleague, Professor G. M. Wickens. . . . [He] has contributed the following foreword [pp. 165-167]."]

31. "Drama: Persian Drama." In Encyclopaedia Britannica, 1961 edition, vol. 7, pp. 586-587. Chicago.

32. "Nasir ad-Din Tusi on the Fall of Baghdad: A Further Study." JSS, vol. 7, no. 1 (Spring 1962), pp. 23-25.

33. "Arabian Nights." In Encyclopedia International, vol. 1, p. 508. New York: 1963; reprinted 1971.

34. "Arabic Literature." Ibid., vol. 1, pp. 509-510.

35.-42. [Eight additional subsidiary articles on Arabic literature and authors, were published in various volumes of this encyclopedia, apparently without their author's signature.]

43. "Bell, Gertrude Margaret Lowthian." Ibid., vol. 2, p. 496.

44. "Iraq." Ibid., vol. 9, pp. 403-411.

45.-49. [Five additional subsidiary articles on Iraq themes and personalities, were published, apparently without their author's signature, in various volumes of the Encyclopedia International.]

50. "Firdawsi." Ibid., vol. 7, p. 124.

51. "Omar Khayyam." Ibid., vol. 13, p. 423.

52.-58. [About seven other articles on themes and personalities in Persian literature appeared, apparently without their author's signature, in various volumes of this encyclopedia.]

59. "Undergraduate Honour Course in Islamic Studies at Toronto." The Linguistic Reporter, vol. 5, no. 3 (1963), pp. 1-3.

60. "Introduction [to] *The Gulistan, or Rose Garden* of Sa^{c}di, translated by *Edward Rehatsek, edited . . .* by W. G. Archer, pp. 35-53. London: George Allen and Unwin, 1964; New York: Putnam, 1965.

61. "Mamluk Egypt at the Eleventh Hour: Some Eyewitness Observations." In *The Seed of Wisdom: Essays in Honour of T. J. Meek*, edited by W. S. McCullough, pp. 140-158. Toronto: University of Toronto Press, 1964.

[Includes extracts translated from Ibn Iyās' *Badā'i^{c} al-Zuhūr*.]

62. "Persian." In *EOS: An Enquiry into the Theme of Lovers' Meetings and Partings at Dawn in Poetry*, pp. 244-247. The Hague: Mouton, 1965.

63. "Islamic Studies at the University of Toronto," *MLJ*, vol. 49, no. 5 (May 1965).

64. "Ḥāfiẓ." In *Encyclopaedia of Islam*, new [2nd] edition. Leiden: [English language edition], vol. 3, fasc. 41-42 (1965), pp. 55-57 = [French ed.] *Encyclopédie de l'Islam*, nouvelle éd., tome 3, livr. 41-42 (1965), pp. 57-59.

65. "Arab Civilization: 3. Literature. Medieval Islamic Literature." In *Encyclopedia Americana*, vol. 2, pp. 153-154. New York: 1968; reprinted 1973, 1976.

66. "Arabian Nights." Ibid., vol. 2, p. 64.

67. "Persian Literature as an Affirmation of National Identity." *Review of National Literatures* (St. John's University, Jamaica, New York), vol. 2, no. 1 (Spring 1971), pp. 29-60. [Special issue:] *Iran, in celebration of the 2500th anniversary of the founding of the Persian Empire by Cyrus the Great*; special editor: Javad Haidari.

68. "*Lalla Rookh* and the Romantic Tradition of Islamic Literature in English." *Yearbook of Comparative and General Literature*, no. 20 (1971), pp. 61-66. Symposium: "Islam in World Literature."

69. "The Imperial Epic in Iran: A Literary Approach." In *Iranian Civilization and Culture: Essays in Honour of the 2500th Anniversary of the Founding of the Persian Empire*, edited by Charles J. Adams, pp. 133-144. Montreal: McGill University. Institute of Islamic Studies, 1972 [released 1973]. Pre-printed in *University of Toronto Graduate*, vol. 4, no. 1 (January 1972), pp. 20-27. Reprinted in *Acta Iranica, 3* = *Commémoration Cyrus*: Actes du Congrès de Shiraz, 1971, et autres Études redigées à l'Occasion du 2500e Anniversaire de la Fondation de l'Empire perse, *Hommage Universel*, III, pp. 261-275. Leiden: E. J. Brill, 1974.

70. "Farabi." In Encyclopedia Americana, vol. 11, pp. 15-16. New York: 1973; reprinted 1976.

71. "Farid ud-Din Attar." Ibid., vol. 11, p. 20.

72. "Firdausi." Ibid., vol. 11, p. 241.

73. "Firuzabadi." Ibid., vol. 11, p. 285.

74. "Hafiz." Ibid., vol. 13, p. 675.

75. "Hamasa." Ibid., vol. 13, p. 733.

76. "Hariri." Ibid., vol. 13, p. 797.

77. "Harun al-Rashid." Ibid., vol. 13, pp. 833-834.

78. "History: 3. Islamic Historical Writing." Ibid., vol. 14, pp. 238-239.

79. "Ibn al-Athir." Ibid., vol. 14, p. 691.

80. "Ibn al-Farid." Ibid., vol. 14, p. 691.

81. "Ibn Battuta." Ibid., vol. 14, p. 691.

82. "Ibn Tufayl." Ibid., vol. 14, p. 693.

83. "Idrisi." Ibid., vol. 14, p. 747.

84. "Imam." Ibid., vol. 14, p. 799.

85. "Imami." Ibid., vol. 14, p. 799.

86. "Ramadan." Ibid., vol. 23, p. 199.

87. "Tabari." Ibid., vol. 26, pp. 204-205.

88. "Arthur John Arberry, 1905-1969." Proceedings of the British Academy, vol. 58 (1972, [1973]), pp. 355-366. Reprinted separately, London: Oxford University Press, 1973; 14 p.

89. "[Letter] to the Editor." IrS, vol. 9, no 4 (Autumn 1976), pp. 314-315.

[Comments on L. P. Elwell-Sutton's review of his Morals Pointed and Tales Adorned [see above, "Books" section, no. 6] in Iranian Studies, vol. 9, no. 1 (Winter 1976), pp. 67-75.]

90. "The Frozen Periphery of Allusion in Classical Persian Literature." LEAW, vol. 18, nos. 2-4 (March 1974, [released 1978]), pp. 171-190.

91. "Introduction to the Middle East." Chapter 1 in Introduction to Islamic Civilisation, edited by R. M. Savory, pp. 1-13. Cambridge, 1976. [See above, "Books" section, no. 7.]

92. "Persian Literature: An Affirmation of Identity." Chapter 7 in *Introduction to Islamic Civilisation* [see no. 91, above], pp. 71-77.

93. "The Middle East as a World Centre of Science and Medicine." Chapter 10 in *Introduction to Islamic Civilisation* [see no. 91, above], pp. 111-119.

94. "What the West borrowed from the Middle East." Chapter 11 in *Introduction to Islamic Civilisation* [see no. 91, above], pp. 120-125.

95. "Khātimah." Chapter 18 in *Introduction to Islamic Civilisation* [see no. 91, above], pp. 189-194.

96. [1] "The Prince of Freedom," [by] Jafar al-Khalīlī; [2] "The Sermon on the Mount," [by] Tewfiq Sayigh; [3] "The Lead Soldier," [by] Bozorg Alavi; [4] "God's Revolt," [by] Forugh Farrokhzad. Translated by G. M. Wickens. In *New Writing from the Middle East*, ed. Leo Hamalian and John D. Yohannan, pp. 47-54; 83-85; 278-292; 375-376. Mentor Book ME 1639. New York: New American Library, 1978.

97. "Little Pharaoh": a short story by Maḥmūd Taimūr. Translated [by] G. M. Wickens. *JAL*, vol. 10 (1979), pp. 109-116.

98. "Literature in Arabic." Chapter 13 in *The Persian Gulf States: A General Survey*, ed. Alvin J. Cottrell, pp. 334-353. Baltimore, London: Johns Hopkins University Press, 1980.

99. "Revolution," by Maḥmūd Taimūr. Translated by G. M. Wickens. *Nimrod* (Arts and Humanities Council of Tulsa, Oklahoma), vol. 24, no. 2 (Spring/Summer 1981), [Special issue:] *Arabic Literature: Then and Now*, pp. 129-134.

100 "W. A. C. H. Dobson" [Obituary notice]. *Proceedings of the Royal Society of Canada, 1983*, 4th series, vol. 21 (Ottawa, 1984), pp. 77-81.

101. "Shah Muzaffar Al-Dīn's European Tour, A.D. 1900." In *Qajar Iran: Political, Social, and Cultural Changes, 1800-1925. Studies Presented to Professor L. P. Elwell-Sutton*, ed. Edmund Bosworth and Carole Hillenbrand, pp. 34-47. [Edinburgh:] Edinburgh University Press, 1984.

102. "Ak̲lāq-e J̌alālī." In *Encyclopaedia Iranica*, 1.7: 724. London: Routledge, 1984.

103. "Ak̲lāq-e Mohsenī." Ibid., pp. 724-725.

104. "Ak̲lāq-e Nāṣerī." Ibid., p. 725.

104A. "Barrasi-i Guzārish-i Naṣīr al-Dīn Ṭūsī Dar Bārah-i Suqūṭ-i Baghdād." [Translated by Ḥasan Anūshah.] In *Shīᶜah Dar Ḥadīs-i Dīgarān*, [ed. Mahdī Muhaqqiq,] pp. 141-166. Tihrān: Bunyad-i Islāmī-i Ṭāhir, 1362 A.H.S. [/1983].

[Translation of item no. 32.]

D. ARTICLES IN PRESS AND FORTHCOMING

105. "Western Scholarship on the Middle East." [In Mutual Perceptions: East and West, ed. Bernard Lewis. Princeton: Princeton University Press.]

106. "Bahārestān." In Encyclopaedia Iranica.

107. "Bostān." Ibid.

108. "Browne, E(dward) G(ranville)." Ibid.

109. "Madīḥ." Encyclopaedia of Islam. New [2nd] edition. Leiden: E. J. Brill.

110. "Mathal" (Persian). Ibid.

111. "Anīs-ol-ᶜOššāq." In Encyclopaedia Persica.

112. "Anvār-e Sohaylī." Ibid.

113. "Auṣāf al-Ašrāf." Ibid.

114. "Alexander the Great: The Persian Literary Aspect of his Legend." Paper in the Symposium, "The Search for Alexander," to be published under the auspices of the Royal Ontario Museum, Toronto.

115. "Persian Language." In Encyclopedia Americana.

116. "Persian Literature." Ibid.

117. "Ḥāfiẓ." In Encyclopedia of Religion, ed. Mircea Eliade. New York, Free Press [Macmillan].

118. "Naṣīr al-Dīn Ṭūsī." Ibid.

119. "Saᶜdī." Ibid.

E. BOOK REVIEWS

120. H. A. R. Gibb, Mohammedanism (London: 1949). CR, vol. 71, no. 1725 (November 12, 1949), p. 146.

121. M. Mīr Fakhrā'ī, Nihuftah (Nahofteh)--Persian Poems, by Dr. M. Mīr Fakhrā'ī, known as Gulchīn-i Gīlānī. CR, vol. 71 (1949), pp. 452-453.

122. A. J. Arberry, Modern Arabic Poetry: An Anthology with English Verse Translations (Cambridge Oriental Series, 1. London, 1950.) CR, vol. 72, no. 1746 (October 21, 1950), p. 52.

123. Gholām Hosein Dārāb, Persian Composition (London, 1948). BSOAS,

vol. 13, pt. 1 (1950), pp. 452-453.

124. S. M. Abdullah (compiler), Catalogue of Persian, Urdu, and Arabic Manuscripts in the Panjab University Library, Vol. 1, fasc. ii--Persian Poetry (Lahore, 1948). BSOAS, vol. 13, pt. 1 (1950), pp. 508-509.

125. J. A. Boyle, A Practical Dictionary of the Persian Language (London, 1949). BSOAS, vol. 13, pt. 3 (1950), pp. 780-782.

126. R. Ettinghausen, Studies in Muslim Iconography, I: The Unicorn (Washington, D.C., 1950). Nature, vol. 167 (1951), p. 167.

127. R. A. Nicholson (translator), Rumi, poet and mystic . . . Selections . . . (London, 1950). LOTS, vol. 5, no. 55 (January 1951), pp. 324-325.

128. J. James, The Way of Mysticism (London, 1950). LOTS, vol. 5, no. 57 (March 1951), p. 167.

129. A. J. Arberry (translator), Avicenna on Theology (London, 1951). LOTS, vol. 5, no. 64 (1951), pp. 153-154.

130. A. J. Arberry, Sufism: An Account of the Mystics of Islam (London, 1950). LOTS, vol. 5, no. 64 (1951), pp. 154-155.

131. A. S. Tritton, Islam: Beliefs and Practices (London, 1951). Blackfriars, vol. 32, no. 374 (May 1951), pp. 235-236.

132. R. J. C. Broadhurst (translator), The Travels of Ibn Jubayr (London, 1953). Blackfriars, vol. 33, no. 393 (December 1952), pp. 536-537.

133. A. Schimmel, Die Bildersprache Dschelâladdîn Rûmîs (Walldorf-Hessen, 1950). BSOAS, vol. 14, no. 3 (1953), pp. 405-406.

134. A. J. Arberry, Omar Khayyám: A New Version Based on Recent Discoveries (London, 1952). LOTS, vol. 7, no. 73 (July 1952), pp. 37-38.

135. J. Wach, Types of Religious Experience, Christian and Non-Christian (London, 1951). LOTS), vol. 7, no. 73 (July 1952), pp. 38-39.

136. A. J. Arberry (editor and translator), The Rubāʿīyāt of Omar Khayyām, edited from a newly discovered manuscript dated 658 (1259-60) in the possession of A. Chester Beatty (London, 1949). BSOAS, vol. 14, pt. 1 (1952), pp. 207-208.

137. P. Humbert, Observations sur le vocabulaire arabe du Chahnameh (Neuchatel, 1953). JRAS (1953), p. 158.

138. F. D. Razi, The Modern Persian Dictionary (Persian-Urdu-English) (Lahore, 1952). JRAS (1953), pp. 158-159.

139. H. Corbin, Oeuvres philosophiques et mystiques de Shihabbadin Yahya Sohrawardi, II (Tehran, 1952). JRAS (1953), p. 1975.

140. E. W. Bethmann, Bridge to Islām: A study of the religious forces of Islām and Christianity in the Near East (London, 1953); D. M. Donaldson, Studies in Muslim Ethics (London, 1953). Blackfriars, vol. 34, no. 399 (1953), pp. 301-302.

141. H. Wehr, Arabische Wörterbuch für die Schriftsprache der Gegenwart, 2 vols. (Leipzig, 1952). JRAS (1954), pp. 185-186.

142. H. Corbin, Avicenne et le récit visionnaire, 2 vols. (Tehran, 1954). JRAS (1955), pp. 98-99.

143. ʿAbdallāh Darwīsh, al-Maʿājim al-ʿArabīya (Cairo, 1956). JRAS (1956), pp. 230-231.

144. Mohammed Iqbal, Reconstruire la pensée religieuse de l'Islam, traduction et notes de Éva Meyerovitch (Paris, 1955). BSOAS, vol. 19 (1957), p. 179.

145. C. J. Edmonds, Kurds, Turks and Arabs: Politics, Travel and Research in North-Eastern Iraq, 1919-1925 (London, 1957). IJ, vol. 13, no. 3 (Summer 1958), pp. 235-236.

146. J. Duchesne-Guillemin, The Western Response to Zoroaster (Oxford, 1958). CJT, vol. 5, no. 1 (January 1959), pp. 64-66.

147. Wilfred Cantwell Smith, Islam in Modern History (Princeton, 1959). UTQ, vol. 28 (1959), pp. 404-405.

148. George E. Kirk, Contemporary Arab Politics: A Concise History (London, Toronto, 1961) IJ, vol. 17, no. 3 (Summer 1962), pp. 327-328.

149. Sylvia G. Haim (editor), Arab Nationalism: An Anthology (Berkeley, 1962). IJ, vol. 17, no. 4 (Autumn 1962), pp. 463-464.

150. Sylvia G. Haim (editor), Arab Nationalism: An Anthology (Berkeley, 1962); Peter Partner, A Short Political Guide to the Arab World (New York, London, 1960). MEA, vol. 14, no. 6 (June-July 1963), pp. 175-176.

151. Mohammad Iqbal, Le Livre de l'Éternité, Djavid-Nama, traduit par Éva Meyerovitch et Mohammad Mokri (Paris, 1962). Books Abroad, vol. 37, no. 3 (1963), p. 360.

152. F. Gabrieli, The Arabs: A Compact History, translated by Salvator Attanasio (New York, Toronto, 1963). IJ, vol. 19, no. 1 (Winter 1963-64), pp. 125-126.

153. P. Avery, Modern Iran (London, 1965). New Blackfriars, vol. 47, no. 546 (December 1965), pp. 165–166.

154. F. R. C. Bagley (translator), Ghazālī's Book of Counsel for Kings (Naṣīḥat al-Mulūk) (London, 1964). JAOS, vol. 85, no. 4 (October-December 1965), pp. 579–580.

155. Lukasz Hirszowicz, The Third Reich and the Arab East (London, Toronto, 1966). IJ, vol. 22, no. 1 (Winter 1966-67), pp. 156–157.

156. J. A. Bellamy, E. N. McCarus, A. I. Yacoub (editors), Contemporary Arabic Readers, V: Modern Arabic Poetry, Pts. 1-2 (Ann Arbor, Mich., 1966). LEAW, vol. 11, no. 2 (June 1967), pp. 186–187.

157. George Makdisi (editor), Arabic and Islamic Studies in Honor of Hamilton A. R. Gibb (Cambridge [Mass.], 1965). JAH, vol. 1, no. 2 (1967), pp. 184–187.

158. Reuben Levy (translator), The Epic of the Kings: Shah-Nama, the National Epic of Persia, by Ferdowsi (London, Chicago, Toronto, 1967). UTQ, vol. 37, no. 2 (January 1968), pp. 203–207.

159. Philip K. Hitti, Makers of Arab History (New York, London, Toronto, 1968). IJ, vol. 25, no. 1 (Winter 1969-70), pp. 230–231.

160. C. K. Zuraik (translator), The Refinement of Character (Tahdhīb al-Akhlāq), by Aḥmad Ibn-Muḥammad Miskawayh (Beirut, 1968). JAOS, vol. 90, no. 4 (October-December 1970), pp. 552–554.

161. al-Zamakhsharī, Pīshrow-e Adab (Muqaddimat al-Adab), vols. 1 (pts. 1-2) and 2, edited by Mohammad Kazem Emam [Muḥammad Kāẓim Imām] (Tehran, 1963-65). JAOS, vol. 91, no. 4 (October-December 1971), pp. 533–534.

162. Majid Fakhry, A History of Islamic Philosophy (New York, 1970). JQRNS, vol. 62 (October 1971), pp. 138–140.

163. David Marshall Lang (editor), Guide to Eastern Literatures (New York, 1971). MEJ, vol. 26, no. 3 (Summer 1972), p. 352.

164. Mahmoud Manzalaoui (editor), Arabic Writing Today: The Short Story (Cairo, 1968); D. N. Mackenzie (translator), Poems from the Divan of Khushal Khan Khattak (London, 1965). LEAW, vol. 15, no. 4-vol. 16, nos. 1-2 (December 1971-June 1972), pp. 908–911.

165. Moshe Perlmann (translator), Ibn Kammūna's Examination of the Three Faiths (Berkeley, 1972). JSS, vol. 18, no. 2 (Autumn 1973), pp. 307–309.

166. Bernard Lewis, Islam in History: Ideas, Men and Events in the Middle East (London, 1973). JSS, vol. 19, no. 1 (Spring

1974), pp. 145-147.

167. Nikki R. Keddie (editor), *Scholars, Saints, and Sufis: Muslim Religious Institutions in the Middle East since 1500* (Berkeley, 1972). *JAH*, vol. 8, no. 1 (1974), pp. 51-52.

168. Tikku, G. L., *Persian Poetry in Kashmir, 1339-1846: An Introduction* (Berkeley, 1971). *JAOS*, vol. 94, no. 4 (October-December 1974), pp. 538-539.

169. Elias S. Shoufani, *Al-Riddah and the Muslim Conquest of Arabia* (Toronto, 1973). *CJH*, vol. 9, no. 3 (1974), pp. 332-333.

170. Daniel J. Sahas, *John of Damascus on Islam: "The Heresy of the Ishmaelites"* (Leiden, 1972). *SR*, vol. 4, no. 1 (1974-75), pp. 75-76.

171. Parviz Morewedge, *The Metaphysics of Avicenna (Ibn Sīnā)* (New York, 1973). *JNES*, vol. 34, no. 4 (1975), pp. 301-302.

172. Peter J. Chelkowski (editor), *The Scholar and the Saint: Studies in Commemoration of Abū'l-Rayḥān al-Bīrūnī and Jalāl al-Dīn Rūmī* (New York, 1975). *MESAB*, vol. 10, no. 3 (1976), pp. 64-65.

173. Salih H. Altoma, *Modern Arabic Literature: A Bibliography of Articles, Books, Dissertations, and Translations in English* (Bloomington: 1975). *Books Abroad*, vol. 50, no. 4, 1976, p. 948.

174. Abū al-Najīb al-Suhrawardī, *A Sufi Rule for Novices: Kitāb Ādāb al-Murīdīn*, an abridged translation and introduction by Menahem Milson (Cambridge, Mass., London, 1975). *MEJ*, vol. 30, no. 4 (1976), pp. 577-578.

175. A. M. Piemontese (compiler), *I Manoscritti Persiani dell' Accademia Nazionale dei Lincei. (Fondi Caetani e Corsini). Catalogo* (Roma 1974); Bo Utas, *Tarīq ut-Taḥqīq: A Sufi Mathnavi ascribed to Ḥakīm Sanā'ī . . .* (Lund, 1973). *JAOS*, vol. 97, no. 1 (January-March 1977), pp. 41-42.

176. L. Fekete, *Einführung in die persische Paläographie* (Budapest, 1977). *JAH*, vol. 12, no. 2 (1978), pp. 174-175.

177. Michael C. Hillman, *Unity in the Ghazals of Hafez* (Minneapolis, 1976). *Ir S*, vol. 9, no. 4 (Autumn 1976), pp. 295-298.

178. A. F. L. Beeston (compiler), *Samples of Arabic Prose in its Historical Development. (A Manual for English-speaking Students)* (Oxford, 1977). *JSS*, vol. 24, no. 1 (1979), pp. 138-140.

179. Hava Lazarus-Yafeh, *Studies in al-Ghazzali* (Jerusalem, 1975); M. Abul Quasem, *The Ethics of al-Ghazali: A Composite Ethics in Islam* (Petaling Jaya, Selangor, Malaysia, 1975). *JSS*, vol. 24, no. 1 (1979), pp. 149-151.

180. L. P. Elwell-Sutton, The Persian Metres (Cambridge, 1976). JNES, vol. 38, no. 4 (October 1979), pp. 294-295.

181. Henry Corbin, The Man of Light in Iranian Sufism, translated by Nancy Pearson (Boulder, Colorado, 1978). MW, vol. 69, no. 4 (October 1979), pp. 277-278.

182. Myriam Rosen-Ayalon (editor), Studies in Memory of Gaston Wiet (Jerusalem, 1977). JSS, vol. 25, no. 1 (1980), pp. 147-148.

183. D. P. Brewster (translator), The Just Balance, al-Ghazālī's al-Qisṭās al-Mustaqīm (Lahore, 1978). JSS, vol. 25, no. 2 (1980), pp. 289-290.

184. Ignaz Goldziher, Tagebuch, herausgegeben von Alexander Scheiber (Leiden, 1978). JAOS, vol. 100, no. 1 (1980), pp. 34-36.

185. Alford T. Welch and Pierre Cachia (editors), Islam: Past Influence and Present Challenge. In Honour of William Montgomery Watt (Edinburgh, 1979). JSS, vol. 26, no. 1 (1981), pp. 153-155.

186. Thomas Philipp, Ǧurǧi Zaidan: His Life and Thought (Beirut, Wiesbaden, 1979). JSS, vol. 26, no. 2 (1981), pp. 338-340.

187. Ignaz Goldziher, Introduction to Islamic Theology and Law, translated by Andras and Ruth Hamori (Princeton, 1981). CJH, vol. 17, no. 1 (April 1982), p. 144.

188. George Makdisi, The Rise of Colleges: Institutions of Learning in Islam and the West (Edinburgh, 1981). JAH, vol. 16, no. 2 (1982), pp. 141-142.

189. Franciszek Machalski, La Poésie persane après la Seconde Guerre mondiale (Krákow, 1980). Ir S, vol. 15, nos. 1-4 (1982), pp. 242-244.

190. V. S. Naipaul, Among the Believers: An Islamic Journey (London, Deutsch; Toronto, Collins, 1981). QQ, Vol. 90, no. 2 (Summer, 1983), pp. 570-572.

191. Yvonne Yazbeck Haddad, Contemporary Islam and the Challenge of History (Albany, N.Y., 1982). JSS, vol. 28, no. 1 (1983), pp. 190-192.

F. BOOK REVIEWS IN PRESS

192. M. G. Carter (editor), Arabic Linguistics: An Introductory Classical Text, with translation and notes (Amsterdam, 1981). JSS.

193. Richard G. Hovannisian and Speros Vryonis, Jr., (editors), Islam's Understanding of Itself (Malibu, 1983). MW.

194. Louis Pouzet (editor & translator), Une Hermeneutique de la

Tradition islamique: Le Commentaire des Arba^c^ūn al-Nawawīya de Muḥyī al-Dīn Yaḥyā al-Nawawī (m. 676/1277), introduction, texte arabe, traduction, notes et index du vocabulaire (Beyrouth, 1982). *MW*.

195. Edward Mortimer, *Faith and Power: The Politics of Islam* (London, Toronto, 1982). *QQ*.

196. Sayyed Mohammad Ali Jamālzādeh, *Isfahan is Half the World: Memories of a Persian Boyhood*, translated by W. I. Heston (Princeton, 1983). *QQ*.

Abbreviations

AOR	Annals of Oriental Research (Madras)
BSOAS	Bulletin of the School of Oriental and African Studies, University of London
CJH	Canadian Journal of History /Annales canadiennes d'histoire (Saskatoon)
CJT	Canadian Journal of Theology (Toronto)
CR	Cambridge Review (Cambridge, England)
IC	Islamic Culture (Hyderabad)
IJ	International Journal (Toronto)
IL	The Islamic Literature (Lahore)
IQ	Islamic Quarterly (London)
Ir S	Iranian Studies (New York)
JAH	Journal of Asian History (Wiesbaden)
JAL	Journal of Arabic Literature (Leiden)
JAOS	Journal of the American Oriental Society (New Haven, Conn.)
JNES	Journal of Near Eastern Studies (Chicago)
JQRNS	Jewish Quarterly Review, New Series (Philadelphia)
JRAS	Journal of the Royal Asiatic Society (London)
JSS	Journal of Semitic Studies (Manchester)
LEAW	Literature East and West (Austin, Texas)
LOTS	Life of the Spirit (Oxford)
MEA	Middle Eastern Affairs (New York)
MEJ	Middle East Journal (Washington, D.C.)
MESAB	Middle East Studies Association Bulletin (New York)
MLJ	The Modern Language Journal (Madison, Wisconsin)
MW	The Muslim World (Hartford, Conn.)
QQ	Queen's Quarterly (Queen's University, Kingston, Ontario)
SR	Studies in Religion/Sciences religieuses (Toronto)
UTQ	University of Toronto Quarterly (Toronto)

Index

All names beginning with al- are indexed under the capital letters immediately following. There are no headings Islam/Muslims or Christianity/Christians in the index; the editors considered that no useful purpose would be served by indexing these subjects which occur with great frequency. There are, however, entries for Byzantines, Greeks, Jews, etc.

In general, the Library of Congress system of transliteration has been followed, but the editors regret that they have not been able to achieve complete consistency in this regard. The variant forms of *ibn* and *b.*; *-īya* and *-iyya*; and *a* or *ah* for the *tā' marbūṭah* will be encountered. The editors have, however, endeavoured to make each chapter internally consistent. The editors take comfort from the thought that *humanum est errare*, and from the fact that E. I. J. Rosenthal (see p. 214) clearly does not consider inconsistency to be a cardinal sin.